Death by Design

By
Lee Urness as told to Dave Racer

airleaf.com

Conventions and Considerations

Top Cop Lee Urness took copious notes and kept thousands of pages of his own records during the chase of serial killer Andrew Cunanan. Given how the case came to preoccupy his every waking hour during those days, its details burned into his memory. Once the case concluded, he wrote a synopsis and timeline, not sure what he would do with the information, but knowing he wanted to retain it. Then he watched in dismay as authors and writers wrongfully portrayed details and observations about the case; too often showing law enforcement in a negative light.

From his notes and records, and from voluminous public records, I was able to help Lee reconstruct an outline of the story. Then, using his notes, Lee filled in minute details during scores of hours of interviews. His memory of the specifics of those events is astounding and electrifying.

Next, we began to contact police officers, FBI agents, reporters and others who were directly involved in each facet of the case. I interviewed these individuals either in person or by telephone. In each jurisdiction, police officers involved in the case expanded on or explained facets familiar to them. They provided me with public reports associated with their part of the case, which we put together like a complex jigsaw puzzle.

I traveled to each murder site to view with my own eyes what Andrew Cunanan saw, walking the streets and visiting the haunts where he spent his time. This adds clarity to the sharing of this gruesome story.

Because this case became so huge, hundreds of individuals had some involvement in the story. Lee wanted to protect the identities of many of them, so we chose to use aliases whenever their names were presented. For the most part, we used the real names of law enforcement officials who publicly became part of the story. As for those private individuals whose real names appear in this book, we believe their own public involvement and pronouncements or family relationships gave us reason enough not to use aliases for them.

I have dramatized this story while sticking to facts. For instance, no one witnessed Cunanan kill any of his victims, except for Gianni Versace. After reviewing voluminous police reports and talking with investigators from each crime site, Lee Urness developed his own theories about why Cunanan chose each victim and how he murdered them. Each investigator had a piece of the story, but Lee was the only person who had the whole story.

To tell The Cunanan story, through Lee Urness' eyes, I have employed description, narrative and dialogue. Except when directly quoting from public documents, all other conversations have been recreated. We do not claim that the words shown in each quote are taken directly from those conversations but are representative of the facts.

Largely, this book is a telling of the story of Lee Urness' challenge while managing such a huge, high profile case.

Lee loved his work and holds law enforcement in the highest regard. He felt that no one had accurately reported the hard work of the thousands of law enforcement officers who had worked on the Cunanan cases; Lee felt driven to set the record straight. As well, his admiration for police work meant he wanted the general public to see what actually happens behind the scenes in such a case that terrorized millions for 79 days.

For me, the case consumed 10 months of my life. For Lee, it consumed the spring and summer of 1997, and large portions of his life since then. Like Lee and me, you will never be the same after reading *Death by Design*.

Dave Racer, St. Paul, Minnesota

Reason for writing

Police work is, to me, among the most noble, fulfilling and exciting of all careers. My great-grandfather, grandfather, and father were all sheriffs, and the example they set during their careers became engrafted into my own character. They were good, hard-working cops who respected the law and the people, and they commanded the peoples' respect.

Without a well-respected police force, communities are made less safe. And the thousands of officers with whom I worked – some on a regular basis and others, perhaps only once – were people who put safety and protecting citizens first.

Police officers know that public criticism comes with the job. Sometimes it is deserved, when mistakes are made or an officer crosses the line. Other times, and I suggest even most often, criticism comes because the citizens do not understand our job. For instance, the public may assume that a criminal is going free because no one has arrested him, when the truth is that investigators are working hard to collect the strongest of all evidence against that suspect. To make a premature arrest can, and too often does, result in losing at trial as a defense attorney pokes holes in hastily collected evidence.

I became the case agent in the Andrew Cunanan chase by chance. Any other member of the Minnesota Fugitive Task Force could just as easily have checked the data wire that day. The fact that it became my case gave me no special stature or claim to fame. I was a cop doing my job. And that is why I chose to write this book.

As the case developed, I became agitated, then angered about how the media covered it. When wire services published how we were triangulating the phone signal in Lee Miglin's car, we were just hours or moments away from catching Cunanan. When the story broke, I knew it bode ill for someone, and that someone was William Reese. Up to this point, the media had just been an irritation, but when this happened, I became incensed. It was very irresponsible for the media to make this information public.

After Gianni Versace's murder, special interest group leaders and others questioned our effort, claiming that we did very little to track down the murderer. I knew differently, and so did hundreds of dedicated local police, highway patrol, state police and FBI agents, men and women who worked thousands of leads and turned over every stone to find Cunanan before he killed again. We did our job and instead of earning respect, these people criticized our effort.

When the case finally ended and the smoke cleared, just weeks after Versace's death, I thought about writing a book. I wanted the world to know what really went on behind the scenes. I felt that if the public really knew what we had done, they would be more patient with police officers, give them more respect, and become more suspect of critical media reports. Then life got in the way and I let the idea go dormant.

Still, every time a new national police chase emerged, and especially during the sniper attacks in the Washington, D.C. area, the media made reference to the Cunanan case. Seldom did they get the story right. Too often, national news reports, and especially cable news, used these human tragedies to exaggerate their viewership, seemingly uncaring about how their reports hurt investigators, suspects, victims and their families.

The time now seemed right to do this book in an effort to let the public know just how hard cops work to protect the public and how thoroughly they conduct their investigations. I wanted it to tell the story from several aspects so that the reader could see what really goes on inside such a case. In this way, hopefully as these happen in the future, they can discern the truth about a case as it unfolds, instead of relying on senseless media speculation.

I am a strong advocate for peace officers and the work they do, and want those who have gone before as well as those still hitting the streets to benefit from this book. That is why a portion of receipts from sales will be going to the National Law Enforcement Officers Memorial Fund, The Minnesota Law Enforcement Memorial Association (LEMA) and Concerns of Police Survivors, Inc. (COPS).

It has been hard to revisit all that occurred during the 79 days of my life that the Andrew Cunanan chase stole from my family and me. But, the task has been made far easier by Dave Racer, as he reconstructed my fractured stories and tied them together, along with the sheaves of paper I laid on his desk. He spent hours interviewing key members of the chase team, and dozens more hours visiting crime scenes. In many ways, watching him work reminded me of how cops do their business. Dave would have made a great cop.

Lee Urness, 2005

Dedication

To Kathy, Lisa, Matt and Kari Urness, my family, for their support and love for me as a police officer, and as a dad and husband; to Ole Urness, Bennie Urness and Howard Urness, the sheriffs who taught me so much about life and law enforcement; to the hundreds of officers who worked on the Andrew Cunanan case; to the families of peace officers who gave the ultimate sacrifice, their lives, to preserve the peace for the rest of us.

Table of Contents

Chapter 1 ~ a dead body surfaced

Most 20-year-old single guys spend their off-duty hours chasing girls, but not Lee Urness, at least during the summer of 1966. Douglas County Sheriff Howard Urness, Lee's father, needed his help.

Two fishermen had ventured out on Lake Ida, a popular walleye lake just north of Alexandria, Minnesota. A sudden storm had blown in and sunk their boat. The sheriff knew they had drowned, and he needed Lee and his friend, Jim Howe, to dive to find the bodies.

Sheriff Howard had taught Lee from his early teens to divorce his feelings from the grim work of investigating felony crime and death. To Lee, despite the grief and suffering of survivors, working with the actual dead bodies of victims really had no effect.

During that hot summer, Lee worked on a bridge crew as his "day job." He reported for work before 7:00 a.m., and worked long, full and arduous days doing grunt labor for the bridge-builders. But after the boat accident occurred, Sheriff Howard gave Lee no time off. "Not 'till we find those bodies. You get right over here after work," Howard said.

For 29 straight days, the routine never changed. Lee left work, drove home to change clothes, grabbed his diving gear and headed to Lake Ida.

"We'll get them today," he told his dad as he dove into the darkness of the 110-foot deep lake. His rubber wet suit fought to protect him from the icy cold waters. His athletic body staved off the crushing pressure created by millions of gallons of lake water. The barren lake bottom had no vegetation, and even fish refused to swim that deep. To Lee, that lake bottom looked like a lunar landscape. It was a desolate and lonely place.

Because of the 29 straight days of diving, Lee's ears had popped so often that he started having hearing problems; but until he found the bodies, he refused to quit.

"You don't stop 'till you're done, no matter what it takes," Howard said, "and as long as those guys' wives and kids are standin' on the shore waitin' for those bodies, we keep searchin'."

Sheriff Howard left the house early each morning during that search to take a boat out on the lake, long before the day's fishermen hit the water. The boat moved slowly, as Howard searched for any sign of the bodies. Whether he chased crooks or searched for drowning victims, Sheriff Urness considered it his job's routine, and he had long since determined not to fail. Lee studied him carefully and felt the same determination-taking root in him.

1

Each day, deputies and volunteers had dragged the lake inch by inch, and as they hit something; they marked the spot. Lee and Jim then dove to the bottom, searching in every direction.

To aid his search, Lee used an anchor tied to a 50-foot rope. He set the anchor in the center of his search area. Then he swam just above the lake bottom in circles around the anchor while hanging on to the rope, expanding the circle five feet at a time. To find a body meant working systematically, but he had no success.

Then on day 30, two fishermen nearly fainted when one of the sunken bodies floated up through the water's surface near where they had dropped anchor. The startled anglers sped to shore and found the nearest telephone to call Sheriff Urness. Urness responded immediately and took a crew out to mark the spot.

As soon as Lee and Jim arrived late that afternoon, they suited up and dove. Each diver had one tank of air – their own personal gear, as was common in rural communities – and they wanted to stay down as long as possible.

They began making circular rounds in the 85-foot deep water.

Suddenly Lee spotted something bulky up ahead. As he swam closer, he saw a 15' boat with a 60 horsepower outboard motor hanging on it; the motor acted as a dead weight. The stern stuck straight up at a 90-degree angle to the bottom. Lee thought it looked like a missile ready to launch. Seeing the boat suggested that he was close to finding the body.

Lee set his anchor near the boat and began a semi-circular swim pattern while his partner did the same on the other side. Swimming five feet above the bottom, he surveyed the area back and forth, hoping to find the body that day, not wanting to let it drag on any longer; but he saw nothing.

He heard the ringing sound that told him his air supply was nearly spent.

Finally, his air all but exhausted, he had no choice but to swim to the surface. He raised his head to start up. He stared into two bulbous eyeballs set into the bloated face of the dead man's body; his momentum nearly rammed him into the floating corpse. Lee jerked backwards. Quickly he took out a marker, tied it on the man and sent the yellow balloon to the surface.

Like it or not, he had to go up. He had barely enough air to get to the surface. Jim had gone up minutes earlier.

"I got him!" he yelled, as he broke though the water and tore off his mask. "He scared the crap out of me, but I got him marked," he said, nodding toward the nearby yellow marker. "But I'm out of air," he told his dad as he climbed into the boat. They carried no spare tanks.

"I hate to leave him down there another day," the sheriff answered. "The family's on the shore."

"You got any air left?"Lee asked Jim, the other diver.

"Maybe three minutes. No more."

"Give me your tank," Lee said, slipping his off. "Maybe I can push him up."

"There's hardly enough air to get to the bottom," Jim protested.

"No, I can do it," Lee insisted. The end of the search was too close to stop, even if it meant taking personal risks. "Back in a moment," he added, diving over the edge of the boat.

Lee dove as fast as he could, following the marker to the body. There he saw the man floating face down, spread-eagle like an angel, about six feet above the lake bottom. As quickly as he could, and breathing shallow, he knelt underneath the obese body. Lee shook his head when he saw that the man still wore a heavy jacket and a full rain suit. The gasses that built up in the body had not given the lift that should have forced him to the surface. Lee hoped he could move him just enough to get him started.

He heard a soft ring coming from the air tank; he had almost no air left. As quickly as he could, he stretched his 6'4" frame straight up and pushed with all his might. After stubbornly rising a few feet, the body flew from Lee's hands, and it jetted upward. The body crashed through the water's surface, flying nearly four feet into the air before belly flopping back into the water.

Lee had no air left. He swam as quickly as possible, passing his bubbles on the way up. He coughed and choked as he broke the water's surface. A wide grin graced his face. His perseverance had paid off; he had snared the man. Finally, the victims' families could find closure.

Lee's mind had drifted to that cool evening at Lake Ida as he sat in the stuffy warm air of the Minneapolis FBI Command Post 31 years later. He waited for the call that could confirm that thousands of FBI agents and police officers had finally gotten underneath Andrew Cunanan, the five-time killer, and pushed him to the surface.

A most dramatic confession

"Lee, line three. It's Evans from Miami," Kevin Rickett told him, snapping him out of his daydream of Lake Ida.

Several Special Agents and their clerks anxiously watched as Lee took the phone in his hand. The cluttered room reflected the chaos of the FBI's manhunt. An overwhelming volume of information collected by cops all across America, recorded on an endless stream of paper and reports, sat in stacks and files on worktables.

"Urness here," Lee said, trying to hide his exhaustion. He fought off hope, fearing yet another disappointment. Once again, the FBI had interrupted him as he coached his daughter's softball game, as they had done dozens of times that summer. He hated losing family time to a perverted killer, but he had no choice until Cunanan had been flushed out of hiding.

The room went dead silent as each agent strained to hear the caller's message. America's most intense manhunt was about to come to an end that night – or maybe not.

Lee braced himself to hear that once again, the lucky killer had slipped through his hands. Never before had someone he chased eluded him like Cunanan, and never before had "one of my guys killed someone on my watch." Lee had totally personalized this case.

The intense pace of the long chase took its toll on Lee's family, personal and professional life. For the first time in 27 years of law enforcement, his emotions had nearly unraveled as the case took control of him. He needed to hear that it was over.

Special Agent Keith Evans had called from Miami Beach with the news. Lee listened carefully to each word Evans spoke, and as he did, his eyes welled up. He sighed deeply.

"He pled guilty," he told the waiting agents. "It's him."

He walked to a nearby easel and wrote in two-foot tall letters on the blank pad hanging there, "D.R.T." – Dead Right There.

In the bedroom of an old houseboat docked in a Miami Beach harbor, curdled blood soaked the nearly naked body of the vicious killer. A single bullet from a .40-caliber Taurus pistol, fired by his own hand, had ended Andrew Cunanan's life.

Cunanan's suicide gave Lee Urness back his own life. For 79 straight days, Lee dove into the dark, cold and perverted mind of the twisted man. His efforts to anticipate each of Cunanan's next moves had failed. Investigators had worked circles around thousands of sightings, but none bore fruit. Yet, his team of agents had closed down all the options until Cunanan could no longer float free, just above the bottom of his barren life.

Cunanan's dead body finally jetted to the surface in the explosive moment when that single bullet ended his life.

It had been an incredible journey for these two men – the enraged killer, and the cop who tried to force him to the surface before he killed again, a journey that began near the Pacific Ocean in late April 1997, and ended 11 weeks later, 2700 miles away, near the Atlantic Ocean.

Chapter 2 ~ Hammering out hits in Minnesota

During late April 1997, 10-year old Kari Urness and her dad Lee drove to softball practice in Prior Lake, Minnesota, an outer-ring Twin Cities suburb. The ballfields had just thawed and dried out, and Minnesotans wasted no time getting spring leagues started. Lee, 51, a Special Agent with the Minnesota Bureau of Criminal Apprehension and a member of the FBI's Fugitive Task Force, coached Kari. He had done the same with Lisa and Matt, his two older children, but Kari showed special talent. Lee knew she had a future in competitive athletics.

Kari, a pitcher, had already developed a nasty 60-m.p.h. fastball and was a key player on the Lakers' 12-and-under "A" team. More so, she hammered the ball harder and more often than the older girls did. Lee felt proud of Kari as he watched her swinging freely and pounding out hits.

Hits with a hammer

Jeffrey Trail, 28, left his suburban Twin Cities apartment sometime after 9 p.m. on Sunday, April 27, 1997 and drove into downtown Minneapolis, heading for the apartment of David Madson. Andrew Cunanan, 27, Trail's former lover who had been visiting Madson, asked Trail to come over for a few minutes to hammer out problems in their relationship. But on that night, the hammering was done by Cunanan, swinging freely and pounding more than two dozen times on Trail's head and body.

Cunanan's bloody barbarism had only just begun that night and soon wreaked murder in the death of four more men. It sent Cunanan cross-country, running just steps ahead of hundreds of American and international police officers who worked day and night trying to chase him down. Kari Urness' coach-dad ran that chase – or more rightly, it ran him – for the next three months as fast-pitch softball child's play gave way to the fast-paced hardball of police work. Lee's life would never be the same again, as Andrew Cunanan wove a design of death that would be remembered forever.

Fickle relationships and souring friendships

David Madson and Jeff Trail had met in San Diego during one of Madson's frequent business trips. They had been casual lovers and good friends, partying together in various cities many times before Trail finally moved to Minneapolis in 1996.

Madson had moved to Minneapolis during the early 1990s, and now lived in an apartment in a rehabilitated office building at 280 North Second Avenue, near Washington Avenue. The building sat in the warehouse district of downtown Minneapolis, just a few blocks from the Target Center, home of Minnesota's NBA team, the Timberwolves. Just several blocks away to the east stood the Hubert Humphrey Metrodome, home of the Twins and Vikings.

Minneapolis had converted dozens of its aging office buildings and warehouses near the stadiums to loft apartments. At street level, artsy restaurants, coffee shops and stores with ambiance had opened up, attracting a large number of gays and lesbians who loved its Bohemian atmosphere.

The neighborhood was peppered with sports bars, coffeehouses, cafes, video production houses, professional theaters and more than a dozen strip clubs. Favored gay hangouts were within walking distance or a short cab ride.

On Wednesday, Thursday and Friday, April 23-25, Madson talked long distance with Reggie Cedar*, 28, who lived in Fredericksburg, Virginia. Cedar dated Madson, despite living hundreds of miles away, and talked regularly with him. Each man spent generously on airfare.

"So what are you doing this weekend?"Cedar asked. "Maybe you can fly out."

"No, Andrew Cunanan is coming in from San Diego," Madson apologized. "I agreed to meet him."

"I thought you didn't like him anymore."

"Well, no, not really. And I'm a bit worried about it," Madson said.

"Why?"

"Well, Andrew told me he hoped that we could be together…" Madson explained.

"Oh, well…" Cedar protested.

"No, no. It's not what *I* want. It's him," Madson explained.

"Well then why…"

---

* The use of the asterisk next to a name indicates that the real name has not been used.

"I don't know. We had good times together, but he kind of scares me. You know he's into something; I don't know what. I thought maybe it was drug dealing, but it's different," Madson said.

"How so?"Cedar asked. Madson had told him how Cunanan loved to always pick up the meal tab, even when it was hundreds of dollars, and how he lavished expensive gifts on everyone. Madson wondered where he got that kind of money.

"I don't know anything specific, but I think it's got to do with some kind of drugs coming in from Mexico. I have no idea what it is," Madson explained.

"Aren't you worried about him coming?" Cedar asked.

"He's only coming for a few days, and then leaving. He's not staying; I can assure you of that. He's got some other guy to see," Madson sighed. "So, don't worry about it. I'm sure it will be okay." In fact, after picking Cunanan up at the airport on Friday, Madson called Cedar to report that everything *was* fine. "We're going out to dinner with some friends."

On Friday, April 25, Walter Jones*, another one of Madson's friends called him from Atlanta, Georgia. "So what're you doing this weekend?" Jones asked.

"Oh, an old friend from San Diego's coming to town. I'm picking him up at the airport later," he answered.

"Ooo, sounds like fun." Jones knew Madson as a fun and giving man, as well as a lover.

"I don't know. He bothers me in some ways," Madson answered. "He's coming to settle affairs with another boy, but then he's heading out east." At least that is what Cunanan had told him.

Even with well-founded apprehension, Madson still showed up on time at the airport that Friday.

"Andrew, nice to see you," Madson said as Cunanan deplaned at Twin Cities International Airport at about 5:30 p.m.

Cunanan and Madson had been steady sex partners for several months during 1996, though Madson claimed it had gone cold later in the year. They had, however, just spent two passionate nights together in March when Cunanan bought Madson a ticket to fly out to California. Cunanan told others that he saw Madson as "the love of my life."

Another love of Cunanan's life had just said good-bye to him the evening before he flew to Minneapolis. Thomas Robins*, one of a string of current and former lovers, along with three others had a going-away party for

9

Cunanan. Cunanan told them he would be moving to San Francisco to live with Sam Taeger*, an attorney he had just met. But first, "I need to go to Minneapolis. I've got some business to tie up," he told them.

Cunanan never told anyone how he intended to "tie up" his business, but he certainly found a way to hammer closed whatever it was he meant to do.

You look different

"So how are you?" Madson asked as they drove toward Minneapolis.

"Oh, I'm all right," the normally ebullient man answered.

"You putting on a little weight?"

"Do I look like it?" Cunanan asked.

"Well, yeah, since we got together you do. Been eating too well?" Madson joked.

"I suppose," Cunanan answered, thinking about the five vials of steroids he had brought along in his gym bag. "I've been pumping a little iron."

Cunanan loved Madson for a variety of reasons, and the man's muscular physique was one of them. The only athletic thing Cunanan had ever done was as an average track and long distance runner in high school. The students at Bishop's School in La Jolla, California, the preppy, expensive private institution from which Cunanan had graduated, remembered him more for being openly gay. Their most vivid picture of him was when he attended his senior prom in drag.

"Let's get something to eat," Madson said, both wanting to cheer up his friend and to minimize his time alone with him. Madson knew that Cunanan still had feelings for him, but he wanted to sever all romantic ties with the Californian. He could be a friend, but no more a lover, especially since hearing all the junk Jeff Trail had laid on him about Cunanan. The fact that a fatter Cunanan had showed up in Minneapolis with a new buzzed haircut only convinced Madson more that this weekend would be the last he would spend with him.

After picking up Cunanan, Madson drove back to his apartment and the two men walked across the street to Café Solo. Cathy Katlein* and four of her friends waited for them.

"Oh, hi David," Cathy said, eyeing the unexpected guest Madson had brought along.

"Hi everyone. This is my friend Andrew Cunanan. He just came in from San Diego to stay the weekend," Madson said cheerfully.

"Nice to meet you Andrew," Cathy said.

"You, too," Cunanan answered and then engaged in a lively conversation with all of them. Katlein thought him to be self-assured and content, though somewhat of a braggart.

"And how long will you be in Minnesota?" Cathy asked as she looked up at Cunanan who sat next to her.

"Oh, I'm going back on Tuesday," he answered casually. Cunanan never told her or anyone else at that table, that he had only bought a one-way ticket to Minneapolis. He had no intention of flying back, and apparently, no intention of flying anywhere, at least without Madson alongside. He had to beg American Express to float the money for his airline ticket because he had maxed out all of his credit cards – $20,000 on this one. On this night he would not, as he usually did, pick up the check for everyone. He had very little money.

Cathy watched Madson and Cunanan leave nearly two hours later and reminded herself never to take this new guy very seriously. Some of his stories seemed just a little too unbelievable.

More partying

Madson had called Sally Monahan*, a Ramsey County (St. Paul) Public Defender and long time friend, earlier in the day. He wondered if she had plans for the evening.

"I'm meeting a couple of friends at Nye's Polynesian Restaurant. Why don't you two join us there?" she suggested.

"Will do," Madson answered. So from Café Solo, he and Cunanan went to Nye's sometime after 8 p.m.

Madson had talked at length with Monahan about Cunanan a few times in previous months.

"Where'd you meet him?" she had asked.

"I met Andrew in San Francisco last fall on a business trip," Madson said.

She had also met Cunanan. He came to Minneapolis several times. She first met him in November, when the man attended an arts fundraiser in Minneapolis. Madson claimed he and Cunanan had already quit having sex by then.

"But before that, you were more than good friends?" she asked.

"Well, yes. But I broke it off."

11

"Why?"Monahan knew at least a few of Madson's string of lovers, so another ex-lover held no special significance.

"He's too secretive; too elusive. I don't know," Madson had told her. Madson said that Cunanan wanted a serious commitment, but Jeff Trail had warned him away.

"Cunanan is a liar; can't be trusted," Trail had told Madson. "And I think he's into drug smuggling; at least he claims he's doing some big-time leveraging of his money. He even tried to lure me into his business. If I was you, I would be very careful."

Madson did break off his relationship with Cunanan, yet the two men had still met several times following that November event.

During January 1997, Dave Roberts* threw a birthday party for Madson at Madson's Harmony Lofts apartment. The guest list included Andrew Cunanan and Jeffrey Trail. Trail dated another man that night. During the evening, Trail talked with Roberts.

"I quit the California Highway Patrol," Trail said.

"Why?" Roberts asked.

"Well, Andrew tried to get me to smuggle drugs, and it somehow caught up to me," Trail said, none too happy with Cunanan.

"You talk too much," Cunanan said.

"So what are you doing now?" Roberts had asked Cunanan that January night.

"Oh I'm being taken care of by two sugar daddies. One of them is from the Midwest, an older man who dabbles in real estate," he answered coyly. He never offered any more information.

During Easter break, 1997, Madson had flown to San Diego to spend time with Cunanan. In his mind, Madson had just broken off a relationship with Roberts, the Virginia man who still believed their love to be exclusive. During that San Diego trip, Madson and Cunanan spent two nights together. Part of their time was shared with Laura Koski* and Will Evert*. Koski saw that Madson was making an attempt to distance himself from Cunanan all weekend. Yet when she and Evert went to the room shared by Cunanan and Madson, they saw many trunk straps, and other restraining items along with candle wax. Friends and former lovers of both men said they were into sadomasochism. Cunanan had paid all the bills for the two men and perhaps saw this as his chance for a long-term relationship with Madson.

On this April 25th weekend, Cunanan meant to give it one more shot, to cement a long-term relationship with the Minnesotan. All indicators pointed to his having left his old life behind, whatever constituted that old life.

Gnawing behavior

"Wow! Looks delicious," Cunanan exclaimed as Nye's waiter set a platter filled to overflowing with relishes in the middle of the table. "I love this place!"

Between drinks and nibbles on celery, carrots, radishes and table onions, they carried on light conversation. Monahan felt uncomfortable with Cunanan. To her he looked shabby and acted tentatively on this night, not like the confident guy, full of bravado, that she had seen during his previous visits. Then, he had dressed in leather, designer shirts and pants, smoked an expensive big black cigar and wore an expensive watch. He dressed to impress potential lovers as a form of costume to embellish his sometimes-irritating flamboyant behavior. Not tonight.

Monahan noticed that Cunanan still had an occasional broad smile break through his two rows of perfectly straight white teeth, but never did he laugh that loud, boisterous cackle that had been his trademark. Usually when Cunanan laughed, everyone knew he was in the room. In fact, usually when Cunanan was in the room, he made sure that he remained the center of attention. This night he acted passive, impatient and preoccupied.

"How long are you going to be in town?" Monahan asked, worried about his intentions toward her friend David.

"I'm leaving Monday morning," Cunanan lied.

"Maybe we can all get together Sunday evening?" she suggested, hoping for a happy ending to the weekend and some finality to this disturbing feeling that nagged at her.

"Yeah, that'd be great. I'm meeting J.T. for brunch, but after that we could get together," Cunanan said, referring to Jeff Trail.

"Great," she said. "David, give me a call tomorrow," she told her friend.

His friends knew Madson as an inveterate partier. So true to form, following dinner he and Cunanan went to the Ya'll Come Back Saloon, a popular gay hangout, just past 11:00 p.m.

"How you doin'?" bar manager Mac Winter* asked Madson, eyeing the man sitting next to him.

"Good," Madson answered. "This is Andrew Cunanan. He's a long time friend from San Diego."

The couple left the bar shortly after and headed to the Gay 90's, a Minneapolis nightclub, and danced past midnight. Madson had too much to drink and sent Cunanan back to the apartment alone. He came along later after dancing off the alcohol's effects. They spent the night together – apparently just as friends. No one knows whether that meant having sex, though Madson denied it to Monahan the next day.

"Did Andrew bother you? I mean, did he put any moves on you?" Monahan asked when she talked with Madson on Saturday.

"No, no. Everything is fine, you know. Nothing like that happened."

"Okay, I just wanted to make sure he wasn't causing you any trouble," Monahan said. She had no idea what kind of deadly trouble lay ahead for her gay carefree friend.

Madson expected company

Cunanan and Madson shopped at a local Target Store and returned to the apartment late on Saturday afternoon. That night they again had dinner with Sally Monahan and headed to the Gay 90's to party. Late that night they split up, but before they did, Cunanan gave Madson a very expensive gold wristwatch. Madson had a boyfriend coming to spend the night with him, so Andrew had to go elsewhere.

Cunanan's plans were expressed in a phone call he had made on the previous Monday. "J.T. It's Andrew calling from San Diego. What ya' doin'? Ah...I can't believe you're not home at 11:00 on a Monday. Maybe you're out of town on business, or maybe you're there and it's too late and you're already in bed. Anyway, I'm coming to Minneapolis next weekend, and I wanna see yaaa...So, if you're in town give me a call. Hmm, either you can leave me a message on my voice mail, 619-555-3539 or you can call me at home which is, 619-555-4424...so yeah...I'm excited. I hope I get to see ya, and umm...okay, talk to ya later. Bye-bye."

Trail invited Cunanan to stay at his place Saturday night, defying logic. He had told others that he despised Cunanan and warned them to stay away from him. Yet he opened his own apartment to Cunanan, and as far as Cunanan knew, Trail would be there waiting for him.

Cunanan found the apartment key where Trail said it would be and let himself in, but Trail had left a note. "Make yourself comfortable. Back on Sunday."

Trail's current lover, Henry Jackson*, had taken him on an overnight date to a "bed and breakfast" out of town. He wanted to celebrate Trail's birthday in a special intimate setting.

Cunanan went to bed alone that night. On Sunday morning before he left, he wrote a note to Trail. He wanted to see him again and told him to call. But before he left, he stole Trail's .40 caliber Taurus PT-100 handgun and a box of .40 caliber bullets. Trail got the gun when he trained as a member of the California Highway Patrol, after he had left the U.S. Navy. At one time, Trail had looked forward to a naval career, having graduated from the U.S. Naval Academy in 1991. The Navy assigned him to San Diego where he met Cunanan during the early 1990s. But Trail left the Navy behind, trying police work until moving to Minneapolis in 1996 to work at Ferrellgas, in Inver Grove Heights, a suburb south of St. Paul.

While Cunanan slept on Saturday night, Madson entertained someone else at his apartment. His upstairs neighbor in #504, Carl Schultz*, heard a "loud yelping noise" coming from #404 sometime between 3 a.m. and 7 a.m. He recognized the sound as two men having sex; Schultz rolled over and went back to sleep.

Sunday, finally a day of rest as Trail ends

Monahan phoned Madson on Sunday to finalize plans for their get-together that evening.

"As soon as I hear from Andrew I'll let you know," Madson answered. "We could go to Buca's."

"Sounds good to me," Monahan answered.

"I'll call a few friends." They joked around for a while and planned to talk later, but they never did talk again. Monahan really preferred staying home Sunday evenings and it mattered little to her that Madson never called her to set finalize the time.

Sometime past noon, Hal Todd* and Eve Daniels* saw Madson with Cunanan at a Minneapolis shopping mall – Calhoun Square. Later, after 5:00 p.m., Mary Tamrack⁺ saw Cunanan on the elevator at Harmony Lofts. No one else remembered seeing either Madson or Cunanan again until Monday.

Whether Jeff Trail met Cunanan for Sunday brunch is also unknown. But they certainly met Sunday night, inside #404, Madson's apartment. The gay meeting turned into a gory bloodletting within minutes.

Sunday date, but with whom?

That Sunday night, the phone rang in Jeff Trail's apartment. The answering machine recorded the message: "Oh J.T., where are you? It's...8:20 so please give me a call when you can. 555-9186. Okay, bye bye. Let me know if you're still coming. I really want to see you. Bye bye," said the voice of Andrew Cunanan.

"What are you going to do?" Henry Jackson asked when he called Trail around 9:00 p.m.

"Oh I promised Andrew I'd go and talk with him," Trail answered without much enthusiasm. "I'm supposed to have coffee with him. He says he wants to do business. It won't take long. I can meet you at the Gay 90's right after."

"Okay. I'll see you there," Jackson said, getting himself ready and heading out the door.

Sometime around 9:30 p.m., Trail parked his green 1996 Honda Civic at a meter on Washington Avenue near 2nd Avenue North. He plugged the meter with a couple of quarters. Later, the meter expired. By the time police found it late Tuesday afternoon, the cops had papered its windshield with several parking tickets.

Looking south, he spied the old grey five-story warehouse building – Harmony Lofts – where Madson lived. He walked past the strip club that sat next door to the lofts. The gay man cared little about the gaggle of pathetic lascivious heterosexual men who normally wandered in and out of the nude club. No one in that neighborhood paid much attention to or cared what anyone else did – they each had their own lifestyle preference.

The Sunday evening streets were mostly empty in the chill of a Minnesota spring night. He smelled stale auto fumes mixed with melting snow as he walked inside the entryway to Harmony Lofts, thinking of making music with Henry Jackson, once he had dispensed with this Cunanan nuisance.

Trail adjusted his red plaid shirt, feeling the ring that hung from his left nipple. His blue jeans covered the "Marvin the Martian" tattoo on his left leg and the "Mighty Mouse" tattoo on his right thigh. He wore "Simple" tennis shoes. Wiggling his toes, he felt the metal of his toe ring. At 9:45 p.m. he pushed the button on the building's security intercom.

"Hello," the speaker crackled. "J.T.?"

"Yes, it's me," Trail answered.

"Just a minute, we'll be right down," Cunanan said. Madson always came down to meet people, thinking that buzzing them in was rude.

A moment later, the two men met Trail at the door, but Madson had Prints, his Dalmatian, with him. "You two go ahead and talk. I'll be back in a little while." He headed out the door to take Prints for an evening stroll and a bit of relief.

Trail and Cunanan rode the elevator to the fourth floor. There they stepped into a carpeted hallway, its walls painted in plain blah colors that tried in vain to cover the cracked plaster. They walked down the long hallway to apartment #404 that sat near to the steel door leading to the back stairway. Shelton Johnstone's* apartment #401 sat across the hall. Johnstone stayed alone that night, planning an uneventful evening.

Cunanan opened the door and let them in, eyeing the athletic and handsome black-haired man as he went ahead of him. They stood the same height – about 5'9".

As Trail entered the apartment, he saw the large room that served as a living room, dining room, kitchen and bedroom. A small bathroom sat to the right. To his left, Trail saw the unkempt bedroom and the messy, busy double bed; he had no intention of sharing it or any other ever again with Cunanan. And he spotted the sofa in front of which sat the dining room table and six chairs.

Trail had met Cunanan at one of a long string of gay parties he had attended. They had partied time together at gay clubs, falling into each other's arms several times. But Trail had long ago written Cunanan out of his love life and urged Madson to do the same. Apparently it had worked. That was the "business" the maudlin gay man meant to discuss with Trail that night. Desperate for someone to take care of him, Cunanan meant to put an end to Trail's interference so he could begin a new life in Madson's arms.

About the time Cunanan opened the door for Trail, Henry Jackson, Trail's boyfriend, waited for him at the Gay 90's. But Trail never came. Jackson called him at Madson's later that night, but a bloodied corpse could never answer the phone.

Trapped Trail

Trail had walked into a trap, and soon after arriving, he and Cunanan began arguing. Cunanan snapped, losing his boyish playful nature in a fit of explosive violence triggered by desperation and steroids.

Jesse Johnstone in #401 heard shouting coming from #404, and thought someone tried running down the hall. Then he heard a pounding sound, but dismissed it.

Cunanan had grabbed a Toolsmith hammer from Madson's red toolbox, and swung it at Trail. In a pathetic attempt to fend off Cunanan, Trail raised his left hand, but the hammer slammed into it, puncturing it deeply. He managed to deflect one shot into the wall near a light switch, offering but one moment of relief.

Cunanan continued his violent attack, slamming the hammer into Trail's head – blow followed by deadly blow on the top and back of his skull. He hit him on the forehead, and near the left ear, pulverizing Trail's skull.

Blood sprayed onto Cunanan's white Banana Republic "Frog" T-shirt, his arms and face; it soaked his pants. Blood sprayed more than five feet high onto the walls near the door. Thud, thud the hammer continued. Somehow Trail got the door open, or maybe it had never closed, and his blood sprayed onto the threshold of #404 and a precious drop hit and stuck to the wall across the hallway near #401. In Madson's apartment, the blood spray looked like embossed red spackled wallpaper.

One blow hit Trail's blood-soaked Wenger watch, stopping it at 9:55 p.m.

Back inside the apartment, Cunanan continued his assault, battering Trail's handsome face into a swollen bloody pulp. He hammered Trail's face and eyes, trying to rid him of his good looks and personality. The former Navy Captain became unrecognizable. Still, in a wild flurry of blows, Cunanan continued to pound on the miserable man. Sixteen times Cunanan slammed the hammer into Trail's head.

Blood pooled onto the scratch-marred wood-planked floor, seeping into the cracks between the boards. Both men tracked and smeared Trail's life-blood on the floor as the assault continued.

Still Cunanan pounded Trail, as if to purge his own sick soul through the shedding of Trail's innocent blood; with every blow trying to cleanse his years of fakery, infidelity and utter depravity. He had meant to close the door to his past life when he left San Diego. This violence sealed his eternal fate. No priest would ever hear this confession nor could Cunanan ever receive absolution.

Finally, in an assault that lasted not much more than a minute, Trail fell dead. His blood oozed from his head as his limp body lay on the floor, and the room went silent.

Cunanan, covered in blood, stood over the blood-soaked corpse. The debased deceiver had now set for himself a deadly course that would leave behind a trail of bodies.

Now a hopeless killer, would he end his own life or take another? If so, whose, where, when?

Chapter 3 ~ Life smashed

Andrew Cunanan felt the hot blood from the claw hammer oozing onto his hand and soaking his shirt and pants. He looked down at the lifeless form of Jeffrey Trail.

It remains unknown whether he intended to kill Trail that night – he had, in fact, stolen Trail's gun. It seems certain he never meant to kill him with a hammer, but it was the item closest to him when he snapped. In any event, a dead body proved that the deed had been done.

Any hope that Cunanan harbored about a new life of joy, love and peace lay dead at his blood-spattered feet. All that remained now was to somehow dispose of Trail's body and figure out how to deal with David Madson.

Cunanan could have fled from the scene, but to where, and how? He had no money. His credit cards were maxed out. He had flown to Minneapolis on a one-way ticket. Most of all he wanted a new life with David Madson, who might walk through the apartment door at any moment.

He stayed.

He pulled off his blood-soaked T-shirt and threw it on the floor. Trail had fallen on Madson's Oriental rug that lay in front of the door, so Cunanan used it like a cocoon, wrapping the body inside. Then he pulled the rug over behind the sofa and near the dining room table, leaving bloody footprints on the hardwood floor.

Trail's legs lay exposed from the knees down. Cunanan found a cream-colored rug and wrapped it tightly around the legs, as though doing so would keep the corpse from moving.

He rushed to the bathroom and tried to wash the blood from his arms, hands and face, leaving the sink smeared in crimson. Then he changed into fresh clothes, stuffing his white T-shirt, a blood soaked towel and other items into a grey Jarmen plastic shopping bag. He threw his bloody pants into a corner of the bedroom. He slipped a pair of Ferragamo shoes on to keep from getting more blood on his feet. Then he surveyed the scene, trying to reason what to do next.

Exactly what time Madson returned to the apartment is unknown. Certainly it was after 10:00 p.m. – after Cunanan killed Trail. As he walked into the apartment, Madson saw blood everywhere and Trail's body wrapped in the rug. Nearly every corner of his apartment showed crimson evidence of Cunanan's vicious attack, with blood even spraying on Prints' dog bed several feet away in the bedroom, and onto the brown overstuffed leather sofa sitting in the living room.

Madson walked toward the dining room table and stopped, aghast at what he saw. He threw his leather key case and billfold on the table, adding it to the mix of magazines, newspapers, mail, and reminder notes. He saw that his red toolbox sat open, but the hammer was missing.

"What the hell did you do?" the stunned muscular, body-builder asked.

"Things just got out of hand," Cunanan said. "Trail threatened me and I had to defend myself."

"This is not *defending* yourself. This is a vicious attack," Madson said, waving his arms wildly, pointing out the blood. "How could you do this?"

"I don't know. I just don't know. I never hurt anyone before," Cunanan said, staring at Trail. "What're we gonna do?" he asked, looking up at Madson.

"We? What do you mean 'We?' I'm calling the police," Madson answered, walking toward the phone.

"No, you can't do that."

"What do you mean I can't do that?" Madson said, turning back toward Cunanan. The barrel of a pistol stared at him.

"I mean, you can't call the police," Cunanan said coldly.

"Andrew, this is no way..."

"There is no way for me anymore, except out of here."

"And you do that. You get out of here!" he screamed, so loud that Jesse Johnstone across the hall heard him.

"No, I can't leave here, at least not alone. You and I have to go away, somewhere where no one will find us. Out east, or south. Anywhere but here," Cunanan said, his eyes emptied of emotion; the raw reality of what he had done settling in. "Like it or not, you are going to help."

"Well, what am I supposed to do?" a confused and frightened Madson asked. He had never before seen such coldness in a person's eyes. It paralyzed him.

"You can help me clean this place up." Whether or not Cunanan understood it, once Madson grabbed a washrag he became an accessory to murder, sealing his own fate. "Where do you keep your cleaning supplies?" Cunanan asked, as he rummaged through cabinets.

"Here in the closet," Madson said as he walked over and grabbed a bucket, paper towels and a bottle of cleaner from the shelves.

"Okay, fill that bucket and open that package of paper towels. We have to clean up the blood," Cunanan said. But they only smeared the thick bloody pools around, soon giving up and not even trying to clean the blood spatters from the walls.

Madson could have overpowered the smaller, weaker man at any time, but he never tried. He may never have had the chance, as Cunanan could have handcuffed him and held him hostage. He may have gone along with Cunanan, looking for a chance to get away. Seeing Trail's dead body and the bloody results of the attack, Madson's decision not to fight Cunanan might have saved his life, at least for the moment. No one knows for certain why he stayed.

By default, Madson had signed on to Cunanan's plans. Perhaps he realized that he had indeed become an accessory to murder. Perhaps Cunanan kept Trail's gun nearby. Perhaps he really was still Cunanan's lover. Speculation abounds, but of the next two days, there was no question. Madson and Cunanan spent them together, mostly inside the apartment with Trail's body decomposing a few feet away.

Madson's apartment bore the earmarks of an active gay man's playground, one who was into sadomasochism. The S&M artifacts could have, however, been Cunanan's. When the two men dated during happier times, according to many acquaintances, they were into violent sex, using trunk straps, candle wax, duct tape and other types of restraining straps. Cunanan preferred this extreme violent sex. Madson told others that he wanted, instead, a gentler and more loving relationship. Friends who saw them together reported that Cunanan was always after sex with Madson, even when the relationship had begun to sour.

A picture of Dave Roberts, a husky black man who claimed he was Madson's current lover, sat on the dresser in a pewter picture frame. Roberts looked down on the shorter, pale white man, with loving eyes as he hugged him close. A bottle of "For Play" lubricant sat ready to ease sexual penetration and enhance sensation.

Madson's slatted head and footboard double bed sat between two big windows. The sheets and blanket were a mess. Madson's bright red bathrobe lay in a heap on the floor.

A recent edition of "People" magazine sat on the shelf of the nightstand. Ironically, the cover story read, "Before they were famous."

Madson's well-stocked closets were filled with smartly hung suits and shirts. His light blue 10-speed bike hung on hooks set into a tough 1' square pillar, a testament to how hard he worked to maintain his physical appearance. He supplemented bike riding with near daily workouts, pumping iron at the Arena Club where he met more than a few new friends.

When Madson tired of physical exercise or encounters, he could go to the living room and power up his entertainment center, plugging in one of the many gay movies that filled its shelves. Perhaps that is how Cunanan and Madson wiled away the time during those two days.

Strangely enough, the others who lived on the fourth floor paid no attention to #404, and no one noticed the blood spot on the hallway wall or the spattering of blood on the apartment's threshold. They showed no interest about what had happened there. Events and sounds that may have seemed odd to straight people drew no attention on the fourth floor at Harmony Lofts, where libertine sex had always produced its own odd sort of misogynous music.

During those two days, Cunanan and Madson, willingly or otherwise, formed a bond that could only end in a lifetime relationship, or death of one or the other – or both.

Chapter 4 ~ Planting seeds of a dark summer

Lee and Kathy Urness spent part of the last weekend in April 1997, planning their summer.

"Maybe we can actually have a family week," Kathy teased Lee.

"Yeah, a slow crime summer. Dream on," Lee answered. "Ah, we'll get some time together, I'm sure."

That spring and summer Lee had committed to coaching 10-year old Kari's softball team just as he had for 17-year old Lisa and 16-year old Matt when they were younger. Next to breaking down a door to arrest a crook, coaching his kids was just about the most enjoyable thing Lee did.

Lee hoped the family could enjoy their lake cabin, located in an isolated area near International Falls, Minnesota. Lee felt glad that many non-Minnesotans think the ice and snow are permanent in this small city near the Canadian border; it gave him more privacy. He knew that the area's summers were warm and beautiful. And despite the influx of fishermen during that time of year, the place offered Lee and his family a quiet refuge. Lee never installed a telephone in the cabin, and it was out of range for pagers and cell phones. A resort a half-mile away had a phone, close enough for *real* emergencies. Just to get to the place meant boating across a river.

Still, his work was too unpredictable to plan ahead. The family usually made plans that excluded him, and then hoped he could come along. At any moment of any day, Kathy knew her husband could be called away to chase a murderer or rapist who had fled from the police. "And he always went. He just has this thing about catching the bad guys," she said. "It's more than a job to him. It's, like, in his bones."

"Yeah, it might be nice to have a few slow weeks," Lee said that morning. They had no idea that the spring and summer of 1997 would soon become the worst of his life.

Maybe David went to the lake

David Madson's parents still lived in Barron, Wisconsin, and from time to time, he would drive to see them. But the weekend of April 26-27, 1997, he stayed home. In fact, he stayed home the 28th and 29th, too, with his friend Andrew Cunanan. Jeffrey Trail lay dead nearby.

Madson earned great respect at the John Ryan Company, the Minneapolis architectural firm where he had worked since 1996. His peers saw him as creative, consistent, considerate and well received by their clients. They also saw him as responsible, prompt, a person who seldom missed a workday, and often worked 12-hour days. To not show up, and especially without calling, was totally out of character. But Madson neither came to work nor called on Monday.

Numerous Ryan employees called Madson's apartment, leaving messages on his answering machine. They wondered about accounts he was working on, setting up meetings, or reminding him of other meetings he had been scheduled to attend. An employee of Storage Services called several times Monday and again on Tuesday, urging Madson to pick up materials they were holding for him. The calls eventually turned to frustration when he failed to show, and then to fear that something had happened to him. John Ryan himself called at 1:45.

That Monday, Ellie Lyndstrom*, a Ryan employee and close friend of Madson's, wanted to know more. "Where's David?" she asked a co-worker. "He missed several meetings today." No one knew. She called his apartment, but no one answered. *Strange,* she thought, but continued on with her daily routine, sensing that something was wrong, but not knowing just how right she was to worry.

But he was there

At 3:30 that Monday afternoon, Sarah Killen*, who lived in #405 at Harmony Lofts, came home from work. She walked to the elevator and pushed the "Up" button. As the elevator doors opened, she saw a dark-skinned man whom she did not know – she thought he looked Italian. Turning the other way in the elevator, she saw David Madson. "Hi," she said.

"Hi," Madson answered. The other man said nothing.

He seems crabby. Oh well, none of my business. She walked to her apartment and paid no attention to the two men who followed her down the hall. Neither did she ask about the blood spot on the hallway wall or the rancid odor that had started to seep out from #404.

Madson's dog Prints, like any dog, needed to take regular walks. Given Madson's long work and play hours, Prints had learned to control his physical urges, but still, he had to be let out at least twice a day. Killen noticed Madson and the dog together on Monday, but paid very little attention to

24

them. She often saw Madson with his dog, and the fact that another man walked alongside seemed normal to her.

Tuesday morning, Killen sat eating breakfast with her boyfriend. She looked out the window and saw Madson and the man walking Prints. Seeing another man with Madson would not be unusual. She noticed that Prints was on a leash, and that was out of the ordinary. Madson usually let the dog run free.

Given that Cunanan was unlikely to let Madson out of his sight, each time Madson walked Prints they did it together. And they were seen having coffee together later that day.

By Tuesday morning, Madson and Cunanan had spent 36 hours in the apartment with Trail's corpse just a few feet away, decomposing and beginning to stink. Still, Madson stayed. Neither did he call anyone. And he never answered the phone.

Lyndstrom persists

On Tuesday, Ellie Lyndstrom again wondered and worried about Madson. She and Hannah Giles*, another Ryan Company co-worker, talked about how unusual it was that he missed work. Lyndstrom called Madson again, but got no answer. Giles also called, and then called Madson's friend, Sally Monahan. "I wondered if you have heard from David," she asked.

"No, not since Sunday morning. Why?" Monahan asked.

"Well, it's just that he hasn't come to work the last two days. We were kind of worried about him," Giles explained. "Ellie Lyndstrom's called him, but there's no answer. I just tried, too, and only got the answering machine."

"That's not like him," Monahan said. Then she called Madson but heard that same answering machine.

"I'm going over to David's place," Lyndstrom said as she headed out the door just after Noon.

Lyndstrom knew about Nelson Grant*, another of Madson's former gay lovers. Grant had just recently been released from a Washington, D.C. prison. A week earlier someone – Madson felt sure it was Grant – had "keyed" and dented his Jeep, and he had left disturbing calls on his answering machine. Madson had obtained a restraining order to keep Grant away from him. Grant, who worked for MCI in the D.C. area, had in fact, visited the Twin Cities during April 19-23. Lyndstrom feared that Grant may have

25

hurt Madson and that was why David failed to answer the phone or report to work.

Grant later told investigators that he had settled a long legal dispute with Madson after the two of them lived together for nearly two years, ending in 1990. Grant said he split from an abusive and violent Madson, when he saw a side of the man unknown to his close friends; a side rooted in the darkest recesses of sadomasochism – S&M. Grant learned firsthand that this was Madson's preferred sex practice, and claimed that Madson had S&M lovers all across the country. He said that was why he split with Madson in a messy separation that cost him thousands of dollars. Of course, Linda Lyndstrom knew nothing about these legal tussles and even if she had heard Grant's side of the story, his description of the caring, sensitive man she knew would not have fit.

At the building, Lyndstrom got someone to let her in and she rode the elevator to the fourth floor. She walked down the hall and stopped at #404. She never noticed the blood spot on the wall or the dried blood on the doorsill. Knocking on the door, she heard Prints' soft barking. She also heard someone whispering inside the apartment, but no one answered her knock.

Nick Terry* stepped off the elevator and saw her outside Madson's door. "Do you know anyone who can let me into David's apartment? I'm worried about him," Lyndstrom asked him as he came closer. "At least I can feed Prints."

"Contact the caretaker," Terry advised, and went on with his business.

Lyndstrom talked with Sarah Killen in #405. Killen said she had seen Madson earlier that day, but had no idea what he was doing or even if he was still home.

She went to the caretaker's apartment and knocked. Willa Jenson* opened to her. "I'm a friend of David Madson's from 404. Have you seen him lately?" Lyndstrom asked.

"No. Why?"

"Well, I work with him. He hasn't come to work in two days, and I am worried about him. I knocked on his door, but all I hear is his dog in there. Can you open it and check on him?"She also mentioned the whispering she had heard.

"Oh no, I can't just do that. I'm sure he's okay," Jenson assured her.

Lyndstrom decided to call 9-1-1. She waited outside for an officer to show up. It was 1:30 p.m.

"First of all, you say there's a Dalmatian in there," Minneapolis Police Officer Hokanson said. "We can't just go bustin' down the door when there's a dog in there. Dalmatians are very territorial. Who knows what he'll do? And besides, just because someone's been missin' from work for a day-and-a-half doesn't mean anything's wrong," he explained. "Talk to the caretaker again."

"Okay."

"And if she needs help with the dog, tell her to call 9-1-1 and tell them to send Animal Control out," Hokanson said before leaving.

Get away

As soon as Lyndstrom left the area, and they knew the hallways were deserted, Cunanan and Madson hurriedly fled from the apartment. No one saw them leave, except Prints, whom they left behind. Leaving Prints suggested that Madson left under duress.

Cunanan left a gym bag with all of his clothes, but remembered to take along Jeff Trail's Taurus pistol. He had loaded the clip with 10 Remington Golden Saber bullets and left the remaining 15 bullets and a holster inside the gym bag. He grabbed his passport before the two men ran out the door and stuffed the passport into another gym bag. He left behind his blood-soaked clothes, making no effort at all to hide or disguise them. They left Madson's driver's license and wallet lying open on the table, but they had taken two sets of car keys on the way out. They were in a hurry.

Out on the street, they went quickly to Madson's 1996 Red Jeep Cherokee, got in and drove away. Cunanan, and perhaps Madson, knew their time was running out and they had to find safety somewhere else. But where should they go?

Persistent friend returns

Later that afternoon, Lyndstrom returned, bringing along another Ryan Company co-worker, Laura Booher. This time she heard Prints in #404 but nothing else. Determined that something was wrong, they went back to Jenson and once again asked her to open the apartment.

This time Jenson agreed, but something told her not to go in alone. Just past 4:00 p.m., she knocked on the door of Del Perryman*, one of Madson's many friends, who lived on the fifth floor. "Del, I'm so glad you're home. I need you to go with me into 404, David Madson's place," she said.

"What? Why?"

"Well, some of his co-workers said he didn't come to work on Monday or Tuesday and they're worried. They came here and knocked but no one answered," she explained.

"Maybe he's gone?"

"Of course, he probably is, but he was supposed to be at work and, well, he never showed up," she said, appealing to him to walk down with her. "And I think he left Prints in there."

They climbed the back steps down to #404 and Jenson knocked on the door. No one answered, but the two heard something stirring inside. She knocked again, and still there was no answer.

"It's the dog," Perryman said.

Reluctantly, Jenson took out her passkey, inserted it and turned it slowly. She pushed the door open slightly and looked in.

"Oh, my God!" the startled woman shrieked. "There's a...body. There's a body wrapped up in a rug!" She started to pull the door shut.

"Wait," Perryman said. "The dog is in there. We better let it out." They called to Prints and he came right away.

"What did you see?" Perryman asked.

"I'm not sure. I'm not exactly sure," she said. "I mean, it could have been, but it might not be." She pleaded with Perryman to go in.

He pushed the door open. His body tingled with fear. Nothing could have prepared him for that sight. The same apartment in which he had attended numerous private parties now felt haunted. Memories of good music, love and drinks were stifled by the putrid odor that assaulted his nostrils.

He saw the rug lying behind the sofa and what looked like a barrel-chested body wrapped inside. Slowly he walked into the apartment as the odor intensified. Maybe the dog had badly soiled the apartment; or Jenson was right and something lay dead in there.

He turned to leave, not wanting any more of what he saw – let the cops deal with it. Then he changed his mind, already having come so far. Fear now raced through his body as he stared down at the rug. He wanted to raise the edge just enough to see what color hair the body had – he knew Madson had blond hair – but his fear of implicating himself in this dreadful deed stopped him. He saw that the hair was so matted with dried blood that it was nearly impossible to tell its color. He walked around the body and nudged it with his foot, feeling a rubbery mass resist his kick. He had had enough.

As he turned to leave, everywhere he saw the blood that had splattered and smeared. On the floor, he saw a swirling stain that looked like someone had quit trying to clean up the blood; or had the dog licked it?

As they walked upstairs to call the police, Perryman remembered that he had seen David Madson on the elevator just a few days earlier – Saturday, he felt sure. It was the day Perryman was showing off his new roller blade skates to his friends. "Got these new blades. Hey, when we gonna go bladin'?" he had asked Madson.

"Oh, you got the graphite blades?" Madson said.

"Right. We gotta go bladin," he said again, eyeing the man next to Madson.

"Hey, this is Andrew from California," Madson said.

"Nice to meet you," Perryman responded. He and Cunanan exchanged smiles, and the two men got off, carrying their groceries. Perryman rode the elevator to the fifth floor and went to his apartment.

Now the memory sent shivers down his spine. He felt certain that the man in the rug was neither Madson nor "Andrew." He remembered that Madson had told him about Andrew, that he was wealthy and a good guy, from California. Madson had always spoken highly of him, never mentioning any trouble. He vaguely knew about a former lover who had threatened Madson, but it was not Andrew. *And David could never do that to anyone.* In any event, the body in the carpet was someone else – of that he felt sure.

"Check the Welfare" came up deadly

Anne O'Connor had spent more than three years working as a police reporter for the Minneapolis *Star-Tribune*. Her working team included Chris Graves, Randy Furst and Jim Walsh. Soon, O'Connor would move on to writing stories on education, but on April 29, her life changed. That day she sat reviewing "Check the Welfare" calls at the Minneapolis Police Department. Police recorded calls from worried family members and friends on this list of people who they reported as missing, or they learned had been harmed. O'Connor knew that sometimes the names on this list turned up as dead bodies. Scanning the list, she saw the name "David Madson," a friend of the *Star-Tribune's* Managing Editor, Pam Fine.

Some time after 4:30 p.m., O'Connor's phone rang.

"Anne "O'Connor," she said.

"You might want to come over to 280 North 2nd Street. We've got another murder," her police source told her.

Arriving at the scene, she saw that she was the only reporter. That suited her well.

She saw cops everywhere, but they would not tell her what was going on, nor allow her access to the building. She saw Harmony Loft tenants coming and going and hoped they could provide answers.

"What can you tell me about what is going on in the building?" she asked.

"I don't know, except that someone found a dead body in David Madson's apartment," the sad and worried tenant answered.

The name jumped out at her. *David Madson!* Her reporter's mind began to conceive a story, but she needed confirmation. Then she saw one of the cops who had been a source for her before. He had just come out of the building.

"So, is it David Madson?" she asked.

"Don't assume anything," he said.

"But I have to file a story. Do I write that you found Madson or not?"

"No. That would be wrong. It's not Madson," he said.

"Well where is he?" she asked.

"We don't know."

"Is he a suspect, then?" she pressed.

"No. We just don't know where he is at this time."

"Then who is the victim?" she asked.

"We do not know. He's beat up pretty bad," the cop said, and ended the interview. "Looks like a gay love triangle, and whoever did it took off."

Anne's instincts told her that things did not add up, but she could only write what she knew, and that was very little. She knew nothing about how the chase of Andrew Cunanan had just become personal and how it would dominate her thoughts in the weeks ahead.

Sgt. Bob Tichich, a Minneapolis Homicide detective, became the lead investigator. He supervised a large contingent of crime scene investigators and officers as they gathered evidence from the apartment. They returned Wednesday to complete their investigation. That same morning, Dr. Garth Burton performed an autopsy on the body and identified it as Jeffrey Trail. He had died from blunt force trauma.

As Tichich and his crew worked the crime scene, just past 11:30 a.m. the phone rang. Chris Graves from the *Star-Tribune* called the apartment to see who would answer. Sgt. Tichich picked up.

"What's going on?"Graves asked. "Why aren't you saying anything? We know who lives there."

"Just don't think that you know what's going on here," he said.

Graves had handled dozens of murder cases and knew not to make assumptions, but with her current knowledge, several scenarios already seemed likely, and that included David Madson wrapped in a rug. Tichich's comments led her to believe that it was not Madson. She also knew that Tichich, like most cops, loved to play a kind of chess game with reporters. They would offer a little, the reporter would offer a little, and they would each try to push the right buttons. Graves preferred cops who simply told her straight up what she needed to know without having to go through this dance.

Tichich let her know that they considered Madson to be part of the problem, though their information was sketchy. With nothing else to go on, Graves set out to learn what she could about Madson.

Tichich continued his search of the crime scene. He had found a dead body lying in a Minneapolis apartment, and he had no sure identity. He understood that David Madson's Jeep was missing, but had no evidence to convince Hennepin County Attorney, Mike Freeman, son of former Minnesota Governor Orville Freeman, to seek an arrest warrant. That evidence did not present itself for almost three months.

Tichich gathered crime scene evidence, including a gym bag that belonged to an unknown person (Cunanan's) and stored it away in the police department's property room. He had to wait a day to confirm the dead man's identity before he could pursue David Madson, the chief murder suspect, and the man who had been seen with him, Andrew Cunanan.

Getting away

Madson and Cunanan had beaten a hasty retreat from the apartment, being long gone before police arrived. No one reported seeing them leaving. People in the warehouse district had learned not to notice other people, because those human interactions common to the area required a high degree of anonymity. To have noticed two gay men leaving together would have meant they, in some way, had acted out of character, looked nervous or furtive. When Cunanan and Madson left, they looked just like any other two gay men driving away. But Tuesday before 4:30 p.m., they *did* leave town. Their whereabouts for the next four days still remains a mystery, but evidence strongly suggests that they spent those days together, emotionally hand-cuffed.

They may have driven to Chicago on Wednesday. Police later found a Chicago parking receipt dated Wednesday, April 30, in the Jeep. This showed that the two men had fled Minnesota directly to Chicago, finding a safe, temporary place to hide. Still, no evidence ever surfaced that proved conclusively where Madson and Cunanan had been from Tuesday evening until Friday just past noon.

Readers of the *St. Paul Pioneer Press* found a curious entry in the paper's "Bulletin Board" section on Friday morning, May 2. Madson loved to read this section, and this made the entry all the more fascinating as the case developed. Someone – Madson? – had written a joke about an architect, an engineer and an artist. The writer signed it, "David, the engineer. I'm OK." Madson was an architect. Trail was an engineer. Cunanan, according to his mother, had been an art major in college.

Some time before noon that Friday, Cunanan and Madson drove around the Twin Cities, perhaps checking out Madson's apartment from a distance. Having been gone since Tuesday night, they had no reason to know what police had discovered, if anything, in #404, and they had left valuable possessions in the apartment.

They may have come back earlier than Friday, finding refuge in the rural areas north of the Twin Cities, at a small, cheap out of the way motel where managers knew not to ask too many questions.

Near 1:00 p.m., Mary Jean Rosen served customers at the Full Moon Bar in Harris, a small town just off I-35, an hour north of the Twin Cities. She saw the front door open and a red sports vehicle parked outside. Madson and Cunanan came in and each ordered Grain Belt Beer and a California Burger Basket. They chose to sit out on the deck while they ate. Chel Carson*, an area resident, saw the Jeep sitting in the restaurant parking lot and pulled in, thinking one of his friends might have been there. Seeing that it was not his buddy's car, he left.

After about 45 minutes, Madson and Cunanan paid their bill and left together.

In the Jeep sat a roughly drawn map, with a route scribbled on the back of a real estate listing from an open house at a south Minneapolis home. The map set two routes. One went up I-35 to Duluth, and the other, east on I-94 to Chicago.

Madson's parents still lived in Barron, Wisconsin, east of Duluth. "My dad can help us figure out what to do," Madson may have suggested.

They were not alone

On an early spring Friday afternoon in Minnesota, northbound traffic is always heavy. Besides people going home from work, fishermen eager to get their cabins ready for fishing opener the next weekend jammed I-35, and all other roads leading out of town.

Scott Anderson left Minneapolis sometime after 3:30 p.m. and drove up the freeway toward his home in Stanchfield. He looked forward to a beautiful early spring weekend. Temperatures had hit the mid-50s – *a spring heat wave in Minnesota* – meaning shirtsleeve weather for the winter-bound natives and with it, an itch to get outdoors.

As Anderson drove near to the bedroom community of Lexington on the northern tip of the Twin Cities, he ran into heavy traffic. Soon after, he saw a red Jeep Cherokee ahead of him. It had a "Vail" sticker on the back. The sticker sat at an angle, and he wondered why anyone would put such a thing on what appeared to be a newly painted truck. Why Cunanan and Madson would have been on that highway during that time is a guess, but there they were, driving north once again.

Traffic flew past Anderson at 75 miles per hour or more, but he wanted to relax and kept his speed at 65. So did the Jeep. They passed each other several times during the next 35 miles, always careful not to go much more than 65.

During the drive, Anderson looked at the Jeep's driver several times. He saw a brawny man in a plaid shirt who had short blond hair. The man reminded him of a co-worker.

Anderson also studied the passenger, an olive-skinned man with short brown hair. Both men looked very serious and Anderson wondered why. Most people heading out of town on a Minnesota spring weekend looked happy, but these two certainly were not.

Then Anderson made eye contact with the olive-skinned man who shrugged him off. *Not very friendly*, he thought.

Just before he came to the exit at North Branch, 45 miles north of downtown Minneapolis, Anderson decided to pull around and take another look. Neither man returned his stare, but as he pulled ahead, he looked into his rear view mirror. He studied the blond man whom, he thought, looked as though

33

he had lost his best friend. *Man, something is sure bugging those two*, he thought as he left the highway. Anderson stopped at the Tanger Outlet Mall in North Branch and bought a pair of shorts and a baseball cap. He saw it was 5:10 p.m. as he left the store and continued his drive toward home.

Those two men in the car *were* solemn for good reason. They exited near Rush City, 14 miles north of Anderson's exit. Some time later, Cunanan drove away alone, using three .40 caliber slugs to permanently divorce himself from Madson, "the love of my life."

Chapter 5 ~ Looking for work

Lee Urness lay in bed early that Friday morning, May 2, 1997. He had made no arrests the prior day, and he knew of none that morning, so he could sleep a little longer, instead of bounding out of bed at 6 a.m. to book "bad guys." The 27-year police veteran loved staying up late, but hated getting up early.

Friday looked like an easy day, unless something broke on one of the handful of cases he managed, or something new popped up on the wire.

He had read about Jeff Trail's murder in a four-paragraph story in the Thursday *Star-Tribune*. The story contained almost no details, save that "the man who rented the apartment on 2nd Av.N. couldn't be reached for comment." Lee saw the reports on the 10:00 p.m. television news as well, but the Minneapolis Police Department had not called anyone at the Fugitive Task Force seeking help.

Lee hoped for an uneventful day and a slow weekend. Lee was on call 24 hours a day and much serious crime happened on weekends.

He pushed back the covers and rolled out of bed, turning on a TV news program. Half listening, he stretched out his 6'4" frame, walked to the bathroom and faced the mirror. His dark weathered skin, the result of years of working the streets on hundreds of crime scenes across Minnesota, stared back at him. As he shaved, he took care not to mess up his carefully groomed grey moustache. He combed his short gray hair, brushed his teeth and quickly changed into his "uniform" – khaki cargo slacks from Royal Robins, a blue polo shirt embroidered with the "MN Fugitive Task Force" logo and FBI seal, and his walking shoes.

He walked downstairs and went straight to the coffee pot, trying to shake sleep from his eyes. He lit a Camel-filter cigarette and took a deep drag, then glanced at the bird feeders on the deck just outside the kitchen. He picked up the *Star-Tribune* and then looked up again at the birds.

Lee loved watching the birds at the feeder as they fought for their territory and daily sustenance. It seemed to him to be a little like the way most people lived – chaotic, frenzied, pushing each other out of the way to get ahead for their portion of the birdseed. And they were like the criminals he chased – jumpy, fidgety, always looking over their shoulder. Birds were like the general population too, in that they spent most of their time chirping, flapping their wings, full of life and mischief, not seeing menaces which often flew nearby. Had he the time, he would have sat there far beyond the second cup of coffee and cigarette he needed to get him going in the morning.

He read the newspaper from cover to cover. That morning he saw no particular crime story that tweaked his interest, so he laid the paper down, drained his coffee mug and snuffed out his cigarette. He grabbed his breakfast – a single muffin – to eat in the car and headed out the door just past 8 a.m. Once again, he would miss rush hour. He hated rush hour.

Lee backed his Fugitive Task Force "company" car out of the garage, a green Ford Aerostar loaded with every imaginable electronic gadget crammed into each nook and cranny. He could monitor a suspect's movements from blocks away using his high-powered video camera, or devices he had planted in or near a building. He loved technology. Other officers called him the "gadget man." From the outside of the van, no one could tell it was a cop car; all the antennas were hidden from view. Lee treated it as his mobile office, and during the next 11 weeks, it often became his sanctuary.

He backed the car out of the garage and turned around, driving down the 28-degree sloping driveway. He hated that driveway in the winter, but willingly paid the price because of the house that he had built atop a hill surrounded by nearly an acre of woods. There he could see Prior Lake two blocks away. Lee considered his house and tree-lined lot an idyllic setting, a place of refuge from the rough and tumble of his daily work chasing fugitives.

Some mornings he drove to the headquarters of the Minnesota Bureau of Criminal Apprehension (BCA) on St. Paul's busy University Avenue. Forensic work might be ready, or reports may be due. Sometimes he just needed to check in. The BCA was his primary employer. He had been assigned by the BCA to the FBI's Fugitive Task Force in March of 1994.

Some mornings he made investigative stops along the route to work. An informer or witness might meet him on the strip in Bloomington, or maybe at the Mall of America. Perhaps they gave him a lead, or told him where to find someone he chased. He had developed dozens of contacts and informants across Minnesota during his years on the BCA's narcotics unit. Now, only murder, rape or armed robbery, – violent crimes against people – that involved interstate flight to avoid prosecution, caught his attention and could end up in his stack of things to do.

That May morning he drove straight to the Fugitive Task Force office in Minneapolis. Traffic flowed smoothly on I-35W going north into downtown.

It was still too early for Minnesota's road construction season, Lee laughed to himself.

Just past the Humphrey Metrodome, where the Minnesota Twins and Vikings played their home games, he exited the freeway and turned west on Washington Avenue. The Twins had been in Toronto the night before, and beat the Blue Jays 3-2. Lee loved baseball, but much preferred amateur sports to the professionals.

His daily route took him a few blocks north of the Metrodome. On game days, whether it was the Twins, Vikings or Minnesota Gophers, the short three blocks to his turnoff could take several minutes – at 8 a.m., it took only a few.

The FBI had chosen a nondescript office for the Fugitive Task Force in an old rehabilitated milling building at 111 Second Street South. Just as he turned off Second Avenue into the huge parking lot, he glanced up and saw Dunn Brother's Coffee shop, one of his favorite stops. On a leisurely day like this one, he might have time for a mug of French Roast – no fancy lattes for Lee Urness.

Just across the street from Lee's parking spot stood the marbled old Federal Building on Third and Washington, the scene of numerous anti-war protests during the 1960s. Lee had little time for the 1960s anti-war sentiment, seeing it as wrong-headed and anti-American. And Lee had little time for the "bleeding heart liberals" who he saw standing against tough prosecution of the criminals he caught. He cared nothing about politicians or politics, but he loved Minnesota and America. He directed his fulltime attention to the bad guys who screwed up society for everyone else.

Parked in one of the 12 spots reserved by the FTF, he walked to the front of the building, climbed the steps and went in. Except for the tan fishing vest that he wore everywhere he went, Lee looked like any one of the other casually dressed people who worked in the many small businesses housed in the building. Some of the others knew that he and his peers were cops, but most knew nothing about them.

The charm of the ancient four-story rehabbed building attracted a number of artists and media production companies. Lee noticed that some of them appeared to be "free spirits," that is, "non-conformist." He had wondered how many gays and lesbians worked in the building. Lee certainly had personal feelings about gays and lesbians, though if they rented offices in his building, he could care less. It was a community of people he knew little about, as he and his FTF teammates had never before worked with them. He knew that there had been several brutal, violent gay crimes in the city, but his job was to chase crooks not investigate those crimes.

He remembered the murder of Minnesota State Senator John Chenoweth down by the Mississippi River flats. At that time, Lee still worked narcotics, and Chenoweth's death and its prosecution meant nothing to him. He heard it was just another act of gay on gay violence, and since it had not involved making a drug bust, it was someone else's problem. In his new job at the FTF, had Chenoweth's murderer fled the state, Lee would have chased him down, never giving a thought to his lifestyle. "A crook is a crook, gay or straight," Lee felt.

He slowly walked around the corner and down the light tan painted narrow hall to the Fugitive Task Force office, a simple two-room affair that said, "Suite 160: AGSG Associates." Pushing open the door, he saw that no one else was there, except for the secretary, JB – Jeanie Burns.

Lee glanced around the room at the eight drab wood desks. There were no cubicles in which to work for these cops; they needed quick communication with each other. Secrets and walls would have hindered their teamwork.

Lee's desk sat on the left, the second one from the door. In front of him sat an empty desk formally used by "Little Dicky," Dick Birrenbach, a 6'2" heavy-set Ramsey County Deputy. One of Lee's favorite co-workers, Little Dicky had suffered a heart attack several weeks earlier and had to retire. Lee missed him, but would miss him more in the weeks ahead.

Lisa Davis, the Minneapolis Police Officer on the team, sat at the desk behind his. Across the room against the wall sat the desks of the other team members; Kevin Rickett and Steve Gilkerson, the FBI agents, Hennepin County Deputy Sheriff Gary Charbonneau, U.S. Marshal Mark "Puttzie" Postudensek, and St. Paul Police Officer Vern Lee. Jeannie's desk sat in the back corner next to the Mobile Data Terminal (MDT).

Two 18" square rough-hewn Cedar pillars stood 10 feet apart down the middle of the room. FTF members had hung a dartboard on one of them, useful while waiting for a lead to call back, or during times of boredom.

Lee barely noticed the clutter of notes, wanted posters and memorabilia hanging on various bulletin boards next to each desk.

Walking into the storeroom, the only other room in the FTF office, Lee poured himself another cup of coffee. The metal cabinets that held FTF case files stood like soldiers in a straight line against the wall. The computer's screen-saver blinked at him from the monitor that sat on the table in the corner.

He walked out to the office and sat down at the MDT. It looked the same as the one in his van and in most every police car in America. Staring at the green eight-inch screen, he began scrolling through the lines of information.

Lee, or any one of his FTF team members, checked the MDT several times a day, fishing for work. Some of their caseload came from local police or sheriff calls, or requests from other FTF jurisdictions. But unlike regular police work, the FTF went looking for cases where their expertise could help track down a criminal and stop him or her before the commission of another crime. Their cases could take any number of directions. They could nab a man in just a few hours, or days, or sometimes, months.

Lee saw criminals as mostly dumb, and they had well-established patterns of giving themselves away. Still, in some cases, the chase felt like riding an angry Brahma bull, and the cop always tried to think and act one step ahead to keep from getting bucked off before subduing the beast. The FTF had captured hundreds of America's worst criminals.

That morning, while Andrew Cunanan and David Madson freely drove around Minnesota, Lee sat at the MDT. One entry caught his eye. He saw that Minneapolis Police were searching for a missing Red Jeep Cherokee and its driver, David Madson. The report said the police wanted to apprehend Madson to question him about a recent murder.

Looks interesting. Maybe we can help, Lee thought. *Today's Friday and the car has been missing since Tuesday. He probably fled the state,* Lee reasoned. He pushed the quick-key on the computer keyboard to print the message. Tearing it off the printer, he walked to his desk and dialed the Minneapolis Police Department. While he waited for an answer, he swiveled around in his chair and lifted up his long legs, planting his feet on Lisa's desk, chuckling to himself. She'd give him hell if she were there.

"Homicide," Lee heard.

"This is Lee Urness, Fugitive Task Force."

"What's on your mind?" the man asked.

"I saw your alert about the Jeep on the MDT and wondered what the deal is. Is there anything I can do to help?"

"No, there's nothing goin' on. We're just tryin' to find the Jeep."

"Well, keep me in mind in case something happens and I can help," Lee said. He never worried about jurisdiction on these cases; that stuff was for TV and movies. The FTF worked every case in tandem with local cops and the FBI agents from jurisdictions across America.

"Okay, will do," the officer answered.

"I see it's been more than three days since the notice was sent. I'm betting your guy's left the state," Lee offered.

"Could be, but we have nothing on it now."

"Well let me know when you finally get the warrant. I'm sure he left the state."

"You got it. Talk to you later," he said.

And they said good-bye.

Lee sat back a moment and re-read the printout. His instincts told him he would hear more about this case, but he had no idea just how loud would be the volume.

The Fugitive Task Force could do nothing until the local jurisdiction issued an arrest warrant, and there had to be probable cause or proof that the criminal had fled across state lines. That meant getting an Unlawful Flight to Avoid Prosecution (UFAP) warrant, difficult without substantial evidence.

Lee looked at the printout again. His hands were tied. *Ah, maybe they'll find the guy*, he sighed, and threw the paper on his desk.

For once, there was nothing else to do. On those rare slow days the task force members took time off, because once something broke, they never knew when their next free day, or hour, or moment, would come.

As Lee headed home around noon, he looked forward to a relaxing weekend, and it *was* relaxing. It was also the last one he enjoyed once he learned that Andrew Cunanan drove that red Jeep out of state.

Chapter 6 ~ Good-bye sweet love

"I think my dad will know what to do," David Madson had told Andrew Cunanan. Staying in Minneapolis was out of the question.

They could hide for a time in a big city – Chicago, New York, Miami – where there was a huge gay population. No one would notice them and even if they did, no one wanted trouble. Turning in a gay man ran its own risks for the snitch. It often meant "coming out of the closet," or violent retaliation.

Gay men believed that cops cared little about solving gay on gay crimes, even murder. Maybe no one would do much about Trail. Still, Madson and Cunanan eventually needed money and a permanent place to stay.

Since William Norman* of San Diego had "fired" Cunanan as his lover and traveling companion the previous summer, Andrew had no real permanent home, nor income. This he sought with David Madson, and the plan, in a perverse way, seemed to be materializing. They drove together up I-35 that Friday, May 2, just hours after Lee Urness had scanned the MDT looking for something to do. (Lee considered that the red Jeep could already have been stopped by a curious highway patrolman who may have spotted the missing vehicle on the NCIC list. Minneapolis Homicide, who had been looking for the Jeep since Tuesday night, had put it on "look out," a local watch list.)

As Madson drove that Friday, he watched his speed carefully, not wanting to attract undue attention from any wondering highway patrolman. Had he wanted or been able to escape from Cunanan's grasp, he could have easily caught a cop's eye by speeding or driving erratically; but he did neither, just as he had, apparently, made no attempt to break free since Cunanan had killed Trail.

Cunanan carried Jeff Trail's .40 caliber gun with him when they fled the apartment. It sat next to him in the car, or perhaps he held it in his hand, still fully loaded. Scott Anderson had only seen the faces of the two men in the car; not the gun.

"Exit here," Cunanan told Madson as he spotted the exit ramp to Rush City.

Madson drove up the ramp as Cunanan scanned the area, trying to decide what to do next. On his right, he saw the pride of Rush City – a 1,999 pound plastic Walleye mounted on a pedestal. A sign boasted that this was the Walleye caught by Paul Bunyan. The huge plastic fish sat on the corner of the Tank & Tackle's parking lot – a local bait shop and gas station. The town of Rush City sat a few miles to the east.

"Go left," Cunanan said, nodding his head.

"Andrew, where are we going?"They had not planned this stop.

"I'm not sure yet. Just drive ahead," he said. "I need to pee." He scanned the fields on either side of the road.

Three miles down the narrow two-lane blacktopped road – Rush Lake Trail – they saw the Rush Lake Resort, a collection of old cabins and mobile homes. Across the highway in an otherwise empty field sat a dozen or so fishing houses, placed there long before the ice came off the lake, awaiting next year's ice fishing season.

Just ahead on the right sat a big red barn not more than 30 feet from the road, ancient but well preserved, and 50 feet after it, sat its twin. On their left a sign said, "State Game Warden, Get Fire Permits Here."

"Keep going," Cunanan said.

On his left toward the lake he saw a big farmhouse. Just up the road he saw the ideal spot to pull off – St. John's Cemetery.

"Pull in there," he said as he nodded toward the opened gates on the east end of the country cemetery. Just after pulling in, they saw that the dirt horseshoe-shaped driveway bent around to the right. "This will do," Cunanan said, as they both got out and did their business. The bare trees that surrounded the cemetery gave them no cover, but standing behind the Jeep, which itself sat parked behind granite grave markers, no one would have noticed them from the road.

"Let's go back that way," Cunanan said, nodding toward the east, the direction from which they had come since leaving the freeway.

Madson pondered what to do next, besides following Cunanan's orders. He had loved this man, physically and emotionally, and for a long time. He had considered him his friend. Madson naturally trusted people. He planned to find a positive way to help Cunanan.

Cunanan had, just a few days earlier, committed a hideous crime out of some sort of rage Madson could not understand. Madson felt pity and sorrow for his friend and wanted to help him. Sure, Andrew boasted and lied, and he might even have been involved in some shady business dealings; Madson knew that. But deep inside, he was just a gregarious, fun-loving boy. Madson still felt himself drawn to Cunanan. Others might have seen him as held hostage, but there were no chains or handcuffs in the car, just Cunanan's need to have someone help him out of the terrible trouble he had created. Howard

Madson, David's dad, had always offered good advice, and David felt glad they had headed in that direction.

Just down the road from the cemetery, Cunanan again saw the farmhouse, noticing that it looked abandoned. Surrounding it, grew dozens of tall leafless trees struggling to awaken from winter's deep sleep. "Turn here," he said, nodding toward the driveway with the smashed mailbox numbered "21B," while ignoring the "No Trespassing" sign that guarded the driveway. Madson obeyed.

Cunanan saw no cars or farm equipment in the yard, and felt certain no one was around. "Stop here," he said. Madson pulled into the driveway well off the road and stopped. George Fahrenholdz had lived in that house for years, but abandoned it after a house fire in 1992. He had moved to the Grant House Hotel in Rush City. Still, he came daily to check his mail and eyeball the place. But neither George nor anyone else was there that evening.

Cunanan surveyed the scene. He saw that the windows on the two-story farmhouse were broken out, and the paint chipped and peeling. Plywood covered the doors and several first floor windows. It looked like no one had lived there for years, and under different circumstances the place might have made a good hideout or even a setting for an erotic party.

The lawn had already turned green from spring rains, the snow had melted. The yard sloped down toward the lake behind the house, and more gradually from the driveway. Someone could easily drive down within 30 feet of the lakeshore which itself was covered in brush, weeds and long grass, even now gasping for the new life spring weather brought.

To his right Cunanan saw a weathered old barn, its brown and moldy green boards bulging at their seams, looking as though it might collapse at any moment. *Hide something in there and no one would find it for ages*, he thought. Closer to the driveway, several feet from the garage, a mature tree grew into and over what had been the concrete foundation of a silo that had been taken down decades earlier. A grey, rusty car sat abandoned in a growth of small trees and weeds.

"What are we doing here, Andrew?" Madson asked.

"I just want to talk, to get out and stretch my legs, and talk," he said. "Let's go down there, by the lake."

Madson started to get out of the Jeep, but Cunanan stopped him. "No, no, drive down there," he said, nodding toward the lake.

Madson drove slowly straight ahead, leaving the dirt driveway behind, making his way down the incline toward East Rush Lake. The Jeep left the grass matted down like a two-rut road.

"Stop here," Cunanan said. He opened the door and got out, walking to a spot in front of the Jeep, where he stood in the 8-inch tall grass, staring out at the lake.

Madson slowly got out and made his way down to Cunanan. He saw that he had taken the gun along with him.

"Andrew, what is this about?" Madson asked. "I thought we were going to my dad's place."

"I don't know. I just don't know. I mean, I did a terrible thing to J.T. I don't see any way out of it," the disconsolate man answered.

"There is always a way out," Madson said, smiling, trying to encourage his friend.

"It'd be better if I just kill myself," Cunanan said sadly, pulling a few blades of grass from their roots and letting them float away in the breeze. "That'll even things out."

"That's no answer and you know it," Madson said, looking at his pitiful friend, placing a tender hand of friendship on his shoulder. Both men looked rough after spending three days on the lam, and they were exhausted both physically and emotionally. "You need rest and time to think. We can get that at my dad's."

Cunanan stood thinking.

"Besides, people who commit suicide are forgotten about as quickly as they die," Madson reasoned. "Your dad's disappeared. You say you have no relationship with your mom, and you have hardly any contact with your brother and sisters. I mean, *I'd* care, but who else? You don't want to kill yourself, Andrew. You need to live and somehow, I don't know how, but somehow all this will work out. I am sure of it."

The stress from lack of sleep, bad diet and the knowledge of what he had done ate away at Cunanan. He felt immense anger and frustration racing through his body. He knew Madson was right. If he killed himself no one would much care, and certainly, no one would remember. Yet, he had debts impossible to pay off, had left friends and lovers strewn in his wake and, now having killed Jeff Trail, he knew it would be just a matter of time and some cop somewhere would catch up to him. A gay killer in prison wouldn't last long. The frustration built as each moment ticked away, leaving him without options.

Cunanan looked across the calm, beautiful Minnesota lake. The ice had gone out early that year and buds on dozens of varieties of bushes, trees and weeds yearned to break free of winter's deathly grasp. It was sometime past 6:15 p.m., and the sun hung at about 30° above the horizon. The air had begun to turn cooler. A light breeze off the lake sent the smell of a Minnesota spring day wafting to his nostrils, the kind of smell that spoke of cleansing, rebirth and reawakening. He stared off into the distance, almost in a trance.

Only one person knows what I did. No one else saw me with the body. Yes, maybe there is a way out of this. Maybe I can make a new life, somewhere, with someone. After all, I'm Andrew Cunanan; handsome, smart, good in bed, likeable.

Cunanan raised the gun up chest high in front of him and stared at it.

"Andrew, now you put that away," Madson urged him. "Killing yourself is ridiculous. You know that. Come on now, let's get back on the road," he said as he turned slightly back toward the car, urging Cunanan to follow.

Pop! Cunanan fired one shot at Madson, hitting him in the lower back, the bullet tearing through his body, the shell casing flying a dozen feet away into tall grass. The impact spun Madson around as he stumbled backward, now facing Cunanan.

"Andrew! What are you doing?" Madson shouted as burning pain ripped through his body.

"What I have to do," he said, raising the gun at Madson's face, the two of them separated by just a few feet.

"No! No!" Madson screamed in terror. "Andrew! I beg you, no!" he shouted, raising his hands in front of his face as if to deflect the bullet he felt sure would fly at any minute.

Pop! The gunshot echoed across the lake.

The slug tore off part of Madson's little finger, and then tore the skin off his right cheek just below his ear. He fell to the ground. Cunanan stood over him, leaned down and – Pop! – fired a bullet through Madson's right eye. In moments, he lay dead.

Cunanan stood there holding the gun, watching the life ebb out of his friend as the blood soaked into the ground. He shook at the visage as he vividly recalled Jeff Trail's battered body, twitching in its death throes just a few days earlier. Two men with whom he had shared sex, his life, dreams and aspirations, had now been terminated by his rage and anger, his sense of hopelessness. Any chance that he might find relief or a way out now lay dead at his feet. He knew that.

Cunanan surveyed the scene. Sure it was isolated and off the road, but the bare trees left no cover. He needed to leave quickly. Madson lay on his back in the rough grass and Cunanan could see he might be visible from the road. He reached down and grabbed Madson's legs, tucking one under each arm, and pulled the dead body down the hill into the brown weeds and stubble, under a small leafless tree, 10 feet from the lake. The rough grass and soil tore at Madson's back, leaving abrasions and scrapes in his dying flesh.

Cunanan reached down and moved Madson's arms so they lay next to his still body, one on either side. Then he stood looking at the body, for the last time taking in the sight of what he had just done. He emptied Madson's pockets save for a bookmark, but he left the Tag Heuer watch, worth thousands of dollars, on Madson's wrist. He took one last look at the "love of my life," and walked quickly back to the Jeep. He turned the car around and drove up the driveway, then east on Rush Lake Trail. He calculated that it could be days or weeks before anyone found the body. He had plenty of time to get away.

Numbed by what he had just done, Cunanan drove robotically back to I-35 and headed south, and catching I-94 east into Wisconsin. Using only rural-located rest stops, he drove directly to Chicago and for an unexplained reason, parked the red Jeep near the corner of North Astor and East Scott, a few doors away from the home of Lee Miglin. Had he been in this neighborhood before, or was his parking there just an act of happenstance? Whatever caused him to choose that specific parking spot, with nothing more to lose, he could put into practice the sordid and sickening rituals he had studied on S&M video tapes he left behind in his San Diego apartment.

And he needed cash.

Chapter 7 ~ Good night in Minnesota

"Maybe I can get the mower out tomorrow," Lee said as he and Kathy got ready for bed that night.

"And wash a few windows," she reminded him.

"Yeah, okay."

No ball games or practices were scheduled that weekend. Only a peaceful retreat at their Prior Lake dream home awaited them, unless he received an "off-duty" tip about someone he was chasing. "Off-duty" was a misnomer. Lee went home every night, but never felt he was *off-duty*. A call could come at any time from another FTF member, a local police officer or the FBI.

On one such Saturday morning, he received a phone call from the FTF office. Rick Pruitt, one of the crooks the team had been chasing for several weeks, called the FBI and wanted to turn himself in.

Pruitt and his friends had robbed an armored car in Prior Lake, Minnesota, and the Minnesota FTF had tracked him to Mexico. The dumb robber had left behind $1.7 million in cash hidden in the attic ceiling of his home. Lee had worked closely with Pruitt's wife and cousins, knowing that eventually he would call one or all of them. Crooks eventually call the people they know best – Lee lived by this rule.

Pruitt had made his way back to Minnesota, tired of running. He desired wifely affection.

"Mr. Pruitt, this is Lee Urness with the Fugitive Task Force. I understand you want to turn yourself in," Lee said when Pruitt answered the phone at the number he had left.

"Yeah, say listen, I'm at the Days Inn here in Burnsville, room 208. I'm tired of running."

"I see," Lee said, already heading for the door, cordless phone held close to his ear.

"But I need a deal," Pruitt said.

"A deal?"Lee asked, as he pushed the high-ride holster and his .40 caliber Smith & Wesson Sigma onto his belt. He pulled his fishing vest over his arms.

"Yeah, you see, I haven't seen my wife for a while and she's here with me. Don't worry, I'm not gonna hurt her. I just want some time alone with her; you know what I mean?"

"Ah, sure. How much time?"Lee said, calculating how long it would take him to get to the motel, just seven miles away.

"Half hour? That should be enough; then I'll turn myself in. I won't give you any trouble," Pruitt said.

"Okay. You've got 30 minutes. Better enjoy it," Lee said, now at his car. He left the cordless phone in the garage, started his car and headed down the driveway. He called Lisa Davis, his FTF partner, the FBI and the Burnsville Police as he drove those seven miles in five minutes.

Once at the motel, with the back ups in place, he reached into his squad car and used the permanently mounted cell phone to call Pruitt. "Look out the back window," he said. Lee watched as the curtains opened slightly. "We're waiting for you. You come out with your hands held high, and then I'll tell you what to do next. You got it?"

"I got it. I don't want any trouble," Pruitt said.

"You get none if you cooperate. Now come on out," Lee ordered.

Moments later Pruitt slowly opened the door and stared at an array of shotguns and pistols aimed at him.

"Come toward me slowly," Lee said, his adrenalin pumping. Lee had made more than 1,000 arrests, but every one still demanded that all of his attention be focused on the moment. He always had to be ready for the unexpected. "That's it. Nice and easy," he said as he watched Pruitt move slowly away from the motel room door.

"Now come on down the steps, real slow," Lee ordered as he watched Pruitt obey his commands. He could see that the man really did not want trouble, and he breathed easier.

As soon as Pruitt got close, Lee told him to turn around. In seconds he had him cuffed and in a police car, sending him on his way to jail.

As he watched the squad car pull away, Lee felt a flush of accomplishment as he always did when he caught someone. Like most of his arrests, this one went smoothly and without incident. Hollywood preferred Dirty Harry, portraying arrest scenes with bullets flying, windows smashing and people being blown away. Lee knew that violence did erupt now and then, but most often, arrests were like this one – a few tense moments but without incident. Still, he never lost the sense of excitement while making an arrest, because there was always an element of unpredictably.

That weekend of May 3, nothing unpredictable happened to Lee Urness. But in Chicago, Lee Miglin felt the violent wrath of Andrew Cunanan. And in Minnesota, two young fishermen who staked out a fishing spot hoped to land Northern or Walleye, but instead snared a body.

This looks like an ideal fishing hole

Kyle Hilken and Carl Schmidt, lifetime friends in their early 20s, drove to Rush Lake early on May 3 searching out sites for the Minnesota fishing opener the following weekend. The two North Dakota natives had never before fished in the area and heard it had plenty of hot spots. They had already checked out East Rush Lake and were deciding what to do next.

"Let's go up to Pine City," Hilken said.

As Schmidt drove down Rush Lake Trail, Hilken noticed a farmhouse and behind it, a clear access to the lake. An open field that led down to the lake lay surrounding the house.

"Maybe those people would let us drop a line out there. Looks like a good place to even pitch a tent," Hilken suggested.

"Let's go see," Schmidt answered, turning his Jeep around and heading back to the place. He turned into the driveway marked by a partially crushed mailbox that said "21B."

Hilken got out of the black Jeep. He saw a "No Trespassing" sign posted next to the driveway, but decided to walk toward the house anyway, hoping to get permission to camp and fish there. Then Hilken saw that the windows were broken out and the house abandoned.

Maybe we can find out who owns it and get permission to camp here, he thought. Before leaving, he decided to check out the lake and took a couple of steps in that direction.

"What the...?" he said, spotting something lying in the weeds and tall grass.

"Come here," he said waving at Schmidt. "It looks like a...a body." Its feet pointed toward the lake, with the arms lying on either side. He could not see the face.

"What?" Schmidt asked as he got out the Jeep and walked nearer.

"Stop there," Hilken said, not wanting Schmidt to mess up the death scene, but it was not necessary. Schmidt had gotten as close as he dared.

Hilken saw tire tracks in the grass that lead back up to the road. He stood about 20 yards from the body. It looked to him like someone was sleeping.

"Let's go down closer," Hilken suggested.

"No, no way. I'm staying up here." Schmidt could see the top of the head and the man's clothes, and that was good enough for him.

Hilken walked down a little closer to the body. "Yup, that's definitely a guy. He looks like he's sleeping."

"Come on, we'd better go call the cops," Schmidt said, not wanting any more of this scene. Hilken joined Schmidt in the Jeep. Schmidt needed no encouragement to get out of that place and drove directly back to the Tank & Tackle. There they called police.

Cunanan thought it would take days, if not weeks, before someone found Madson. Instead, it had only taken several hours. That left hope for the cops who soon descended on the scene en masse.

Sorry to spoil your weekend, but...

Jon Hermann, a Minnesota BCA agent, member of the SWAT team and good friend of Lee Urness, had just started making his lunch when the call came. "We got a body out at Rush Lake," Lt. Tom Alvin, from the Chisago County Sheriff's Department, told him. Hermann wrote down the directions to the site and immediately headed out, leaving lunch on the table.

By the time he arrived, yellow crime scene tape had been stretched all around the multiple acre site. He saw two men sitting in a black Jeep, learning later that they were the ones who found Madson's body.

Investigators began to process the site. Hermann, a veteran homicide detective, methodically began collecting evidence along with the BCA's crime lab team he had called to the scene. Joël Kohout, his partner, worked alongside him. As gruesome as was the murder, it was just another crime to solve, so thought Hermann. With some luck, they would catch the killer quickly.

He carefully studied Madson's corpse. A corpse that had been lying for a long time would have dry eyes, but he saw that these eyes still had moisture on them. Every indicator from the color of the skin to the clotting of blood pointed to a time of death within 12 hours.

He saw tire marks in the grass when he first arrived. Most of the matted grass that formed two ruts in the lawn still laid perfectly flat, bent over by Madson's Jeep as it drove in and out of the place. Immediately adjacent to the bent grass, the grass stood straight up, even though the sun now shone directly above them. To Hermann's trained and experienced eyes, that solidified his certainly about time of death. If it had been days earlier, the bent grass in the tire ruts would have already pretty much stood straight. In fact, as the day wore on he noticed that the bent grass quickly lost its distinction and began standing tall like the surrounding grass.

"I'd say late last night or early this morning," Hermann opined.

"I agree," Kohout said.

Sometime after 4:30, Hermann and his partner checked Madson's pockets looking for some form of identification. No one had a clue who lay dead in the grass. They found his pockets empty, save a bookmark from the Solar Light Book Store in San Francisco.

"Well, that's odd. A Frisco bookmark on an unidentified stiff in Minnesota," Hermann observed, holding the bookmark in his hand. It had a phone number. "I'm going to call the store," he told Kohout, and walked back to his car. There he dialed Helen Larson*, identified as one of the owners of the bookstore. He left a message for her on the answering machine. She returned the call within five minutes.

"Agent Hermann," he answered.

"Ah, hello. This is Helen Larson from San Francisco. You left an urgent message for me to call. Is something wrong?" she asked, her voice shook from anxiety.

"Well, I just needed to ask you a few questions." Hermann described the incident and the victim, to which Larson breathed a sigh of relief.

"No, he doesn't sound like anyone I know, but he could have been a customer or something," she answered. "My husband might know him. He's there in Minnesota now."

"Oh, why would he be here?"Hermann asked.

The Larson family had lived for 15 years in the Twin Cities before moving to California and going into the book business. Their son Jack*, an athlete, went to school at St. Paul's Hamline University where he ran track. Donald* Larson, her husband, had flown to Minneapolis on Thursday to watch Jack in a Friday track meet and to visit his parents.

"Donald and Jack will probably be at his folks out in Coon Rapids tonight. Here's the phone number if you want to talk with them," she said, dictating the number to Hermann.

"Thank you very much Mrs. Larson. I will be calling them right away," Hermann said. And he did, before the wife could tip them off that cops were looking for them.

Hermann felt they had gotten lucky. "Think about this," he said to Kohout. "A man from California comes to visit his jock son, finds out he's hooked up somehow with this guy, and in a fit of rage, kills the man, dumping his body. It sounds plausible."

"Yes, you could be right," Kohout offered.

"We might get lucky and wrap this up in a few hours," he added as they drove to Coon Rapids.

An hour later they pulled up in front of Evan* and Sara* Larson's house and went to the door. The Larson's invited them in and served them coffee and something to eat.

Donald explained that he had, indeed, flown to Minnesota the prior day. The family attended Jack's track meet – Jack's coaches could easily confirm this – and they met at Grandpa and Grandma's.

"We give out thousands of those bookmarks every year, with each book we sell. I can tell this one was printed in 1996. Either this guy or someone he knew must have bought a book from us. That's all I can suggest," Larson said. None of them recognized the picture of the dead man.

Thanking the family, Hermann and Kohout drove back to Chisago County, disappointed but determined. So, it would be tougher than an immediate arrest. Most homicides went that way, but Hermann felt certain he'd nail the killer quickly enough.

After 10 p.m., Todd Rivard, the chief investigator for the Chisago County Sheriff's Department, called Hermann. He mentioned that Sgt. Tichich from the Minneapolis police department had called, having seen a TV news story about the dead body found in Rush Lake. Tichich felt it could be either David Madson or the man who traveled with him. Hermann called Tichich right away.

"They left the driver's license of a David Madson on the table. Let me describe him to you," Tichich said.

"Sounds like our guy," Hermann answered after hearing the description.

Tichich condensed what they had learned about Madson and his friend, someone named Andrew Cunanan. "We talked with San Diego PD, and they've been to this guy's place and picked up a lot of stuff," he told Hermann.

Tichich had talked often with the media since they found the body of Jeff Trail that Tuesday afternoon. Unlike most cops, he apparently loved to talk to reporters, and it always bothered Lee. Lee worried that giving the media too much information, or slipping about something that should be kept secret, could hurt a case; worse yet, someone might get hurt because of what a cop leaked to the media.

Hermann had now become convinced that the name of the dead man was David Madson and obviously, this murder was tied to that of Jeff Trail. He saw the prime suspect as Andrew Cunanan, about whom he knew very little, and he spent his day Sunday learning what else he could.

The news reports about Madson's murder had played Saturday night without a name. A small article about a body having been found appeared in the Sunday papers, duly noted by Lee Urness, but filed away in the recesses of his brain.

One of the investigators called the *Star-Tribune's* Anne O'Connor with the news. "That story about the body they found at Rush Lake," he said.

"Yes."

"It's David Madson. You might want to get to work on it," he said.

A story about murder in Minneapolis had no media play outside of the Twin Cities, even if it seemed likely that two men had been killed by the same person. Although that person had apparently fled the murder scene in a stolen Jeep, the story still belonged to "Murderapolis," as the *New York Times* had recently labeled the city. For the first time in its history, the city's soaring murder rate had hit 100 in a year, far fewer than New York's 2,000 plus, or Washington, D.C.'s "highest murder rate in the nation" status. Still, 100 was a shocking number in the newly insecure Midwest city. And no one knew that Cunanan had plans to kill again, next in Chicago. For all the Minnesotans knew, the sad story of Jeff Trail and David Madson remained a local lover's triangle gone badly.

Dr. Lindsey Thomas performed an autopsy on Madson on Monday, May 5. By then, there was no doubt that whoever had killed the erstwhile gay man had fled the scene – and probably the state. Agent Hermann called his BCA friend Lee Urness.

Chapter 8 ~ Death developed

Speculation abounds about how or when Andrew Cunanan met Lee Miglin. In reality, only those two men knew the answer. To investigators and reporters early on in the case, it seemed likely that Miglin had a secret life that could have been hidden from his wife, son and business associates. Yet, soon after digging into case details, Chicago cops and Chicago Fugitive Task Force members came to believe that their meeting was "happenstance;" the kind of serendipity life throws at analytical, suspicious investigators and soap-opera hungry voyeurs. They labeled this a "crime of opportunity."

The Miglin family denied that the man had any ties to Cunanan. While eventually, Lee had to accept the official line that "no" connection existed, he remained unconvinced.

Cunanan earned his keep by prostituting himself to rich gay men. One sure way to meet these types was attending meetings of Gamma Mu, the La Jolla, California-based organization that catered to their exotic and erotic tastes. Thanks to William Norman, Cunanan had often traveled in their circles and held his own membership in Gamma Mu.

Gamma Mu staged fabulous "meetings" in exotic settings for their rich clientele and young, virile male prostitutes prowled those settings looking for scores. Investigators needed to answer the question, "Did Cunanan meet Miglin at a Gamma Mu event, or at some other gay meeting?"

Following Miglin's murder, Lee Urness asked to see Gamma Mu's membership list, and the organization held it tightly. Lee wanted to know if Miglin's name appeared there, and he needed to see if there were any other ties to Cunanan on that list. Keith Evans made the contact in Miami.

"I need to see your membership list," Evans explained, "to see if Lee Miglin was a member."

"Just a moment," Billy Price*, the Executive Director said. Price scanned the list, and then said, "No, Mr. Miglin's name is not here."

"Ah, may I see that list?" Evans said.

"I don't think so," Price answered. "I'm afraid that you would be pretty surprised to see who's on it."

"Well, I need to see for myself if Miglin's name appears."

"Tell you what," Price said. "I'll run it past the board and see what they think. We'll help you if we can."

"Okay, you do that, and I will check back with you in a few days." It took four weeks, but Gamma Mu found a way to work with the FBI. They allowed Evans to see the "M" section of the list. Miglin's name did not appear on the list. Still, the effort paid a side-benefit in that Gamma Mu members had become aware of Andrew Cunanan's danger to them.

Magazines found at Cunanan's last known San Diego address included two articles about Beitler-Miglin, the architectural firm owned in part by Lee Miglin. Cunanan acquaintances acknowledged that he had an interest in architecture, and that interest could easily have been sparked by his love affair with David Madson – or designs on Lee Miglin.

News reporters, in search of the sensational nature of the case, or perhaps just out of morbid curiosity, turned every possible stone to find the Miglin-Cunanan link. None ever did.

Given no other proof, investigators who spoke on the record have settled on "happenstance" as the most likely reason for Cunanan's May 3, 1997 meeting with Lee Miglin.

Lee Urness speculates

Lee Urness remains convinced that a link existed between Miglin and Cunanan. One link, however, that he discounted completely was that Miglin was some kind of closeted or high-rolling gay. "If that was true, within hours, and certainly days of his murder, Chicago gays would have come forward; even some on the national scene, like William Norman. But no one did." Norman denied knowing Miglin.

Actually, two men eventually came forward, but not until after the Versace murder. Lee discounted those sightings as nothing more than "folks who wanted to be part of a big case. We could never establish the gay link because it does not exist."

Lee resents the way the media treated Miglin. "The man was dead, and the media kept bringing up these rumors about his being gay. Why do that to a dead guy? It serves no purpose except to sell newspapers."

Lee spent countless hours replaying the various possibilities of how the two might have met previously. Any one of them could have unlocked a name or place that would lead him to Cunanan.

Cunanan had knowledge of architecture. Madson had been an architect, and certainly, Madson would have known something about someone of the stature of Lee Miglin. Cunanan had magazines with articles about Beitler-

Miglin, so he certainly knew the name. "What if the reason Cunanan had the magazines was so that he could get closer to Madson? So that Miglin's being in the magazine was happenstance."

Perhaps Madson knew Duke Miglin, or Cunanan did, and Duke had mentioned that his family lived in Chicago. Duke always denied knowing Cunanan, but that meant nothing. If they had only a brief meeting anywhere at any time, Cunanan would use Miglin's name if he had a need, and claim they were best of friends. "Maybe they had met briefly at a party," Lee suggests.

The first day following the murder, Lee spent a great deal of time trying to figure out where Cunanan had been since Tuesday. Perhaps he really had murdered Madson on Tuesday night and drove directly to Chicago. That gave him four days to find Miglin, whether on purpose or by accident. It leaves unexplained what seemed to be reliable Cunanan sightings on Friday in Minnesota.

"So suppose that Cunanan drove to Chicago and stayed at the Westin or the Omni," Lee asked. The hotels were close to Miglin's home. "Suppose that Cunanan saw Miglin sitting in the bar or a restaurant there and recognized him from the magazine article. It would be nothing for him to strike up a conversation with Miglin; that's how he got himself picked up; how he made his money." During such a conversation, Cunanan could have learned that Marilyn Miglin would be out of town that Saturday, and the location of Miglin's home. "This made it possible that Miglin even let Cunanan in the front door, thinking he was a friend of Duke's. And it had nothing to do with sex."

Miglin's name did not appear in Cunanan's small phone book (even though Lee learned later that he had the wrong book, but the name did not appear in the right book, either; neither did Duke's). There were no phone records of calls between Duke or Lee Miglin and Andrew Cunanan or David Madson.

"It makes no sense for Cunanan to just happen to be in that neighborhood and pick that particular house," Lee conjectured. "Think of it. Here's an out of town car parked several days in an upper class neighborhood, and nobody notices. It must be a neighborhood where no one keeps an eye out for the other neighbors."

It made so sense to Lee that Cunanan would just park on that corner unless he had a plan. "He needed money. He certainly must have realized that the cops would be looking for the Jeep, at least sometime soon. So he needed a ride. But he was not a car thief or a burglar. It is unlikely he would seize on someone unless he knew them."

Lee remains convinced of a link, but one that will never be known.

For the purposes of this book, Lee accepts the official story, that it was a murder of opportunity and happenstance. This, then, is the best guess of how the murder occurred.

Video training tapes?

When investigators searched Andrew Cunanan's San Diego apartment they found it stocked with numerous sadomasochist tapes – hard-core violent gay sex. Cunanan had ventured deep into S&M. Ever increasing in intensity, it drove him to continuously riskier levels of behavior. The soft, fun-loving sex partner had become rough and violent. David Madson had rejected him, at least in part, because of his rough sex play.

The images of murderous violence played across Cunanan's mind as he fled from Minnesota. He had bludgeoned a man to death and shot another in the face, making sure to destroy the good looks that had attracted him to both of them. During 60-seconds of brutal hammering and the instant brutality of three .40 caliber slugs, Cunanan took two lives and forever changed his own life's design.

He had made for Chicago with just about enough cash left to buy gas for the trip and eat a few meals. He needed money, companionship and a place to hide.

In the past, he had never had trouble picking up a man at a gay bar or club, and when money ran short, he trolled for rich older men, lonely men. They provided a place to stay, meals and more, just as had William Norman back in San Diego. Cunanan knew that there would be no long-term relationship building in Chicago, at least not until the murder investigators gave up pursuing him. But if he found the right man, he could, perhaps, convince him to help him out on his journey, maybe even out of the country.

His mother Maryann, one of his sisters and his brother lived in Illinois. They provided no real option in that his relationship with family members, save for Gina in San Francisco, was very strained. There would be no safe haven there.

He needed to score in Chicago where he had his favorite hotels, motels, bars and clubs. He knew enough about Chicago to recognize that some of its most prosperous people lived in an area known as the "Gold Coast." He headed there.

In Chicago where whole neighborhoods often spawned violent crime, the Gold Coast stood out as a safe haven for its residents. Few crimes against persons were reported there, but many crimes against property. Nearby bar patrons were often seen wandering its alleys and streets, searching through garbage cans; their most serious crimes were usually breaking and entering its houses and garages. Residents employed security services for assistance. Still, risking the loss of property as opposed to fear of physical violence meant that the area was a relatively safe place to live.

Cunanan drove the streets between North Lake Shore Drive and North State Parkway, on East Scott, Division, Goethe, and North Astor. There he saw expensive townhouses built side-by-side, close to the sidewalks on both sides of the narrow streets. The curbs in front of the homes were jammed bumper to bumper with parked cars. Street signs warned that anyone parking there between 6:00 p.m. and 6:00 a.m. without a parking sticker would be towed.

Unlike Minnesota, Chicago's trees had already sprouted leaves. Hedges and shrubs had turned deep green, and flower boxes burst with tulips, daisies and lilies. The wrought iron security fences that guarded the fronts of the townhouses stood stark and black, reminding intruders to stay out. The neighborhood shouted "wealth." Cunanan felt had he chosen well.

He searched for a place to park and saw an opening near the corner of Astor and Scott. Once parked, he reached under the seat to check for the Taurus pistol, feeling its cold steel on his hand. He looked around him and felt safe. Few people were on the streets. How to find the right target remained a mystery, but first, he laid the seat back and took a short nap.

Prowling the alleys

72-year old Lee Miglin had "built half of Chicago," public officials often said. Beitler-Miglin, the successful real estate company of which he was a partner, had business and political power; it owned and developed much property in the city.

Miglin often used Saturdays to putter around the garage. When the cleaning lady had left around noon on May 3, she saw him in the den. Everything looked normal. He had the afternoon and evening to himself.

Around 2 p.m., Miglin talked by phone with his wife Marilyn, who had called from Toronto. Her Marilyn Miglin cosmetics line had provided the family with a second thriving business. She had traveled to Toronto on a business trip, and checked in just to see if he was all right. Miglin told her that he was going to putter around the garage. He planned to go out and get a salad for dinner.

None of the neighbors talked with him that day, though two noticed him in his garage before 5:00 p.m. If he had left his hearing aids in the house, it would have been impossible for them to chat anyway, as he was virtually deaf without them.

He owned a 25 x 40 foot garage on East Division that sat across the alley and one door up from the Miglin townhouse. The garage housed three vehicles: a Jeep, parked tightly behind a 1982 Silver Bitter along one wall, and a 1995 dark green Lexus. Even with all three cars in the garage, he had ample access to the workbench and supplies stored against the front wall.

As he worked in the garage that day, he left the overhead door open. He wore a brown leather car coat to fight off the chill.

Cunanan awoke from his nap in David Madson's Jeep Cherokee. He had parked a half block from Miglin's house. With no criminal record or years of street smarts as a guide, Cunanan knew nothing about how to burgle a home. He knew only that to survive, he needed money; and he had a gun.

He walked south down Astor, crossing Scott and then a short half block to the alley that separated Miglin's house from the garage. He saw no one in the alley, but could see that a garage door on his left sat open. He walked quietly toward it and there he saw Lee Miglin. Without his hearing aids, Miglin never heard Cunanan enter the garage, but he did turn as Cunanan flashed the yawning barrel of Jeff Trail's .40 caliber Taurus in his face. Cunanan closed the garage door; it locked behind him. He turned the lights on.

"Move over there," Cunanan motioned with the gun.

"What do you want? I have money in my billfold and more in the house. I can give you money," Miglin said, reaching into his pocket and pulling out his billfold. Cunanan took it from him.

Cunanan faced the same problem with Miglin as with Madson. They were both witnesses to a crime. All that mattered to him was survival, and that meant that Miglin had to die.

He looked around the garage and spotted the instruments of death that he needed. "Over there," he said, motioning Miglin toward the corner where a small workbench sat.

"What are you going to do?" Miglin asked.

Still holding the gun in his hand, Cunanan pushed Miglin hard, and he fell, hitting the back of his head. Cunanan tied Miglin's feet together with a heavy-duty orange extension cord, knocking his right shoe off and onto the floor. Miglin lay still, stunned and immobilized as Cunanan put his gun down a few feet away and pushed his prey over onto his back.

Cunanan saw a roll of heavy-duty masking tape and grabbed it off the workbench. Walking around to Miglin's head, he knelt down, one leg on either side.

Working quickly, he pulled off a length of tape and tore it loose. Taking the strip of tape in one hand, he lifted Miglin's head up and pulled the tape across his face. Then he pulled it around behind Miglin's head. He had seen similar scenes in the S&M videos that littered his San Diego apartment.

"What are you doing?" Miglin tried to yell as he regained consciousness, but the masking tape muffled his voice.

Cunanan tore off another piece of tape and wrapped it the other way so that it went all around Miglin's head. Then he tore off another piece, and wrapped it around Miglin's nose and completely around his head, leaving his nostrils exposed. He had no intention of suffocating Miglin – his intentions were far more sinister.

"Please! Please stop!!" Miglin's body thrashed about, and he continued to try to scream.

Cunanan saw a pair of white and black cotton work gloves on the workbench. Grabbing one, he shoved it into Miglin's mouth, muffling his screams.

He continued wrapping tape around Miglin's head, covering every inch of it to just above his hairline down to his chin, leaving only the nostrils uncovered. Being so wrapped created a cruel claustrophobic feeling that would leave Miglin gasping for air.

Cunanan found a box of dark green plastic bags and laid them out on the floor. He rolled Miglin on top of the bags.

Miglin strained against the increasing oppression as panic overtook him. But Cunanan had only begun his hideous ritual. He clenched his fist and beat Miglin several times on his checks, near his eyes and nose.

Cunanan pulled Miglin's white shirt and T-shirt up, exposing the man's chest and he yanked open the fly of his jeans, slightly tearing the zipper, but he stopped short of molesting him.

He grabbed a Phillips screwdriver from a small toolbox. Then he began jabbing it into Miglin's chest, causing the helpless man excruciating pain. Blood began to pool on Miglin's chest, soaking his shirts and running down his body.

Cunanan continued to stab him, deeper and deeper, twisting and turning the screwdriver as he did, magnifying the pain. With one violent thrust, he punctured Miglin's aorta in two places. With another, he punctured his heart and a lung.

Miglin could not scream as the masking tape held his mouth and chin in place. He could only breath heavier through his nostrils as his body contorted and writhed in painful convulsions. Cunanan had killed Jeff Trail in a 60-second barrage of hammer blows: now he stretched out death for several minutes, as though wanting to pay Miglin back for being rich, or just being in the wrong place at the wrong time.

He thrust the screwdriver into Miglin's right neck, just below the ear, but missed the artery. He poked him on the torso a few more times.

Now blood pooled everywhere as Cunanan began to tire of his terrifying task. As though he wanted to make sure that Miglin never again got up, he took a sack of powdered cement and dropped it on the man, causing all of Miglin's ribs to break twice, and for a short time, forcing the man to try to breathe through the pain of shattered bone.

More than 700 cc's of blood poured into Miglin's chest from the wounds to the heart, lung and aorta. He lost consciousness.

Cunanan saw a red-handled bow saw on the workbench, the kind used to trim hedges and small trees. Seizing the handle on either end, he pressed it down on Miglin's Adam's apple, drawing it back and forth, as though intent on sawing the man's head off. But he stopped.

Cunanan laid the saw down near the screwdriver.

He dragged Miglin's body to its final resting place in front of the 1982 Bitter on top of brown wrapping paper he had laid out on the floor. Leaving the cement bags leaning against Miglin's body, he retrieved a blue jacket from the Jeep and laid it across the masking-taped face. He put the bow saw into a nearby trashcan, but put the screwdriver, the toolbox, and Miglin's shoe into the trunk of the Lexus.

The closed garage door had protected Cunanan from prying eyes and apparently, no one heard Miglin's muffled screams. Cunanan had once again killed in private, his victim the only witness.

With any luck, he figured that he would be long gone before anyone found Lee Miglin. He needed to complete his task and get away from there. He had no idea that two fishermen had already found David Madson's body or that his name had already been connected to those two murders.

Feast, then flee

Covered in blood, Cunanan needed to clean up. He took Miglin's keys and went across the alley. He walked across the parking apron that abutted the brick wall that guarded the townhouse. He could see the townhouse rising three stories above the wall. He opened and walked through the wrought iron gate and into the home. He closed the blinds.

Inside the house, he tore off his blood soaked clothes and put them into a bag that he later threw into the Lexus. He showered away the blood that stuck to his body, and he shaved his face. As he did this, a neighbor couple came home, sometime after 5:00 p.m., and noticed the wrought iron gate had been left open and the blinds closed. It registered as odd, since the Miglins usually kept the gate closed and the blinds open. They left again at 6:30 p.m. and neither saw nor heard anything else.

Dressing in fresh clothes, Cunanan went to the kitchen and realized his hunger. In the refrigerator, he found a large chunk of ham and took it out, slicing off generous pieces from which he built a sandwich. He opened the refrigerator again and retrieved a shiny red apple and a can of Coke. He saw a bottle of cranberry juice and poured himself a drink in a paper cup, leaving the bottle on the counter.

He chewed on the sandwich and took a bite from the apple, walking quietly around the first floor staring at the beautiful, well-decorated home. He saw the gold-print drapes on the big front bay window, and the beautiful black baby grand piano sitting on the nearly pure white carpet. A white satin chair and matching footstool sat near the piano. It had been 10 months since he lived in such beautiful surroundings. The thought made him sick with frustration and anger.

Back in the kitchen, he set the apple and sandwich down and continued his tour of the house. He needed more money. He had already cleaned out Miglin's billfold.

He searched the first floor. Then he climbed the stairs and entered the front room. There sat a gold-embossed black secretary's desk in front of louvered blinds that covered the bay window – they were closed. No one could see him standing here.

During his search, he found a 9-mm. handgun, but closer examination revealed that it was only a replica. He left it on the counter next to the bathroom sink.

Back in the kitchen, he took another bite of the sandwich and left it on the table next to the unfinished can of Coke. He found a carton of ice cream and sampled its contents.

Soon he needed to leave, but before he hit the road, he took a short nap. (Somehow, never determined by investigators, Cunanan knew that Marilyn Miglin would not be home that evening.)

When he awoke, he went out into the alley and walked up to the end, looking in both directions. A man working nearby noticed him, but wrote it off as just another bar patron walking the alley.

Just past 11:00 p.m. he did a mental inventory. He had all the money he could find in the house. He had found a few gold coins, which he admired for their beauty and value; they provided a potential source of cash if he needed to pawn them. Taking other items of value to fence made no sense; he had no clue how to sell stolen goods.

His belly felt full, his body rested. He had everything he needed. Night had fallen and that was his favorite time of day.

He went back to the garage, trying to look as though he belonged to the neighborhood. "This'll do just fine," he said, smiling as he threw his gym bag into the Lexus and slipped the Taurus under the front seat. Another of Miglin's leather jackets and a few shirts had been added to his prizes.

His hand and body felt the fine leather on the Lexus' seats as he adjusted it to fit his body. He saw that Miglin's body had been hidden enough so no one looking in would see it.

He gave one last look at the garage before pushing the button on the remote door opener, started the car and slowly backed out. He closed the garage door and drove up the alley, the car purring quietly, granting a sense of peace and prosperity. As he turned on East Scott, he threw a glance at the red Jeep Cherokee. He wondered if a cop had ticketed it yet, but the windshield held nothing but wipers.

As quickly as he could, he found Route 41 and drove south to I-90. He had already decided to head to New York City, a city he knew well and had visited often. He felt sure he could blend in there until he could figure out what to do next. His newfound wealth would bring him a few hot dates and, with any luck, someone else willing to pay for his services.

It would be Marilyn Miglin's fate to discover the next day that her husband had become the third victim. Like the Trail and Madson families, her life laid shattered by the hands of Andrew Cunanan, a man with no purpose, no hope and no plan, an elixir of disaster that would soon explode on a quiet, unassuming New Jersey cemetery worker and create chaos for an intense Minnesota cop.

Awful homecoming

Marilyn Miglin came home Sunday morning and saw that things looked wrong. She noticed a gun sitting on the counter in the bathroom, and then saw food items out on the counter. She called police.

Two officers entered the home and inspected the gun. They saw that it was a replica, but Mrs. Miglin knew nothing about it. Seeing the food warned them that a burglar could possibly still be in the house, and they searched carefully, finding no one. They did see remnants of someone cleaning up in the bathroom, as well as the partially eaten food.

Lee Miglin was not around.

They decided to check the garage and here confronted a horror beyond imagination. The officers called for help and a crime scene team.

In an apartment building on East Scott, 27-year old Eric Ferkenhoff rolled out of bed. He showered, dressed and left for his job as a rookie crime reporter for *The Chicago Tribune*. Using the apartment building's west door, he left the neighborhood unaware that a small crowd of cops had gathered just 100 feet east of him on Scott.

Ferkenhoff felt tired that day and hoped for a break – a quiet news day. Soon after arriving, his assignment editor told him of a Gold Coast death. Ferkenhoff figured one of the quirky area residents had committed suicide and so, took his time about looking into it. Then his fiancé called. She worked for a city wire service and saw a story about an elderly man having been found dead, that it might not be suicide. Ferkenhoff recognized the address easily enough, but there was no name attached to the wire, and he never personally knew the neighbors.

When he arrived at the scene he saw a small army of police officers, and they were not sharing information, not even the victim's name. He leaned against a car and waited. Upon reflection years later, it occurred to him that he, or any number of gawkers, cops or other reporters, may have used David Madson's Red Jeep Cherokee as a backrest that day. But no one spotted or reported the Minnesota plates.

Ferkenhoff had covered dozens of murders and violent crimes in his short tenure at the *Tribune*, and had learned that Chicago cops were relatively good about cooperating with reporters, but not on this case. He discovered that the cops treated this case "close to the vest," unwilling to share details.

Still, he had his sources inside the department, and later that morning one of them shared that some sort of garden implement had been used in the murder. Ferkenhoff then wrote the first murder story about the elderly victim, unaware that an out-of-town gay killer had been the perpetrator and that evidence of his complicity sat parked a short distance from Miglin's front door. It would be the Medical Examiner who revealed Miglin's name to the world the next day.

Chicago police began canvassing the townhouses, apartments and businesses in the area. No one, they found, had heard or seen anything useful. Those few who reported seeing anyone in the alley described a family that had been moving away, or the vagrants and drunks common to the area. The cops meant to treat Miglin's murder just as they did any of the other hundreds of homicides they investigated each year, pursuing evidence and looking for the murderer.

Miglin and his partner, J. Paul Beitler, were powerful political players in the windy city. Reporters speculated that this, along with the celebrity stature of the men, resulted in the near media blackout.

(Once the chase began, Lee felt fortunate that a Chicago police officer, Terry Thedford, worked on that city's Fugitive Task Force. Only through Thedford did he win the help of the big city's cops.)

On Monday, Dr. Edmund Donoghue, the Chief Medical Examiner for Cook County, performed an autopsy on Lee Miglin. Donoghue had learned about the murder on the prior day as he left Mass. He could have assigned the case to any of the doctors on duty, but chose to do it himself. Part of his job was handling the more difficult cases, and this one had its own certain peculiarities. As he witnessed the intensity of the media in covering the Miglin murder story, Donoghue saw right away that this case would be different from others. A powerful man brutally murdered made big news, more so than a drug abuser beaten to death in a deal gone bad.

Donoghue performed a thorough examination of Miglin's body. It bothered him that police had already labeled the murder as some sort of torture, implying that the killer had dragged out each step of the process. He saw it differently. Though Miglin certainly suffered the terrorizing effects of being wrapped in masking tape, and though the punctures made by the screwdriver and associated with the broken ribs certainly were painful, they were short-lived.

Donoghue ordered a thorough toxicology screen, performing numerous tests on Miglin's hair, fingernails and blood. One test he did not order, because he had no reason to, was an HIV or AIDS screening. Nothing about Miglin's body suggested to Donoghue the need for such a test, and on that day, no one knew about Andrew Cunanan.

At the *Chicago Tribune*, veteran reporter Andrew Martin took the lead on the Miglin murder case, assisted by Ferkenhoff and John O'Brien. They saw right away that it was big news in the windy city as police tightened the noose on information flow. Martin began a long, frustrating and unfulfilled search for the link between Lee Miglin and Andrew Cunanan. That same day, a Chicago police officer noticed a Red Jeep Cherokee parked illegally on Astor, near Scott, and wrote a ticket; but the cop never ran an NCIC check.

Chapter 9 ~ TV news becomes Lee's story

All weekend Lee had chewed on Saturday night's TV news of a body being found up by East Rush Lake. He felt in his bones that soon he would be involved, even though he had no idea yet that it connected to David Madson's murder. All he knew was that Madson's Jeep was missing and Jeffrey Trail laid dead.

He sat at his desk late on Monday afternoon. His phone rang.

"Fugitive Task Force, Agent Urness," he answered.

"Lee, it's Jon Hermann," the BCA agent said.

"Hey Jon, what's up?"

"Well big guy, I've got a case for you. You said you were good, so let's see what you can do with it."

"What is *it*?" Lee asked.

"The body they found at East Rush Lake was a David Madson, the…"

"…owner of the missing red Jeep," Lee finished.

"You got it," Hermann said.

"What do you know?" Lee asked, readying his pen. He scribbled notes on a white legal pad, the first of dozens he would fill in the next 11 weeks.

Hermann described the crime scene at East Rush Lake, what they found on Madson and his discussions with the Minneapolis Police Department. Hermann said he believed Andrew Cunanan killed Madson and fled in the Jeep.

"It sure sounds like this Cunanan guy," Lee said. "You know much about him?"

"Nope, not yet, but I'm working on some things."

"Well, let's go get him," Lee said, confident that like any other case, he'd find and capture Cunanan quickly.

"Okay. I'll get going on the local warrant," Hermann said. Before Lee could do anything officially on a state crime, someone had to get a judge to issue a local arrest warrant, and it would be for Second Degree Murder. Minnesota law required an indictment for First Degree Murder, and Lee knew they could get that later, once they captured Cunanan.

"You got what you need to get the warrant?" Lee asked.

"Well, I'm not so sure. Anything you can turn up will be useful," he said. Lee could hear the pause as Hermann spoke and could imagine him frowning. "I wish we had more, though."

"Keep me posted. I can't do much without the warrant, you know." Actually, officially, Lee could do nothing.

"I will have it tomorrow," he said.

"I know you will. When you've got your ducks in a row call me right away. In the meantime, I'll get ready." Lee knew that if Hermann said it would be ready on Tuesday, only God, or a reluctant judge or county attorney, could stop him.

They said good-bye.

Lee went to the MDT and typed the Jeep's license plate number into the National Crime Information Center (NCIC) database. Nothing came up. "What?" he said aloud, exasperated. He tried again; and again, nothing came up. "I don't believe it," he said, picking up the phone and calling Hermann.

"Jon, you'll never believe this," Lee said when Hermann answered the phone. "MPD never listed the Jeep on the NCIC database!"

"You gotta be kidding me. I thought they had it in," Hermann answered.

"I wish I *was* kidding. You'd better get it listed right now," he said.

"This county will have it in as soon as I'm off the phone," Hermann answered as Lee heard him hang up.

Lee sat at his desk, staring at the blank wall directly ahead of him. *Who the hell is Andrew Cunanan? Where's he going? What will he do next.* At the last thought, a shiver ran down his spine as a fearful memory flooded his mind.

An unsuspecting cop

On August 27, 1994, a beautiful sunny morning, Lee had been on his way to the office around 8 a.m. when he heard a call on a police radio. A cop had been shot in St. Paul, and officers were in pursuit of the killer at that moment. He turned on his siren and lights and roared toward St. Paul's East Side.

Just off busy Johnson Parkway, he pulled into the pot-holed parking lot at Johnson Brother's, a liquor warehouse that sat next to I-94. As he got out of the car, he heard helicopter blades beating the air and scores of sirens coming from all directions.

By now, he knew that second generation St. Paul Police Officer Ron Ryan Jr. had been gunned down point-blank in the parking lot of Sacred Heart Catholic Church. Ryan had gone there to check out a car that had been parked in the church lot overnight. Walking up to the vehicle, he looked into the window at a "slumper," a man sleeping in the car. Ryan walked to the back of the car to check the license plates and started toward his squad when a flurry of gunshots sent him sprawling.

Guy Harvey Baker got out of the Red Plymouth Sundance and walked to where Ryan lay, flipped him over and stole his service revolver. Satisfied with his diabolical deed, Baker climbed into his car as a neighbor began shooting at him. He sped away, wanting none of the neighbor's action.

A short time later, two boys spotted Baker's abandoned car in the Johnson Brother's parking lot. Now there, Lee walked up to St. Paul Police Sergeant Vern Lee. Sgt. Lee, a fellow member of the Minnesota Fugitive Task Force, stood next to his squad car, directing police officers on a hand-held radio as squads began closing in on the site.

Lee stood there waiting for other officers to arrive, anxious to get the shooter before he hurt anyone else. Then he saw K-9 officer Tim Jones and his dog Laser as they started searching the edge of the thick woods on the lot's north side.

"Maybe I should go with him," Lee said. "I hate to see him go in there alone."

"No, no. Those K-9 cops *like* working alone," Vern Lee answered.

"Well, he oughta have a backup," Lee insisted.

"No, he wants to work alone. You go and do house-to-house checks when Bergsgaard gets here."

Lee watched Jones and Laser work their way along the woods and then go in deeper, disappearing into the thick trees. He had bad vibes about cops working without partners, especially when an armed and dangerous killer hid who-knows-where in the woods.

Larry Bergsgaard, a fellow BCA agent and SWAT team member arrived. Vern Lee sent him with Urness to Wilson Avenue, just a few blocks away. There they began their house-to-house search, slowly and carefully moving down the street, always watchful for the slightest out-of-the-ordinary movement. They worked their way to the end of the street, a dead end that overlooked a high hill covered with thick trees.

"Pow! Pow! Pow!"

They heard gunshots echoing from somewhere down below. Running to Lee's van, they jumped in, tearing around the corner and onto 3rd Street, turning into a driveway that led down into a parking lot near three Little League ballfields. But there would be no games that morning, just serious and deadly business.

71

As Lee stopped the car, he grabbed his MP-5 submachine gun. He and Bergsgaard bolted from the van. They looked up ahead toward a house surrounded by trees that sat on a low hill overlooking the ballfields. The shots seemed to have come from behind the house. As Lee surveyed the scene, he could hear sirens coming from all directions, converging on the spot.

Behind the two-story grey house, and across an aged and rutted road, stood a 40' high hill that rose sharply to the back yards of the homes above. Trees covered the hill giving the sniper invisibility if he was up there, aiming to pick off cops one at a time.

Lee's eyes searched the perimeter of the site. Lying just behind the home, not too far from what looked like a fish house, he spotted something he would never forget. Officer Jones lay motionless in a pool of blood. Laser lay dead by his side. The shooter had gotten them both. The sight both sickened and angered Lee. He had no way of telling whether Jones was still alive, and it really made no difference. Protocol called for him and the others to get to the fallen officer and get him out of there. That meant venturing into the line of fire.

A bevy of cops had formed up on both sides of the house by then, and radios crackled as they debated what to do. The call went out, "Blast the fish house." Lee knew what that meant, and he didn't like it. He took a position behind a small bunker of dirt and grass and watched and listened to the roar of gunfire that decimated the fish house, and then the garage. If anyone had been in there, they would be dead for sure.

Lee's eyes constantly surveyed the area around and above where Jones laid, his MP-5 ready to fire, giving cover to the cops who hurried to Jones' body. Lifting up the bodies, the rescuers quickly took them to a nearby ambulance, where paramedics tried to revive them as they hurried to Regions Hospital's emergency room.

With the bodies removed, the cops still needed to flush the shooter out of the house, if he was still there. A SWAT team fired tear gas through the window but still, no one appeared. He had escaped.

Lee had encountered death many times, but never before had the victim been a fellow officer. That day, two officers in the same neighborhood had fallen to a killer's bullets. The reality hit Lee. It hit him hard.

Lee had wanted to patrol with Jones. Perhaps if he had, they could have killed the shooter before he struck again. Or the shooter could have killed him as well as Jones and Laser. And the shooter still sat somewhere, waiting for his next victim. Lee knew that once the guy killed Ryan it mattered little to the sick puke whether he killed again – his fate had been sealed.

Several hours later, early that afternoon, police found Guy Baker hunkered down under a piece of plywood in a stand of trees. He had three handguns with him, and he wore camouflage. Despite what he had done to those two officers and a police dog that day, the cops extricated him without incident, other than a few scrapes, and took him to Regions Hospital for medical care. Then they booked him for the vicious murder of two of their peers and a police dog.

Lee never forgot that morning or the sight of Tim Jones and Laser. It haunted him each time he thought about a killer on the loose who could strike at any time, like Andrew Cunanan, someone about whom he knew almost nothing save that he probably had a .40 caliber gun and enough anger to kill two men. And he was out there somewhere, driving a Jeep no cop knew was stolen, just waiting to be stopped for speeding. Lee shuddered as he envisioned a highway patrolman walking up to the window of that Jeep, just as Ron Ryan had done, and being blown away. It made his blood boil.

Lee could not stand stupid mistakes, and not listing that Jeep on NCIC was stupid. He resolved to track down this homicidal idiot before he killed someone else, especially a cop.

Religion played almost no role in Lee's life, but every night while Andrew Cunanan remained at large, Lee fell asleep praying that God would protect the cops who might run into the killer. And every morning, when his night had been uninterrupted by such a phone call, his first words were, "Thanks, God."

Tuesday waiting game

Lee had handled hundreds of fugitive cases and always got his man, with one exception. Alonso Carasco Chavez, wanted on a First Degree Murder warrant, still remained at large in Mexico, but he knew he would get him eventually.

The idea of apprehending Andrew Cunanan, now a two-time killer, seemed routine. He would do what he had always done: "Put the crook in the bubble and shut down his options, close the window on him, until he calls someone."

Jon Hermann had talked with the San Diego Police Department and so had the Minneapolis PD. Hermann said they had recovered quite a bit of stuff from Cunanan's apartment and that the San Diego PD had it at their office.

Lee knew that the more he could find out about a man, the easier it would be to catch him. This one sounded easy enough.

He called Hermann on Tuesday and learned that the local warrant had not yet been issued. Hermann was having trouble getting enough information together to convince County Attorney Jim Reuter to send the warrant to a judge.

"I'll keep working on it. I'm sure we can have it no later than tomorrow morning," Hermann told him.

Lee needed to get a UFAP warrant as quickly as possible. Then he could get to work catching Cunanan. Each minute of delay made his job harder.

"One thing kind of concerns me," Hermann said.

"What's that?"

"San Diego tells me that some of Cunanan's friends said he had told them his family owned a house or something on the French Riviera."

"Oh man, he could be long gone," Lee said.

"Right."

"Maybe I can get something going on that. You get that warrant and let me know as soon as you have it. I'll get mine ready so I can fly to the judge right away," Lee said as they hung up.

As Lee contemplated his next move, another Chicago cop spotted the Red Jeep Cherokee on Astor Street and wrote a second ticket, slipping it alongside the first, underneath the windshield wiper.

No problem for Sniz

Lee put his feet up on Lisa Davis's desk. He tried to reason how he could get the French Embassy to help. One of the other agents told him the routine. "You call the D.C. FBI office. You put in the paperwork. They contact the U.S. State Department. Then State contacts the French Embassy. That's the procedure, and you have no choice. Oh, and I hope you're not in a hurry."

Lee frowned at the news. Like any cop who lives for the bust, he hated paperwork and time lost. He saw Cunanan's potential flight out of the country as a major risk. He dialed the FBI office in Washington, D.C.

"This is Lee Urness, Minnesota Fugitive Task Force. I wonder if you could connect me to the French Embassy?" he asked.

"Just a moment," she said. Then, "Here it is." He heard a click and then the phone rang.

"French Embassy. How may I direct your call, please?"

"I am a police officer with the FBI Fugitive Task Force in Minneapolis. I need to talk to someone about a murderer who may have fled to France," Lee explained, hoping for a break-through.

"I'll connect you with our Police Attaché. Just one moment, please," the woman said.

"This is Helene Martini. How may I help you?"

"Miss Martini, my name is Lee Urness, and I am with the FBI Fugitive Task Force here in Minnesota. I am looking for an American citizen, a murderer, whom I have reason to believe might be going to France or might even be there," he said.

She asked for specifics and Lee told her what he knew.

"Can you help me?" he finally asked.

"Oh yes, I am sure I can. Do you have his passport number?" she asked.

"No, sorry. I just got the case. I've been told by San Diego police that he claimed his parents had a place on the French Riviera, and other than a photo, that's about all I have right now," he answered. He had secured Cunanan's California driver's license picture. He faxed it to her.

"Okay, I have the description now and we can check all points of entry for Mr. Cunanan right away," she explained. "I'll also see what records we have of him trying to enter the country. This might take a couple of days," she apologized.

"No problem. That would be great. Let me give you my phone number and pager number. Best to try the pager – I have it on all the time," he explained. Lee liked working with her. He liked working with anyone who saw the expediency and urgency of his work.

Martini agreed to call Lee as soon as she heard anything.

"Thank you so much," Lee said after recording Martini's direct phone number. He hung up, leaned back in his chair, threw his legs back up on Lisa's desk and smiled. This is why the others had nicknamed him "Sniz," short for "snizzle," as in "a person who is able to find ways around red tape to get the job done." It felt good to expedite these problems and stop the crazed killer before he hurt someone else. He hoped Cunanan stayed stateside, but if not, felt confident that Helene Martini and her allies would find him.

Lee checked his watch. He still had plenty of time before his daughter's double-header softball game that night in Bloomington. He decided to get everything ready for Jon Hermann's eventual call, maybe even later that day before he had to leave the office.

He took out his tape recorder and dictated the FD-65, the form used by the FBI to summarize data that is then entered into their computer system. Then, using the information provided by Agent Hermann, he dictated the UFAP Warrant and the Complaint. This he left on his desk for Jeanie Burns to type the next morning.

If the FTF had been a sports team, Lee might have called Jeanie Burns the Most Valuable Player. Average-sized, she could be tough as nails and very demanding when necessary. Through her beautiful smile, she could charm work out of Lee. By an angry, arched brow and a sample of her most shrill voice, "She could make grown men melt," Lee said. Lee especially hated it when he fell victim to Jeanie's fiercest look, the one he saw whenever he objected to doing paperwork the right way. Team members called her, "the boss," because she knew the way the FBI wanted things done, and she insisted on it.

"Lee, get over here," were the slow, deliberate words he hated to hear the most. It meant he had fallen victim to Jeanie's wrath. She meant to set him right. At the same time, though, he also knew that she would fix all his mistakes and get his paperwork perfect.

"I'm so glad the FBI saw fit to send you to us," Lee said to her more than once.

"Why?" Jeanie asked, not sure if it was a compliment.

"To keep us on the straight and narrow," he explained, and he meant it.

Moving that UFAP along

He called Agent Hermann again and told him the UFAP was ready to take to the judge to be signed.

"I'm sorry; I still don't have this done. Reuter is pushing us for more details," Hermann said, referring to the Chisago County Attorney. "But I promise you, I will have it on Wednesday by 10 a.m."

"We've got SWAT Team practice at the range in St. Cloud tomorrow," Lee reminded him.

"No way will I make it. I gotta get this warrant done."

"Okay, well I'm going, but I'll check in with you. As soon as you have it, I'll get the UFAP," Lee said. "Oh, I talked to the French Embassy," he added. "She was great. If he went to France, we'll get him pretty quick I should think."

Once again they said goodbye. Agent Hermann went off to solve a murder and Urness prepared to search for the murderer – two related tasks but with a very different focus.

With nothing else to do, Lee reviewed his other active cases and decided to leave for the day. Spring softball practice waited.

Sure sign of Minnesota spring

Lee drove casually out to one of the dozens of lush green softball fields in Bloomington, the home of the Mall of America. Kathy, his wife, would be bringing Kari, his 10-year old daughter to the park and he would meet them there.

Kathy Urness had found life with Lee to be predictable only in that it was unpredictable. She had long ago grown used to his crazy hours and intense, focused personality. Many moms taxied their children around – she knew that – but few lived with the uncertainty of a schedule that belonged to criminals, not her or Lee. She had seen him leave home any time of the day or night, any day of the week, holiday or no holiday. During his time on the narcotics squads, she knew he could be gone for days, and she knew little about where or what he was doing, just that he had this intense desire to track down and arrest the "bad guys." She knew, too, that he insisted on being the first guy in the door, and the risk that carried for her and her family.

Since he had joined the Fugitive Task Force, Lee tried hard to keep Kathy and the family in the dark about specific cases, not wanting to worry them. Perhaps more importantly, he needed his home to be a place of refuge from the dark world of rapists and murderers. Now with this new assignment, this Cunanan guy, Kathy knew that Lee would not rest until he caught him. She had no idea how invasive would be Cunanan's effect on their family during the next 11 weeks. Even if she had known, she also knew it would make no difference to Lee. Cunanan had become his job – no other questions need be asked or answered.

Softball, like home, provided a break, a refuge for Lee. Arriving at the park, he got out of the car, smelling the fresh mown grass and clean air of the state he loved so much. The fresh damp air reminded him of his days in Alexandria where he grew up amidst dozens of Minnesota's 10,000 lakes. He loved it, and coaching his kids was easily his favorite pastime.

He slipped out of the fishing vest that held all his important cop paraphernalia and pulled his FTF polo shirt off, laying it on the back seat of the van. He pulled his holster off the belt and placed it carefully under the seat, making sure it was well hidden from view. Then he pulled on his Prior Lake Lakers coach's jersey, grabbed his baseball cap and headed for the field. There he worked the first base coach's box and instructed the girls on the 12-and-under team how to bat. Kari, he knew, had a huge future in softball and he looked forward to every one of her games that season.

This night's double-header, though, would be his last uninterrupted one until late July.

While Lee Urness enjoyed a Minnesota summer evening with his family, Andrew Cunanan left the confines of New York City's West Side Bath Club where he stayed, to stalk the city's gay clubs. Not a single news story had appeared in New York City's media about any of the three men he had killed. To make the New York City papers meant killing someone there, and he had been developing a plan to do just that.

None of the men Cunanan seduced in New York City that week had any idea that they could be his next victim. In the high energy, pulsating gay clubs, being bludgeoned to death with a hammer, shot in the eye with a pistol or tortured with a screwdriver meant little – not when hot sex presented itself in the form of this handsome, glib sophisticate from California, or whatever he claimed on those nights.

Jeep seals it

Just past midnight, in the wee Wednesday morning hours, Chicago Police Officer Dana* Dickey noticed the Red Jeep Cherokee parked illegally on Astor Street. She also saw three parking tickets had been written and stuck under the wiper.

Dickey went to her police car and ran the Minnesota license plate number on the car's computer keyboard. She watched the MDT as it reported back to her that the car was wanted in Minnesota, associated with two homicides.

Dickey notified her district supervisor who, in turn, notified two nearby detectives. They immediately recognized the car's proximity to Miglin's house and notified Area 3 detectives. Sgt. Steve* Sappanos then called Sgt. Voss at Minneapolis Homicide.

That morning, *Chicago Tribune* reporter Eric Ferkenhoff heard the news about the ties to Cunanan, too. He boarded a plane to Minneapolis to learn what he could about Andrew Cunanan and the murders of Jeff Trail and David Madson.

Bernie Grace, a veteran crime reporter for KARE 11 TV news in the Twin Cities, also headed to an airport the moment Cunanan's name had been linked to Lee Miglin. Perhaps he and a small army of Minnesota reporters passed Ferkenhoff and a small army of Chicago reporters in mid-air. Soon Grace and a cameraman joined the media pack that sensed in this string of murders something far beyond that of the two gay men in Minnesota. The murder of a powerful and well-known Chicagoan, married to an internationally known businesswoman, packed the kind of pizzazz and interest loved by reporters.

As Grace stood in front of Miglin's townhouse, a police investigator came out. The reporters were eager to learn the connection between Miglin and Cunanan, and to their questions, the investigator answered, "Yes, they knew each other," but the officer refused to say those words on camera. That story did not align with the official police and Miglin family claims, and no reporter ever did establish a link beyond pure speculation. Every official pronouncement thereafter denied a link, especially a sexual link.

The cop described the crime scene as gruesome, though few other details were released to the public. Much public information existed about Lee Miglin and his family, but none of it told of what had happened inside that garage and house that day.

Chicago and Minnesota police officials needed to share information, and CPD sent a copy of their working police reports to Chisago County, where Madson had been found. Minneapolis *Star-Tribune* reporters, eager to learn the contents of the Miglin file, learned later that the county had the reports and sent Chris Graves to retrieve them. There she made a copy, and found lurid details about the crime scene. But they contained nothing firmly establishing a Miglin-Cunanan link, other than the Jeep and a murder.

Reporters' hands were tied. Unable to establish reliable and verifiable sources, despite their personal conjecture, they reported that no link existed between Miglin and Cunanan. Miglin's survivors delivered a denial of any link as they spoke of their horror and sorrow at a press conference. When Ferkenhoff later wrote a feature story about the case that contained speculation about various scenarios linking Miglin and Cunanan, his editor redacted that portion of the story, telling Ferkenhoff that the *Tribune* did not want to be the originator of rumors.

Chicago reporters, though, through years of working with local police, had developed sources unavailable to out-of-towners, and two days later, their news leak proved costly to a New Jersey cemetery worker.

Chapter 10 ~ Elusive UFAP becomes chaotic investigation

Wednesday morning Lee rolled out of bed just past 6 a.m. He looked forward to a good day; good because he knew he would soon have a warrant in hand on a new case. It beat waiting for something to happen, and Lee loved action. He also knew that he had SWAT training scheduled at 8 a.m., and that meant a long drive to St. Cloud, 90 miles from home.

He went to the bathroom and had just lathered his face when Kathy called him. "Isn't this the case you were working on?" she said, nodding toward the TV.

He walked back into the bedroom with shaving cream covering half his face, a razor in his hand, and a towel draped over his shoulder, gaping at the TV.

"Damn!" He watched the story about the discovery of Madson's Jeep. He wiped the lather from his face and went to the phone, calling Jon Hermann, his BCA friend.

"Hey," Lee said as he aroused Hermann from sleep, "They found Madson's Jeep in Chicago."

"No kidding?" Hermann said.

"There's more."

"Oh?"

"Yeah. It seems as though the Jeep is parked close to the house of another homicide victim, a Lee Miglin, a big time Chicago developer. He had been pretty brutally murdered," Lee added. "Maybe worse than Jeff Trail."

"I'll be damned," Hermann said. "Well, I'll get on the warrant right away. I'll have it this morning."

"You going to the SWAT shoot?" Lee asked.

"Nope. I need to get this done. I'll call you later," Hermann said, and hung up.

Lee quickly dressed and headed out the door. Before driving away from home, he pulled out the list of names associated with Andrew Cunanan that he had started to put together. He searched for "Miglin," but it was not there.

He cranked toward St Cloud. As he drove, he called "Young" Rickett – Kevin Rickett – the youthful-looking FBI agent he worked with at the FTF. "They found Madson's Jeep in Chicago near the home of some guy named Miglin. Cunanan might have murdered him, too."

"They get him?" Rickett asked.

"No, and I don't know much about it. Hermann is working on the local warrant and I left a tape for JB, so we ought to be able to roll on this today. Just wanted to let you know so you can get your ducks in a row," he said. "I'll call Chicago's FTF and see what I can find out."

He got to St. Cloud just before 8 a.m. Before heading to the firing range, he called Jeanie Burns. "I left a tape on your desk with the FD-65 and the Complaint and Warrant for this Cunanan case. Get them typed and ready for my signature. Jon Hermann says he'll have the local warrant this morning."

"Okay. I'll be ready," JB answered, optimistic as always. Lee really liked JB's willingness to get things done, and to bail him out from his otherwise flawed paperwork routine. With Rickett as his partner, – an expert at FBI procedure – Lee smiled, knowing that at least the paperwork wouldn't slow him down too much.

"Oh, call the court and find out who the signing magistrate is. Will you see if you can get an appointment for this afternoon?" he asked.

"Will do. Shoot well," she said, hanging up.

Just after getting on the range, he was paged by Rickett. Rolling his eyes at Phil Hodapp, the range trainer, he headed back to his car to use the digital cell phone. Lee worried about inadvertent release of confidential information that could affect his task, and so never trusted any phones but landlines that had FBI encryption. When he talked on the cell phone, even though digital signals are hard to intercept and monitor, he took great care not to say too much; someone might be listening. He considered all these calls to be top secret.

"I gotta go first today. Got a hot case," he told Hodapp when he returned to the range a few minutes later.

"Oh sure! Hey, you're not getting out of cleaning guns again. No way," Hodapp snarled at him. "Just forget leavin' early."

Lee shrugged and smiled playfully at the man he called "The Bowling Ball," given Hodapp's short, stocky frame.

Again his pager sounded. This time it was BCA communications wondering about the case. Lee's bosses wanted to be kept in the loop, to understand the case as it developed. They wanted to know if he needed additional resources or if they should intercede to solve problems beyond his authority. The fact that he chased a guy who had murdered three times already added urgency to the case, but Lee's bosses figured that he would catch Cunanan before long.

"Everything's under control," Lee explained. He said that because it is how he felt, and because it was still several hours before the "blur" began.

Lee went to the first firing line with his .40 caliber Smith and Wesson. Just as he began firing, again his pager sounded. He headed back to the van. "Jon, you called?" he said, returning Agent Hermann's call.

"Just want to let you know that at 10:00, I'm going to the County Attorney. I should have the warrant then."

"Thanks, and keep me posted," Lee said. He left the van and headed back to the firing range.

He finished the pistol round and got set for the next weapon. His pager sounded. This time it was Hermann asking for a clarification on a detail. "I'll call you later, as soon as it's signed," Hermann said.

Lee went back to shoot the MP-5 submachine gun, but again, his pager sounded. He laid the weapon down and, under the angry studied eyes of Instructor Hodapp, walked back to the van. "What's up?" he asked Kevin Rickett.

"Fred Tremper called and wants to know the status."

"Okay, I'll get on it." Lee called Tremper, the supervisor of the Minnesota Fugitive Task Force, and explained the status of the case. This procedure, informing all agencies of what was going on in a case, was routine enough, but the urgency of these requests left Lee a little nonplused. He sensed this case had already grown beyond reasonable proportions. Sure, the guy had killed three times, but Lee knew he'd get him. Why all the fuss? And besides, he could do nothing until he had the UFAP.

He went back to the firing line. No sooner did he lift his weapon and his pager nagged again – at least it had begun to feel like nagging. This time it was his boss at the BCA – Don Peterson.

After talking with Peterson, he finally started his MP-5 practice. Again the pager nagged. He saw that again, it was Jon Hermann. "Screw it!!" he yelled. "I've had it. I'm out of here," Lee said as he walked over to Hodapp. "I gotta go sign a federal warrant."

"Damn it, you gotta stay and clean the MP-5," Hodapp snarled, albeit somewhat in jest. He knew the routine and the special demands on the Fugitive Task Force members. And he knew nothing would dissuade Lee Urness, once he made up his mind.

"Nope, I'm leaving, and by the way, I qualified," Lee smiled. "Write it down."

Lee tore back toward Minneapolis. He called Hermann on the way. "How's it coming?"

"I should have it signed within the hour," Hermann answered.

Lee did a fast drive directly back to the Fugitive Task Force office, hoping everything would be ready to go when he got there. It was and it wasn't.

"You're set with Judge Arthur Boylan, but over in St. Paul, at 3:00," Jeanie said, knowing it would bug Lee. Going to St. Paul meant an extra hour of his precious time. He never wanted to waste time, especially when it meant stopping a killer.

Jeanie had, as usual, done an impeccable job of preparing all the paperwork and had faxed it to Deb Long, her counterpart at the US Attorney's office. Long had finished her side of the task, and faxed everything back. "Here's the Complaint and Warrant. The U.S. Attorney's signed off," Jeanie said, handing Lee the paperwork.

"What the hell? What's holding up Hermann?" he said, flopping back into his desk chair. He hated this, wanting to get on with his job, but he also knew that getting the federal warrant signed prior to getting the local warrant would spoil the case, once he caught Cunanan. He had no choice but to do it right, so he called Hermann.

"We got a delay but I'm working on it. Reuter still thinks we need more," Hermann said. "Look, I will go over and I guarantee we'll get it done. What time's your appointment with the judge?"

"We're on for 3:00," Lee said.

"I'm going over now," Hermann said, convinced he could beat the deadline. "I'll have it by 2:00 p.m. And I'll call you as soon as I have it in my hand."

Once at the Chisago County Courthouse, Hermann found Jim Reuter, the Chisago County Attorney, still a hard nut to crack. Time wasted away; 2:00 passed and he still had no signed warrant.

In Minneapolis, a progressively more agitated Lee Urness looked at his watch just after 2:00. "I gotta go," he said, standing up and turning toward Jeanie. "JB, have Hermann call me the moment he's got the warrant."

He started out the door, and turned back, "Can't be late for a judge, you know." Lee had learned the hard way. Judges kept tight control of their schedules. If Boylan said 3:00 p.m., then it had to be 3:00 p.m. If Lee missed it, he might lose another day of the chase, so he drove to St. Paul, parked his car and headed into the Federal Court Building on Kellogg and Robert, hoping for Hermann's page.

Hermann finally got in front of Reuter and laid the case out again, adding what little new information he had gleaned. "Look, here's the deal. We've got two bodies and Hennepin County's not doing anything on this. Cunanan is tied to both murder sites; we know that. And now they found the Jeep in Chicago a block from another murder. You gotta go out on a limb on this," he urged. Reuter took the papers and began to scrutinize them.

Lee walked into Judge Boylan's office at 2:45 p.m. and announced himself. He pulled his pager off his belt and held it, as if that would make it beep, but nothing happened.

"The judge will see you now," the secretary announced.

Man, I hoped he'd be running late! Still no page, but he had to go in. He knew nothing about Judge Boylan, but he knew that some judges were sticklers about every nit-picking detail. He had no idea what to expect.

In Chisago City, Hermann stood nervously watching Reuter study the local Warrant and Complaint.

In St. Paul, Judge Boylan took the federal Warrant and Complaint in his hand and began reading it. Lee wished he had written a multi-page complaint as he nervously watched Boylan review the four pages he had just handed to him.

Lee kept his hand on his pager, but nothing happened.

In Chisago City, Reuter said, "Well," as he took his pen in hand, "I trust you guys. I know you know what you're doing, so, okay." He signed off on the Warrant and Complaint, and then together, they walked it into the chambers of Judge Linn Slattengren who signed it moments later.

Judge Boylan picked up his pen. "Hope you catch this guy soon," he said, as he signed the UFAP.

"We're gonna try," Lee said, as the clerk took the document, time-stamped and dated it.

As soon as Lee walked out of the office, he paged Hermann with the message, "Hey, you signed the warrant yet?"But it would be 3:15 before he heard back.

"Lee, we got it," Hermann told him. "Reuter did us a favor."

"Good. I've got the UFAP signed already." His voiced dropped. "Ah, what time is your's signed?"

They had both been signed at almost exactly the same moment. Lee breathed easier, that is, until he stepped back into the office 30 minutes later.

Cunanan cruised

Cunanan left Miglin's house sometime before 11:30 p.m. on Saturday, May 3. Before getting too far down the road, he turned on the cell phone that

Miglin had permanently mounted in the car. A computer linked to a tower in Michigan registered the activation. But to place a call required a password and Cunanan had no idea what it was, so he turned the phone off. At midnight, he tried again with the same result; a computer linked to a tower in Pittsburgh recorded the activation.

Cunanan paid the phone problems no attention, but their activation created an opportunity for Chicago police. On that Sunday, they had no idea who drove the Lexus, but they knew it had been stolen. Now they also knew in which direction it headed, thanks to reports from the mobile phone service company. Monitoring that phone signal and triangulating on it once Cunanan tried it again gave them their best hope of catching Lee Miglin's killer.

Late Sunday afternoon, Cunanan arrived in the New York City area and found a place to park in one of the scores of parking ramps that service the Big Apple. He used the subway system and cabs to get around the city.

He knew New York City well, and he knew he could find good, anonymous sex. Staying at the Rihga Royale or Four Seasons was no longer an option – he loved those places and felt he deserved to enjoy them, but the thousands of dollars in his pocket would last but a few nights at either one of them. Instead, on May 5 he checked in at the West Side Club Bathhouse on West 20th Street. From there he could get anywhere in Manhattan without much notice.

Anyone could get lost in the Big Apple's gay clubs; even a guy who had killed three men. As yet, the east coast did not know about Lee Miglin. No one would study him that closely in the darkly lit, noisy gay bars and clubs of New York City. He might score with a pretty blond boy or pick up a few bucks performing for an old, rich sugar daddy. Maybe he could not stay at the Four Seasons, but he could still go there and prowl for a lonely man who was anxious for companionship. It had worked before, and though he had added 20 pounds to his handsome frame, he could still charm men who did not know him.

He knew that William Norman was due in town that weekend and he knew where he would likely stay. If Norman had been one of his targets in some sort of payback scheme, it would have been simple enough to locate and kill him. He had also heard that Gianni Versace was due in town. Cunanan believed that Versace owned a residence in the city. Versace regularly threw lavish parties and they were open to many men and women who knew how to charm their way onto the list. Cunanan had met Versace like this at a 1991 party. Cunanan may have believed that he owed Norman payback, but Versace offered him a chance for immortality. He had no reason to believe that a task force of cops searched for him there, given that the New York media were mute about his case.

Cunanan knew that gay men feared cops almost as much as they feared being "outed." News stories about him would inevitably require gay men to go public, and that was a small risk. But, he could easily change his appearance, like a chameleon, by choosing to wear his glasses, grow his beard, and comb his hair differently. His mixed race allowed him to look Asian, Italian, Hispanic or just plain Heinz 57 American. In any event, no cop in America knew where he was anyway. They would be looking in California or Texas – just about anywhere. The only link to him was the Lexus, now legally parked in an obscure ramp in America's most crowded metropolitan area, along with hundreds of other dark green luxury cars. And, he had money in his pocket.

As far as Cunanan knew, cops would only be chasing him for two killings in Minnesota – a hammer bludgeoning and a gun shot. That did not match the profile of a serial killer, at least in the traditional sense. Both men had been gay lovers, and perhaps the cops would not give it much effort. By blending in with the millions walking New York City's streets, he felt safe.

Soon his mission would end, and so might his life. Until then, he needed companionship and anonymity. New York City offered him all that, and more.

Using time, while wasting it

Officially, Lee's hands had been tied without the UFAP. He knew without a doubt that Jon Hermann would eventually prevail; timing had been the only issue.

So before he had the UFAP, he began planning, starting by asking himself questions.

In most FTF cases, the agents had very little information with which to start. If they were lucky, they might have a name, or a picture, maybe a fingerprint or a witness, or a partner in crime who made a deal and squealed on the fugitive. Sometimes they had nothing.

Lee assessed what information they had on Andrew Cunanan. He knew that Minneapolis' Homicide unit investigated Jeff Trail's murder, and though the warrant would specify only Madson, Lee felt sure that Cunanan had driven Madson's Jeep to Chicago and killed Lee Miglin there. He probably had killed Trail, or at least helped Madson do it. He called Sgt. Bob Tichich at Minneapolis Homicide and made an appointment for the next morning.

Hermann told him that the San Diego PD had been to Cunanan's apartment and picked up a box of stuff. He made a note to call San Diego later in the day.

He looked at a map of the United States. Earlier that morning when he talked to the Chicago Fugitive Task Force, he had told them that he would have the UFAP signed that day and wanted to share information immediately.

"The guy must be really sick," Scott Bakken of the Chicago FTF told him. "He nearly sawed the man's head off."

"Why? What's their connection? Why would he have gone to see this guy? Do you have any ideas?" Lee asked Bakken. While he had no part in solving the murder, the motive for being in Chicago meant everything to Lee. His job required reasoning where Cunanan would head next, and that meant understanding why he had been in Chicago.

"All's we know is that he stole Miglin's car, a black 1995 Lexus, and some cash," Bakken answered. "We think about $2,000. The family says they never heard of Cunanan." Later, the family claimed the stolen dollar amount was $6,000. Lee scratched down the $2,000 figure and then added another $1,000, thinking that sounded more reasonable. From this, he calculated that Cunanan had enough money to last 60 days before he would run out. Once he ran out, he would have to try something again, and that meant he would surface.

"Any sightings?"Lee asked, wondering if CPD had noticed anything yet.

"No one's seen him, but we are tracking him with Miglin's car phone." Bakken reviewed the information about cell phone activities and saw that a telephone tower in Michigan and another in Pennsylvania had picked up Miglin's code just past midnight the prior Sunday. It gave them some help in trying to figure out Miglin's time of death as well. The first calls placed him in Chicago sometime near 11:00 p.m. "So it looks like he's headed east. Maybe we can catch a break when he turns it on again."

Chicago PD had already retrieved Miglin's car-phone password and had the cell phone service company remove it, allowing Cunanan to make calls. Without the password, Cunanan could never have used the phone. It explained why he had just turned it on and off a couple of times.

Lee recorded the contact numbers for the Chicago FTF office and the CPD on his rapidly growing contact list, knowing he would be spending many hours talking to them in the days ahead. He posted the list on the bulletin board near his desk, and put another copy in his case file. Each day it seemed he had to add another jurisdiction to the list of contacts. Every note he took was fed into his case file, a manila folder that became his constant companion during the next several weeks, though Lee quickly supplemented it with a large brown accordion file filled with notes written on dozens of legal pads.

Lee studied the U.S. map, looking at Chicago, situated like the hub of a wheel whose highway spokes pointed in every direction. "Which way did he go?" he pondered. Crooks almost always used the interstate highway system. He surmised, based on the telephone information that Cunanan most likely had gone toward New York City. But from there he could go almost anywhere – and he already had at least a four-day lead.

Chapter 11 ~ Blur begins

After speeding back to Minneapolis from the judge's chambers, Lee walked into a buzz saw of activity back at the FTF office.

"Lee, lines two and four are for you," one of the agents said, "and you better check the calls on your desk."

Lee saw a short stack of yellow call slips sitting near his phone and the two blinking lights waiting for him. "Take four for me and get a message. Anyone know who's on two?"

"Newsies," JB said.

Lee shrugged and hit the button. Having seen the finding of the Jeep in Chicago on TV news, and concerned about how Minneapolis cops continued to talk to Twin Cities media about the Jeff Trail murder, Lee clenched his teeth and picked up the phone. Before he could even push the button, someone said, "Lee, line five."

"Agent Urness," he answered line two.

"Officer, this is Meg Wilson* with ABC. About this Andrew Cunanan chase…"

"Miss Wilson, I'm sorry, you'll have to call Coleen Rowley at the FBI. She handles all media inquiries…"

"I'm sure that's true, but I wondered if…"

"No ma'am. I have no comment. You call Rowley," he said forcefully and hung up.

Coleen Rowley gained unwelcome fame following September 11, 2001. She became an FBI whistleblower, accusing the agency of mishandling warnings of the impending terrorist attacks. *Time* magazine named her, along with two other women, "Person of the Year for 2002." She gained additional notoriety during the 2003 war in Iraq when she publicly criticized the FBI's plans to prevent domestic terrorism. But in 1997, she served as the official communications spokesperson and legal counsel for the Minneapolis FBI office.

"Look, no newsies get through. Send them all to Rowley," he told his team members. "Now which one do I take?"

This time it was the FBI Headquarters in Washington, D.C. Next, it was Peterson, his BCA chief. Lee needed to talk to the San Diego Fugitive Task Force, but first he had to field all the legitimate calls from police agencies and his superiors. The volume of calls refused to let up. He felt as though a tsunami had flooded over him, with wave after wave, in a roiling storm of inquiries.

"Hey people, I need some space. I gotta go outside and make my calls. Take messages, and page me only if anything is really important," he said as he slipped out the door. He headed down the back hall, climbed down two flights of stairs and out the rear door to the building, the same route he and the others took when they had to hurry to catch a crook. He pushed open the big metal door as bright sunlight nearly blinded him. For a moment, he thought about the beauty of a Minnesota spring day, but just for a moment. He walked quickly to his green van and climbed inside, taking a deep breath. "Man oh man, what is this all about?" he asked himself.

He checked his notes and found the phone number for the San Diego Fugitive Task Force. "This is Lee Urness with the Minnesota Fugitive Task Force. I'd like to talk to an FTF agent who might know something about an Andrew Cunanan."

"Just a minute," he heard. The office clerk announced the call.

"A call from Minnesota FTF looking for help on the Andrew Cunanan case. Who wants to take the call?"

Special Agent Ann Murphy sat near her partner, Special Agent John Hause. Hause had just come back from dealing with a militia problem in Montana. Four other FBI task force members were working fugitives at the time. One agent was on temporary duty, and another was at Quantico. Yet another had been on vacation. For the previous two weeks, Murphy was the only FBI person taking calls. She felt exhausted.

"John, take it," Murphy said.

"No, you take it," Hause responded.

"It's yours," she said again.

He pushed the phone button. "This is John Hause," he said. By virtue of this draw of the lot, Hause became the San Diego FTF Case Agent on the Cunanan case.

Lee explained who he was, and that he had just gotten the signed UFAP. "I understand that the San Diego PD already searched Cunanan's apartment and talked to his roommate, an Erik Erickson. An agent here says that Erickson gave them a whole box of Cunanan's and that it's at the San Diego PD."

"We'll go get it right away. What do you want us to do with it?" Hause asked.

"Call me back and let me know what's in there. Oh, let me give you my pager number. It's gone crazy here and that's the best way to get me," he said. "Page me day or night when you have something," he added, knowing that Hause would ask the same if he were chasing someone and needed Lee's help.

Lee continued calling other FTF offices and police departments, often ignoring his pager unless he saw something that really needed immediate attention. A short time later, San Diego paged him. He knew it was urgent by the 9-1-1 code added to the message.

"Urness here. What've you got?"

"San Diego PD says there's a bunch of bills and a phone book, plus a lot of other stuff. Credit card bills, letters. We're going over now to get it." This time Ann Murphy called. She and John Hause worked the case together from then on.

"Great. Can you fax the phone book to us, and the bills? We can get started on those right away," Lee asked.

"Will do. We should be ready in about two hours. We can FedEx the whole box there if you want," Murphy offered.

"Do it, but I still want those phone book pages and bills," he answered. "Good work. Talk with you later." He gave them the fax number and hung up.

Lee felt good about his chances of catching Cunanan, given what Murphy had just told him. This actually was a good amount of information. Having the phone book meant knowing who Cunanan would try to call, because criminals on the run always call people they know. They usually end up going to a family member's or lover's house to hide.

Having Cunanan's credit card bills in hand would be a huge break and speed up the chase.

As soon as the fax came in, Lee sat studying it. As he paged through the phone book the first name he searched for was "Miglin." He saw no such entry. *Curious. If he had serviced Miglin, you'd think his name would be in here.* He wrote a note to tell Chicago about it. He saw Jeff Trail and David Madson's name, and dozens of others that meant nothing to him. In the days ahead, be meant to know something about every name in that book.

The FTF had developed a relationship with a contact that could get credit card information for them. Lee wasted no time calling him. He easily convinced the man of the urgency of his request and gave him Cunanan's social security number. Within a few minutes, a fax arrived in the Minnesota FTF office that listed all of Cunanan's credit cards and his activity.

Before leaving the quiet safety of his van in the middle of that parking lot, Lee wrote several notes and tried to think through what he would do next. He had anticipated that there would be another stack of calls sitting in the office, but he felt ready for them, and he had other calls he wanted to make right away.

"Lee, line two wants you now," he heard as he walked in the door. He went to his desk and threw a quick glance at a half-inch deep stack of yellow call slips as he grabbed the phone. As soon as he could, he dispensed with the call. Then he called the FBI Information Technology Center (ITC) in Butte, Montana.

"So I need everything you can give me on this Cunanan guy. I'll fax the paperwork to you immediately," Lee said, signing off on it just after 5:00 p.m. He asked the ITC to search for all of Cunanan's prior and current addresses, and those who lived nearby. He planned to have agents contact everyone who knew or had known Cunanan. And he asked for Cunanan's work history, discovering it was woefully short – one stint at a quick stop grocery store. *How the hell did he survive?* Lee asked himself.

As it got closer to 6:00, amidst the constant ringing of phones, Lee said, "Listen everybody, here's the plan for today. This thing is crazy. He's got a four-day head start on us, and we've got a lot of work to do tomorrow. Tonight I'll have my ducks in a row. I suggest everyone go home right after work and get a good night's sleep. Rickett and I meet with the MPD at 9:00 in the morning, and then let's get together and I'll lay out the plan for you." He told them about the faxes from San Diego. "Expect to work late tomorrow night."

No one argued about going home while Lee stayed behind, collecting and studying the faxes as they came in, mapping a strategy, deciding which agent should do which task. He had a great team with which to work, and each had skills ideal for what needed to be done. Experience told him that this case had all the appearances of sucking up their time and energy in a hurry.

Okay. It was a bit nutsy here today. And now that the guy's killed three times, it'll be a little crazier than others. But his killing days are over; we'll get him. Maybe a week on the outside.

So how do you really feel about this?

Talking to the media had always been an issue with Lee. He felt they usually got critical facts wrong or gave away information that he needed kept from criminals. So he avoided them as a group, but he had another group he avoided even more, and with more passion. He knew he had to confront this, or it would severely affect the way he did his job.

Lee had no time for homosexuals. In fact, he despised their lifestyle and had personalized his feelings. It turned his stomach to think about what homosexuals did to each other. To be successful in this chase forced him to confront those strong negative feelings. It was not unlike the strong feelings he had about sexual abuse of children and it is why he refused to work child abuse or porno cases – because he could not keep an open mind.

As he started talking to different west coast officers, he learned that Cunanan had been openly gay since high school. In fact, he had gone to his high school prom in drag. The thought disgusted Lee, but to do his job, he had to find a way to set all this aside.

None of his fellow FTF officers, as far as he knew, had had any experiences working with gays. The attitude Lee wanted to foster in his own spirit and that of his team was, "I don't really care what he is or who he killed. He's a murderer and we have to catch him no matter what."

Lee sat thinking about this that Wednesday night. He had worked on and off with one gay drug informant, a man he called "Simply Gary" because of how he addressed himself. Simply Gary talked and acted effeminately, the way that drew so much derision from straights. Simply Gary often turned in his lovers for drug abuse when he tired of them, or they did something he just didn't like, and he had been useful to Lee during his undercover narcotics work. So Lee knew he had the ability to work with gays and lesbians while gritting his teeth about their personal foibles.

Lee decided to talk to his dad to gain perspective.

"Dad, it's Lee," he said when he called Howard Urness at his northern Minnesota home. "You see this thing on Andrew Cunanan on the news?"

"Yeah. You got something to do with it?"

"I'm the case agent," Lee answered.

"How you gonna work with all those queers?" Howard asked. Howard had spent a lifetime in law enforcement. He had, in many ways, trained Lee. He knew his son well, certainly well enough to know that venturing into the high-flying world of gay men would give Lee trouble.

"I don't know. It will be a different deal," Lee said. "I've got no choice but to work with the gays around town."

"I know some in Alex and I had to work with them," Howard said, referring to Alexandria, Minnesota. "No one knew they were gay except me, and I worked pretty well with them. It makes no difference what they are. It is how they act that mattered."

"Yeah, I know you're right," Lee said.

"I know a lot of secrets about people, but you got to keep it to yourself and not let it affect your case. You treat everyone like a human being. But be careful. This guy's crazy. If you find him, be careful," Howard advised.

"Well he's never coming back to Minnesota. That's what worries me. He's got a big head start."

"Never give up, son. Stay after him like you always do. You'll get him sooner or later," Howard said.

"Well I hope it's sooner, before he kills again," Lee said. After hanging up with his dad, he had to smile. Howard Urness had always been his tutor, and as the chase dragged on, Lee found himself regularly reflecting on his dad's advice, or calling him for more. This advice, though, about setting his feelings and prejudices aside carried life and death implications. He set his mind to do so. And he knew the agents working with him had to do the same.

Late that night he drove home, relaxing as he took a deep drag on a cigarette. At home, he sat in his kitchen staring out at the birdfeeder, illuminated now by moonlight. He envisioned the birds as they fussed about landing and finding their feeding spot. "Andrew Cunanan, enjoy it now, 'cause there's no place you can land safely after tonight."

He snuffed out his cigarette and headed to bed, setting his alarm for 6 a.m., sleeping peacefully on that night of May 7, the last good sleep he enjoyed until late in July.

Cunanan partied

Wednesday evening, Cunanan walked to the Chelsea Theatre and watched "Liar, Liar." The pathological lying character played by Jim Carey hit too close to home. Cunanan had always been a liar, and his recent murderous activities only intensified that awful truth.

Images of brutality continued to play across his mind, images he could never overcome or dispel. The fact that he had made it this far, four days, without anyone noticing him secured his decision. He would try to find his way into a Gianni Versace party and complete that part of his plan. If needed, he could move on to another place where he could blend in and still finish his design, and that place was Miami Beach.

I'll stay another day and see how it goes, he told himself as he lay back on the bed in the middle of the night. The boy next to him had no idea that he had been in the grasp of a brutal murderer and weeks later, felt relief greater than sex when he heard news accounts about Andrew Cunanan, the "gay spree killer."

Birds always return to their nests

Early Thursday morning, Lee sat once again watching the birds pecking at their seed on his birdfeeder. He wished he could sit there all morning, but Andrew Cunanan beckoned.

He noticed that one cardinal looked just like another, and it reminded him how easy it was for a bad guy to blend into the crowd if he wanted to avoid detection. Yet, most often, the same cardinal returned to feast at the birdfeeder each day at about the same time. Birds are, he thought, like fugitives; they are creatures of habit. Their habits made them predictable and able to be captured and put into cages.

He pondered the patterns he had practiced hundreds of times during the last few years. Cunanan would try to telephone his parents, siblings or closest friends, or he would travel to one of their houses. That meant that Lee, or some other local FTF agent, would have to get close to these people, develop a relationship with them. To win their total cooperation they would use every psychological trick in their bag. Lee could hear himself talking to Cunanan's dad, which he planned to do once the FBI found him.

"Mr. Cunanan, I am sure you don't want your son to get hurt, and I can assure you that if he comes peaceably, we will not harm him."

"Mr. Cunanan, your son has killed three times. I know you do not want him to hurt anyone else."

"Mr. Cunanan, you *are* going to cooperate. I want to be perfectly clear about this. If Andrew calls you or comes to see you, and you fail to notify us, you will be guilty of aiding and abetting a fugitive. *You* will go to prison."

"Mr. Cunanan, do not force my hand on this. If I have to, I will get a warrant and check every phone bill, every credit card purchase, every move you have made since this all started. And I will make sure that we know everything you do. It's your choice. Cooperate and help us catch Andrew, or we come after you."

Through regular, even daily contact with those closest to Cunanan, Lee knew that eventually he would get a solid lead.

Most bad guys he chased had committed a crime in their home state and fled to another, or to a foreign country. The FTF office in the home state usually got the case, meaning they were closest to the bad guy's friends and family. This case was different.

Cunanan was from San Diego, and had killed in three locales in two states. He left no one alive in Minnesota or Illinois who really knew him or, apparently, had witnessed the crimes. That made Lee's job harder. He felt certain that he would never personally get to do face-to-face interviews in Illinois or California. For that he would rely on the local FTF agents, and they all knew that all interviews must be done face-to-face. The investigator had to see the face and body language of the interviewee, and also, by their physical presence, provide a sense of the threat of police authority residing in a cop's badge.

Lee considered his assets, other than the national team of agents that, he felt sure, would work enthusiastically with him. He had skimmed the phone book pages faxed to him from San Diego. These would be prime leads and immediately handed out to his FTF team for calling. Every person in that book would hear from his team, that day if possible. And every contact would create more contacts, and all of them would be called. "We will talk to everyone Cunanan ever knew in his whole life, no matter where they live or what they do," he told his team later that day. They were to learn that in the dark closets of some gay men, turning on the bright lights of an investigation created its own set of problems; special threats were needed, and a special understanding of their need for privacy.

Since Cunanan had been nice enough to leave behind his personal phone book in San Diego, Lee reasoned that the only persons left for Cunanan to call were those with whom he was closest, whose phone numbers he had memorized. At best, it would include a few intimate friends and family members. As the FTF got into Cunanan's life and learned just how extensive were the entanglements of this active gay man, they saw that "intimate" and "close" meant something different than with heterosexuals – even promiscuous ones. But like all humans, Cunanan would surely have his favorites, like Madson and Trail. *He'll eventually call one or more of these people,* Lee thought.

The copies of Cunanan's credit card bills were especially valuable.

He felt sure that Cunanan belonged to some kind of group or club, though it was unlikely to be Rotary or a Baptist men's group. Eventually,

Cunanan would try to contact one of them, especially if he began to run out of money. *We'll find out who they are and tip them off.*

He could widely distribute "wanted" posters to any place Cunanan might appear. *Several hundred "wanted" posters might be needed for this one*, he figured, given that two states were involved, and most likely, Cunanan had fled to yet another state.

He had the UFAP, he had the authority and he had quite a few tracking tools, more than he often had at the beginning of a chase. In many cases, he had nothing but a name and a crime. "Fly free while you can," Lee said, smiling at the birds, "because, Andrew Cunanan, you will soon be a bird in a cage."

He grabbed his muffin and headed to the car, ready to do battle. As he drove up I-35W that morning he thought, *Give me one week. I'll have him.* But the confident cop couldn't possibly yet conceive how wrong he was until disordered days exploded into wretched weeks.

Chapter 12 ~ Let's Roll

Just before 9:00 a.m. on Thursday, Lee met "Young" Rickett at the police department housed in Minneapolis' historic Municipal Building. Each time he entered that ancient structure he felt as if he was walking into a bygone era, into a British castle. The granite-walled building raised several stories to the red-tiled shingles that covered the sharply sloping roofline. Its clock tower peaked at 345 feet and held what was, when it was built, the largest clock in the world, four inches bigger than London's Big Ben. The four-sided clock told the official time to all the city's neighborhoods. Lee could almost imagine a moat and drawbridge at the old structure had it been built in England instead of this Midwest American city.

As an undercover narcotics agent with the Minnesota Bureau of Criminal Apprehension, Lee had worked with police departments in numerous jurisdictions. Once he joined the FTF, he saw how the close-knit camaraderie of intercity and interstate police and sheriffs, FBI and other federal law enforcement agents, all worked seamlessly to hunt down and capture dangerous criminals. Lee took pride in being a part of such a network. The FTF's, formed in the early 1990s, and had proven to be a boon to city and county cops who usually lacked the resources to chase across the world to catch a bad guy.

Lee and Rickett looked forward to taking a giant step toward capturing Cunanan as they walked past the huge bluish "Father of Lakes" statue that guarded the Municipal Building's lobby. They rode the elevator to the second floor and sat in a cubicle with Sgt. Robert Tichich and Detective Greg Gordon of the Minneapolis Homicide Division. Lee opened his case file and laid out a legal pad as he and Rickett sat ready to take notes.

"So, what have you got so far?" Lee asked, once the niceties and small talk had concluded.

"Well, a lot. There's no question it's Andrew Cunanan. Several neighbors saw Madson on the elevator with him, and walking the dog together," Tichich explained. He laid out the rest of the crime scene evidence.

"Do you have any leads, any idea where he might be?" Rickett asked.

Lee watched Tichich and Gordon carefully, how they sat, the way they spoke and the words they used. He saw that Tichich had taken control of the case and something in his demeanor let Lee know that he was frustrated. Lee sympathized with the difficult task homicide investigators had, not just with sifting through evidence, but in persuading prosecutors to give them the lee-way they needed to nail crooks. Tichich, Lee felt, had already said too much to the media about the case, something he personally avoided. He meant to guard what he shared with the Minneapolis cop just so that Tichich would not accidentally let slip a critical fact in their case.

"Okay, well, we've done a ton of telephone work on the case in San Diego. San Diego PD got a search warrant of Cunanan's apartment. Cunanan's roomie, an Erik Erickson, gave the San Diego cops a big box of stuff, including a black address book," Tichich explained.

"Yup, we got it coming today," Rickett offered.

"You do? Okay, well we also called a lot of Cunanan's friends and asso-ciates in San Diego, but didn't get much from them," Tichich said.

"Well, it's hard to get much unless you do face-to-face interviews. Too easy to lie on the phone," Lee said. "Okay, I can send task force agents to do the face-to-face interviews and we'll copy you on them."

"Good," Tichich went on. "Cunanan's favorite hotel in New York City is the Townhouse Regents. Stayed there often with his boyfriends." Lee made a note to call and get their records, something much easier for him to do than for a city cop.

"We talked with San Francisco PD. They sent us this fax," he said, show-ing them one of the documents in their case file. "We talked with this Liz who says Cunanan used to live with her and her husband."

"I'll get someone out to see her right away," Lee said. He knew Liz was the exact kind of person to whom Cunanan would appeal once he ran into trouble.

"So, we haven't talked with all of these people yet, but we're working on it," Tichich said. "There is one guy we can't find. Maybe you can help. Name is Dave Roberts from D.C. Supposed to be one of Madson's lovers or something."

Lee wrote it down.

"Can you give us the fingerprints from the apartment?" Rickett asked.

"We don't have any," Gordon said.

"What?" Lee asked, astounded.

"The place was never dusted for prints," Tichich said. "But we did talk with a lot of people here in Minnesota, but almost no one really knows Cunanan."

"Any idea where he might be headed?" Lee asked.

"No. Not a clue. No one in California's seen him since the 25th," Tichich answered.

"We think he's headed east, but who knows where?" Lee opined. "What do you think? Where do you think he might go?"

"I haven't a guess. That's your department," Tichich answered.

"You get a warrant yet?" Lee asked.

"No, the assistant prosecutor won't sign off on it," Tichich said, letting his frustration be known. "So, it looks like I gotta go pick the guy up myself and deliver him to Minneapolis to make my case for a warrant."

The meeting had lasted nearly an hour and Lee had learned very little. He had learned to guard against any local cop arresting Cunanan, though. The arrest was a federal concern; he wanted the U.S. Marshals there, not a local cop. Lee looked at his watch, anxious to get back to the office and jumpstart the chase.

"I would appreciate it if you could do this for me," Lee said. "Anything that doesn't fall within the city of Minneapolis, call me right away. I will have it followed up all over the world."

"No," Tichich answered matter-of-factly, "I don't know if I'll have time to give you a call."

"What?" Rickett said, astounded.

"If I find anything, I may or may not call you. We'll see," Tichich said. "And I hope you'll let me know if you get this guy cornered someplace."

His words stunned the veteran cops.

"Sure, ah, we'll keep you informed," Lee said as he and Rickett turned to leave. They headed quickly for the hallway outside the PD.

"What the hell was that all about?" Rickett asked.

"Beats me. He sounds really frustrated, though. Maybe Lisa can explain it," Lee said. "I get the feeling he's not happy with the way this is going, I mean, with no warrant. And I think he feels like this is *his* case," Lee observed. "But I've got the warrant, not him."

Back at the FTF Lee explained his strange encounter with Tichich to Lisa Davis. One of the reasons the FTFs were carved out of differing jurisdictions was for this purpose, to make it easier for them all to get along and work together.

"Sure, I can work with Tichich," Lisa answered.

Lee felt glad to get that task out of his hair and in her capable hands.

The plan

Lee and Rickett walked into the FTF office just after 10:00 a.m. The team sat waiting for them, although most were fielding phone calls. A thick stack of yellow phone slips sat on Lee's desk, and the FedEx box from San Diego sat on a table.

"Okay," Lee said, after grabbing a cup of coffee, "here's the plan. First of all, I want all calls relating to possible sightings to come to me, no matter the day or time. I will be the clearinghouse of information. Second, any newsies call, send them right to Coleen Rowley. I don't care who they are…"

"What if it's Rowley calling for you?" someone asked.

"Well, okay, I *want* to talk to her," Lee said. He needed to know at all times what the media was saying about the case, and Rowley could be his conduit. "No one here talks to the press. Everyone understand?" he asked, looking around the room. They all shook their heads, feeling the same way he did.

"Now this guy's gay," Lee said. "We haven't had much experience working with the gays and someone's gonna have to make contact with them. Any personal feelings you might have about gays must be set aside. This guy may kill again, once his money runs out or he gets cornered by some unsuspecting cop." He looked at Steve Gilkerson and asked, "You know any gays?"

"No, can't say as I do. Not my cup of tea," Gilkerson laughed.

"Well, see what you can find out. See who can help us contact them and such," Lee said.

"Will do."

"We got Cunanan's phone book from San Diego. We'll all work on that," Lee said, knowing that phone numbers were like current events, whereas credit card and bill information was history. Having that phone book was a great advantage. "And when you get a lead, call it out to the local FTF office for a face-to-face interview," he said, laying the photocopied sheets of phone numbers out on a table.

"Lisa and Putzie can start working on the credit cards and bills. We've got faxed copies here, and the originals are probably in the box. If he stayed in a hotel or went to a club – any place – we need someone over there to find out what he did. We will pull the phone logs from his apartment…"

"What about subpoenas?" Lisa asked.

"You just tell them that we will get them, but they gotta know the urgency. This guy's killed three men already. Brutal murders. Tell them that, and assure them that we will get the U.S. Attorney to sign off on it, but we can't wait," Lee explained.

"I'll talk to the bosses here and keep them posted," Lee continued. "Refer them to me right away if they call. And I'll keep in contact with Chicago, San Diego, L.A. and San Francisco. And have the important callers page me."

Lee checked the notes he had written on his legal pad on Wednesday night.

"Look people, this is no different than any other bad guy we chased, except he's done three now. We'll get him in days, a week, maybe two. But we'll get him," Lee said confidently. They all shook their heads in agreement.

He told them about Tichich and the Minneapolis PD. "Hennepin County refuses to issue a warrant even nine days after they found Jeff Trail. Chisago County got one in a couple days, so maybe Tichich is frustrated. But he wants to make the arrest," Lee said, shaking his head. "Ain't gonna happen."

Lee worried that the day some local cops picked up Cunanan, cops from Minneapolis and Chicago would fly in and try to haul him back to their jails. "When we get him, we call the marshals and they are to take him *in comunicado* until I get there. No one talks to him and I will decide who gets him, when they get him and how. We can't have any screw-ups because some damn local cop wants to win a merit badge."

"Lee!" Jeanie Burns said in her shrill, most accusing voice as she pointed to the tin can on her desk. "That's a quarter."

Lee retrieved a quarter from his pocket and tossed it to Jeannie. She put it in her "Swear Can." Anytime anyone in the office used profanity, she collected a fine. Most swear words were 25 cents. Some were a buck.

"I think we're gonna have a real big party thanks to this case, Burnsie," Gilkerson laughed as he watched Lee toss the quarter her way. All the proceeds in the Swear Can accrued toward "company" parties where, of course, no swearing was allowed.

"Okay, now, where the hell is he?" Lee asked after the chuckling subsided (there was no fine for saying "hell"). "Does anyone have any ideas? Any hint?"

"Not a clue yet, except I say east coast," someone answered. They talked about the highway system and possible directions Cunanan might drive, or nearby airports.

"All right, what didn't we do? What did I forget?" he asked, once he felt they had exhausted their current options. Then he sent them scurrying to their assignments.

Lee sent Gary Charbonneau to the Hennepin County Sheriff's Department crime lab. They had the best facilities in the Twin Cities for making wanted posters. Charbonneau carried with him four different color photos they had obtained, and Cunanan's vital statistics.

Charbonneau discovered a busy crime lab, but convinced them to drop everything they were doing and make the posters, given the urgency of the case. He returned to the FTF in the early afternoon, ready to run multiple copies.

Passing the test

Lee began calling other jurisdictions, putting together his interstate team. He quickly developed a checklist to evaluate FTF agents who answered his call. He wanted the best ones, the out-going, self-confident, go-get-them agents.

"This is Lee Urness, Minnesota FTF, case agent on the Andrew Cunanan case," Lee would say as he began building his national team. "Tell me a little about yourself." He wanted to know their police experience, and whether or not they were on a SWAT team. He asked if they had ever done undercover work, and how many arrests they had made.

"Now you know this Cunanan's a homosexual. How do you feel about doing face-to-face interviews with gays and lesbians, or going to their clubs and bars?" became a standard question. Lee needed to know how they would react.

"What about you?" they would ask him.

"Well, I've been a cop for 27-years. SWAT team and undercover narcotics for more than 20 years. Joined the FTF in 1994. I've made thousands of arrests. Only one of my guys is still loose, and I've never had one commit a serious crime while I chased them." He did this not to build up his ego, but to show that he knew what he was doing and win the respect of the other agents. They needed to have confidence that he could do the job, and they also had to know how intense he was about doing it quickly. Because he was not an FBI agent, it seemed even more important that they knew his background.

Lee had to make sure that these agents understood they would be talking to everyone Cunanan knew in his entire life, no matter their sexual preference or status in life. And there would be no phone interviews. "You gotta hit the streets and do face-to-face interviews," he told them.

As soon as Lee finished his instructions, the teams went to work. Before he finished, he had called Chicago, San Diego, L.A. and San Francisco. The conversations were similar, updating the locals on what he had learned and asking them if they had anything new.

Now that Cunanan had been identified as the prime suspect in the killing of Lee Miglin, intense national TV and radio coverage had begun. Twin Cities' news reporters were quickly dispatched to Chicago to join the legion of reporters from seemingly everywhere who were covering the case. Lee shook his head as he saw newsies who had been swimming like hungry minnows suddenly explode into hyperactivity, like piranha attacking a warm body. But here they attacked three dead bodies and the gay man who killed them.

Lee heard one radio report where an FBI spokesman called Cunanan a "spree killer."

"What the hell?" Lee said, looking at Rickett. "What is a 'spree killer? Now they have to invent a name for him. Just call him what he is. He's a killer!" Lee grunted.

Mapping out a Chicago strategy

After studying the wall map once again, he picked up the phone and called Chicago. "Urness here," he said as Terry Thedford picked up. Thedford was a former Chicago homicide detective assigned to the task force. "Just want to know if you've got anything new? Any more phone calls?" he asked, referring to cell phone calls placed from Miglin's Lexus.

"Nope, nothing new on that. If he tries, we get a fix on him, but there are no calls on that cell phone since Sunday," Thedford said.

"I say he's somewhere secure and hunkered down. Sure seems he headed east, maybe New York or Boston. Anyone could blend in there," Lee said. "The agents will have to go into the gay bars and clubs out there and in your town, too. Oh, we'll have wanted posters soon, maybe this afternoon."

"Send me some as soon as you can," Thedford asked, "and don't worry about the bars and clubs. We'll get there right away."

"Done," he said, then changed gears. "So where is he? Did he flee the country? Is he gonna try to flee the country and if so, where?"Lee asked this not so much because Thedford might actually know, but to help him think through every possible escape point.

"Maybe he's roughing it," Thedford suggested, seeing Cunanan holed up in the woods or mountains somewhere.

"Naw," Lee said, "I can't see this guy taking a tent to the woods. He's too used to fancy digs and stuff. And he's not a thief or burglar."

"Well he stole from Miglin, that's for sure," Thedford said.

"True enough. But he had to have gotten desperate, you know, like pushed over the edge. Maybe he begged for something and Miglin told him to go to hell, and that set him off. He sure did a number on Jeff Trail, so he's capable of being set off," Lee said. "I think the money was just an extra. I mean he needed money. He's spoiled and never had to work for anything."

"Well he's got $2,000, we figure," Thedford told him.

"Okay, that buys him 40 days; 50 on the outside. I'll give him 60. Sometime, then, he's got to hit someone else, unless he can find a sugar daddy. Maybe that's why he hit Miglin..." National news media continued to allege that Miglin was a closeted gay. No other real reason could be found for him knowing Cunanan.

"But everyone we've talked to says Miglin is not gay," Thedford answered.

Lee asked Thedford to try everything to see if there was any connection whatsoever between Cunanan and Miglin.

"There's a lot of politics in this case, Lee. Miglin built half the city and he was well-connected," Thedford said. "And the cops are getting a lot of pressure to solve the case, quick."

"I just want to catch the guy. So what do you think? Was he gay?" Lee asked.

"If he was, the family won't admit it."

"Well, that's their problem. I really don't care how they feel. If the old man was gay and it helps find Cunanan, I want to know. I just need to find Cunanan. It's all I care about," Lee emphasized. "You think he's dead?"

"Don't know. Would he commit suicide?"

"Unlikely, unless he gets real desperate. And with that, I can help," Lee chuckled.

"What have you done about international?" Thedford asked.

"I got the French Embassy looking and the alert's gone out worldwide. They posted a lookout on Interpol yesterday. It's all they can do until we get the 'Red Notice.'" This notice told Interpol to give priority to a chase, and it required hours of painful preparation of paperwork. "Maybe we'll catch a break and get him before that," Lee said, seeing in his mind's eye the mountain of paperwork already stacking up – the least favorite part of his job.

"We've already talked with Toronto's FTF. They're really good about watching the borders," Thedford added. "He's got a good jump on us."

"Yup, that's our biggest problem. We're four days behind him. So we gotta put him in the bubble; cut off all his escape routes, friends and family. Which brings me to the point. Cunanan's mother, and a sister and brother living down near Springfield or something. Can you do face-to-face interviews with them right away?" Lee asked.

"Well, they've got an RA down there," Thedford said, referring to an FBI Resident Agent. Chicago had one of the biggest and busiest FBI District Offices, but all of these offices had Resident Agents assigned to other, smaller and less busy locales.

"But I want *you* to go down. You're the best guy to do this instead of some agent who never chased a fugitive. We need constant contact with the family," Lee said.

"Okay, I'll get it set up for tomorrow. Scott Bakken and I can go. He's FBI. Will that work?" Thedford offered. Thedford and Bakken found a nervous and unstable Maryann Cunanan and two of her children, extensively interviewing them.

"Just fine. Then stay on it. Put the fear of Uncle Sam into them. And you know how mothers can be," Lee reminded the veteran cop. Just like a professional coach, Lee had no problem reminding his FTF team of the basics, too easily forgotten.

"Sounds like you've got it under control," Thedford said.

"Well, where do *you* think he went, and what is he doing?" Lee asked. "Where is he heading? What have I missed?"These questions he repeated every day to dozens of agents as the chase continued.

"Okay, make sure you have my pager number," Lee added as their conversation came to an end. "The phones here are going nuts, so it does no good to call the office. I'll call you back ASAP. Any interesting leads, let me know about them. I just need to know what you're doing so I can be a like a clearinghouse for everyone. Use the phone and get an agent on it right away. Paper is too slow. Talk to somebody and get their butt on the street. You get a hot lead, go after it, but let me know what you're doing," he explained as they said good-bye.

Willing help comes quickly

Andrew Cunanan had two older sisters and an older brother, but had almost no interaction with them, save Gina. Gina lived in San Francisco, and Andrew occasionally visited her, the last time during March.

Gina contacted San Francisco FBI Special Agent Rich Anderson on Thursday, May 8. Minneapolis Police Sergeant Tichich had called her the prior day. As well, a friend from San Diego told her about the news stories concerning Andrew. She first called a San Diego TV station that referred her to San Diego police.

Gina said that Andrew seldom talked about his personal life with her. She suggested that he perhaps wanted to shield her from the truth about his homosexual lifestyle. Because of this, she had no knowledge of his friends.

Gina saw her herself as the one person in the Cunanan family who had contact with him. She held out hope that he would try to call her and if he did, she would make sure to call the FBI.

When Lee learned of this conversation the next day, he smiled. "This is exactly what we need," he said to Kevin Rickett. "When the family wants to help, we win."

The formula for catching crooks always included help from the family, whether or not they were willing helpers. With Gina, they had a willing helper. Lee felt he could shut this one down in a few weeks at the most.

Informing everyone, even the boss

Lee called Fred Tremper, Squad 6 Supervisor who supervised the Minnesota Fugitive Task Force. "And so, I'm telling everyone, no one talks to the media. We know we can track Cunanan by his phone calls, and we don't want him tipped off," Lee said.

"You got it. It's a good plan. Just keep me posted and let Rowley handle the media," Tremper said.

"Ah, right. I will do that," Lee answered, laughing to himself.

In between calls to FBI and BCA agents, Lee talked with police and sheriff's departments across the country, quickly discovering that like Tichich in Minneapolis, Chicago PD was very closed-mouth. "Lee Miglin was a powerful man, well-connected politically. The heat is really on us to catch him," Lee heard. "We're willing to work with you, but we're doing our own chase. Anything you hear, we want to know."

Lee asked the same of them. "Yeah, okay. We'll do that," he heard.

Lee talked often with Jon Hermann, the Minnesota BCA agent on the Madson case. Hermann, like Lee, knew that good things happen when cops work together, and they trusted each other. He was a tenacious and vigorous investigator. "Nothing new," Hermann said when they talked on Thursday. "How about on your end?"

"No, not really. We got the stuff from San Diego and we're working it. Got stiffed at MPD, though," Lee said, explaining his experience earlier that morning. "I'm not real confident in their investigation either," he added.

"Well, I may swing down there again and go through their stuff. Maybe I can find something. If I do, I'll let you know," Hermann said.

"Good," Lee said. He asked Hermann about his opinion of Cunanan's whereabouts. Like the others, Hermann had little to offer. Lee reminded him to keep a closed mouth with the "newsies, and I'll talk to Rivard, too," Lee said. Deputy Sheriff Todd Rivard headed up the Madson investigation for Chisago County.

Lee knew that his best source of cooperation would be the FTF agents in each locale, but local cops had to be included in the circle, even those that were aloof and uncooperative. The issue was to catch Cunanan, not catch glory for an arrest.

It made no difference to Lee whether Andrew Cunanan were arrested or was "dead right there" – DRT. If a cop shot and killed him, if he killed himself or if they arrested him, it made no difference. Lee saw that his job was to stop Cunanan any way he could before he hurt someone else.

Progress amidst chaos

Steve Gilkerson hit the mother lode when he phoned the Gay Lesbian Community Action Council – GLCAC – an organization of activist gays and lesbians based in Minneapolis. There he talked with Constance Potter who headed up the organization. She agreed to do everything she could to work with the FTF to alert gays and lesbians nationwide. Gilkerson passed the message on to Lee for his Friday stack of calls.

Lee saw a call slip from Coleen Rowley. He dialed her number.

"Coleen Rowley," she answered.

"Lee calling. How are you? You called?" Lee said.

"I've got media people all over me on this Andrew Cunanan thing," she said.

"I'm sure you do. We're sending them all your way," he chuckled.

"Do you want to talk to them? I can help you," she suggested.

"No way. I won't talk to any newsies. That's your job," he answered.

"Fine. But they want to know where we think he is. What do I tell them?" she asked.

"Tell them we don't know. Tell them he could be anywhere," he answered.

"In the world?" she asked.

"No, I don't think so. Tell them he's in the U.S.," Lee answered.

"Line 5 for you, Lee," Vern Lee shouted from across the FTF office.

"Who is it?" he said, muffling the phone. "Just a minute," he said to Rowley.

"San Diego," Vern said.

"Okay, tell them to hold," he told Vern.

"I've gotta run. You need anything else?" Lee asked Rowley.

"You haven't given me anything."

"Well, this is all we know," Lee answered. "And you know, I don't want to discourage leads from anywhere in the country. Logic gives me an idea where he may be, but I don't want to stop someone from calling who thinks they saw him," he explained.

"Okay, I can work with that," Rowley said. "But we'll have to give them more eventually."

"That's your job, and I wish you well. I gotta go," he said.

"Talk to you later then," she said as they hung up. Rowley immediately set out to make sure that the FBI both got credit for what it had done right and kept the media focused on the story. When the media began going down a bunny trail that looked as though it would hurt efforts to capture Cunanan, she tried to steer them back on course. She assisted all the FBI spokespersons in what they should say. She kept a summary of all that the FBI had done during the time since Cunanan killed Jeff Trail, tracking the extensive manhunt. On May 12, she had Cunanan's picture posted on the FBI's website. She saw immediately the potential for a misunderstanding of how hard the agency worked on the case from the beginning.

At the FTF office, Lee punched line 5. Two other phone lines sat blinking back at him, and his pile of call slips continued to grow like grass pushing its way up through fertilizer on a warm spring day.

Chapter 13 ~ May sweeps story into limelight

Donna Brant, an Executive Producer at the Cable TV program America's Most Wanted, needed something hot and spicy for her May 10 show. She knew that May was "sweeps month," and AMW needed to score huge points to prove to the network that they were justified in keeping them on the air. Just the previous year, Fox Network had cancelled the show. It took an outpouring of more than 80,000 viewer phone calls, letters from 32 governors and a torrent of calls from cops all across America to get the show back on the air. AMW staff was still searching for the kinds of stories that would win them a broader audience and ensure their continuity – and jobs.

Wednesday's stories linking Andrew Cunanan to Lee Miglin's murder in Chicago sounded ripe to Brant. She had developed a nose for news at NBC where she worked as a reporter for 10 years, and this story smelled to her like it had legs. Besides, John Walsh and his crew were already scheduled to be in the Chicago area that week. Doing a Cunanan story seemed a perfect fit to her. Like Lee Urness, her curiosity about Cunanan soon turned into a life-changing and all-controlling venture.

Brant recruited Evan Marshall, one of the young Production Assistants who had been hired since the shows near demise the prior year. Strangely enough, it was the cancellation and resurrection of AMW that 1996 summer that won Brant her new position with its increased authority and responsibility. The demanding job in a production company less than flush with cash offered her the kind of rewards she relished – catching bad guys, using all of her skills and resources to get stories done, no matter the limitation.

Brant and Marshall began collecting information about Cunanan and Miglin. Convincing AMW's program committee could be a tall order, but the sensationalism of the Miglin killing and its apparent ties to two Minnesota murders gave Brant an edge. Cunanan killed a powerful man in Chicago and was on the run – a story made for AMW.

Normally she would have to pitch her story to a programming committee as they gathered together in the big conference room just down the hall from her tiny work cubicle. There the committee would vote, and if she had done a good enough job, her story might win a feature. But with Cunanan, the convenience of Walsh's location (saving money) and the need for something sensational (sweeps) gave her the edge she needed. Cunanan would be featured on May 10.

Brant contacted Colleen Dudgeon, a contract video producer in Chicago, and gave her marching orders to get the show put together. Dudgeon went to work immediately.

Meanwhile, Brant had Evan Marshall contact the FBI who directed him to the agent in charge, Lee Urness. Marshall called and left a message for Lee, hoping for a quick call back and even quicker cooperation.

Here's some news you'll like

Lee saw the note to call Evan Marshall at "America's Most Wanted." He pondered it. He had never had good luck working with any media and was not sure this was the time to start trusting them.

"Hey," he said to everyone in the office, "any of you know anything about this America's Most Wanted? Are they worth talking to?"

"Yeah, they're good," Rickett said. "They've helped catch a lot of crooks."

"That's right," Charbonneau added. "You'll get a lot of leads."

"Not all good, though," Davis suggested. "You can get some crazy ones, too."

"But they're good to work with? You can trust them?" Lee asked.

"Sure, I think so," Rickett offered.

"Mr. Marshall, this is Lee Urness, Minnesota Fugitive Task Force," he said when Marshall answered his call.

"Thank you for calling me. We've decided to go with the Cunanan story this Saturday night," Marshall announced. Such immediacy was nearly unheard of, Lee knew. But he had recognized the day before as activity surrounding him exploded, that nothing about this case was normal. "We just need everything you've got," Marshall said. "The more you give us the better job we can do."

"Okay, but I'm afraid I can't add much to what's already out there," Lee said. He refused to reveal anything the FTF was doing or where they were concentrating their search. He did not know Evan Marshall. All he knew is that newsies screw things up. Lee refused to risk anything of value. His single concern was how to handle the leads, how they would help him catch Cunanan.

"We can have a local film crew talk with you right away on Friday..." Marshall began.

"Oh, no, no. That can't happen. I've got no time to talk to the media. You'll have to do it without me. You call Coleen Rowley," he said, rattling off her phone number.

"You sure?"

"Absolutely. Just send me the leads," Lee insisted. "And I want them right away."

They made arrangements to talk again on Friday when everything was finalized.

"Hey, thanks for your help," Lee said before hanging up.

"You bet. We'll do what we can," Marshall said.

Marshall gave his report to Donna Brant, who was both intrigued and frustrated by Lee's obstinacy. No cop would stop her from getting the information they needed to make this AMW show a winner. Brant wrote a note to call Lee on Friday.

Lee wrote a note to remind him that everybody had to be notified about the AMW program. That meant his agents and all other agents everywhere, because Cunanan could have been anywhere in the world by then. A hot lead could develop into a late night chase, and a quick arrest. "Great!" Lee said as he headed to the phone.

Making credit deals

"How's it going?" Lee asked Lisa later that afternoon.

"Good. We've got all the stuff in the boxes from San Diego, and we're working the credit cards now," Lisa said.

Copies of the bills revealed that Cunanan loved oriental food, and visited some of California's finest and most expensive restaurants. Knowing where he liked to eat gave the FTF more leads to check, and Lisa called these leads out to west coast agents.

"You know," Lisa said, staring at Cunanan's credit history, "he's maxed out a lot of these cards. And he's got a collection company chasing him. What if we got the credit card company to extend some credit, then if he uses the card, we know where he is."

"Great idea, let me call on it right away," Lee said. As he called the credit card companies, he asked them to extend Cunanan's credit by $500, "and the FBI will cover your losses. I'll get a letter out right away," he told them. "Flag the card and as soon as he uses it, I want you to call me, any time of the day or night. I can't overemphasize how important this is. He's killed three times already, and he'll likely kill again if we don't get him first."

This was like setting cheese in a mousetrap. With the "Snap!" of a credit card through a card-reader, Lee would catch the rodent.

With that detail done, Lee and the team worked on calls to hotels, restaurants and anywhere else Cunanan had used his credit cards. The routine was similar to what he had done with the credit card companies.

"So, I need you to check every record for his name. He may be registered as Andrew DeSilva or Drew Cunningham, too," Lee explained.

"What about a subpoena?" he'd be asked.

"Don't worry; I will get it for you right away. But we got a killer running loose, and I need this stuff right now," Lee said.

"No problem. Just get me that subpoena."

"Will do. Now I want everything. All his food bills, room charges and especially, any phone calls he made. Just the phone numbers."

At the same time, others were calling Pacific Bell, and long distance service providers. Having a record of all Cunanan's calls meant knowing who he called most often, and it steered investigators to more face-to-face interviews.

Each time the FTF picked off yet another of Cunanan's friends, they closed his window another notch. Soon there would be no air of freedom left for the man.

These kinds of calls and the interviews that followed took hundreds of agent hours, but they were essential to shutting down Cunanan's options. And Lee had set his jaw, as he always did, focused on catching this guy before he hurt another person. When Lee searched for a missing man, he never gave up. He always got his man, and when Lee chased a crook, that crook never again hurt anyone, that is, until he chased Andrew Cunanan.

Chapter 14 ~ Chasing Cunanan while meeting gays

During the day on Thursday, *Chicago Tribune* reporter Eric Ferkenhoff worked Minneapolis city streets near David Madson's apartment. He searched for anyone who had known him, Trail or Cunanan. And he had talked with Chris Graves at the *Star-Tribune*. Then he heard about a breakthrough story at the *Chicago Tribune*.

One of the *Chicago Tribune* writers had talked with a Chicago Police Department source that day. The source said that the cops were tracking Cunanan by triangulating on Lee Miglin's cell phone. This gave them a great chance to find the car, and that meant finding Cunanan.

Ferkenhoff could hardly believe that someone actually gave up such information to the newspaper. He called his own police department source to confirm the story; it checked out. Soon, the newspaper released the story. Wire services quickly picked it up. Given that it said Cunanan had headed east, toward New York or Philadelphia, news media in that area began making inquiries with local cops.

Chicago police became very angry about the leak, working hard to find the person or persons responsible. Everyone linked to the case pointed fingers at others; even the phone service company that worked with the police could have leaked the story, they said. No one ever stepped up to take the blame and no reporter ever gave up his source.

Since the story said that the signal had come from a Philadelphia tower, police knew that the Lexus likely had been somewhere in the area. They wanted their squads to watch for it, and it followed that a dispatcher put out an alert to all squads in the area. In some cities, those calls are encoded, but in many, anyone with a police scanner could hear the dispatch. News organizations often monitor police chatter, making it likely that a reporter in the area heard cops talk about tracking Cunanan by his cell phone. A responsible reporter would have next called the Philadelphia PD to verify the accuracy of what they had heard.

Sometime on Thursday, a wire service report stated that law enforcement officers believed Cunanan had headed east. They had based their suspicion, the report said, on two cell phone calls he had attempted on Miglin's car phone the previous weekend. The cops had been monitoring Miglin's cell phone, the story revealed.

"Son of a bitch!" Lee shouted when he heard the news. "Our best chance to catch the guy, and the newsies broadcast it!"

It got worse.

Philadelphia's Deputy Police Commissioner Richard Zapille felt that the best way to satisfy the reporters and warn the public was to hold a press conference. Then the officer laid out the facts, that police had monitored two calls the past Sunday, and that Cunanan appeared to have been in the Philly area. He said they were still monitoring calls, hoping Cunanan would use the phone.

KARE TV reporter Bernie Grace, still working in Chicago, heard about the press conference. He shook his head wondering why the cops would put out such information. He feared that someone might get hurt as a result. So did Lee Urness.

"This is bad! This is real bad," Lee said to his FTF members. "Let's just hope Cunanan's having sex with someone with the TV off. This just tells us how careful we have to be. We gotta keep our mouths shut." More than that, they had to make sure that they never gave out any damaging information accidentally, and that meant talking "business" only on encrypted phone lines. Few police radios were encrypted, and eager reporters, he knew, could possibly even eavesdrop on calls between two digital phones.

He sat back in his chair and started thinking about how dangerous these leaks could be.

Devastating leaks

Lee had worked with informants making drug buys and doing deep undercover work in the Hibbing, Minnesota area. He shared his mission with one Hibbing cop and another in the Iron Range city of Virginia. No one else knew.

After three months work, the day came to make the bust. Lee got out of bed early that morning, his adrenalin pumping as he rehearsed the day ahead. He checked everything before leaving his motel room, making sure he had the warrants in hand.

At the same time, the Hibbing cop sat with this family eating breakfast. "What's up for today?" his wife asked.

"Oh, big drug bust, with an undercover agent," he said, shrugging his shoulders. "Should be fun." He left for work.

When the cop's son got to school, he casually mentioned to a few friends what his dad had said at breakfast that morning.

Finally, the moment came. Followed by the local cops, all of them wearing full protective gear, Lee broke the door down. They found an empty room. The crooks had cleaned it from top to bottom. Three months work was flushed down the drain.

On another occasion, in the small western Minnesota city of Fergus Falls, Lee held about half a dozen search and arrest warrants on a case he had developed over a month's time. Ready to move, he got the County Attorney to sign off on the warrants and only needed a judge's signature.

The opportune time to make the bust came one evening after working hours, so Lee headed to the judge's house. "Your honor, we heard the guy's got a pile of drugs in his house right now. We want to take him right away, so I just need these signed," Lee said when the judge opened the door to him.

"Come on in," the judge said, leading him to the kitchen where he sat down at the table, just recently cleared of supper.

"Can we find some place a little more private to talk?" Lee asked, remembering Hibbing.

"No, let's do it here."

"This is pretty confidential," Lee said.

"Naw, we'll be all right here," the judge insisted, and then began asking Lee tough questions about the warrants. Lee rattled off the names of the alleged crooks and the addresses they planned to hit.

The judge's son, who had overheard the conversation, quietly slipped out the door.

Later that night, when Lee led his crew through the door, just as in Hibbing, everything had been scoured clean and the bad guys were gone.

As bad is all this had been, even more than his anger about losing the busts, Lee feared how armed crooks who had been warned about the cops could have opened fire and murdered them as they stormed the door. And a leak could cause that to happen; could cause someone to be killed needlessly.

Because of his experiences, Lee wanted nothing to do with leaking police information to anyone, especially to the media. He insisted that everyone on his team stayed tight-lipped – it was a life and death issue. And now, someone had given away their greatest chance to stop Andrew Cunanan. The anger welled up in Lee and his phone calls now carried a warning he hoped he would never have to give.

119

Sugar Daddy's gone

Lee called the San Diego FTF office. "Urness here."

He told John Hause about the Philly leak concerning the cell phone calls. "It really fries me, and it might cost a cop his life. We all have to keep our mouths shut," he said.

"No argument here," Hause answered.

Lee told him about the upcoming America's Most Wanted show. "So you want to alert your agents, because we may get a flood of calls. Anything new out there?"

"Nothing earthshaking. We tried to get ahold of William Norman, Cunanan's erstwhile sugar daddy, but he's out of town."

"Nuts," Lee said, thinking the man would be a key to finding Cunanan.

"Norman's friends say he's working his way to New York City where he's taking the Queen Elizabeth II to London. Supposed to be leaving this coming Monday."

"Okay, that makes some sense. Maybe Cunanan will try to link up with him there," Lee said. He had no idea what role, if any, Norman still played in Cunanan's life, or if somehow, he might even be connected to what the killer had already done.

"He's got a place in Phoenix somewhere and they're trying to find him. As soon as we do, we'll let you know," Hause reported.

"How about the other interviews?" Lee asked.

"Well, we're working our way through the list. I think we'll finish what we have by tomorrow."

"Any luck?"

"No, not yet," he sighed. "These guys are something else. I tell them what Cunanan's done and tell them they must cooperate. And they say, 'Yeah, I suppose I will. But I know Andrew, and I really can't believe he killed those people. You know, I still really love Andrew.'"

"Sick! Don't they understand what he did to their gay buddies?" Lee asked.

"Sure, but they say it's out of character..."

"Well it is!" Lee said. "The guy they knew is dead. At least it's like Cunanan left his old self behind in San Diego. The new Cunanan is vicious, a killer without hope. He'd kill any one of them if they provoked him, just for provoking him. Make them understand that!"

"That's what we've been doing," Hause answered.

"Are there any we have to watch?" Lee asked. Many close associates of bad guys refuse to give them up if they have contact with them, so the FTF often tails them.

"There's this one attorney who simply refuses to help. I think he's afraid of letting people know he's gay," Hause said.

"Well let him know that being exposed is a lot better than being disbarred, jailed or dead," Lee said.

"He's one we may have to tail later on," he opined. "We've been going non-stop on this, and every lead gives us more leads."

"Any help?"

"Yes and no. I mean, they all call him the life of the party, the center of attention. But they also call him a liar and braggart," Hause said.

"A real winner," Lee chuckled.

"One guy told us that they were driving around together during high school and Cunanan sat in the back seat. All of a sudden, he pulls out a .45 caliber gun and sticks it in the back of the driver's head," Hause said.

"Jeesh," Lee answered. "What about drugs. He a dealer?"

"No, we can't find anything like that. They tell us he used steroids, smoked crack and did cocaine, but dealing? No, no way," Hause said. "He had guts, but not for that kind of thing. He might get hurt!"

Hause explained that Cunanan had lived with Norman for a long time and they traveled all over the world together. Norman had bought him a new Infiniti.

Lee began to understand that Cunanan really was a nobody, a nothing who never had a real job. He failed at college and had no close family. Cunanan's occupation was "party boy" and prostitute, whose partying had ended abruptly when Norman "fired" him. Cunanan wanted more money, and Norman said, "No, get out."

"He prowls the gay bars and clubs at night, and prefers young blond guys," Hause said.

"Oh how lovely," Lee said.

"And he's never been arrested or convicted of a crime, so there are no prints other than the thumb print on the driver's license."

"Okay, good work. Well, let me ask you what you think about this. I mean, where is he?" Lee asked. Then he rattled off his list of questions, repeating this so often as if it was a religious mantra to be said so many times a day as to ascend to a higher level of consciousness. Only this wasn't religion, it was good police work.

Lee had Steve Gilkerson call Norman's San Diego home that Thursday and left a message. "This is the FBI; we have to talk to you. Call any time day or night," and he left Lee's phone number. Cunanan had talked and partied with Norman recently, so the line between them looked straight and taut.

Lee called San Francisco and talked to Rich Anderson, the FTF agent there and learned about "Liz, this woman he used to live with."

"What? Does that make sense?" Lee asked.

"Well, she says they'd been friends since junior high. There was nothing else between them, but Cunanan lived with Liz and her husband for a long time. In fact, he used to baby-sit their daughter."

"How'd you like to have a three-time killer as your babysitter?" Lee said, shaking his head.

"Well that's the thing. Liz says she just can't believe Andrew would do this, that he was never violent or anything like that," Anderson said. "In fact, all his friends keep saying that they can't believe he did this. We've been hearing that a lot."

"Well this Andrew ain't the old one. That's for sure." The more Lee heard and the more he thought about it, the more he got inside Cunanan's head, at least to the extent he could understand this bold, brash gay man, the more he felt that the old Cunanan had died. The new Cunanan had become a murderous monster.

Next Lee called L.A. and talked with Jeff Knotts.

"Nope, nothing new. His friends say he told them he was going to Minneapolis. Then he's supposed to go to San Francisco. That's what he told them," Knotts said.

"And others he told he's going on to New York or Miami," Lee said, staring up the U.S. map on the wall. "Well, where do *you* think he is?" Lee asked yet another time that day. Sometimes the routine of repeating the same questions got monotonous, but like a football lineman who keeps repeating his blocking routine, doing so eventually paid off in winning the game, only this game meant life and death, not the Super Bowl.

"Listen, make sure you've got my pager number and use that first. If you call my cell, it will roll over to my pager in three rings. You'll never get through on the office line," Lee explained to each FTF agent.

"That bad, huh?"

"Worse! I've got to fly. Remember, call me if anything breaks," Lee said.

Feasting on a serial

Lee continued to compile everything he knew for the massive dispatch of information he planned to send out on May 9 – it would be the ninth of his dispatches, labeled "Serial 9." Lee sent a priority copy of the report to every FBI office in the world, giving them notice to assist in the chase. The FBI's "Priority" designation required the cooperation of every receiving office.

The Serial 9 begin with the words, "ARMED AND DANGEROUS; ARMED WITH A .40 CALIBER HANDGUN," in bold print.

The Serial 9 "Lead to locate and apprehend," carried a case synopsis, warrant information and suspect description. It listed recent lead information and a list of conclusions about Cunanan, as well as his descriptors. It set a lead for all FBI offices worldwide, meaning that each office has been officially requested to take action. The action Lee requested, in particular, was that FBI agents everywhere contact local gay and lesbian organizations and local media for assistance.

The Serial 9 concluded with the words, "ARMED AND DANGEROUS; ARMED WITH A .40 CALIBER HANDGUN," in bold print.

With the Serial 9 in hand, every FBI office had to respond to Lee, through the Minnesota FTF, within 24 hours and provide continuous reports. In this way, Lee could make sure that maximum attention was paid to the case.

The Serial 9 also included two copies of the wanted poster. That meant that every FBI agent in the world now had a picture of Cunanan to carry with them at all times. The Cunanan chase would carry a high priority, meaning all field agents would be working together.

"Lee, line 3 for you," Vern Lee said yet again. The phones refused to quit nagging him.

Lee took a deep breath and looked around the office. Every agent worked on some aspect of the case. The noise level had increased, even accelerated all day. Lee felt as though he sat inside a snare drum, with the constant rat-a-tat-tat of noise starting to give him a headache. Always calm, cool and under control, he felt his orderly world crumbling around him. He had to get out again.

"I'm going to the car to make calls. Page me if it's important," he said, heading to the parking lot.

Lee started catching up on his calls, interrupted by the nagging of his pager and then headed back into the office an hour later.

"Take line 1," Vern Lee said as Lee walked into the office. "It's your buddy Rowley."

And so another round of calls began that continued non-stop until Lee saw it was time to call it quits for the day. Late that afternoon, he got the team together to review everything.

"America's Most Wanted runs the Cunanan show on Saturday. We need to be at the FBI by 6:00, and ready to work late. I need three volunteers," he said. "Now it's almost 6:00. You people go on home and we'll hit it hard again tomorrow."

Lee, though, stayed on, fielding a few calls, calling the west coast once more, before their day ended. Then he sat pondering his notes and the chaos he had experienced the past two days.

For the first time in his 27-year career, he felt that a case had taken over his life, that it controlled him, instead of the other way around. And no matter how hard he tried, he could find no way to shake that feeling, but he steeled himself to regain control, a nearly hopeless battle.

The day ground to a close

After 6 p.m., the clamor started to subside. The east coast agents had gone home; so had Chicago. Lee knew that in California, agents were still on the street, and that they would call if anything important happened.

The room fell quiet.

He pulled out his case file and notes and set them on the desk. He set an empty legal pad next to him, ready to write a "to do" list. Then he picked through every piece of paper, every scribble on a note pad, making sure he knew every name, every fact, every timeline. He wrote phone numbers of all his FTF contacts on the back of a 6 x 9 white envelope and stuck several copies of Cunanan's picture inside. Once he finished, he reviewed it all again.

As chaotic as the day had been, he felt they had made a lot of progress. Stacks of information sat around him and on the desks of his fellow agents. He studied those piles and smiled. Somewhere in there, he knew, lay the single element that would flush Cunanan out of his closet and into the bright light of a shiny police badge.

Exhausted, but encouraged, just after 10 p.m., Lee drove home, listening as he always did, to police radios monitoring Twin Cities activity, and KQQL 107.9, the "Golden Oldies" station he loved the most.

Once in bed, Lee said a prayer for his fellow police officers, and he fell asleep.

Good movie

Andrew Cunanan pulled the bill of his baseball cap down on his fore-head, put on his sunglasses and left the solitude of the West Side Club Bath-house. The chilly evening had brought dark skies, but the bright lights of New York's streets pushed that darkness from the sidewalks. At any other time in his life, wearing sunglasses at night would have been preposterous, but now Cunanan needed the anonymity they brought to him. The loud, brash partying stud that always drew self-attention had been reduced to acts of camouflage. It grated on him, but the completion of his murderous assign-ment required it.

He walked quickly down West 20th Street toward 8th Avenue and then up to the Chelsea Theater at 260 West 23rd Street, nine long blocks away. No one noticed him as he passed among the thousands of people scurrying here and there. Even if a passerby had focused in on him, so many of them looked just like him that there would be no reason to notice. News anchors across America had been telling and retelling his sordid story for days, yet the only picture available to them was a profile, and it left much to the viewer's imagination. Had someone studied that picture it is unlikely they would have matched it to Cunanan's appearance on this early spring night. The extra body weight and concerted effort to conceal his identity simply sealed his public anonymity.

At West 23rd Street and 8th Avenue he crossed the street in front of the New York Sports Club, a place at which, under any other circumstance, he might stop for a quick work out, or to meet someone nice. Instead, he crossed the street to the theater that stood 100 feet west of that intersection, and bought his ticket for "Devil's Own." Harrison Ford's good cop character contrasted with the evil lurking in his own heart, yet he, like Sean Penn's IRA character, had a crusade of his own, one that would bring him immortal-ity. At least, Cunanan hoped it would be a better movie than Jim Carey's "Liar, Liar," the one he saw at the same theater the night before. A character known for being a consummate liar came too close to Cunanan's own reality, and the fateful hammering of Jeff Trail back in Minneapolis ended all chance whatsoever of his own redemption.

Hidden in a crowd of ebullient men flocking to the Chelsea, Cunanan bought his ticket and slipped into the darkened auditorium, unnoticed by boys more preoccupied with their own dates than with him. Good fortune smiled on those men assembled for the show that night in that Cunanan had not yet heard or seen the TV news about how the FBI was tracking him. If he had, he would most certainly have found himself trolling for a new ride out of town, not a new date.

What mattered to him that night was finding someone to hold, to love and with whom to laugh.

After the movie, he and his lover could have slipped next door to East of 8th, the night club where men came and went, enjoying a naughty live stage show and having a few drinks. He and his date might have crossed the street to the Chelsea Gardens Apartments. Or to travel to an apartment or hotel room, they need but make an easy 100 foot walk to the subway stairs that climb down to the tracks carrying the A, C and E trains. From there they could connect with just about any New York City site. Slipping into the dimly lit, though always busy subway stations carried very little risk. Hardly anyone looked at anyone else down there, rather simply intent on getting on the right train.

Cunanan knew that William Norman might arrive in town that night, or perhaps the next. Norman planned to take the Queen Elizabeth II to London the following Monday. Most likely, Carter Peterson* would travel with him, unless he had met yet another companion. Getting from the dingy West Side Club Bathhouse to the exotic Rihga Royale or Four Seasons' hotels was a matter of a short subway or cab ride, and these were Cunanan and Norman's favorites in New York City. Cunanan needed to but make a simple phone call to find out if Norman had checked in. But he made no direct attempt to find Norman.

Cunanan still needed to get himself invited to a Gianni Versace party, and that would win him a legacy about which no one would ever forget. But on that Thursday night, he needed the warmth of a hot blond boy. Tomorrow would take care of itself.

Chapter 15 ~ Laying the foundation of a chase

The alarm screamed at Lee at 6 a.m. Friday morning. He shook off sleep and got out of bed, refreshed and ready to catch Andrew Cunanan.

"Thank you God," Lee said in a simple prayer. Since no phone calls had interrupted his sleep, he figured Cunanan had not killed anyone else.

He read the newspaper and glanced at TV news, grateful that neither carried a story to destroy his day. He hoped that this day, the end of the week, would give him a major breakthrough and, if he was lucky, an arrest. He had done everything by the book, and even ventured into the gay and lesbian world.

Too bad that Lee had it all wrong, because there would be no peace that day, only an explosion of death and mayhem.

An hour later, Lee walked into the FTF office and went straight to the dartboard that hung on the second wood pillar, an 18" square rough-hewn oak post that stretched to the high ceiling above. On the dartboard, he hung a 5x7 color photo of Cunanan.

Hanging a bad guy's picture on the dartboard was nothing new. The agents regularly did this with other crooks as sort of an office joke, but Lee saw nothing funny about Cunanan. During the next weeks, every dart he threw at this sick man carried fresh intensity aimed between the childlike eyes on that picture. In-between phone calls at particularly frustrating moments, throwing darts replaced the urge to punch something or someone. But he had no time for darts on this day, just time to hang Cunanan on the dartboard. Soon enough, he would hang handcuffs and shackles on him, he felt sure.

Have a gay time

Lee called Emilio Blasse, an FTF agent in New York City. The FBI operation there was huge, with ties to field agents all over the Big Apple. Dozens of Special Agents worked out of offices connected to the New York City division.

"Blasse here," Emilio answered.

"This is Lee Urness from Minneapolis. I'm the case agent on the Andrew Cunanan case, file number 88A-MP-47461. I need your help," Lee said.

"What do you need?" Blasse answered in the brash blunt way of New Yorkers.

"I've got some leads on him in New York City and I'd like you to check them," Lee said. "Can you check The Townhouse on East 58th and the Regents on East 53rd?"

"Oh yeah, those are gay hangouts. Classy places," Blasse said.

"But you'll check them?"

"Sure."

"I've got a few more places," Lee said, adding high-class hotels and other places. Lee really knew very little about New York City, but he knew that Blasse did: that was how the FTF worked, with agents who knew their own towns.

"Okay, I'll VIGIT the photos to you as soon as I can this afternoon," Lee said. On Wednesday, Lee had learned how to use the FBI's VIGIT program. The operator who was supposed to help him wasn't there, so Lee, impatient as always, had done it himself. VIGIT allowed the transmission of photo quality pictures anywhere in the world, and he needed to do that for Emilio Blasse as soon as possible.

"Okay, I'll get on it as soon as I get the photos," Blasse said.

"Also, this guy had a sugar daddy back in San Diego. His name is William Norman and he is due into your town, we think Friday night. When I hear from him, I want you to go see him," Lee said.

"Okay, I can do that."

"Where do you think he'd go?" Lee asked.

"Beats me. I don't know much about homosexual hang outs," Blasse laughed. "Not my kind of place."

"Mine neither," Lee laughed. "But it's what we've got to work with."

"Wonderful," Blasse answered.

"I'll get the photos to you ASAP, and keep me posted," Lee said. "Here's my pager number." Lee got all of Blasse's numbers, too, as he had done with all the other agents. "Call the moment you get anything," Lee said.

"Consider it done," Blasse added. The New York City FTF office produced hundreds of copies of those photos and distributed them to gay establishments all over the Big Apple.

Lee liked Blasse's attitude. He sounded like a go-getter, a man of action. Lee found his New York accent to be humorous.

"But tell your people to be careful," Lee cautioned. "The guy's got a .40 caliber Taurus. He's already killed three, and he apparently doesn't care who's next. Watch yourself."

"Will do…"

"Okay. I'll be calling you later. Gotta call my new lesbian friend in Minneapolis now," Lee laughed. He dialed the GLCAC office.

"Miss Potter, this is Lee Urness with the FBI Fugitive Task Force. You talked yesterday with Steve Gilkerson," he said.

"Yes, I did."

"I am the case agent in charge of the search for Andrew Cunanan, and wanted to let you know that anything you can do is greatly appreciated, as well as give you my phone number, just in case you hear something. Don't hesitate to call at any time, day or night," he urged.

"Okay."

"How many wanted posters can you use?" Lee asked.

"As many as you can spare. I'll send them out all around town and across the country, if you'd like." Potter explained that GCLAC had contacts with similar groups all across America, and even with those in foreign countries. That thought fascinated Lee, who never knew such a gay network existed.

"Great. I can only get you photos now, but as soon as I can, I'll get you a bunch. Would it work for you to pick up pictures at the FBI office in Minneapolis?" he said, giving her the location. She agreed to pick them up as soon as they were ready.

"Well thanks for all your help. We need to stop this man before he hurts someone else, and you can help us do that," Lee said.

"You can count on it. And thanks for letting us help, and for going after the guy," Potter said, as they hung up.

Lee felt relieved by the conversation and pleased with himself. With the gays and lesbians on board, he felt confident that he was closing down Cunanan's options. With Potter contacting her network, and the law enforcement surveillance that was even now quickly increasing in size and scope, Lee felt sure they would soon spot Cunanan somewhere, as they cut off all avenues of escape. As the window slowly closed on Cunanan, he would become more desperate, forcing him to turn to his few real intimate friends and family members. By then, Lee or some other FTF agent would have made contact. The formula always worked.

Lee headed over to the Minneapolis FBI headquarters to leave pictures for Constance Potter. By mid-June, she would have more than 1,500 of them to distribute nationwide. He felt pretty chipper about his chances.

Barring advances

As he drove to the FBI office, Lee's pager went off. He saw that Emilio Blasse had left a message for him. Dialing the FBI office on his cell phone he asked to be patched through to Blasse.

"Urness here. You called," Lee said when Blasse answered.

"You son-of-a-bitch!" Blasse began.

"Hey, what's the matter?"

"I'm sitting here in a gay club over in a corner using the manager's phone, showing my badge and handing out posters, and these guys started hitting on me!"

"They what?"

"They are eyeing me up and down like a piece of meat; like they could care less why I'm here. I never saw anything like this before," Blasse went on.

"What do you expect? You must fit their profile," Lee laughed harder. "They must think you're cute."

"Enough already," Blasse said. Lee could tell he enjoyed the teasing.

"Oh well, it's one of the perks of the job," Lee added.

"You owe me big time," Blasse razzed him.

"Right. Any time," Lee said. "Okay, good work. Hey, maybe you can do a face-to-face interview with the club patrons," he laughed all the harder.

"Thanks so much," he growled. "But of course I will, I'll talk to anyone who ever knew this guy. Count on it."

"Good. Keep me updated and have a good time," Lee said.

"You S.O.B.," Blasse laughed as he hung up.

Lee parked next to the building that housed the Minneapolis FBI. The office sat a few blocks away from the FTF office on Washington Avenue and, ironically, just a few blocks west of David Madson's apartment.

Lee checked in with the security guard at the Second Floor desk, and took the elevator to the 11th Floor. With a feeling of accomplishment and great confidence that this would make a critical difference, he gave the receptionist two Cunanan pictures for Constance Potter, the lesbian activist, to pick up.

"You can run, but you can't hide," Lee said. He still had no clue about how reclusive, diverse and closeted were gay men. He had no understanding of how they loved to live on the edge, to take chances and risk clandestine and anonymous sexual relationships.

The pictures Potter was about to send out showed Cunanan in four different poses, and in each, he looked like a different person. Combining his chameleon-like appearance, his insatiable sex drive and the habits of the gay community in which he thrived created a volatile mixture ready to explode at any moment.

Through his years of successful police work, Lee proved that he understood thugs, crooks, murderers and rapists. And he knew that Cunanan had changed from mirth-maker to murderer since leaving San Diego. But his lack of understanding about how gays interact with and treat each other would help Cunanan avoid apprehension in what dragged on into Lee's single most frustrating case – and more murder.

Afternoon filled with facts

Back at the office, Lee surveyed the FTF team, all busy calling out leads to local agents, or following up on calls they initiated. Everything seemed perfectly harmonized, like one of Lee's favorite Golden Oldies tunes.

Lee officially got the case on Wednesday, and unofficially on Monday, so he felt no tinge of frustration or panic. In fact, he felt they had made great progress. Given the stacks of information already on file, his confidence level rode high.

A call came from Donna Brant, identified as "someone from America's Most Wanted."

"This is Lee Urness," he said as he took the call, reluctant only in that he had so much else to do. While he knew that AMW had helped capture many bad guys, he still did not want to talk to any newsies and he had repeatedly told that to Evan Marshal, the AMW Production Assistant with whom he had spoken the prior day.

"Mr. Urness, this is Donna Brant. I am the Executive Producer of the Andrew Cunanan segments."

"Donna Brant?" he said, writing down the name. "Give me your phone numbers, will you? All of them."

"Sure," Brant said, rattling them off. "Now about tomorrow's show," she began, "we are hoping that you will come in and…

"Not a chance," Lee said. "I can't leave here. Too much to do."

"But it makes all the difference if the lead officer can be here in the hot-line room," she said.

"Tell me about the hotline room," Lee said.

"Well, we have about 25 operators who come in before the public airing of the show. They watch a tape of the show so they know what's coming, and they have a set of information about each person who we are featuring. Basic facts and such, with contact numbers. You can see all this if you come in…"

"I'm sure. So what happens then?" he asked.

"Well, they take the calls and record them on a form; a call sheet."

"You have a fax there?" Lee asked.

"Sure."

"Then why can't you fax them out right away. I'll have a team up here to handle the faxes, and you can have someone call us if you get a hot lead, you know, like 'Cunanan is standing here right now.' Won't that work?" Lee asked.

"Well, yes, but not as well if you are here with us. You know, that's what most of the officers do," she insisted.

"Well that may be, but I am not most of the officers. There is no way I can come out there. I simply do not have the time," he said firmly, sealing the deal.

"You're sure?"

"Absolutely!"

"Okay. Well, can we go over some details in the case. Our files are pretty sketchy," she said, hoping to salvage something good from the call.

"If you agree to keep some of these things to yourself, and they will be helpful in catching my guy, yeah, I can talk to you," he said.

Lee felt good about Brant from the beginning. They talked often during the next several weeks, and Lee used her to gain insights that helped him as he tried to narrow Cunanan's options. He learned that Brant was a thorough reporter who really did her homework, and Brant learned that Lee was a dedicated and intense cop, sure in his ways. Lee gave her inside information and she protected it, and her source. No one else knew about their connection, save for Evan Marshal.

"So the plan is that we will assemble at FBI headquarters here in Minneapolis and watch the show. Then we'll take your calls and faxes. That a deal?"Lee asked.

"Sure, unless you change your mind and come out," she tried once again.

"Nope. How can I call you tomorrow night, just to make sure everything is still moving ahead?" he asked.

Once their plan had been set, Lee said good-bye and turned to his FTF team. "I need three people tomorrow night at the FBI office. From 6:00 p.m. until we are done. And it will most likely be a long night," he said.

"I'm in," Lisa Davis said, as did Kevin Rickett and Steve Gilkerson.

Chicago calling

Lee's pager told him to call Scott Bakken, an FBI member of the Chicago FTF.

"Urness here," he said as Bakken answered. "What do you have?"

"Well, Terry and I met with Maryann, the mother; Elena, the sister and the brother, Chris," Bakken said.

"Good. Any luck? He call them?"

"Nope. No one's heard anything from him. And they all said they'd cooperate, although the mother's unstable," Bakken said.

"Unstable?"Lee knew that very few close relatives of those he chased believe their loved one would be capable of a felony.

"Yeah. Well of course she can't believe her precious Andrew could be in trouble, but she is just a bit out of it. Not all there," Bakken explained. "I mean, nice enough, but not a clear thinker."

"Will she help?" Lee asked.

"I don't know. I mean, she says she will, but also refuses to believe her Andrew could be in trouble," Bakken opined.

"Stay close to her. Couple times a week at least," Lee advised.

"Will do. Elena says Andrew called her earlier this spring, but neither of the siblings has heard from him since," Bakken added. "They'll cooperate. What about the dad? Is there one?"

"Yeah, he's somewhere in the Philippines. I think he's Philippino by birth and we got word he left the family and went back there," Lee said. "We're trying to get someone to him now."

"Cunanan likely to go there?"Bakken asked.

"Possibly, but we're watching the borders and there's nothing yet, at least that we know of."

"Any other siblings?" Bakken asked.

"Yes, a sister in San Francisco. Her name is Gina. She's already talked to our agents," Lee said.

"Okay, well keep me posted and I'll call you if anything breaks," Bakken said.

"Good. And good work," Lee said and they hung up.

Then the newsies called

Anne O'Connor and Chris Graves sat together in their crammed and cluttered workspace at the *Star-Tribune*. They were trying to find some unique angle to work, something no one else had done.

"I wonder about his mother," O'Connor said.

"I haven't seen any stories on her," Graves answered. "Why not call her?"

"You mean just like that?"

"Sure," Graves answered.

They had learned that Maryann Cunanan lived in Illinois and it took O'Connor but a few minutes to find her phone number. She felt a rush of excitement as she dialed.

"Hello," Maryann Cunanan answered. The reality that Anne had so easily gotten her on the phone startled the young reporter and while she listened she caught Graves' eyes, pointing at the phone receiver and mouthing the words, "It's her!"

"Mrs. Cunanan, this is Anne O'Connor. I am a reporter with the *Star-Tribune* from Minneapolis," she said as kindly as she could. "I wondered if I could ask you a few questions about your son."

"Well, sure, I guess so," she said, sounding bewildered.

"Mrs. Cunanan, have the police come and talked to you yet?" O'Connor asked.

"Well, yes, yes they have."

"And did they tell you than Andrew was in trouble?"

"Yes, they said that he had bounced some checks and they were looking for him. They wanted to know if I had talked to him," she explained. Her words froze in O'Connor's mind.

"They said he had bounced checks?" O'Connor asked, incredulous at what she had just heard and startled by the realization of what she was about to do. She debated with herself as she said the words, *What do I do? My God, she doesn't have a clue. How can I tell her this?*

"Yes, they said he had bounced checks and they wanted to talk to him," she repeated. Bakken and Thedford had told her exactly why they wanted

Andrew, but either she did not hear them, ignored them or was unwilling to tell O'Connor.

"Well," O'Connor said, swallowing hard, "I'm afraid it's a little more serious than that, Mrs. Cunanan."

"Oh?"

"Yes, well, actually they want to talk to him in conjunction with three murders," O'Connor said as calmly as she could.

"With three murders?" Maryann answered. "I don't understand."

"The police have reason to believe that Andrew has committed three murders," O'Connor said, regretting for the rest of her life that she had to be the one to break it to the woman.

"Oh my, well…I haven't talked with him since Easter and I haven't seen him for a long time," Maryann said.

O'Connor talked a while longer with the woman, and also called other family members. She felt that Maryann really did not grasp what was being said during this interview.

Maryann, however, started calling Andrew's old friends out west once the news had broken. She told Laura Koski her belief that Andrew could never do such a thing. She wondered if Koski had heard from Andrew. But the Andrew they both had known before April 25 had changed, from an irresponsible, fun-loving gay prostitute into a vicious killer.

On May 18, Maryann Cunanan moved to National City, near San Diego, in California. There, Special Agents Ann Murphy and John Hause began checking with her on a regular basis. No evidence exists that Andrew ever tried to contact her, nor did she add anything to apprehending him, except frustration.

Sugar daddy could attract the killer

Lee felt fairly sure that Cunanan would eventually try to contact William Norman, his former sugar daddy. Steve Gilkerson had called Norman's San Diego home on Thursday, but only got an answering machine. Lee decided to give it another try.

"This is Lee Urness. I'm the case agent in charge of finding Andrew Cunanan. I have to talk to you. It is critical." He left the toll free number of the Bureau of Criminal Apprehension. "Please, call me right away. They will page me any time of the day or night."

Though Norman's friends claimed he had left for New York earlier that week, Lee knew better than to trust them. There were dozens of reasons friends might cover for him, and none of them good, at least from Lee's perspective. Norman could even have been an accessory to Cunanan's murders. Just because they said he had left town didn't make it so. Lee wrote a note to remind San Diego's FTF to keep on eye on the Norman residence.

"Lee, take line 2. It's Kari," Vern Lee called from across the room.

"Hi Bear, what's up?"Lee said as cheerfully as he could muster to his young daughter. An early season warm-up softball tournament was set for Saturday, and Kari would be playing. He planned to be there, having calculated that he should have time to get back for the America's Most Wanted show on Saturday evening.

"I just wanted to tell you what they had on CNN," the 10-year old girl said. Lee had always insisted that his family be kept out of the loop on his cases. That made it possible for him to relax at home, and protected them from knowledge that could put their lives at risk. But after the media explosion on Wednesday, his wife Kathy and daughter Kari became his news monitors. Kathy did day care and it was easy for her to leave a TV on, and the two of them could monitor cable TV news. The FTF had no such capability.

"That Minneapolis police officer talked to the media again," Kari reported. She knew her dad would not like to hear this.

"Oh, and what'd he say?"

Then she rattled off the details as Lee's blood pressure swelled. He wished that all the cops would just keep their mouths shut. He thanked Kari and felt sure that media calls would spike within minutes.

"Lee, it's Coleen Rowley on line 5," Vern called out. Every time some new detail emerged, her phones rang off the hook, hence the call to Lee. The questions were always the same: "Where is he? What new can we tell them?"But Lee had no new information to give. Still, the cycle of inquiries continued unabated.

Chapter 16 ~ Media breach means murder

Andrew Cunanan rose late in the morning on Friday and walked out of the lobby at the West Side Club. Before leaving the area, he picked up a copy of the *New York Times, USA Today* and *Philadelphia Inquirer.* To his delight, none of them carried stories about him. Minneapolis murders never received news coverage in the Big Apple, and even a distinguished man like Lee Miglin meant nothing to New York papers.

Cunanan had learned that Gianni Versace would be bypassing New York City and heading to Florida upon his return to America (but Versace did, in fact, briefly return to New York City in July). He decided it was time to head south even though William Norman was due in town that same night. If Cunanan had planned to murder Norman as some later suggested, he could have stayed in the city and waited for him, but he chose to leave. Versace would give him what he really wanted.

Packing his gym bag, he stuck the three newspapers under his arm and headed to the subway. From there he went to the parking ramp where he had left the Lexus.

Within hours, FBI agent Emilio Blasse would spread Cunanan's picture all around town, in every gay bar, hotel, club, restaurant and haunt. A lesbian group offered a $10,000 reward, and the New York City Police Department added $1,000 to the fund. By these actions, Cunanan would be forever excluded from the Big Apple.

Though he had never been there, Cunanan set a route for Miami Beach, a place where he knew there was a huge gay population. Cops would struggle to find him mixed in among the tourists. More importantly, Versace had a mansion there.

As he crawled into the dark green and grey two-toned Lexus he had stolen from Lee Miglin, he ran his hand across the white leather seats that surrounded him. The tightly built engine purred quietly as the smooth riding car headed down I-95 out of the New York City area. He smiled at this feeling of luxury, the elixir of power available to him at a simple nudge of his foot on the accelerator, and knew it was what he deserved.

New Jersey's continuous string of small cities gave way to rows of plush trees that had burst into a chorus of green. The sweet smell of springtime filled his nostrils on that warm day. He turned on his radio, playing soft music in the background as he drove carefully, not wanting to alert a highway patrolman. Thousands of cars roared past him, irritated that he refused to speed and weave as they did in their vain effort to get somewhere a minute or two sooner.

Looking around him, he spotted scores of cars that looked like the Lexus, dark colored luxury cars common to that stretch of freeway. Just as in gay clubs, he felt sure he could blend in and remain unnoticed as long as he did not do something stupid, or no one else did. Cunanan saw himself as smarter than anyone else, and only an idiot would get stopped for speeding after doing what he had done in the past two weeks.

He itched to talk to a friend, maybe even catch up with William Norman, whom he knew would be in New York by then. When he had tried the cell phone the prior Sunday he could not get through, but decided to try again. He pulled off the road at a rest stop in northern New Jersey, went in and bought a cup of coffee and headed back to the car. At 1:27 p.m., he activated the phone, dialing 1-609-306-9522. It seemed to work. He input the numbers of a Discover Card, but the credit card company refused the charges.

He decided to try once more a few minutes later, at 1:31 p.m. This time he dialed 1-609-306-9551, but he had the same results. It would have done no good if he had gotten through. His brilliant mind had recalled two bad phone numbers that rang nowhere. The phone numbers that he could most easily recall, those of his closest friends and family members, might be tapped and he could not risk calling them. That meant calling one of his second or third tier friends, and for that he needed his little blue phone book, the one he had left behind in Minneapolis.

Not wanting to sit exposed for any length of time, he drove back on the freeway, heading south until he could cross over to I-295, toward Delaware.

At the moment he activated that phone, FBI agents in Chicago were notified by the cell phone service company that Cunanan was somewhere in northern New Jersey. They went to work.

"Lee," Scott Bakken told him in a quick phone call, "we got two cell phone activations at about 1:30 in northern New Jersey. He's probably on I-95 or 295, driving south. We've got every available officer on the way. Looks like we got our lucky break. We'll keep you posted."

"Great! Get on it," Lee said, smiling broadly. He stood up and grabbed a dart, throwing it straight for Cunanan's face. "Gotcha! Your luck is running out!"

The calls suggested that Cunanan drove south. Lee visualized the net of agents and police officers closing in on the Lexus. New Jersey Highway

State Police cars would take up positions along the freeway's shoulders. Deputy sheriffs would join them in a mobile patrol, supported by town cops from the many small cities that lay alongside the route. Other cops would go to the service areas. This small army of cops would surely find him. He felt certain it would be just a matter of hours, even minutes, when he would get the good news.

Bakken called back a bit later giving hope, but no good news. "He hasn't tried the phone again, but we're pretty sure he's driving south. They've set up a net and if he tries crossing either of the toll bridges, they'll be at the tollbooths. No way he gets out of Jersey," Bakken said.

"How hard is it to spot a green Lexus?" Lee said, imagining Minnesota's busiest rush hour.

"Just about impossible," Bakken laughed. "There's thousands of look-a-like cars out there. Everybody's getting out of town, you know, and it's absolutely nuts. But don't worry, they're closing in on him."

"Well where could he be? I mean, where could he pull off and hide, and why would he do it?"And so the conversation went for a few more minutes.

Cunanan continued to drive south, now within minutes of crossing the Delaware Memorial Bridge, – a toll bridge – thrilled, and yet nervous about the increased media stories about him. He turned up the radio and flipped channels to KYW 1060 to listen to the news at the top of the hour.

"Local FBI agents and police officials continue to search for Andrew Cunanan, alleged to have killed a wealthy Chicago businessman and two former lovers from Minneapolis," he heard. His ears perked up as a sly smile filled his face – they had no clue where he was and at that very instant he was once again slipping through their hands. "But officials know that Cunanan is somewhere on the east coast, and they are tracking him by cell phone calls he is attempting to make from the stolen Lexus he is driving…"

The words stunned Cunanan. He turned the cell phone off, and then yanked the receiver cable from the phone. He started looking in every direction in his rear view mirror, at the cars alongside him, on the side of the road, ahead of him. Each Crown Victoria looked like an unmarked highway patrol car. He saw shadows on a cloudless day. Panic welled up inside. He hoped he could get safely across the Delaware Memorial Bridge and out of the state as quickly as possible.

Finally, he saw the bridge up ahead. The highway sign hanging across his lane said, "Last exit before toll – Route 49."

He cursed. Cops would certainly be lying in wait for him at a tollbooth where, at the very least, he would have to slow down. They could easily cut off his egress from the other side. He could not cross that bridge in the Lexus.

He jerked the Lexus onto the exit to Route 49. To the south lay Pennsville, and he headed in that direction. He saw a rest area on the south side of the highway and made for it, but it was too busy, and too easy for a cop to check. He headed back to Route 49. Somewhere down that road, he thought, there must be a place to stop without being seen.

So if they tracked him by the cell phone, he needed to get rid of the cell phone. He needed a ride to go to Miami Beach. Where and how would he get a new ride? He knew nothing about stealing cars. He would have to find someone somewhere from whom he could steal the keys, and it would have to be unseen from the road and away from people.

He drove south on Route 49, but instead of finding a refuge he found continuing suburbia. Instead of a stand of trees or a forest, he found standing buildings followed by more buildings, a forest of strip shopping centers on both sides of the road.

One mile became two, then three, then four. Still the unending strip centers gave him no refuge. He tried turning onto side streets, but they were neighborhoods of homes packed closely together. Back on Route 49, his pulse now increasing as fear mounted, he continued south.

Finally he saw a welcome word – cemetery. A simple sign hanging on a light pole pointed west toward "Finn's Point National Cemetery," "Fort Mott State Park" and "Three Ports Ferry." He turned west, hoping to find a stretch of open and quiet land in which to stop.

Once again, one mile became two, and there was more open land, but there were also houses and buildings. Two became three, and it got no better. He drove past a busy softball field, and then stopped at Route 632. A sign to the cemetery beckoned him to turn right, and he continued on.

A small bunker of tall cane stood guard on his right, but on his left were more open fields and a few houses – no place to hide. He saw a fork in the road that directed him toward Fort Mott and the cemetery. He drove toward the fort, still searching for some secluded place. Finally, he spotted the old fort, a series of open fields, boarded up barracks, a few houses, and not much activity. He saw an old abandoned artillery battery on his left, and continued south a bit farther. He saw a parking lot and pulled in. Those additional four miles had left him nearly frantic. He stopped the car, then grabbed hold of the cell phone base and yanked it from its moorings.

A man drove past, noticing someone in a dark car "fiddling with something on his dash." Cunanan did more than fiddle: he angrily pulled the wires that led to and from the cell phone, tearing them off from their moorings. He reached up and tore the antenna wires from the headliner, pulling the lining down with it. He got out of the car and tore off the external antenna: then threw all of the phone equipment in the trunk. Unknown to him, the base unit in the trunk would remain connected, leaving law enforcement a chance to try to signal the car and, thereby, locate it. In fact, at that very moment, an Ameritech engineer was attempting to triangulate his location.

Something caught his eye. A red pick-up truck had just driven from the east, down the road that led to Finn's Point National Cemetery. Cunanan watched a middle-aged man get out of the truck and retrieve the mail from the post box. Then the truck turned around and headed back toward the cemetery. Cunanan followed at a safe distance.

The one-mile long road quickly was soon reduced to one lane, surrounded on both sides by oak trees and bunkers with tall cane grass standing guard. A small creek on his left that followed the road flowed silently.

Cemeteries, he knew, were silent places and seldom visited. He and David Madson had visited one in Rush Lake, Minnesota. No one noticed and no one would notice this time, either. The peace that shrouded that cemetery would soon be shattered by the crash of a .40 caliber slug through the head of an unsuspecting and innocent caretaker.

Steeped in history, now with a black mark

Cunanan watched from a distance as the red truck drove through an opening in the 30-inch tall stone wall that surrounded the cemetery. The truck turned up the circular driveway, past one of the beautiful sculptured pine trees that sat amongst the old, knurled oaks. It came to a stop in front of a newly painted blue garage and storage shed. The man got out and walked into the lodge that sat some 30 feet away.

Cunanan glanced to his left and saw a small white gazebo, imagining it to be a place used for memorial services. It served as a memorial to the Union Soldiers buried in that cemetery. Ahead, reaching up from behind a stand of tree he saw the 85-foot tall white granite obelisk built by the federal government in 1910 as a memorial to the Confederate Soldiers buried nearby.

In 1875, the United States government had designated Finns Point, located inside Fort Mott, as a national cemetery. During the Civil War, both Union and Confederate soldiers had been buried there, although in separate sections. The Union Army had buried 2,436 Confederate soldiers there, men who died while in captivity. The Union had also buried 135 of their own in a separate section. During World War II, the United States buried 13 German POWs at Finns Point who died while in captivity. (In modern times, the federal government still buries military veterans there, but limits these to cremains.)

The cemetery sat surrounded by that low stone wall and behind that, on all sides, stood bunker-like hills upon which grew thick groves of tall cane. He could not see beyond those hills, and that meant that no one could see in either. The place offered total seclusion. The only way in or out was the road on which he and the red truck had come. Here he saw the opportunity to secure a new ride.

He drove quietly up the circular road and stopped next to the two-story Meigs L-shaped lodge alongside the red pick-up truck, parked facing the garage. He glanced over at the lodge. The stone walls and fresh white painted trim gave it a comfortable, almost home-like appearance. He looked in the rear-view mirror to check the road behind him. He saw no one.

He slipped the Taurus pistol into his belt, pulled his sweatshirt over it and quietly walked to the door of the lodge. He heard a radio playing softly inside and saw that the door sat open, so walked in. He saw a man sitting at a desk reading Bible verses from the Old Testament, Deuteronomy 21:1-7.

"If in the land which the LORD your God gives you to possess, any one is found slain, lying in the open country, and it is not known who killed him, then your elders and your judges shall come forth, and they shall measure the distance to the cities which are around him that is slain; and the elders of the city which is nearest to the slain man shall take a heifer which has never been worked and which has not pulled in the yoke. And the elders of that city shall bring the heifer down to a valley with running water, which is neither plowed nor sown, and shall break the heifer's neck there in the valley. And the priests the sons of Levi shall come forward, for the LORD your God has chosen them to minister to him and to bless in the name of the LORD, and by their word every dispute and every assault shall be settled. And all the elders of that city nearest to the slain man shall wash their hands over the heifer whose neck was broken in the valley; and they shall testify, 'Our hands did not shed this blood, neither did our eyes see it shed.'"

"Hello sir, may I help you?" William Reese asked, looking up from his desk. Reese, 45, worked as the cemetery's caretaker. A meticulous man and a Vietnam War veteran, Reese took pride in the appearance of the remote graveyard.

"Yeah, thanks. This is sure a beautiful spot out here," Cunanan said.

"That it is."

"And quiet."

"I like it like that," Reese said. "You a veteran?"Reese knew that any military veteran could have his ashes interred there, even young ones like the man who stood in front of him. Authorities encouraged veterans to make arrangements in advance.

"No, no I'm not. I was just out driving and saw the sign, and thought I'd stop here," Cunanan said.

"I must admit we don't get many visitors out here except for funerals," Reese said.

"You have them often?"

"Oh no. Once in a while, but we haven't had one for a while," Reese answered.

"Nice truck," Cunanan asked, nodding toward the parking lot. "Is it yours?"

"Sure is."

"So you're alone?"

"Yes sir, just me and the clients out there," Reese answered.

"I need the keys to your truck," Cunanan said as his two eyes turned cold and bore in on Reese.

"What?"

"The keys to your truck. Where are they?" Cunanan asked.

"Well, on the desk there, but…"

Cunanan pulled out the Taurus and aimed it at Reese. At the same time, he looked around the room and saw two doors leading off in different directions. He saw a hallway. "Where's that lead?" he asked.

"Downstairs, but…"

"Move," Cunanan said, pointing the gun at Reese.

"What?"

"I said move, there, down those stairs," Cunanan ordered, nodding toward the stairway.

"But…"

"Just do as I say and you won't get hurt," Cunanan lied. "Now move," he added, raising the gun.

"Okay. Okay," Reese answered, moving toward the stairway and then slowly walking down, his hands held up above his head, ever so often turning and looking at Cunanan. The barrel of a .40-caliber Taurus that pointed at his head made the nightmare real.

Cunanan noticed that he could lock the door and leave Reese down there alone. By the time someone found the man, he would be miles away. Images of Lee Miglin played across his mind. He could have left Miglin alive too, and Madson, but he didn't. He followed Reese down the stairs into the cool, musty basement.

"Over there," Cunanan ordered, and Reese moved toward one of the walls. "Now turn around and face the wall."

Reese turned, expecting to be knocked unconscious. He knew it was senseless to resist a man holding a gun so close to his back.

"Kneel down," Cunanan ordered, and Reese complied.

Cunanan raised the gun and at close range, fired one round into the back of Reese's head, spraying brain tissue, blood and bone onto the wall as the body fell limp on the floor. Blood pooled everywhere on the pock-marked and rough cement floor.

Cunanan quickly raced up the stairs and closed the basement door, locking it behind him. Grabbing the truck keys, he went outside, relieved that no one was around. He reached inside the Lexus and grabbed a gym bag filled with his clothing, passport and a few other items he felt he would need. Slamming the door, he cursed his bad fortune.

The 1995 Red Chevrolet pick-up, like the cemetery, was impeccably clean and neat. He stuck the gun under the seat – six bullets remained in the magazine. He threw his stuff inside the truck, climbed in and drove away, giving one last look at the beautiful Lexus left behind.

He headed north on Route 49 and then turned on I-295 South, a route that would take him across the Delaware Memorial Bridge. Putting on sunglasses, he drove past a parked State Police car and across the bridge as cautiously as he dared, stopping momentarily to pay the toll. No one paid any attention to him. The clerks had all been warned to watch for a dark green Lexus, not some country guy in a red pick-up truck. To the tollbooth operator, he was just one of thousands who crossed during rush hour. On the west side of the bridge, he drove past other cops who sat watching for the Lexus.

Cunanan drove south through Delaware, on his way to freedom. The red truck camouflaged him as much as if he had changed his own appearance. He ran his hand across the vinyl seat covers and studied the truck's sparse features. Like his own life that had once been the center of attention, the debonair man whom everyone loved, being resigned to this truck represented his own plunge into obscurity – from a gilded Lexus to a gaudy pick-up truck, from a highly paid stud to a despised queen.

At least the truck offered him some more time to achieve his ultimate goal. Only one problem remained, and that was the license plate. Cunanan knew that within minutes of finding Reese's body, the cops would list the truck on their national database. Many hours and hundreds of miles later, he pulled into a South Carolina shopping center and there stole the license plates off a 1984 Toyota. The owner assumed they had just fallen off, and a few days later, went to the county and bought replacement plates.

Other than stopping at a quick stop or drive in restaurant, he drove straight through to Miami Beach, confident that he had lost the cops, all the time plotting his future, a future that he had calculated would win him a macabre immortality. He designed a plot to go out in style, in a way that the world would never forget, and that would end his own gay misery.

He needed to think, plot and wait; he needed a place to hide during the day. Like a vampire, he could venture out at night in a place where no one would much pay attention to "just another gay tourist" in a red pick-up truck with South Carolina license plates.

Overdue hubby

William Reese's wife wondered where her predictably prompt husband was when he did not come home on time, and around 5:30 went to the cemetery looking for him. There she found the man of her life lying dead in that bloody basement, his life crushed by the cruel hands of Andrew Cunanan, a maniacal murderer who killed for a ride.

As Lee would label it later, in a perverse chain of events, William Reese's life had been snuffed out by a wire service writer who saw fit to give away the FBI's best hope of catching the killer *before* he struck again.

A despairing wife called local police to report the crime.

Chapter 17 ~ Flurry of activity out east and back home

Unaware of Cunanan's deadly deed, FTF teams across America continued to work their local leads, hopeful that at any minute they would hear from Philadelphia. Then, if they were lucky, they could finally pull together their evidence and turn it over to prosecutors. They could go back to capturing less aggressive murderers and rapists than Cunanan.

In Minnesota, Lee Urness waited for the good news. "We got him," the call he expected at any minute, would send him to the airport for a ride on the next plane, ready to look Andrew Cunanan in the eyes.

Having received no such call, Lee left for home just after 6:15 p.m., confident that before the evening was out, the boys out east would have Cunanan in custody.

As he walked into his kitchen just before 7:00, Lee's BCA pager went off. He called immediately.

"This is Lee Urness. You paged?"

"Police in New Jersey are looking for Andrew Cunanan regarding a murder in New Jersey. Is this your case?" the operator asked. Lee almost dropped the cordless phone. Kathy and Kari saw outrage consuming his face as his body tensed. He began pacing angrily back and forth in front of the breakfast bar.

"What the hell you talking about?"Lee shouted.

"We just got a teletype that he's a suspect in a murder in a national cemetery at Fort Mott State Park, and he's stolen a red pick up truck."

"Damn! That's got to be my guy," he said, slamming his hand on the wall. "Cunanan killed again," Lee said to Kathy and Kari.

"Does that mean you won't be at my games tomorrow," Kari asked with sad eyes.

"Might be," Lee answered, distracted by what he had just heard from New Jersey, becoming more agitated by degrees.

In a few minutes, the FBI called. "We just got a call from New Jersey and they are looking for Cunanan."

"Who's got it?" Lee asked, anxious to talk to someone out east as soon as possible.

"A Resident Agent in Cherry Hill is handling it," the operator said.

"Fine," Lee said, shrugging in frustration. "Connect me with Philly. They'll know who it is." The operator transferred him immediately.

"This is Lee Urness with Minnesota FTF. This murderer in New Jersey is my guy. Who's got the case?" Lee asked.

"Well, Jeff Covington of the FTF is out at the site now."

"Page him and have him call me right away," Lee demanded. He had lost his cool.

Immediately his pager began sounding. Unable to return the calls as rapidly as he liked, he grabbed a cup of coffee and went out to the garage. Climbing into his van, he held the cordless phone in one hand, and his own personal cell phone in the other. His "company phone," mounted in the van, gave him three lines and he tried to keep one line open at all times. His teenagers glared at him for taking their phone out of the house. Girlfriends and boyfriends had to stand in line that night.

Protocol required that Lee first call Fred Tremper, the Minnesota FTF supervisor. Lee hated making the call, having to tell him that "my guy killed someone," words that he had never before had to utter. Finished with that, he called Kevin Rickett at home.

"Guess what made my day?" he asked Rickett.

"You got Cunanan," Rickett answered.

"No. He just blew away another guy," Lee said, and explained what he knew, which wasn't much. "That's all I know, and I'm waiting on calls back from New Jersey."

"This is bad, real bad," Rickett said. He, like Lee, hated the idea that a crook he chased had killed again. "What do you want to do?"

After discussing their mutual frustration and still waiting for a call from Covington, Lee called out to John Hause in San Diego to alert him. "You might want to keep an eye on his friends out there. This would be the time he might call someone," Lee suggested.

Then he called Agent Scott Bakken in Chicago, and repeated the routine. "Better call his mother and the siblings," Lee suggested.

Jeff Covington paged him from New Jersey. Lee called him immediately.

"Covington," Jeff answered.

"This is Lee Urness from Minnesota. I hear my guy did another one."

"Yeah, and we got your Lexus here, but not your guy." Covington worked out of the Philadelphia FTF office and had been to the murder scene.

Lee knew that it would take investigators many hours to process the crime scene and the Lexus. It made no sense to ask about them in this call.

"What's this about a pickup?" Lee asked.

148

"He stole the guy's pickup," Covington answered, and he paused for a moment that seemed like minutes. "You know," he went on, "I've been in this business a long time and seen a lot of dead bodies. But this one made me want to throw up."

"Oh?" Lee asked.

"He marched the guy down to the basement and made him kneel facing the wall and executed him. An unbelievable mess. I had to go outside to get air," Covington said.

Lee visualized the strong man as he tried to deal with the death scene. As many times as he had dealt with dead bodies and as detached as he had become, it never got easy and sometimes it was just plain worse.

"Who's got the case?" Lee asked.

"It's a crime on a federal reservation – national cemetery – so it's a federal case. FBI agent is Paul Murray, a really good cop. It'll be his case. He's on his way."

"What is going on with trying to find Cunanan?" Lee asked as he wrote Murray's name and phone numbers on his legal pad.

"Every cop on the east coast is looking for him," Covington said. "At best he's got a couple hours head start."

"Who is William Reese?"

"Just a caretaker. A Vietnam vet, and *not gay*!" Covington answered.

"So Cunanan just needed a new ride," Lee observed.

"Right. The cell phone is totally ripped out of the Lexus. He even pulled out the antenna wire," Covington added.

"So he heard the reports how we were tracking him…"

"…and then he killed the caretaker," Covington said, finishing his sentence for him.

"Damn! The newsies killed him!! Do they know that?" Lee said, his anger percolating.

"I'm sure they don't see it that way, but…"

"But nothing! They're responsible, and that's why I don't talk to newsies," Lee said. "I mean, why did the reporter put that information on the wire? He obviously got it from somebody in the know. And it was *not* newsworthy. Now it's killed somebody," Lee said. "So he's gonna have to live with it."

The idea that competition for market share or ad sales or some other media prize had caused this to happen made Lee livid with anger. "Well, with another dead body, the newsies will have a field day," Lee sighed, already seeing in his mind's eye the call slips piling higher.

"You got that," Covington said.

"Look, we need to stay in constant contact. If anything breaks, anything at all, I want to know right away," Lee said.

"You got it."

"And I'll be calling the FBI agent in charge, too, but not until he's done processing the scene. So where do you think Cunanan's going?"

"Well, you would think if he crossed the Delaware Bridge that someone would've seen him. Granted he's driving a different car, but we got pictures everywhere," Covington said.

"Maybe he went north? He could almost be in Canada by now," Lee said, making a note to call Canadian authorities.

"There's lots of places to hide out around here, too. Woods, beaches, in the city. You name it, we got it. And of course he could've gone to New York City," Covington suggested.

"Well, keep after him. Check everywhere and let me know. Thanks for your good work," Lee said. "Talk to you later."

As a courtesy, Lee called the Chicago Special Agent in Charge (SAC). The Chicago SAC had called Lee after Miglin's murder and asked if he would personally brief him on any significant developments. Lee recognized the significance of the request and even though it required one more call, he meant to fulfill his promise.

Lee sat in the van thinking, *what the hell else could I have done to stop this guy?* But the phone and pager kept going off; interrupting any real chance he had of reasoning it all out. He called everyone in his line of command, or who was related to the chase. Or they called him; he had trouble keeping up with the calls.

Between calls, he thought through the timeline. *Intercepted at 1:30, they found the body at 5:30 or so. So when did he kill him? There were some sightings around New Jersey this afternoon, so given the time lag, where could be now? They had been looking for a green Lexus, not a red truck. How far could he have driven?* Lee decided Cunanan could have had a three-hour head start, so he checked his atlas, trying to find what cities lay near freeways within 150-200 miles.

He paged Emilio Blasse. And so continued the difficult task of calling all the FTF and FBI agents already working on the case, in New York, Philadelphia, Boston, Chicago, San Diego, Los Angeles and San Francisco. In each jurisdiction, Lee replayed the events in Pennsville, and each time he told the story, his anger at the media increased. "We just have to keep close-mouthed about all of this," he told the agents. "Slips get people killed."

Irish cop

Paul Murray sat at home helping care for his elderly mother. Murray's family had been saddled with the difficult job of caring for a mother with Alzheimer's, and with four very active children, it complicated his life. Family played a central role for Murray, and he fought for time to spend with his children and wife, sandwiched around the unpredictable demands of his FBI job.

Murray had come to Cherry Hill, New Jersey in 1977 and now served as its Resident Agent. Now 20 years later, he handled federal crime investigations for three counties, including Salem County, the home of Fort Mott State Park.

Three of Murray's brothers, like him, were FBI agents and a fourth brother, an attorney, worked as a prosecutor. Law enforcement fueled his blood.

The phone rang sometime past 7:00 p.m. The message said to get out to Finn's Point Cemetery to investigate a homicide. Murray, the veteran cop, had never before done a homicide, but since the crime took place on a federal reservation, the federal government had jurisdiction, and that meant he had to go.

"Who's out there now?" he asked.

"The Philly Fugitive Task Force is at the sight," he heard.

"That's not right. Why did they get the call instead of us?"Murray was a results-oriented cop and cared little about jurisdiction, credit or turf battles. All the same, the rules were the rules and he meant to let his superiors know he was not happy.

"So is the FTF doing the crime scene?" he asked.

"No, they say that's your deal."

"What the hell? Tell the guy to read his job qualifications. They're the same as mine. They can get going on it," he said.

Twenty minutes later, he pulled into Fort Mott State Park. A bevy of news reporters had already swarmed around the site, although a police line held them back to the parking area near the cemetery road. Seeing those reporters reminded him of a beehive, packed together, all pursuing the same interest. He had no time for them, and after identifying himself, drove the mile-long route into the cemetery area.

Now outside the lodge, he saw several squad cars and soon learned that Thomas Conavo from the New Jersey State Police Crime Scene team from Buena Vista, New Jersey, was on site.

"Whose case is it?" Conavo asked after Murray identified himself.

"Well, it's a federal site inside a state park. So that makes it federal," Murray said. The tiny cemetery sat land-locked inside the much larger Fort Mott State Park. Any observer would have thought it was just another corner of the state property. In fact, the federal government had, years earlier, tried to deed the cemetery to the state, but New Jersey officials refused.

"It's my case, I guess," Murray sighed. "But do what you are doing. Let me know how I can help."

Murray followed the investigators into the lodge and then to the basement. There he saw the grotesque bloody remains of Bill Reese. "This never had to happen," he growled. "Damn media. The poor guy was just in the wrong place at the wrong time."

Murray and the investigators worked the scene all night and on into the morning. They found a spent .40 caliber cartridge, the slug and the Lexus.

The Lexus told them much about Lee Miglin, but little about Andrew Cunanan. In the trunk, they saw the demolished cell phone and wires Cunanan had torn free. A toolbox held a screwdriver that appeared to have body tissue on it – Lee Miglin's, Murray learned later. A pliers and a short length of 12-guage wire also had Miglin's tissue smeared on them. They saw one shoe, Miglin's, lying in the trunk.

In the office, Murray read, re-read and stared at the Bible verse Reese had left open on his desk: "If in the land which the LORD your God gives you to possess, any one is found slain, lying in the open country..." It seemed to Murray that Reese had been trying to send a message; to let people know that he knew he was going to die. The words sent chills down the experienced cop's spine.

"Let's find this son-of-a-bitch," he said to the investigative team. Somehow, sandwiched around caring for a wife, four children and an ailing mother, Murray purposed to catch the slime-ball who had murdered a good man who did not deserve to die. Like Lee Urness when he first saw the story of a missing Jeep on May 2, Murray had no idea just how consuming would become the search for the gay chameleon, Andrew Cunanan.

New York City yields nothing

While Murray and the New Jersey team began to get acquainted with Cunanan's handiwork, Lee Urness continued to make his calls. Given the location of this latest murder, Lee worried that Cunanan might be heading back to the Big Apple. He called Emilio Blasse.

"We're not doing any good here," Blasse said, when Lee got him on the phone. "We got cooperation, and talked to everyone, and spread his picture around, but no one's seen him or is willing to admit to it."

"Well, here's the bad news." Lee gave him the update on the new murder and the red pick-up truck with New Jersey plates. "So see what you can find, and you might want to go back and warn those gay friends of yours."

"Thanks a lot," Blasse said, "Yeah, I'll go warn my gay friends." But he was resolved to do whatever it took to stop Cunanan.

Lee jotted everything down on the note pads he kept in the car, and filed them into his case file. Up until then, he had kept pretty good mental control over names, dates, locations and other facts, but in this rush of bad news, he felt it getting away from him. *There's just too much!*

The time from 7:00-8:00 p.m. fled past as a blur of phone calls, anger, frustration and more phone calls competed for Lee's attention. He needed to stretch. Getting out of the car, he reached his long arms high into the air, trying to work out the tension. He walked into the kitchen and reached for a bottle of Jack Daniels. He nearly filled a large glass with the liquor, added a little 7-Up and went back to the van. As he sipped the drink, he tried to turn his mind off and relax. His pager went off, and the message said, "William Norman calling for you on the 800 line."

"This is Lee Urness. You paged me to contact a William Norman," he said to the BCA operator who picked up. "Patch me through to him right away." He listened impatiently as the phone rang on the other end.

"Hello," William Norman said from his New York City hotel room.

"Mr. Norman, this Agent Lee Urness. I am in charge of the manhunt for Andrew Cunanan," Lee said.

"Oh yes. Thank you for returning my call. I understand you were trying to get hold of me," the polished gay man said.

"Yes I was, and thank you for calling back. Did you hear that Andrew killed another man today?" Lee asked, and noticed the strong edge that had crept into his voice.

"Yes, I just heard it on the news," the sad man answered.

"Well, you may be at risk and we want to protect you," Lee said, hoping to gain Norman's complete cooperation. Lee had no idea if Norman was on Cunanan's hit list, or even if Cunanan had formed such a list. He also had no idea that Cunanan had been in New York City for the past several days.

"Thanks. I heard about what Andrew had done and so I checked into the hotel under an assumed name. I must admit this has me shook up," Norman confessed.

"Hey, it's very important you help us as much as can. He's killed four already and he'll kill again. I've got two agents in New York I'd like you to talk to. I'll have them come right over," Lee said, not leaving the man any wiggle room. Since Norman obviously felt Cunanan to be a real threat, Lee could shelve any of his tricks to win cooperation – staying alive gave Norman all the incentive he needed. The man with whom Norman had so often shared his bed had turned into a maniacal murderer, someone to fear, not harbor or coddle.

"Fine, I'll be sure to cooperate," Norman offered.

"Good," Lee said. "Where do you think he'd be going right now?"

"Well, he doesn't really know anyone south of here."

"Like where?"Lee asked.

"Like Florida. We know a lot of people around the country, but we don't really have any friends south of here." Lee found it interesting that Norman referred to Cunanan as "we," as though they were still somehow joined together. "I have really no idea where he'd go."

Lee felt certain Norman held back information, and it irked him that he could not be there and look the man in the eye. "Well sir, thanks for your willingness to cooperate. Cunanan (Lee had taken to purposefully mispronouncing the name as COO-na-nin, as fast as he could say it, instead of coo-NAWH-non) will most likely try to contact someone he trusts, and you would be high on his list."

"Yes, I suppose that is true," Norman answered, once again, very sadly. "By the way, you should say the name as coo-NAWH-nun."

"Yeah, I know," Lee said, not willing to explain himself. "Look, Agent Emilio Blasse will be contacting you shortly. He'll do everything he can to protect you, but you *must* cooperate fully, understand?"

"Oh yes, I understand. Look, I don't want any trouble from Andrew or from the police. I came to New York to take a cruise, and I just want to get on with my trip," Norman said.

And they hung up with that clear understanding.

Lee paged Blasse and sent him to Norman's hotel right away. Blasse found Norman very cooperative as he told him about every friend and associate he and Cunanan knew while they were a couple. He made suggestions about where Cunanan would go and his likes and dislikes, the kind of information vital to catching him.

Blasse and his partner shadowed Norman that weekend, following him to parties and to dinner – anywhere Norman wanted to go. They hoped that Cunanan might show up.

Lee called Jeff Covington once again and learned nothing new. "They're doing the crime scene search now and I'll call if anything breaks," the investigator said. Lee knew that processing a murder scene could take hours, even a day or more. It would provide little if any immediate help.

"Okay, thanks. I'll hook up with Paul Murray in Cherry Hill on Monday, unless something breaks right away," Lee said.

He sat back in the van again, picking through his files. No matter how many times he looked at those pages, nothing new jumped out at him. They had Cunanan in their sights for a few minutes and then they lost him. He killed again. And he fled again. *And it happened on my watch!!* He slammed his fist on the steering wheel in anger.

Lee went back to the house and poured himself another Jack Daniels laced with a hint of 7-Up. He seldom had two drinks on the same night, but tonight was different.

Back in the car, he replayed his conversation with Jeff Covington and the scene the agent had described. It brought back the memories of slain officers Ron Ryan Jr., Tim Jones and Laser that fateful day on St. Paul's east side. The idea that a civilian had died because of a news leak, and that Cunanan might do it yet again, especially to an unsuspecting cop, made him shudder with anger.

I hope some cop finds the jerk dead right there! he said, drinking deeply from his whiskey.

He felt angry with himself. *What did I miss? What should I have done? What could I have done?*

"I wish we could have prevented it," Lee said when he called Kevin Rickett again, anger mixing with sadness.

"We need a break," Rickett said. "But we'll get him, don't worry. Those east coast cops are all over the place. Just hang in there Lee."

Lee took out his file and began again at page one, reviewing everything. He saw nothing he could have done to prevent this.

155

He drew two columns on a sheet of legal paper, and wrote "Good News" above one and "Bad News" above the other.

Under "Bad News," he wrote "luck." He added, "not caught speeding – no accidents." Then, "No one visited cemetery." "3 vehicles across the country and no cop saw him!" "Extensive news coverage and no sightings on the east coast." "Fled 4 crimes undetected." "LUCKY!!"

His "Good News" side had many entries, but lacked the one most needed – he still had no idea where Cunanan was or where he was going. All he knew is where he had been and what he had been driving. With this murder, Lee had lost ground only to find another body.

This is the first time on my watch my fugitive committed another crime! he shouted at himself again. He took the blame.

Now what do we do?

William Reese's death created problems for more than Reese's survivors and the cops who chased Cunanan. Anne O'Connor, the *Star*-Tribune reporter got a call at home Friday evening just like Lee's. "We just heard that Cunanan killed again in New Jersey," she heard.

"Oh my God," she exclaimed. She called Chris Graves.

"Chris, Cunanan's killed again!"

"What? Killed who?"Graves asked.

"A cemetery caretaker. A guy named William Reese. That's all I know."

Because Cunanan's name had been linked to Reese's murder, the *Star-Tribune* dispatched veteran reporter Randy Furst to New Jersey. With Jim Walsh still in San Diego, O'Connor and Chris Graves worked the local angles. O'Connor's days were consumed by endless phone calls to cops on the east coast who had nothing to say. Graves continued to work the local cops. On top of their own work, they became inundated with calls from national and local media pleading for information for their own stories. They began to feel a sense of ownership – it was "their story." O'Connor, after all, had been the first reporter on the scene of the first murder. The busyness they had felt since Miglin's death ratcheted up several more notches.

In Washington, D.C., at the Fox TV building that housed America's Most Wanted, a debate had broken out. AMW had already taped the Saturday segment about Andrew Cunanan and the Miglin murder. Everything had been completed and by the time the editing team had added the music and graphics to John Walsh's report, it was just too late to change it. And AMW needed the show to pump up its points during "sweeps month."

Donna Brant talked it over with her bosses. They made the decision. "We go with it as it is," knowing that it would disappoint at least one Minnesota cop. But given everything, they had no other choice but to let it run. It would be the first of seven such stories that came to dominate Brant's life, just as it consumed the cops.

No relief

His drink and spirit exhausted, Lee went back into the house to catch the 10 p.m. news. He flipped from CBS to NBC to ABC – Channels 4, 5 and 11. Each station featured the Reese murder. His stomach burned with frustration and anger.

"Dad, did he really do that?" Kari asked, as she monitored CNN. "You gotta catch this guy quick!"

"The death penalty is too good for him," Kathy said.

And the calls continued.

He told the west coast they should call it a night unless there was something new. For sure, Cunanan was not on the west coast, but he might try to call someone out there.

Lee thought about what to expect on Saturday. Though he had never worked with America's Most Wanted, he felt certain this new murder would generate scores of fresh leads. He hoped that maybe one lead would break open the case. By his "Serial 9" notice, Lee had notified law enforcement agencies all across America – and the world – so that "Lee Urness" and "Andrew Cunanan" were now linked together by cops everywhere.

Finally, close to midnight, the calls stopped, but he wondered for how long? The call he longed for would be a highway cop telling him that they had found Cunanan "Dead Right There!" But there would be no such call that night.

Lee tried to sleep, but could not. All he could think about was some poor cop or another civilian who surprised Cunanan and bought a bullet. He prayed for the cops.

Chapter 18 ~ Softball gives way to hardball police work

Lee found himself checking the clock every few minutes, longing for sleep but being denied. Finally, he saw it was 6:00 a.m. Kari played her first game at 8:00 and there was much to do to get ready. Batting and throwing the ball around, watching Kari do her softball magic, he hoped, would snap him out of the black mood he felt overwhelming him. Perhaps he could hide away at first base, leaving all the trouble back in that van, but to do that meant leaving his pager at home, and that is something he never did.

With a body and eyes that screamed for more sleep, Lee willed himself out of bed. Fifteen minutes later, he was provisioning a cooler for the long day ahead, filling it with snacks, sodas and lunch. By 7:15 Kathy, Kari and he left for the softball fields, but in two cars. Lee wanted his squad car ready in case something broke and he had to fly back to the office.

Wearing his Prior Lake Lakers uniform shirt, he packed a fresh FTF shirt and his vest in the car just in case he needed to make a quick change. His hid his gun under the seat and wore his pager on his belt. He knew the likelihood of that pager going off at least a few times during the day was high, but hoped it would be manageable and that one of the pages would let him know Cunanan had been caught – or was dead.

On the way to the game, he called Kevin Rickett and asked him to check to make sure that America's Most Wanted was still on for that night.

"Will do," Rickett said.

"Maybe we can catch a break and have the night off," Lee chuckled, hopeful that Cunanan would be found even that morning, but not feeling very confident about it.

"I'll get back to you or have them call if there's any question," Rickett said.

Lee saw the ballfield up ahead and pulled in, finding a spot where he could see the field from the car. He coached the Lakers' batters, and at first base when they were up to bat. When the Lakers took the field, Lee sat in the dugout and gave Kari her pitching signs. Though she could already chuck a 60 mile-per-hour fastball, he needed to help her become more than a thrower, to be a pitcher, choosing each pitch carefully. Kari seldom gave up a hit, and she led the under-12 team in hitting. Lee could not stand the thought of missing a moment of her budding softball career.

Just after the Lakers came up to bat in the first inning, Lee's pager beeped. He saw that America's Most Wanted had left him a return number. He had already warned the other coach that he might have to answer pages from time to time, so he signaled for a parent to replace him at first base, and headed toward his van. There he called the FBI and had them patch him through to AMW. He lit up a cigarette and opened the window while he waited.

"Urness here. You paged me?"

"Thanks for calling. I needed to talk to you about tonight's show," Evan Marshall said.

"Okay, everything still on?" Lee asked.

"Oh yes, but I needed to check something with you. We got a call from the Cherry Hill FBI office and they want the information from the show sent to them," he explained.

"No way! You can cancel that. This is my case and all the information will come to Minnesota. We can send them a copy," Lee said bluntly.

"Well, it's your call."

"Yes it is, and we'll be following up everything out of Minnesota," Lee instructed.

"You want to let them know?" the man asked, sounding as though he would rather not do it himself.

"Bet on it. I will personally contact them and do all the follow up and thanks for calling," Lee said, writing himself a note to call Jeff Covington in-between games. It ticked him off that New Jersey had done this because he could not afford duplication of effort and leads. The last thing Lee wanted was to call some highway cop in Georgia and find out New Jersey had already called. The chase had already gotten too complicated to let this happen.

With that settled, Lee got out of the car and stomped out his cigarette, grinding it hard into the ground in frustration. By the time he got back to the game it was the second inning, and Kari had pitched flawlessly without him.

Totally preoccupied

Lee loved the kids on the "A" level softball team and he felt jealous about his time with them. He was a good and popular coach, the kind who could tease a young girl into performing better, and yet protect her delicate self-image.

From time to time during the game that day, Lee's eyes would float up into the stands, seeing no one in particular. Suddenly he focused on a man sitting two rows up on the opponents' side of the field. *Could it be?* he asked himself. *Andrew Cunanan sitting on those bleachers?* He stared even harder, finally shaking his head to clear his mind. *There's no way! Pull yourself together, man!*

Never before had a case begun to run him like this one did. This case refused to do what he told it to do. He felt he had lost control.

The sound of a batter making contact with one of Kari's pitches caught his attention. She had hit the ball sharply to second, but the fielder let it go through her legs.

"Come on," Lee yelled, "You gotta execute that play!" The word stuck in his mouth. "Execute!" That's what Cunanan did to Reese.

During her turn at bat, Kari hit the ball hard and as she rounded first he yelled, "Run, run harder." That's what Cunanan was doing, only not to a predictable place like second base. Lee shook his head, trying to rid himself of the thought.

"Strike three!" the umpire yelled, as Kari threw a fastball past the batter and into the glove of Carly Nelson, her personal catcher. Another strike out. Lee felt like he struck out with every step along the way in this foul and deadly game Cunanan played.

As usual, Kari's team won the first game. *And I'm going to win this game with Cunanan,* Lee assured himself.

This was just a warm-up tournament, more like a series of scrimmages, so victories carried no bearing on league standings. Still, the Lakers always played hard.

The next game began at Noon, so Lee had time to make some calls. He knew there would be three games that day. His body felt the effects of no sleep, his mind felt clouded, and the day had gotten very warm. He felt miserable.

Lee went back to his van and began making calls. First, he called Jeff Covington in Philly.

"How you doing today?"Lee asked.

"Really dragging. We finished up about 4:00 a.m. at the murder scene," he explained.

Before they began their crime scene investigation, they had to get a warrant to search the property. They got started after 7:00 p.m. Their search was meticulous. Lee knew it would be so and had not bothered them the night before, knowing Covington would be up all night.

It would do no good to call Paul Murray, the FBI Agent on the case, until he had processed all the crime scene evidence. Murray's job was to solve the murder case, to find evidence strong enough to convict Cunanan, though the fact that Cunanan did it seemed obvious to everyone. Lee focused entirely on the chase and what he wanted to learn from the murder scene was different from Murray. Lee needed to understand Cunanan's mindset, his capabilities and tendencies. He needed to predict how dangerous Cunanan really was, and what he would attempt. The crime scene details could tell him much of this. More important than all this, was Lee's need to establish a pattern of where Cunanan would go following a criminal act and how he would react once the police had him cornered. The more he knew, the more likely it was that he would catch him sooner.

"So how in the hell can a thousand cops not find a red Chevy pickup?" Lee asked Covington, honestly frustrated.

"Hey, you know it's Friday and rush hour on the East Coast is ridiculous," Covington answered.

"Yeah, but he didn't have that big of a head start."

"Apparently he had enough. Who knows, maybe he's still around here somewhere," Covington offered.

"I gotta tell you, I'm really glad I didn't get any calls in the middle of the night. You know if someone stops him he's gonna shoot first and he could kill a cop," Lee said.

"Yup. Well, we'll just have to find him before he does that."

"Say, about America's Most Wanted. Let New Jersey know that all the leads will come to me and then I'll send them out," Lee explained, trying to save himself another call.

"I'll let everyone know," he answered.

"Were there any sightings in the area?" Lee asked.

"Some locals say they saw Cunanan driving the Lexus around the area around 4 p.m. but none after, at least not so far," Covington answered.

"Well, maybe it was him and maybe not, although the time fits," Lee said. "Hey, I gotta keep going. A lot more calls to make. You call me with anything, okay?"

"Will do. Maybe we'll get lucky."

"Yeah, maybe," Lee said, without much conviction.

Sometimes, though, luck did break these cases.

Gassed

Years earlier, a man from the Southwestern Minnesota town of Pipestone had shot his pregnant girlfriend to death on a Wednesday and fled the state. The Bureau of Criminal Apprehension agent in the area got the local warrant on Thursday and Lee had the UFAP the same day and went to work.

He got a hit on the car license plate in Indianapolis, Indiana. The killer had pulled into a gas station there, pumped his gas and drove off without paying. When Lee heard the news, he rolled his eyes, reminding himself that most killers were not only bad guys, but also stupid. The station owner reported the car license to local cops who saw the warrant listed on the NCIC and called Lee. All this told Lee that the man had headed east. Lee focused his search. Then he got a call from Myrtle Beach, South Carolina.

Some would call what happened next a "lucky break," but the fact is that good, solid police work usually creates lucky breaks. By putting the word out on the street everywhere that the felon had fled, the chances of "luck" falling Lee's way increased.

"This is Lee Urness," he said that Saturday morning, answering a page from an eastern area code. "You paged me?"

"Hey guess what? I got a hit on your license plate on that murder case in Minnesota," Myrtle Beach police officer Mike Berndt* told him.

"What happened?" Lee asked.

"Strangest thing," Berndt said. "I had some down time and was in the office going through Friday's reports and saw a gas drive off. Usually we just blow these off. But I was thinking, I'll check into it and I ran the plate and saw your fugitive. It bugs me that these guys do this."

"Friday?"Lee said. "He could still be around there. He must know someone there. But we found no one he knew in that area."

"Maybe he just pulled off the freeway and is laying low," Berndt suggested. "Well, I know the newspaper guy here. What if you give him an interview?"

"Yes, as long as he promises to put it front page." Lee may have hated what the newsies too often did to his chases, but he knew there were times they became his tool.

That afternoon a Myrtle Beach reporter interviewed Lee and a story appeared in the Sunday paper under the headline, "Murder Suspect Spotted in

Area." The article that followed included all the gory details about the pregnant girlfriend the bad guy had shot and how he had fled police.

On Monday, Berndt called him back. "We got him."

"What happened?" Lee asked.

"A newspaper reader was in a convenience store, saw the license plate, and called the cops. Then he followed the guy while he talked to the cops on his cell phone until they caught up. Then the cops chased him and he crashed. Took a shot at the cops as they chased him, but missed. Then as he tried to out-run the cops, he stuck the gun in his mouth and shot himself. Blamo! Right into a tree with his head sprayed all over."

"Dead right there," Lee said, smiling. "Good work and hey, thanks a lot"

But there was no Myrtle Beach here

As Lee thought back to that Myrtle Beach case, he pictured Cunanan and wondered if he would ever put a gun to his mouth. He made a note to talk to the FBI profilers about it. But in South Carolina, at least, a combination of good cop work and "luck" had finished the earlier chase. Again, Lee shivered as he wondered if, in the Cunanan chase, it might be the bad guy shooting the guy with the cell phone.

He looked at the cell phone in his hand and then his list of contacts. He needed to check in with his immediate supervisor at the BCA, Don Peterson, and if he could squeeze it in, Nick O'Hara, the Chief of the BCA. He wanted to keep them all informed. The news had spread to every media outlet in the world and he knew the bosses needed a comfort zone, to know that everything was being done to catch Cunanan.

During the second game, and the last game at 3:00 p.m., his pager sounded several times forcing him to leave the game. The FBI told him to call ASAP because the *Chicago Tribune* wanted him. He quickly referred them to Coleen Rowley and headed back to first base. Other jurisdictions called with questions or updates; he only wished they could wait until between games.

Finally, the games ended.

"You going home?"Kathy asked him.

"What?" he said as he gathered up the cooler. His mind was miles away, chasing Cunanan.

"I said, are you going home?"Kathy had seen Lee distracted before, but never like this.

"Sure, gotta shower. Then I'm going in to work. It'll be late," he said as he walked to his van. At least Lee had managed to stay at the ballfield all afternoon.

After cleaning up, he had just enough time to drive into Minneapolis and hit Cuzzy's for dinner before settling in at FBI headquarters. Cuzzy's sat a mile west of the FTF office, and only a few blocks from David Madson's apartment.

Lee pulled into the small lot alongside the neighborhood restaurant that sat in an old 1880s building. A sandwich board sign on the front sidewalk said, "Open 'Til Closed."

He walked in and went to the back of the place, near the narrow hallway that led past the restrooms. He sat at a table just under the green "Corona Street" sign mounted on the wall. This was where the cops usually sat.

Lee loved the offbeat, friendly place.

When Cuzzy's had opened a few years earlier, John Lee, one of the owners, asked his first customer to decorate a dollar bill which he promptly stuck on the black wall behind the bar. Several minutes later, relatives and friends of John Lee and his partner Bob Goral, asked if they too could decorate dollar bills. By this day in May 1997, the walls and ceiling of nearly half the restaurant were papered with $1 bills decorated by patrons. The offbeat artwork had long ago covered the wall behind the bar and had bled over to the side walls covered in blond knotty-pine panels and onto the black-painted ceiling.

An old worn floor that ran downhill from back to front held the Formica-topped stainless steel tables and wood chairs. Waitresses slipped beer coasters or matchboxes under the table legs to level them out. A 30-foot long bar sat on the west wall of the narrow restaurant, and several people were sipping drinks.

Lee looked up at the "Specials" listed on the board just above the window to the kitchen. "1/2# Cuzzy's Burger topped w/crumbled Bleu cheese, lettuce, tomato & Onion. $6.00" Cuzzy's made the best burgers in the Twin Cities and served them with a plateful of hot fries.

On a Saturday evening, the place was busy with its usual eclectic mix of college students, blue-collar workers and clerks from the retail businesses located in the warehouses that surround the place. Their noisy conversation was serenaded by upbeat music coming from the speaker just above Lee's head. He glanced up at one of several TVs that hung from the ceiling, not really looking at it – just seeing it. The bar noise covered anything said by the TV talking heads anyway. Blue smoke from dozens of cigarettes, Lee's included, filled the air.

"So, do you know anything about this Cunanan guy?" John Lee asked as he walked over to Lee.

"Yeah, too much. I'm the case agent," Lee said.

"What's that mean?"

"I'm the unlucky guy who's in charge of chasing him down."

"Too bad about that guy in New Jersey," John Lee said, shaking his head. He saw Lee's eyes go sad, and glass over.

"That it is," he said. "That's the first time anyone ever died on my watch, and I can assure you, it won't happen again."

"Where is he? Do you know?" John asked.

"Naw, no one knows. We have some ideas, but nothing firm. Every cop on the east coast is looking for him. Hey, you gotta watch America's Most Wanted tonight. They're doing the story," Lee said. "It'll hopefully generate some good leads. I say give me two weeks – a month at most – and I'll nail the sucker."

"I wish you well," John said as he walked back to the bar.

"Yeah, I wish myself well," Lee muttered. If he had come at the end of that day's work, he might have lingered over a Jack Daniels and 7-Up, but not this evening. Soon, he hoped, he would hold the single perfect lead in hand that would nail Cunanan forever.

His pager left him alone long enough to enjoy his supper, but all the time he could not shake the idea that at any moment, Cunanan would walk through the door. The idea was ridiculous, he knew, but at that point, he needed to grab hold of anything that seemed like hope.

As he drove the half-mile back to FBI headquarters, he kept thinking and hoping that maybe, just maybe it would be "the" night. Surely, someone somewhere in America had spotted Cunanan and would call America's Most Wanted.

Bring on the hits

In Washington, D.C., Donna Brant had been at her desk since 5:00 p.m., anticipating that evening's show. She felt sure that it would be a smashing success. AMW needed a boost during sweeps month, and her instincts told her that Cunanan would make the difference.

Downstairs, in the hotline room, Wanda Witherspoon made sure everything would be ready for AMW's operators as they reported that evening. Packets of information several pages thick had been stapled together, each packet giving information about the segments they planned to air that night.

The entire show had been blocked out in minute detail, each time element broken down so that the operators could anticipate when the calls would most likely begin. One thing that those callers had proven repeatedly was that they were loyal and that they *would* call. If any of them had seen Cunanan at any time, anywhere, the phones would light up.

By 7:00 p.m. Eastern Daylight Time, the operators had assembled for the one hour screening of that evening's show. It aired at 9:00 p.m. EDT, but seeing it early gave them time to make sure they were ready for an onslaught of calls, should they be so lucky. Their best shows generated perhaps 10 calls about the most sought-after criminals. Cunanan might generate more, given the murder of such a high-profile person as Lee Miglin.

Each operator kept a stack of three-part call report forms nearby, ready to write the tips. Witherspoon reminded them to be careful with the callers, assuming nothing but reporting everything, and not to push for a name. Many callers wanted anonymity, and AMW granted it. Witherspoon collected the call reports and decided which ones to send along immediately and which would wait.

"Remember, this Minnesota cop wants them faxed right away," Brant reminded Witherspoon.

Back in Minneapolis, Lee, along with Kevin Rickett, Steve Gilkerson and Lisa Davis, rolled into the FBI office at 6:30 p.m. Lee went directly to the phone and called AMW.

"Donna Brant, please," Lee said. "This is Lee Urness from the Minnesota Fugitive Task Force."

"This is Donna Brant," he heard in a moment.

"Lee Urness here. Everything ready to go?" he asked.

"Yes sir."

"Well, here's our direct dial number," he said, rattling off the digits. "You'll call us with all hot leads?"

"Sure will, and we'll fax the others," Brant said. Brant really appreciated that Lee wanted those leads right away. He was the kind of cop she liked best – ready and eager to go. She said nothing to him about the "old news" that awaited AMW's viewers.

"Okay, let's test the fax." Lee gave her the number and stood next to it, talking with her as the paper came out of the machine. "Okay, looks good. We're all set, then," he said, hanging up.

They set up TV monitors to watch the show. He explained to the team that hot leads would come by phone and be called out immediately. All other leads would be faxed into the office and evaluated.

A hot lead would be one where someone said they were looking at Cunanan at that moment, or had just seen him within minutes or a few hours. Other sightings older than a few hours, but that still appeared to be real and sensible, would be called out after the hot leads. The remaining leads could be called out on Sunday or Monday, depending on how urgent they seemed.

Lee briefed the communications center operator to give him the high sign each time a lead came in by fax and each agent took up a position near a phone. Lee knew there might not be a break for several hours, and he needed a cigarette. The office rules banned smoking in the building, so he rode the elevator to the second floor, went to the first floor lobby and walked outside. As he lit his cigarette, he pondered what the night could bring. This would be his first experience with America's Most Wanted, and the other agents had told him it could be a real help catching Cunanan. He checked his watch; it was time to go back upstairs to the Eleventh Floor FBI office.

Everyone watched the TV monitor as the program started.

John Walsh stood in Chicago with its well-known skyline in the background. He began talking about Cunanan fleeing in a Green Lexus, and that he had apparently headed east.

"What the hell?" Lee said as his mouth dropped open. He watched in angry astonishment. "This is yesterday's news!"

And it *was* yesterday's news. It said nothing about the assassination of William Reese or Cunanan's theft of the red Chevy pick-up truck.

"Damn!" Lee shouted. "You could at least give the right car. What use is this?" he yelled at the TV.

"Give me Donna Brant," he demanded as he called the show right away. "Hey, what gives? That's old news you're showing."

"Yeah, it was put together yesterday," she admitted. "I'm sorry."

"Can't you throw something on the air to show what he's driving now?"

"No, we're just set up here in the hotline room taking calls. There's no broadcasting going on in the studio," she said.

"Damn!"

"In fact, the first calls we got were about the truck," she added. "Folks wanted to let us know we had blown it, I guess.

"Great. Just great," Lee said.

Despite the "old news," AMW and Donna Brant had scored a ratings winner. They knew it when more than 60 leads came in that night. "That's about six times more than any other good show," Brant said, smiling at the results. Standing in AMW's hotline studio, Brant watched in amazement. She began plotting for a second segment the following weekend.

Lee grudgingly took the calls and assigned the leads. They had no choice but to work them, even if they were cold. Every lead meant generating another piece of paper, another FBI report. The faxes reported calls from all across the United States. Seemingly, Cunanan lurked in several states at the same time.

"This jerk's got more than luck. He's got more than one body," Lee laughed snidely.

There were a couple of hot leads, though.

Could this be your guy?

Right after the show a caller in Sayreville, New Jersey said he was sitting at the Coliseum Bar. "Hey, Cunanan's sitting in this bar right now."

Lee put him on hold and called Jeff Covington. "Get someone out there right now," he told the agent. And he did, but there was no Andrew Cunanan.

Then a caller said Cunanan sat in The Rascals Bar in New Hope, Pennsylvania. Lee again called Covington, but there was no Cunanan.

Another caller saw Cunanan at the Court House in West Palm Beach on Wednesday; he was sure of it. He saw Cunanan sitting outside with four other obviously gay men who rode away together in a 1994 dark-colored Lexus with Illinois plates. He thought that Cunanan acted strange, like something bothered him. Lee sat this lead on a pile for Monday follow-up. It made no sense that Cunanan would be in West Palm Beach on Wednesday and kill Reese in New Jersey on Friday.

Some leads were very strange, though well intentioned.

"You gotta hear this one," Lee said reading the latest fax. "We got a lead from a guy who says Cunanan is riding around the country in a car on the back of a car carrier." As crazy as it sounded, Lee still had to ponder its credibility and write the paperwork.

Another fax said the caller had spotted Cunanan in Norfolk, Virginia on the previous Wednesday. "Unlikely," Lee chuckled, as he rubbed his forehead in frustration.

One caller reported that a man who had just been released from the Cook County, Illinois' jail claimed that Cunanan still sat in that same jail on a burglary charge. "Unbelievable," a partly bemused Lee Urness said as he called Terry Thedford, sending him out to check on it. He knew that in some locales, cops seldom checked warrants and someone he chased really could be sitting in a jail on some minor violation.

Lee had once chased a rapist who had eluded him for several weeks. One day as he talked with the bad guy's Minneapolis friends, they said they had just heard from him. He had called from a New Orleans' jail.

"Say, this is Lee Urness with the Minnesota Fugitive Task Force," he told the duty officer at the jail. "I'm chasing an Arnold Pendergast*, a rapist, and his buddies up here say you got him in your jail."

"Just a moment," the jailer said. "Yup, we might have your guy."

Lee gave him the descriptors.

"Sounds like your man. Been here about 90 days," the officer said nonchalantly.

"What? Don't you people check NCIC?" Lee asked, astonished.

"No, we're just too damn busy down here, and have no time to check them all," the officer answered matter-of-factly.

On this Cunanan lead, Lee asked Thedford if in Chicago they run NCIC on all arrested individuals. Unlike New Orleans, Chicago made it part of their routine.

"Well for your information, I got a lead that Cunanan is sitting in Cook County jail right now," Lee said.

"No kidding?" Thedford answered, unconvinced.

"Well, I don't think it's our guy, but check it out, will you?" Lee asked.

"Will do, just to be sure."

A fax came across that said a New Jersey woman and her girlfriend had bought gas at a truck stop just north of Pennsville late on Friday afternoon. They swore they saw Cunanan come in and get a cup of coffee, then drive away. It might have been Cunanan, but by the time they called, it was a day too late. Lee decided to wait until Monday with this lead. It made him think about the possibility that Cunanan had headed north.

"I think this is bogus," he said to the others. "He wouldn't stop at a truck stop and get coffee if he had just murdered someone in the area. But he could be heading to Canada."

"Yup, you're right," Davis said. "We better check it out."

"Here's a live one," Rickett shouted from across the room. "This fellow says he flew on an airplane with Cunanan into Chicago."

"Oh *really?* "Lee asked, already getting tired of these crazy reports.

"Well, it might not be so crazy. The guy's an air traffic controller. He said he just got off a plane with Cunanan and when he got home he saw the show."

"Where was he coming from?" Lee asked.

"Said he flew into Chicago from L.A. and sat next to the guy and talked to him. Said he was weird and elusive, and the suspect told him he was from the north side and has a wife and kids."

"No, that's too weird," Lee said. "Did the guy give him a name?"

"Nope."

"Give it to me," Lee said, calling him back directly.

The man claimed they had flown together on Southwest Airlines from L.A. to Las Vegas, through Omaha and then into Chicago Midway.

"Tell me about the man," Lee said.

"He's about 5'10", loud and obnoxious. Said he had a lot of money and he talked about violence. Said he had a divorced wife in North Chicago," the traffic controller said.

"What'd he have on?"Lee asked.

"Light blue jeans, tucked in blue long sleeved shirt and Doc Martin imitation shoes."

"When was the flight?" Lee asked.

"May 6", he said. "I'm absolutely sure it was Cunanan."

"Well, it may have been. But it's kind of old news now," Lee said.

"Could you do me a favor? When this is over and done with – I know you're gonna get him – will you call me and let me know if this was Cunanan on the flight?"

"Ah, sure, I'll make a note of it. And thank you for calling," he said, hanging up.

Lee felt sure this was a false sighting. It did not fit the few facts they knew. Still, he made a note to call Southwest Airlines on Monday to check the manifest. (Southwest had no record at all of Cunanan, Drew Cunningham, or Andrew DeSilva ever flying with them.)

One very close associate called

Kurt Demars called America's Most Wanted that evening, too. He told the operator that he knew Cunanan personally. Demars, from San Diego, said that Cunanan had told him he would be back to California in "six to eight weeks." But Cunanan had kept extending the trip. Demars had known Cunanan as Andrew DeSilva, which he labeled his "gay name."

Demars had met Cunanan during the summer of 1996. At the time, Cunanan said he planned to move to San Francisco where he wanted to get into the parking lot business.

Cunanan wanted Demars to become his roommate in San Francisco, but the man had refused; he claimed they had never been lovers. Demars believed that Cunanan was well networked in the city. Demars had an undeveloped roll of film that he believed contained photos of Cunanan.

The night's onslaught finally ebbed

AMW's switchboards closed down when the calls stopped, sometime past 1:30 a.m. EDT. They turned on their automatic answering machine; the recording told callers to leave a detailed message, or call back the next day.

Donna Brant slept well during what was left of that night. She had scored a hit, but like a string of cops, she would soon discover that Andrew Cunanan had just begun to run her life.

In Minneapolis, the calls also slowed down and finally stopped, although more came on Sunday. The FTF crew gathered up all their leads and evaluated them. Then they did their paperwork, getting them ready for Monday transmission to local FBI offices.

Those that they thought to be hot leads were immediately called out to a local jurisdiction. Lee cared little about waking cops form their sleep. "Get up and on the street. The guy may be 10 minutes from you now," Lee would say.

Some leads they could ignore, and those had to be a gut call. The location, physical description, freshness and the story itself determined the priority. A cop's experience determined which calls were followed up and which were dropped.

Lee had been a cop too long to get very excited about every lead. He knew that people attached themselves to big stories in bizarre ways, although in the weeks ahead, he would find some of the craziest and most unusual of these he had ever encountered. He hoped that somewhere in this pile of crazy leads, though, might lay the one that would lead him to Cunanan. So, all leads had to be at least put through a validity test.

The sleepless Friday night and long Saturday at the softball field left Lee close to exhaustion, but he pushed on, just as he had when he dove for that body at Lake Ida. With luck and hard work, he just might bump into Cunanan at any moment.

Chapter 19 ~ Forget Sunday rest

At 4:00 a.m. Sunday, Lee finally left FBI headquarters for home. His carry-along file folder had grown a half-inch thicker from the leads gathered during and right after AMW aired. He made notes about calls to make on Sunday and those that could wait until Monday, and those notes were stuffed into his case file, already getting dog-eared from near continuous handling. He kept a legal pad open and sitting on the driver's seat next to him in case an idea popped into his head. Years earlier, he had perfected a form of short-hand allowing him to write and drive at the same time, though he had to write clarifying notes to these notes once he arrived at his destination.

The chaos created by America's Most Wanted – the frustration that they were a day late with their story – and the bustle at the office had taken an additional toll on Lee, so much had it hindered his feeling of making progress. All he felt he had done for the last four days was sit in the office or car and talk on the phone; no personal face-to-face interviews. Lee liked working the streets not the phones.

All this played like a bass drum in his head as he drove away from FBI headquarters. The cacophony of thoughts that pelted his mind competed for his attention, and combined with the clatter coming from the police radios he always monitored while driving. The "Golden Oldies" on KQQL 108 sounded like white noise.

Lee needed to think clearly, but his mind could not sort out the noise from inside the car with the flood of thoughts that haunted him.

As he drove, he never noticed time or miles passing. He rehearsed every detail of the case and all that had happened. Then he rehearsed it again. His tenacious drive to catch Cunanan sent him deeper into reflection. The sense that he had already lost control of the case and it now owned him particularly nagged him.

He reminded himself that even if he had specific information about Cunanan partying in New York, Lee knew nothing about the city. He had no connection to the place. And there was no evidence whatsoever to even prove that he had stayed in the Big Apple. As far as Lee knew, Cunanan could have been in Philadelphia, Boston or even Rhode Island. All he knew for sure was that Cunanan had been on I-295 in New Jersey, and that he had killed William Reese in a New Jersey cemetery. He knew that Cunanan had, for a time, driven a red pick up truck, and even at that, he had no way of knowing if he had already ditched the truck – maybe even killed someone else who as yet lay dead without anyone having found the body. The options were too numerous to consider, and he could only rule out a few of them.

He knew that Cunanan had driven a stolen Lexus for five days, a car listed on the NCIC, but not a single sighting had been reported. Now he probably drove a red pick-up truck, but no one had spotted him. He knew that Cunanan had to be driving carefully to avoid attention, but hoped that some calamity – a fender bender, being run off the road, even a flat tire or running out of gas – would lead some cop somewhere to spot the truck.

"He's a genius, so smart, and it'll be really hard to find him," Cunanan's friends claimed.

"BS!" Lee said aloud. "If he was so smart, why did he kill? So he's got a 160 IQ. I'm smarter than him, and I'm just a dumb cop."

"He's always the life of the party. Rich and smart," they'd say.

"Well he isn't rich. He isn't smart and he's a no-good murderer," Lee told himself. "This just isn't the same guy they knew."

He kept driving, thoughts assaulting his mind like the fast firing of a machine gun.

He noticed that he was already on the Burnsville Bridge, a long expanse of I-35W that crosses an industrial area and the Minnesota River. No other cars were to be seen.

His brain's hyperactivity left him feeling as though he was on a roller coaster at the Valley Fair Amusement Park a few miles west, in Shakopee. That ride had a 14-story drop followed by ups, downs, twists and turns; just the way he felt. And worse, he could not stop the tumbling feeling. He pulled off the highway, stopped and turned off all his police radios, silencing the incessant clatter.

"What the hell is going on?" he asked himself. "I can't survive this thing if it stays like this all the time. This is my case and I'm going to work it methodically," he promised himself. "This guy is just another fugitive!!"

Say what he would, he just could not shake the frustration.

After a few moments, he reached down and hit the scan button on his FM radio, finding KPRM 99.5 FM, Minnesota Public Radio, the classical music station. He heard violins; smooth, soothing violins playing in perfect harmony, leading an orchestra that itself seemed calmed by their sweet melodies. The tough cop, the first-through-the-door cop, the bird-watching cop, remembered how Sheriff Howard Urness, his father, used to take out his own violin and play soothing music to help him relax.

In those few seconds, as the rich tones of a great orchestra played across his senses, he regained mental control.

No matter how crazy or demanding this case had started, Lee knew that he had to remain calm. He could not allow Andrew Cunanan to control his life or create the kind of barbarous mayhem for him that he had done for Trail, Madson, Miglin and Reese.

"No, no matter how crazy this gets, I am in control, not you, you son-of-a-bitch," Lee said, as he pulled back out on the highway.

"Give me two weeks on the outside, and your luck runs out and you're mine," he said just before pulling into his garage.

He slept soundly for the next few hours, ready to rise early and win the battle against his "lucky, not smart" foe.

The sad truth was, had Cunanan been playing the lottery, he would have won the jackpot that weekend. His string of luck continued to play out for several more weeks, leaving Lee Urness feeling like the poor slob who just spent the food money on the Powerball Lottery, and then had to face an angry wife.

Sunday no day of rest

Lee managed to sleep until 8:00 a.m. on Sunday. His pager woke him. Paul Covington reported on his Philadelphia leads. None of them checked out. Cunanan had not been in any Pennsylvania bar, at least none reported by an America's Most Wanted caller.

After getting dressed, Lee made a round of calls. First to Emilio Blasse, but Blasse still babysat William Norman and his date. Nothing had happened.

Then he called Chicago. Next, he called the West Coast. There were no sightings and worse, from Lee's perspective, Cunanan had not tried calling anyone, at least anyone on the FTF list. Lee had felt sure that having Cunanan's phone book so early on in the case would have been the key to catching him – crooks always call someone. Then again, maybe Cunanan could not remember the phone numbers and needed that book.

Goes south

Andrew Cunanan drove south along the freeways that parallel the Atlantic seacoast. No highway or other law enforcement officer saw him, or that red Chevy pick-up truck.

He finally arrived in Miami Beach.

The small city of 7.1 square miles sat on an island accessible by bridges from the west and north. Less than a mile wide from east to west, its north-south streets had been overbuilt and bustled with thousands of people who crowded its narrow sidewalks. Even the wider streets, like Washington or Collins, were jammed with people any time of the day or night, and the traffic flowed slowly.

During May, the tourists had begun to disappear, to leave the city to its 85,000 permanent residents. During the tourist season, the population swelled by 250,000 each week, and all of this was policed by a sworn force of about 350 Miami Beach officers. Since most of the party action occurred south of 15th Street, most police action focused on that area, called South Beach.

Fabulous restaurants sat next to family restaurants; bars next to coffee shops and bakeries. Upscale clothing stores stayed open late, as did stores for the huge number of middle-income people who visited. Every toy imaginable, including some of the most exotic sex toys for both genders, lined the shelves of dozens of stores.

The 75° to 80° winter days had already begun to give way to the sweltering 80s and 90s of summer by the time Cunanan arrived. Unlike murderers who had to hide out, the nearby Atlantic Ocean, accessible by hundreds of boats and yachts for rent, offered residents and tourists a break from summer's oppressive heat and place into which Cunanan could easily blend without being noticed.

Under any other circumstances, Cunanan could have attended a continuous party, choosing from hundreds of anonymous sex partners. But on May 11, he needed sleep. First, though, he went to Joe's Sporting Goods on Collins, in the South Beach area, and bought a couple of clothing items. In that area sat numerous hotels and he crashed at one for the night.

While he rested, a New Haven, Connecticut man contacted the FBI. He felt sure he had spotted Cunanan that day in Misquamicut, Rhode Island at Pattie's Restaurant. He had followed Cunanan outside and saw him drive away in a red Ford Taurus. Cunanan wore a long green raincoat, had short hair and a two-day growth of beard. Lee sent agents out immediately to check the lead. After all, Rhode Island sat just hours from Pennsville.

While FBI agents and local police officers chased phantom leads that weekend and on Monday, May 12, Andrew Cunanan searched for affordable long-term lodging, at least long-term enough to complete his deadly plan. He found the Normandy Plaza Hotel near 71st Street and Collins later that day.

Mirian Hernandez, the desk clerk, checked him in. He used the name "Kurt Demars." Demars had been a close California friend of Cunanan's. The hotel was an extended stay hostelry and he paid in cash. He climbed a half flight of stairs to room 105 and crashed, somehow able to put out of his mind the horror he had created for four men and their families, and the disruption of the lives of hundreds of cops chasing him. In the weeks ahead, he moved two more times in the building, eventually settling in Room 322.

As he walked into the room, he saw the dingy, outdated and worn surroundings, unlike the five-star hotels he preferred. A small sink, refrigerator and stove sat along one wall, meaning he could conserve cash by buying food and preparing it in the room. A 13" color TV provided entertainment, which he would soon supplement with newspapers, magazines and books. He purchased some books at a nearby discount store, and used the public library that sat just a few blocks north of the hotel.

The three-story pink building was bordered on the west by Collins Avenue, on the north by the Crystal Court, another rundown hotel, and on the east by the beach. On the south lay yet another hotel, waiting remodeling. A small, grassy backyard surrounded by the hotels on the north and south provided some refuge from the throngs cruising Collins Avenue.

Now in the room, Cunanan stuck the Taurus pistol under his pillow, laying there, pondering what he would do if the cops broke down his door. He had six bullets left, and he could take a couple with him before they ended his miserable life.

He needed time to plan his next move, and he needed sex, readily available to him in South Beach, just five miles away, where thousands of anonymous gays would welcome him warmly, oblivious to the deadly danger into which they put themselves.

Chapter 20 ~ Cunanan, the Chameleon

Lee Urness needed to get inside Andrew Cunanan's head, to think like him, to be able to simulate his actions and reactions. In order to be successful at this, Lee learned everything he could about the man.

Andrew Cunanan had many friends and a vast stable of sex partners, many of them anonymous. Those who knew him over a period of time variously described him as fun loving, the life of the party, good looking, witty, intelligent, caring, boastful, occasionally boorish, and self-centered. He loved dropping names of famous people he knew or places he had been. No one knew for sure if he really knew those people whose names he dropped so freely, or had visited those places.

He claimed to be an heir of or related to wealthy people. He demonstrated extravagance in the clothes he wore and he loved to pick up a dinner tab that sometimes exceeded $1,000. He paid for pricy hotel rooms for one-night or weekend sexual romps. He maxed out all his credit cards.

He told various stories about what he claimed to be his immensely successful business ventures. At one time, he said he had an importing business. At another time, he held property. To others, he had a manufacturing or parking lot business.

Even after he began murdering people, many of his friends continued to believe his stories and to defend him. They could not believe that their handsome intelligent friend Andrew would ever purposely hurt anyone, at least outside of an S&M bedroom.

No one knew the real Cunanan, not during his life nor following his death. It is likely that he did not even know himself.

He had very little contact with his mother, father, or his siblings, save his sister Gina. He had no job, no home and no property. Yet he had friends, seemingly everywhere.

FBI and FTF agents interviewed dozens of Cunanan's closest friends and relatives on more than one occasion. Lee eventually culled this list of close contacts to 16 key people. If Cunanan would have called anyone, these were the most likely.

The people with whom he fraternized or shared a bed sincerely believed the stories that they related to the agents, which, taken in their entirety, showed Cunanan to be a chameleon who adapted to each person, or the circumstance of his life at the moment – the profile of an out-of-control pathological liar.

The following are some of his friends, family members and lovers, and their comments about Cunanan.

William Norman

William Norman was rich. He lived in a million dollar San Diego-area home formerly owned by Lincoln Aston, whom someone had bludgeoned to death in 1995 (much the same way that Jeffrey Trail had died). Norman also owned a home in Phoenix, Arizona.

Norman met Andrew in July of 1994 while Cunanan had been renting a room from a Rancho Bernardo woman and her daughter. Cunanan worked part time at the Thrifty Pharmacy across the street from the boarding house. After a long period of dating, Norman invited Cunanan to move in with him during August of 1995.

Cunanan told Norman that his parents lived in Rancho Santa Fe. He said that his wealthy father had retired and lived part of the year near San Francisco, while the rest of his family lived in New Jersey. Cunanan claimed that his parents threw him out of the house because he was gay.

Norman believed that Cunanan's parents sent him money to keep him going, and that he supplemented that with his pharmacy job. Cunanan drove an older Cadillac, claiming his father had given it to him, and he told Norman that he had successfully completed a drug and alcohol treatment program.

Norman paid Cunanan to live with him at a rate similar to what he could have earned at a professional job – claimed to be $4,000 a month. He wanted Cunanan available so that they would be free to travel at Norman's whim. They traveled together all across continental America, and to Hawaii, Florence and France. They were together nearly every day while Norman was at home.

On Cunanan's birthday, Norman gave him a Cartier watch and later, a new 1996 Infiniti valued at $30,000.

In July of 1996, Norman found a note from Cunanan that said Cunanan was leaving him, that they were "too different." The abruptness of the dissolution shocked Norman who claimed he had no forewarning.

Norman then feared that Cunanan would file a paternity lawsuit against him. Unwilling to take a chance that a court might hand Cunanan a huge monetary settlement, Norman wrote Cunanan a $10,000 check as severance pay.

Since their split, Norman occasionally ran into Cunanan at parties or on trips. He had heard that Cunanan planned to move to San Francisco.

He did know that Cunanan planned to leave San Diego in April, and had talked with him by phone early during the week of April 21. But he claimed he had not attended any of the going-away parties.

Cunanan called Norman on Sunday, April 27, before he killed Jeff Trail, to tell him "good-bye." Cunanan claimed he was moving to San Francisco.

Norman told Lee Urness on May 9 that they knew no one in Miami, but in June, he told an FBI agent he had a hunch Cunanan might head there once he left New York City.

Carter Peterson

Peterson knew him as Andrew DeSilva. Cunanan told Peterson that he had been born in Israel and came to the United States with his uncle and aunt. He said that his wealthy father owned a parking lot business in San Diego, and that he lived with his family in Rancho Santa Fe. Cunanan claimed to have a sister living in Minneapolis, another in Chicago and a brother in Hawaii.

Cunanan said he planned to move to San Francisco where he had left behind a wife and daughter.

Peterson said that Cunanan was deep into sadomasochism. Peterson's Chicago friends also told him that Lee Miglin was deep into S&M, a never-established fact that continues to be aggressively denied by the Miglin family.

Peterson saw that after Norman and Cunanan split up, after Cunanan sold his Infiniti, he seemed "somehow different." Peterson felt that Cunanan had money problems.

Once Cunanan began killing people, Peterson feared for his own life because he had taken Cunanan's place with William Norman.

Thomas Robinson

Robinson knew him as Andrew DeSilva. DeSilva was a well-known name of a wealthy California family, although Cunanan had no ties to them, other than stealing their name.

Robinson met Cunanan at the University of California, before Cunanan failed and left school. They also spent time together "socially."

Cunanan claimed he lived in Rancho Bernardo and worked at the Thrifty Pharmacy – the truth. He also claimed his family lived in Rancho Santa Fe – a lie.

Cunanan told Robinson that he had moved out of Norman's house because the man was tight with his money. So he moved in with Erik Erickson.

In 1997, Cunanan told Robinson that he was bored with his life and so, had decided to move to San Francisco. Robinson believed, instead, that Cunanan was running out of money and yet wanted to maintain his lavish lifestyle. He had sold the Infiniti, and spent the "$15,000" Cunanan said Norman had given him. The lack of money left him stressed. Finally, Cunanan claimed he had found a San Francisco apartment and felt excited about moving there to live with an attorney.

Robinson, along with three others, attended a going-away dinner with Cunanan on April 24 at California Cuisine. Cunanan told them that night that he was flying to Minneapolis and then later, would move to San Francisco. In Minneapolis, Cunanan said he planned to see his sister and Jeffrey Trail. Robinson was to pick him up at the San Diego airport on Tuesday, April 30. Then Cunanan would leave for San Francisco.

Before flying to Minneapolis, Cunanan gave Robinson his suits, claiming he planned to purchase a new wardrobe. Cunanan had also given away his cashmere overcoat to Dennis Richards*, and gave his Cartier watch to yet another lover.

On or about April 30, three days after killing Trail, Cunanan called Robinson and left a simple message: "Thomas, this is Andrew, I'll call you later." He never did.

Investigators in New Jersey found a picture of Thomas Robinson that Cunanan had left in the Lexus. In it, Robinson stood in front of a pick-up truck. Robinson claimed it was the only copy he had ever made and that Cunanan had taken it. Since it was the only copy of the picture in existence, it offered positive proof to New Jersey police of Cunanan's presence at the New Jersey murder scene.

Robinson considered himself to be one of Cunanan's closest and best friends. He simply could not believe Cunanan would hurt or murder anyone.

Garth Davidson*

Attorney Garth Davidson practiced in San Diego, and he met Cunanan during the spring of 1993. He noticed that Cunanan's friends were high class, and that he was smart and witty.

Cunanan claimed to be Jewish and born into a wealthy family. Cunanan seldom carried cash, but used credit cards frequently, and Davidson believed that his money came from a trust fund.

As far as Davidson knew, Cunanan met William Norman during the summer of 1995.

Davidson once bought an airline ticket for Cunanan for a trip together to Vancouver, but he bought it in the name of Andrew DeSilva. Cunanan told him to get it reissued under the name, "Cunanan." While in Vancouver, Davidson saw the name "Cunanan" written on the hotel bill printout. He dismissed this discrepancy believing that it was something a wealthy person had to do to protect his identity.

In 1996, Cunanan told Davidson that he planned to move to San Francisco and work for Dennis Richards in his financial services business. Cunanan said that he broke up with William Norman because the man was not giving him enough money.

During early April of 1997, Cunanan called Davidson and said he had reserved a $650 a night hotel room in San Francisco. He wanted Davidson to join him there. Cunanan claimed that David Madson would be there as well, and Cunanan wanted to visit his daughter while they were there. Cunanan had previously shown him a picture of a little girl that had been taken in front of an expensive home.

Davidson agreed to go to San Francisco for a "one nighter," and met Cunanan at the hotel. Madson never came. The hotel rejected Cunanan's credit cards. The two men went instead to the Mandarin Hotel where Davidson paid the bill. Cunanan wanted Davidson to meet him in Los Angeles the following weekend, but planned to stay with his daughter in San Francisco for a few days.

On April 24, Davidson went to California Cuisine to meet Cunanan for the going-away dinner, but was surprised to find three other men there as well.

Once Cunanan began his trail of violence, Davidson feared for his own life. Cunanan knew Davidson's daily routine. Davidson also feared that news of his relationship with Cunanan would force him to be "outed," a fact he feared nearly as much as Cunanan's violence.

Neil Stoker*

Stoker met Cunanan in 1992 and they became fast friends, though never sex partners. Cunanan called Stoker his little brother and invited him to the

April 24 going away party at California Cuisine. At that time, Cunanan said he was moving to San Francisco.

Stoker claimed that Cunanan bragged about hiring "boys" for sex, and that if he ever contracted AIDS he would kill himself. Cunanan told him that he was a part-time pharmacist. Stoker knew that Cunanan used Vicadin and may snort cocaine, but never drank to excess.

Cunanan claimed he visited friends in Vancouver, San Francisco and Cabo San Lucas, Mexico.

Tyler Dorgan*

Dorgan met Cunanan in 1991 and they had been occasional friends since then. He last saw him during the week of April 17. He knew Cunanan as De-Silva until recent weeks. Sometimes Cunanan used the name "Andy," and at other times, "Drew." Though they did not date, they did have dinner together often. Cunanan told Dorgan that he was a Spanish Jew from the Philippines.

Once he saw Cunanan with a young girl who he claimed to be his niece from Sacramento. Dorgan heard that Cunanan spent that April 17 night with a lover who described Cunanan as "weird when it came to sexual encounters." Though Dorgan said he and Cunanan were casual friends, he described his violent actions as "weird and uncharacteristic."

Cunanan told Dorgan that his parents provided him with money, and that he had served in the Israeli navy. He had also heard rumors that Cunanan had been involved in the murder of Lincoln Aston and another gay man, Robert Johnson, whom he thought was from San Diego.

He saw Cunanan as very intelligent, a man who knew a lot. He never saw Cunanan drink alcohol, though he did see him smoke an occasional cigarette.

Gary Elly*

Elly said he had last seen Cunanan during April 18-20, 1997. Cunanan told him that he had been in Cap Farrar, France and New York recently, but Elly never believed his claims of worldwide travel.

Cunanan told Elly that he was a college student, and Elly provided him a place to stay off and on for three years. Cunanan liked everything first class, so Elly believed he would not live in a pick up truck or in the back woods. He saw Cunanan as an underachiever.

Elly believed that Cunanan had family in Philadelphia and heard that his father had a shady legal past, somehow related to the troubles of the Marcos family.

Elly said that Cunanan was intelligent and charming, with a great understanding of the arts and an absurd sense of humor.

Cunanan told Elly that he had a relationship with an older gay man from Chicago, but Elly never knew the name of the person.

In a prophetic statement, Elly said he believed that Cunanan would never allow himself to be arrested. He believed he would commit suicide, rather than face life in prison.

Will Evert

Evert knew Cunanan through Laura Koski, Evert's wife. He had met Cunanan many times and saw him as a mysterious kind of person, and a pathological liar.

Cunanan told him the reason he spent so much money was to offset high taxes, and that he was in the real estate business.

Cunanan told Evert that he had designed and built movie sets with Duke Miglin, Lee Miglin's son. Cunanan claimed they were building sets for another "Jaws" movie. Cunanan preferred wearing gold watches and expensive leather jackets.

Laura Koski

She and her husband, Will Evert, were close friends of Cunanan's and he often stayed with them. Cunanan told her that he saw them as a normal couple who could put stability in his life.

Cunanan told her he was in the real estate development business in San Diego, and she said his house was all white inside, with a lot of marble. She said that Cunanan was infatuated with blond men like Duke Miglin, and he often prostituted himself to make money.

Garfield Strom*

Strom knew Cunanan for seven years. They dined together whenever Cunanan came to San Francisco. Strom and Cunanan talked about S&M sex, and Cunanan often talked about latex masks and a "cock cage." Strom never had sex with Cunanan, though Cunanan did make a pass at him the last time they met in April 1997.

Cunanan told Strom that he had just bought a company with 60-70 employees. The company, Cunanan claimed, built sets for Hollywood movie companies, but did so from Mexico because the worker laws were more lax.

Strom saw Cunanan as a person who would never get his hands dirty, who would get manicures and pamper himself. Cunanan told Strom that he came from New Jersey and had attended Choate Rosemary School in Connecticut.

Dennis Richards

Richards was the President of Horton Financial Group, a financial services business based in San Diego. Cunanan told him that he was moving to San Francisco where he had an apartment, many friends, relatives, a daughter and ex-wife. Richards had met Jeffrey Trail through Cunanan.

At one time, Richards offered Cunanan a job at Horton Financial Group, but Cunanan refused.

The last time he saw Cunanan he had acted normally.

Abner Paulson*

Paulson, a rich Detroit resident, met Cunanan in 1995 through his long friendship with William Norman. Norman had been Paulson's Detroit neighbor for more than 30 years before moving to San Diego. Norman had brought Cunanan with him to a get-together Paulson held at a house he kept in East Hampton, New York. Paulson knew him as DeSilva.

DeSilva told Paulson that he had been born in Israel but grew up in Connecticut, then attended a New England prep school. DeSilva claimed also to have attended a prestigious Connecticut college.

Paulson had understood that at one time DeSilva had been married to the daughter of the Chief of the Israeli Secret Service. Eventually, Paulson came to believe that DeSilva exaggerated many of his claims.

Ned Williams*

Williams moved to San Diego after graduating from college in 1993. He lived there three years and met Cunanan the first day he arrived. They became close friends, seeing each other practically every day, but never became lovers, Williams claimed.

He knew that Cunanan lived with a rich boyfriend who he believed was in his late 70s. He had a hard time believing that Cunanan prostituted himself. As far as he knew, Cunanan and Jeff Trail had never had sex.

Williams saw Cunanan as a nice guy who never gave the appearance of being easily agitated or violent. And he never saw him use any illegal drugs, save for Valium. He suspected Cunanan used crystal methamphetamine because it was the drug of choice within the gay community, and that Cunanan always seemed shaky and hyperactive, able to stay awake long hours for days on end.

Williams remembered Cunanan as always carrying a roll of money, and paying for dinner and drinks, and that he took many airplane trips. Cunanan told him he had a friend who owned an expensive New York City condominium.

During his last night in San Diego, Williams gave Cunanan his home phone number at his new east coast residence. He told Cunanan to call him if he ever came to town.

Morrie Roberts*

Cunanan told Roberts that he had been in the Israeli Army and was the son of a wealthy family. Roberts knew him as DeSilva, and graduated with him from The Bishops School.

Al Miller*

Miller knew Cunanan as DeSilva, and the two of them had planned an April trip together to Australia. A third man planned to join them. Cunanan then planned to go to Minnesota to take care of some business, and afterward, fly on to London.

Wayne Patrick*

Patrick had met Cunanan in San Diego, but moved to Minneapolis during February of 1997. Cunanan told him he planned to go to Mardis Gras in Sydney and then on to Amsterdam.

Wally Moberg*

Moberg tended bar at the West Coast Production Company, and considered himself a good friend of DeSilva's. Cunanan bought him cologne and a camera for one of his birthdays. Cunanan told Moberg that he had served in the Israeli army.

Moberg had dated Jeff Trail for a time and considered Cunanan one of his mutual friends, along with Lincoln Aston.

Cunanan told Moberg that he dated an older wealthy woman who did not know he was gay. Cunanan had planned to marry her, but she broke it off.

Rob Ketherton*

Ketherton knew Cunanan for about 18 months. He worked at Flicks. (Flicks website defines itself thusly: "FLICKS [flicks] *noun*; 1. a place to find the hottest guys and girls in the area. 2. where you can see the boys in their wet undies on Saturdays. 3. a cool place to just kick it...")

Cunanan told Ketherton that he was going to San Francisco because he was "HIV Positive" and he did not want his San Diego friends to see him suffer.

Ketherton heard from others that Cunanan had an ex-wife and daughter in San Francisco.

Cunanan spoke fluent German, French and Turk. He thought Cunanan might use heroin.

Candace Parrott

Parrott was Jeffrey Trail's sister. Cunanan told her and Trail's family that the Cunanan family lived in Rhode Island and that he was a friend of the Kennedy's, in fact, he planned to attend a Kennedy family reunion.

Cunanan told her that he had lived in Israel. She saw him as a rich, well-bred socialite.

Kurt Demars

Demars met Cunanan during the summer of 1996. Cunanan told him that he had been a suspect in the murder of Lincoln Aston.

For a time, Demars planned to move into an apartment with Cunanan, who claimed that he had worked for the University of California system – but had not worked since 1992.

Cunanan said he had saved up enough money to buy a parking lot or garage.

Cunanan had a San Francisco friend named Laura and he loved $600 a night hotels. Demars thought Cunanan was a drug dealer.

Frank Stiles*

Stiles lived in Pasadena. He and Cunanan spent time together during March of 1997.

Cunanan claimed he and his mom were close friends of Debby Harry, a singer with the band, "Blondie." In fact, Stiles claimed they vacationed together.

Ken Erickson*

Erickson met Cunanan while they were both young kids. They graduated together from The Bishops where both of them ran track and were good friends.

During those younger years, Cunanan always talked like a child of a wealthy family. Cunanan claimed that his Pilipino dad was a stockbroker who specialized in tax shelters. He claimed his mother to be a homemaker.

Cunanan told Erickson that he modeled his life after Sebastian Flight, a character in the Evelyn Wagh book, *A Bride's Head Revisited.* Flight eventually self-destructed, both physically and mentally.

Erickson moved to Boston to attend college and settled there, but he did go home to visit during December 1995. There he met up with Cunanan as they joined other high school friends for dinner. Cunanan picked up the dinner tab for everyone, and later, he bought expensive wine and cigars for the group. They partied at William Norman's house, but Cunanan never told Erickson he was prostituting himself to the rich man.

During high school, Erickson had been convinced that Cunanan was gay, but he had never hit on him, his brother or any of his friends.

The last time Erickson saw him, Cunanan claimed he would be traveling to France on vacation and while there, would be dealing in European art.

Eleanor Schillaci

Eleanor's late husband had been the brother of Maryann, Cunanan's mother. Aunt Eleanor recalled that Cunanan first announced to the family that he was gay during a 1983 wedding they had all attended.

She had last seen him during 1990 when she visited the family in Rancho Bernardo, California. It bothered her that Cunanan had become extremely spoiled and self-centered. She noticed that Cunanan slept in the master bedroom, relegating his father to a living room couch and Maryann to the guest bedroom.

Jackie Michels*

Michels was a lesbian activist who called the FBI about Cunanan. She claimed that a gay male friend had lived in Cunanan's condo building and that Cunanan was a "gym bunny," addicted to working out. He did this because at age 27 he was three years past his prime as a gay prostitute. Taking steroids and bodybuilding would make him more popular and, therefore, "employable." She saw him as a "queen desperate for attention."

Michels said Cunanan used cocaine and ecstasy. He preferred establishments where he would be more likely to meet older gay men, like "The Numbers." Cunanan also met men at weekly circuit parties, a series of clandestine bashes for high profile rich gays who sought the services of expensive male prostitutes. Especially popular for circuit parties were "The Black" in San Francisco, "The White" in Palm Springs and "Labor Day" in Los Angeles.

From police working papers

Police investigators interviewed dozens of others who knew Cunanan. From these, they compiled a profile of "Claims made" by Cunanan; all were lies.

He had property in foreign safe deposit boxes and bank accounts that amounted to millions of dollars, except they had been confiscated by federal agents.

At one time he arranged to have someone (unidentified) killed.

He was a computer consultant whose work often took him on business trips across America.

He once threw someone out of a car after having sex with him.

He attended Yale as an undergraduate and the University of California at San Diego as a history major.

His wealthy family lived in the Philippines and that was the source of his own money. His parents lived on a large sugar plantation they owned there.

So who was Andrew Cunanan?

None of Cunanan's friends really knew him. He kept the real Cunanan hidden from them, telling them only what he wanted them to hear, or what would get him what he wanted. To some he was a brilliant and successful businessman; to others, a great sex partner. To still others, he was a drug dealer or into some form of illegal business activity that made them both excited and wary.

None of them knew the truth about his father Modesto, who abandoned his family after his own business failures, and moved to the Philippines. They knew nothing of his mother, who had moved to Peoria, Illinois, and who struggled with her own mental demons.

Lee had learned this about Cunanan: The pathological liar never had a wife or a child. He never had full time work or a career. All he had was his sexy body and his glib mind, and once his body began to give in to the rigors of age and the abuse of an overactive gay sex life – even at 27 years old – he began to lose his edge. He became a time bomb, set off by depression and disappointment. He was a nothing, but he became a vicious killer, a chameleon who remained at large, and wanted to leave his mark on the world so as never to be forgotten.

Chapter 21 ~ Apprehension about apprehending

Lee willed himself out of bed just before 5:30 a.m. Monday, truly the middle of the night for a man who preferred crawling *into* bed at that time. He could not recall a single time during his long career where he felt so exhausted at such an early point in a case. He threw a glance out the window and saw that it was still dark. "Ugh!" he grunted.

As soon as his eyes opened, he began searching his mind for new answers, but his head felt empty, as though filled with stale air that needed to be bled off before he could think clearly. His body ached from the stiffness of fatigue, and he felt far older than his 51 years. Yet his will to win this challenge of wits with the killer Cunanan quickly pushed him past exhaustion and into the kitchen.

One cup of coffee, one cigarette, no time for bird watching and a muffin in hand sent him motoring out of the driveway before 6:00 a.m. He meant to beat the traffic. More so, he meant to call New Jersey exactly at 8:00 a.m. Eastern Daylight Time.

The FTF office sat perfectly quiet as Lee walked in just after 6:30. He stared blindly at his cluttered desk that overflowed with paperwork, a thick stack of yellow phone slips awaiting return calls and a pile of Andrew Cunanan wanted posters. The floor near his desk was strewn with notes, reports and files, with but a thin clear path leading to his chair. He saw that the desks of the other agents were not much better.

He walked to the storeroom and made a fresh pot of coffee, all the time strategizing his day. He resolved to set his *own* agenda, working methodically, calmly, and not letting Cunanan control him.

He stared blindly out of one of the two small windows into the empty parking lot. The city had just begun to come to life. He had no bird feeder to watch, but the chaos and clamor of cardinals seemed, to him, much like the snare of cars, trucks, buses, and people who moved hurriedly on their journeys just outside the window. He reminded himself that Andrew Cunanan could not possibly be among that bustle of people.

He got a cup of coffee, went out back and stood on the landing, smoking a cigarette, all the while urging the clock to move more quickly toward 7:00 a.m.

He had decided to pull his team together once he finished his round of phone calls, and so, reviewed a mental list of the issues he wanted to address.

He pictured his team sitting around the office, and it drew him back in time to his childhood days at the Douglas County Jail and Urness family home.

You call this home?

Twenty-one year old Ole Urness had left Norway and stepped on American soil in 1861, promptly enlisting in the Union Army. In 1867, he left the army and began farming in Douglas County, located in West Central Minnesota. In 1876, Douglas County citizens elected Ole as their sheriff, a position he held until 1888.

Ole's son Bennie, also a farmer, became Douglas County Sheriff in 1931, and served until 1959. Bennie's sons Howard and Luther both served as his deputies. Upon Bennie's retirement, Howard immediately ran for sheriff and easily won the election, holding the job until he retired in 1974.

A rural Minnesota sheriff's job sharply contrasted with that of urban sheriffs. The job came with a family residence in the aging county jail building shared with the prisoners, surrounded by the simple law enforcement equipment of the day. Use of the jail as a home was considered a benefit of a job that paid only a modest income, though it demanded a lot.

Lee was 13 years old when his dad became sheriff. The odd circumstances created by living in a house that held a jail fascinated Lee. Douglas County seldom produced violent or dangerous criminals, but it had a steady stream of local miscreants and wrongdoers incarcerated for short amounts of time, or held over until delivered to one of the state's prisons. Big city crooks loved to ply their trade in the area's small towns, and provided most of the real excitement at the jail. Lee spent hours playing cards with the prisoners, albeit through the bars.

Each morning he helped Maxine, his mother, serve meals to the prisoners, meals she was expected to provide as the sheriff's wife. The county paid her at the rate of $2.50 per day per prisoner back in the 1960s, and that meager sum included the cost of the food as well. She, too, did the prisoner's laundry and kept clean what they left soiled in the musty old jail cells. Cleaning the cells also fell on her.

The county built the old jail and sheriff's residence in 1890. The block-sized two-story brick building had bars on the windows toward the back on one side. These contrasted with the delicate drapes that "guarded" the other windows. A side door opened into the Sheriff's Office and off that, a main door opened into the jail. Inside the jail sat four men's cells in two tiers with their steel bars and hard steel bunks. There was one woman's cell, a one-room affair – and they seldom had women "customers."

Their most common residents were drunks, men known around town who on one day would viciously curse out Sheriff Urness as he booked them, only to beg for forgiveness the next morning when they were sober. Lee marveled at his father's patience with those drunks. Howard always treated them with dignity and respect, no matter what they said to him.

The jail always smelled like disinfectant and rotten cigarette smoke. Those prisoners who stayed around a while got one bath a week in a big cast iron tub set inside a small room. The Sheriff would send them in one at a time, lock them up and give them 15 minutes to get clean before he would march them back to their cells. Once in a while Lee had to help delouse the jail. Being the child of a rural sheriff brought added duties, not privileges.

All the rooms in the living quarters were oversized and comfortable. The huge jailhouse kitchen, with its 10-foot tall walls and its tin ceiling tiles, served as the hub of activity. A large, old Formica-covered stainless steel table sat in the middle of the room on a plain, well-worn linoleum floor. The stainless steel tube chairs with their cracked red vinyl padded cushions and backs sat in disarray around the table.

A huge teletype machine sat on a table near the wall by the window, and a one-channel police radio sat near it. A large microphone rested on top of a short steel mike-stand from which Sheriff Urness could dispatch either one of his two deputies. Or he might call them on one of the two phone lines provided by the county.

The Urness kitchen served as the de facto law enforcement center of Douglas County. Every waking hour, police officers from several jurisdictions sat around the kitchen table talking about active cases, telling stories about the "old days" or discussing county gossip, the kind that kept them all informed of potential problems – or a peaceful resolution of an old problem. These officers wanted to know what was going on in their jurisdictions. Lee sat in the corner and listened to a Minnesota Highway Patrolman, an Alexandria policeman, the local game warden, or the two sheriff's deputies talk with Sheriff Urness. Usually, the country attorney or one of the local judges would stop and chat awhile. At times, they were joined by an FBI or BCA agent.

And every day, Maxine's wifely duties included making sure the cops had their coffee and treats. And they had to be fresh. Even had store-bought goodies been available, she never could have afforded them on a sheriff's salary and the county had no donut budget.

Everything started with fresh coffee, but not just any coffee. She made Norwegian egg coffee, breaking fresh eggs over dry Hills Brothers coffee grounds. She added those grounds to cold water in a two-quart Norwegian coffee pot on which a rosemaling artist had hand-painted colorful flowers. This she sat on a burner turned up high. Once the water and coffee boiled, she turned off the burner and added cold water to the brew, forcing the grounds to the bottom so that she could pour out the fresh flavorful coffee into a large urn.

With the tasty Norwegian coffee, she served freshly baked chocolate chip cookies or homemade donuts. Especially popular were the donuts with fresh whole pitted prunes stuck in the hole.

The cops hardly noticed Maxine as they talked about the known crooks in the area, burglaries, domestic problems, troubled kids. They shared information about unsolved crimes and speculated on "whodunit." They talked about where crooks might be hiding and what they would do once they caught them. They speculated on the big city crooks that might come out to burglarize the small towns in Douglas County. During the summers, small horsepower motors were a favorite target of thieves, and always, the small town hardware and food stores.

Often the noisy teletype clanked out an alert, which Sheriff Urness pulled off and dealt with right away. With half the county's police forces sitting in the room, these alerts could get instant attention.

Lee loved these daily discourse and sat like a mouse in the corner, soaking it all in. He developed a deep kinship with the cops who helped his dad put away the bad guys, and loved the camaraderie of these simple and honest men. Howard Urness taught him much during his teen years about police work, but it was here at these daily gatherings where he learned the most, and it was in watching these men work together that he decided to be a cop.

"But don't get involved in politics," Howard warned him. "It's tough and you gotta run for reelection every four years. Move away and do something else."

Lee did move away, working as a deputy sheriff in Fillmore County south of the Twin Cities, before signing on with the Minnesota Bureau of Criminal Apprehension in 1972. At the BCA he did undercover narcotics work. This kept him in the field, moving from place to place, arresting hundreds of bad guys, leading teams, being the first in the door. The job demanded action, and it fit him perfectly. But just as with the Douglas County Sheriff, the job required cops working together, a valuable lesson he had learned in a kitchen years earlier.

For 44 years in a row, an Urness had served as the Douglas County Sheriff, and Grandpa Ole had served 12 years. Lee broke that string, taking his father's advice to avoid politics, choosing instead the world of a street cop. He never regretted it. Howard proudly pinned the badge on Lee when, at the age, of 21 a county clerk of court in Alexandria swore him in.

On Monday morning, May 12, 1997, in the midst of the most frustrating and challenging case he had ever handled, Lee smiled thinking about those old days, counting himself lucky to have learned such important lessons. He felt sure that this FTF group would have been just as happy as those Douglas County cops sitting around the kitchen table drinking Norwegian egg coffee, talking about how they were going to catch Cunanan. He wondered if any of them had ever enjoyed or appreciated a fresh prune donut.

New Jersey and a new friend

Finally, the clock rolled past 7:00 a.m., and he made the call to Cherry Hill, New Jersey, the office of FBI Agent Paul Murray.

"Agent Murray, this is Lee Urness, the case agent on the Andrew Cunanan case," he said as Murray came on the line.

"Earnest did you say?" Murray asked.

"No. Urn'-ess, like a coffee urn, which I am enjoying now. You got a cup?"

"Ready to go," Murray answered and within minutes, filled Lee in on his long FBI experience. Lee could tell by Murray's attitude and words that he was a street cop, not a paper-jockey, and he knew they would get along well. Murray worried more about putting bad guys away than dotting his "i's" and crossing his "t's," and Lee liked his sense of humor.

"This is my first homicide," Murray confessed. "The FBI is sending me a four inch thick manual on how to properly build a homicide case. I'll be sure to read it, after we catch the jerk," he laughed.

Murray had a loud and sometimes sarcastic laugh. Still, he was a serious man who kept a relaxed perspective on his cases. He felt confident that eventually they would catch Cunanan, even though they might take some heat during the days ahead. He was not used to the rush of media he witnessed at Fort Mott on Saturday nor had he yet experienced the crushing demands faced by Lee each day, but this attitude of doing police business in a routine manner appealed to Lee. They quickly became friends.

"I'm the Resident Agent in Cherry Hill, and it's a small shop. We sort of run ourselves," Murray explained.

"Where in the hell is Cherry Hill? Do you grow cherries there? What kind of a name for a town is that?" Lee asked, chiding him.

"Yeah, well they got lots of stuff going on here. But it's a nice place to live," Murray answered.

"Oh, sort of a retirement job?"

"Ah, no. That isn't me. Ask headquarters. They know my name around there," Murray answered trigger-like. Lee liked that.

"Whatever needs to get done we will get it done. Period!" Murray said, describing his work style. He could talk to the bosses after the fact if acting right away meant catching someone before they committed another crime. Protocol could wait.

Murray became Lee's first call each morning. He confided everything to Murray, and asked him dozens of questions, playing and replaying different scenarios. Murray gave him an objective perspective, unfettered by the constant pressure Lee faced each day in Minneapolis. So close did they become, that information Lee even kept from his own Minnesota agents he shared with Murray.

"Well, where is Cunanan?" Lee asked. "Did you find my truck yet?"

"Hey, this is a rough area out here. You got the whole east coast. And the area's remote, heavily wooded with thousands of vacation homes," Murray explained.

"Oh great. He might have already found a new place and killed the homeowners," Lee said. "He could be right in your back yard."

"Could be, but if he is, we'll find him. Now if he's at all suicidal, we got these quarries over in Pennsylvania. He could drive in there and sink to the bottom. They'd never find him," Murray chuckled.

"Oh yippee! I may be stuck with a dead-end case for the rest of my life. Well, as long as he doesn't kill anyone else," Lee said.

"Or he could drive off a cliff into the ocean and we'd be lucky to ever find him," Murray said, further needling Lee. "I hate to be the bearer of bad news, but this is all possible."

"Listen, I want you in charge of the entire east coast. Deal?" Lee asked.

"Sure, fine with me."

"Now, what can you tell me?" Lee asked.

"Like what?"

"Like, where is my pick-up truck?"

"I don't *know*, but we'll search every airport and parking lot and ramp within miles of here. If he ditched that truck, we'll find it," Murray said, as a starting point. "But if he headed to the woods, it's pretty rugged out there. Hard to find anyone intent on staying hidden."

"Hey, in Minnesota we sometimes use the National Guard for this. You could ask some troops to do a training mission in the woods and at the same time, they can comb the place for Cunanan," Lee suggested.

"I don't know how that'd work out. Having army guys tramping through the woods," Murray laughed. "I guess it might not be so dumb, though."

"How about the choppers? You can do aerial searches," Lee suggested.

"Yeah, that we might do. I'll call Quantico and see if we can get the FBI air force out," Murray said, referring to the agency's squadron of planes and helicopters. They always needed training missions.

"But you really need foot soldiers to check out those woods," Lee urged.

"I'll get it done. Every place will get checked," Murray answered. Lee's concern for detail appealed to Murray. He filled Lee in on the Lexus, the crime scene and the reports he had already reviewed about possible Cunanan sightings in the area.

"Oh, we got an America's Most Wanted call from some girls who said they saw him at a truck stop north of Pennsville," Lee said, giving Murray the details. "It's a cold lead, but should be checked out."

"Okay, will do."

"Maybe he just turned around and headed north, once he knew we were on to him," Lee said.

"Yeah, that's logical. But he could have gone in any direction. There's a lot of major cities nearby," Murray said. "There's a huge gay community in Boston; maybe he went there. What about New York?"

"Well, Emilio Blasse's got his poster plastered everywhere there," Lee laughed. "Don't know if he'd go there again. Of course, he could go to Canada."

As for Canada, Terry Thedford had told Lee that the Toronto FTF office was one of the best in the system. They were already checking every entry point. Lee had talked with the lead agent in Toronto and was assured of total cooperation.

The longer they talked, their more personal became their conversation.

"Bet you had a long weekend, too," Murray said.

"Yeah. It got real late with AMW and I coach my daughter's softball team, too. We had a triple-header Saturday and…"

"No kidding?" Murray interrupted. "I got a daughter who's a fast pitch star and I ump fast pitch…"

"Really? My kid's only 10 and throws 60 already."

"Fantastic…"

"But I had to run off and handle pages most of the day. I missed a lot of innings," Lee said.

"I understand. Well, maybe we can catch this creep right away and you can enjoy the rest of the season," Murray said.

"Say, you got a warrant?" Lee asked, getting back to cop business.

"The prosecutor says I don't have enough yet. I need some prints or something. We're waiting on the results from the Lexus."

"The guy has no criminal record, so the only print we have is the driver's license," Lee said.

"I heard, but how do you know it's even a real license and really his thumbprint?" Murray asked.

"True enough. Minneapolis never dusted for prints. Chicago PD doesn't want to share much. So we have to go with what we have for now."

"We have a shell casing and the slug," Murray said.

"Well, Minnesota has shell casings. The Jersey cops could compare them," Lee said.

"Yeah, the state police lab has the evidence," Murray answered.

"Have the Jersey lab get ahold of the Minnesota lab and see if there is anything that will help," Lee said, giving Murray the phone numbers.

Their talk ended with yet more personal coincidences. Both of their mothers were gravely ill and had just entered nursing homes. This added stress to their already stressful jobs, but they found that this common experience, like their children softball players, made it easier to work together.

"Listen, I'll be calling you first every day, and I need all your phone numbers," Lee said, writing them down as Murray listed them. "You call me any time of the day or night if something breaks," he told his new friend.

"You're on."

"And find my pick up truck," Lee teased.

"Sure. Today," Murray said, as they hung up. *Sheesh. This guy is obsessed with that truck,* Murray thought to himself as he reasoned where it might be.

Lee looked at the clock. They had talked for more than an hour, and though neither of them could say they got an inch closer to Cunanan during that time, they had made progress. At least Lee knew that if Cunanan still hid anywhere in or near New Jersey, Paul Murray would nail him soon, and that felt good.

Working with little information

As soon as he hung up with Murray, he called Terry Thedford in Chicago. As he had suspected, Thedford found no Andrew Cunanan locked up at Cook County Jail, and nothing else new had turned up. The Cunanan family members swore they had not heard from Andrew, and Thedford believed them. Chicago PD had yet to obtain a warrant, like New Jersey and Minneapolis, still lacking specific facts sufficient to put to rest the mind of a wary prosecutor.

"Okay, well keep me posted," Lee said as he hung up.

Jeanie Burns came into the FTF office and stared at Lee with a look of amazement.

"What?" Lee said, frowning at her.

"What are you doing here?" she asked, knowing Lee never got in before 9:00.

"Ah, this damn case…"

"I figured you caught him this weekend," she laughed as she walked to her desk.

"Yeah, we caught him all right," Lee muttered, only partly amused.

Lee noticed that the answering system had been jammed to capacity with messages and he assumed most came from newsies. He left the job of clearing them to Jeanie.

The others came in one by one. Lee studied their faces and body language just as much as hearing their words. All of them looked and sounded ready to get back to work.

By 9:00 a.m., everybody was there. Lee called them together – they settled for donuts from Mr. Donut, without egg coffee – but first he "busied out" all the phone lines, so the calls would roll over to the automatic answering system. He wanted no interruptions.

"All right folks, we gotta get our ducks in a row and catch this guy," Lee said as they began their meeting. "It's high gear time, and we really have to talk to everyone, no matter how crazy the leads." He threw a stack of faxes on the table. "These are from AMW Saturday night. There's about 60 of them here."

"Man, they sure screwed that up," Putzie said, referring to the fact the show had made no mention of the William Reese murder.

"Right, they taped it ahead of time," Lee said. "By the way, I say that the media killed Reese. I can't over-emphasize that we have to be careful what we say outside these walls, and no one, absolutely no one talks to the newsies. You send all that to me or directly to Rowley."

"AMW gonna do another show about it?" Lisa Davis asked.

"Let's catch the guy before then," Lee said.

"If they do, maybe we should have someone screen these calls," Putzie suggested as he picked through the leads, some of which appeared to be just plain crazy. "Can we send someone to their studio during the show?"

"Yeah, maybe. The producer begged me to come down, but there is no way. Maybe someone else from here can go," Lee said, writing himself a note. He knew an experienced agent would have a better chance of weeding out the hot leads than a TV producer or phone receptionist.

"Lisa and Putzie, you keep working on the financials. Something's got to turn up," Lee said. "And Lisa will prepare all the subpoena's," he said smiling at her as he lifted his leg up onto her desk. She pushed it off.

"Let's do an inventory on the calls and leads. Where are we on that?" Lee asked. They brought him up to date. They still had many leads called out to other jurisdictions that needed follow-up, plus the new leads from the AMW calls.

"When you talk with the cops remind them that Cunanan is gay, and maybe into S&M, but we can't let that interfere. We need the help of the gays to find him. And when you talk with gays, make sure they know that he does not discriminate; he'll kill gays or straights," Lee said.

"What's been done with the local gays, Constance Potter, I mean?" Gilkerson asked.

"Oh she's been a great help," Lee answered. "She's sending out stuff all across the country, and of course, letting everyone here in Minneapolis know about Cunanan."

"Now, remember that all leads have to come through me first as the case agent," Lee reminded them. "I have to be the clearinghouse. Someone's got to know everything that's going on, and that's me."

"Hope you can keep up with it," Vern Lee said.

"Yeah, well, it's already tough," Lee said.

"Have you thought about using Rapid Start?" Rickett asked.

"What's that?" Lee asked.

"It's the FBI's in-house data base, very sophisticated and self-contained. All computerized case management system," Rickett explained. "It'll help you track leads and set timelines, too. It'd be a great help."

"What's involved?"Lee knew that the FBI had paperwork for everything, and saw no need to add volumes of busy work when there was a bad guy to catch.

"You have to apply for it, but I can help you," Rickett answered.

"Okay, let's go for it, but I think we'll catch him soon with the media playing this as they are. Man, the guy's picture and story is on dozens of times a day. Someone's got to spot him. Maybe one more week, if we can keep on narrowing it down," Lee still believed. "Every fugitive calls somebody, and we have to find 'the' somebody. We have to keep closing down his window and keep him in the bubble so he can't go anywhere. Then he gets desperate and we get him."

Everyone agreed.

"Young Rickett's going to be my partner and will handle all the paperwork that has to be reported to the FBI, and in my absence he runs the case," Lee said.

"Now, I'm hoping we can wrap this up quick, but I've already cancelled my first trip to the cabin." He looked around the room noticing a few eyes dropping. "And we go nowhere until we catch this guy. Better get ready to cancel any vacation plans, just in case."

"Except me," Vern Lee said.

"Right. We *might* let you retire," Lee laughed.

Jeanie had cleared the answering system calls from earlier that morning and handed Lee and the others a stack of yellow call slips. Though many of the calls had come from newsies, others came from law enforcement officers in dozens of jurisdictions. They, too, had gotten AMW leads called in directly to them and needed information.

Before their meeting broke up, the team reviewed every detail of the case. This became their normal routine – digesting the data, reviewing the routine, reflecting on referrals, rejecting the bizarre, but holding on to and following up every remote possibility.

"Now, what have we missed? Where'd this guy go?" Lee asked yet again, as they reviewed all options. They all felt Cunanan had to be on the east coast somewhere, "but where?"

He released the team back to their workstations and they began plowing through their notes, call slips and reports. Jeanie again cleared the calls on the answering system.

"Okay people, I've got to go talk to Fred Tremper, but you keep working on these leads," Lee said as he stood to leave.

"Lee," Vern Lee said, "Jon Hermann on three. Thought you'd want to talk to him."

"Hermann the German. What's up?" Lee asked his friend as he pushed the flashing phone button.

"I'm heading over to Minneapolis to review MPD's case. Just wanted to let you know," the BCA agent said.

"Good."

"Anything new?"

"Naw, not really," Lee said, and told him some of the more bizarre stories. "Nothing worth much yet. New Jersey's got a top cop on it, though. Name's Paul Murray; our kind of guy."

"Okay. Well I'll call you if I find anything new at Minneapolis," Hermann said. And he did find something truly remarkable, something that nearly sent Lee through the roof. But not until after Lee faced his FBI boss.

Boss, we are doing everything

The Twin Cities metropolitan area is the fourteenth largest advertising market in the country, with a 1997 population of nearly 2.8 million people. It is home base for more than a dozen Fortune 500 companies, and has a long history of nurturing and growing innovative businesses, processes and products that become national and international mainstays.

More than 70 professional theaters are housed in the Twin Cities. Its professional orchestras are known worldwide. All of this mixed with its progressive politics and numerous higher education establishments created an attractive haven for gays and lesbians.

In the last three decades, bustling suburbs exploded with new growth as inner cities fought to survive, and since the 1980s, those cities had attracted a new kind of citizen, less tuned to Minnesota's Scandinavian and Germanic heritage. Minnesota had become a magnet for the down-and-out crowd; many crooks had moved in from Chicago, Gary, and Detroit. Likewise, a flood of new immigrants, especially Southeast Asian and Hispanic, struggled to understand Minnesota's laid-back culture. Many came because of Minnesota's easy and generous welfare programs.

Gangs had begun to flourish during the 1980s and violent crime increased well into the mid-1990s, though tough cops and statewide task forces worked hard to clamp down on the gang-bangers.

Still, Minnesota's communities remained relatively safe compared to the criminal climate in cities like New York, Chicago, or Miami. While New York City struggled with 2,000 homicides a year, during the mid-1990s, Minneapolis set a new record with just more than 100. Yet, Minnesota's cops were kept busy by a constant flow of criminal activity.

Minneapolis served as an FBI divisional office.

In 1997, Fred Tremper, a 30-year FBI veteran and a former FBI field agent ran Squad 6 at the Minneapolis FBI office. His unit focused on burglaries, but the FBI had also assigned him supervision of the Fugitive Task Force, an effort he fully supported.

Lee looked forward to talking to his FBI supervisor, even if he had only a few positive results to report. He knew that Tremper would deal straight with him.

Lee walked into the elevator at the Minneapolis building rented by the FBI, and pushed "10." Once there, he walked into the busy Squad 6 offices, moving past rows of government-issue desks in various levels of disarray. He heard the hum and clamor common to police offices as cops talked to informants, suspects or other cops while their fingers clicked away on computer keyboards.

As he walked toward Tremper's corner office, agents and their assistants sitting at those desks pelted him with questions that followed a predictable pattern. They all knew he was the case agent on the Cunanan chase.

"You get any good leads yet?"

"Any sightings?"

"Where do you think he is?"

"How's he avoiding apprehension?"

"You think he's coming back to Minnesota?"

Lee had no answer but, "I don't know," and it bothered him that he had to say it to these desk cops. Walking into Tremper's office and closing the door behind him gave him a moment of peace.

Tremper stood and walked out from behind his huge wood desk and firmly shook Lee's hand. Tremper's desk sat loaded with case files and the paperwork which he, too, despised. Like Lee, Tremper preferred street work, but his managerial career at the FBI kept him in the office as his mandatory 57 retirement age neared. His corner office was well lit by the sunlight pouring in through two sets of huge windows, giving the place an almost cheerful feeling. Tremper was soft-spoken, but tough. He seldom needed to bully anyone, especially cops eager to do their jobs and who did them well.

"Lee, good to see you," Tremper said, studying the man, searching for signs of stress or weakness. He saw none. "Sit down and fill me in."

"Right. Hey, this is a tough case, but I wanted to bring you up to date," Lee began, and filled Tremper in on the details. Lee had felt refreshed that morning by his conversation with Paul Murray and the spirit of the FTF team bolstered his confidence.

"Oh, you'll catch the guy. I have no doubts about you or your ability. Now, what can I do to help?" Tremper asked.

"Well, this has turned into a really big case. He's already killed four, and I'm sure he'll try again," Lee said.

"I think you're right, unless you stop him first."

"I'd like to stay on as the case agent…"

"Absolutely," Tremper said.

"And I'd like Kevin Rickett as my partner. He is an expert on the FBI paper system, and he's a great cop," Lee said.

"You got him. And I'm sending over three more agents to help you. They'll be there this morning, and they know you're the boss. You use them any way you want," Tremper said. Later that day Tremper assigned Greg Jones, Jay Hardy, and Joe Basille to the FTF and as the days passed and the pace quickened, they were kept very, very busy.

"Great," Lee answered, sitting up a little straighter in his chair. "Tell me a little about them, if you know."

"Well, they're green, but eager. Been through the basic stuff, but not much field experience," Tremper said, "but you can help us there," he smiled.

"Okay, glad to do it."

"What else do you need?" Tremper asked.

"Help with the newsies. You know, they killed Reese with their news leak. Damn!" The thought sent anger tremors through Lee's body. "We have to control the leaks. They can be deadly."

"I will do what I can. Is Rowley helping you?"

"Oh yeah, she's great. I'm letting her handle it all," Lee said.

"Okay, and if you have any problems with anyone anywhere, I'll help," Tremper offered.

"Good," Lee said, smiling inside. This is what he loved about police work, especially working on the FTF. Almost to a person, cops set aside egos and their hopes for a merit badge to work together to catch the bad guys, and that was all Lee ever wanted – and keep others from being killed.

"I wondered, since we have to do a Red Notice [to provide Interpol with all it needed] and we have to get all that stuff together, maybe we could get Cunanan on the Top Ten list," Lee suggested.

"Yes," Tremper said, chuckling a little. He knew the volume of paperwork and myriad regulations with which Lee would have to contend, and he knew that Lee was a street cop. The process of putting this all together would be excruciatingly difficult for him. "You want to use Rickett and Jeanie Burns on that, and we'll help you all we can. I say go for it now. It takes a while to get on the Top Ten. See what happens this weekend then go for it."

"Okay, I'll get started on it this week, that is if the phone quits ringing for a few minutes…"

"Hours…"

"Right, hours." Lee checked his notes to see if he had forgotten anything. "Listen, I want you to understand that this guy's been lucky. We get within hours of him and he slips through. But he can't hide forever, and we will get him!"

"Oh I know you will," Tremper said, standing to indicate that the interview was over, "but keep me posted. That's all I ask," Tremper said, walking him to the door.

Lee walked out of the office as the eyes of every FBI staff person searched his for clues to what was said behind closed doors. Lee left them wondering like a well-seasoned poker player who just suckered a huge pot of money.

"Lee, you see the paper yet?" one staffer asked.

"No, why?"

The agent handed him the May 12, 1997 *Star-Tribune*, Minnesota's highest circulation newspaper. The headline on page one burned into him and he erupted with a string of curses.

"Hunt for suspect lacks strategy," the headline screamed.

He shook with anger as he read the story.

"As Andrew Cunanan continues to elude authorities, it appears that there is no coordinated strategy among local enforcement agencies to help catch the man suspected in a nationwide killing spree that began in Minneapolis."

"Those assholes," he muttered. He read the next paragraph, wanting to scream at each word.

"No single agency is assuming overall responsibility for processing information, directing the investigation or developing an approach for finding the 27-year old San Diego man who has been wanted since the first of the four victims was found April 29."

He stared at the story's byline – Chris Graves, Randy Furst – and immediately memorized their names. Glad that they were not in the room with him, all he could think of was how their buddies out east had caused the death of William Reese with their ill-advised reporting, and now they had the audacity to accuse local cops, him especially, of not assuming "overall responsibility" for the chase.

"Can I have this?" he asked the agent.

"Sure. I guess they don't know what they're talking about," the man said.

"No, they sure don't," he said, storming out the door. As he left the room, he realized that there was a good side to this story as well. He muttered to himself, "They don't know what's going on because I don't want them to."

He knew that not talking to reporters made him vulnerable to these kinds of attacks, and as he read the article more closely, he saw that Coleen Rowley had told the reporters exactly what he wanted them to hear. But the audacity of them accusing him – him! – of not doing anything when he had already worked his body to the edge of exhaustion and his mind to near insanity really irked him. His resolve to win this case had always been strong, but this kind of "newsie crap" made him even more intense. He looked forward to the day he would gloat in the face of these upstart reporters who "don't know diddly about what goes on."

In the FBI Com Center, Lee put together packets of information about Cunanan, ready for immediate transmission anywhere in the world. These were simple; posters and personal descriptors (age, weight, color of hair, height, thumbprint), plus other pertinent information and Lee's contact numbers. He included Cunanan's photo, done in several versions to ensure the best quality of copy on the other end. He knew that faxed pictures often printed out blotchy, or black and nearly impossible to see, so he made different qualities of pictures with different densities. Laser fax printers were still rare, so in this way, no matter the quality of fax equipment sitting at the end of the phone line, the receiving agent would have good copy. Anything less might make the difference between stopping Cunanan and the commission of another murder. Every packet concluded with the statement, "ARMED AND DANGEROUS, ARMED WITH A .40 CALIBER HANDGUN," typed in bold-faced capital letters.

Now, no matter the time of day or night or where Lee might be, he could be sure to get information into the hands of a cop within minutes. He had also prepared an Electronic Communication (EC) and the enclosures for the Com Center to send immediately to all FBI offices worldwide. Later that day, he had higher quality photos of Cunanan sent by US Mail to every FBI office.

On rare occasions, Lee could get info-packs sent out faster by doing it himself, so he carried one with him in his van at all times. He had developed a close friendship with Cris Olson, an officer with the Prior Lake Police Department. Olson worked with him on the Pruitt chase and, in fact, was the officer who had found a stash of money in Pruitt's house. The Prior Lake PD sat just minutes from Lee's house and, as a result of his close relationship with Olson, Lee had the access codes to their building, giving him use of their fax any time of day or night.

"I'll show you who's taken responsibility," Lee growled as he drove back to the FTF office.

As soon as he walked in the door, he heard the clatter of the busy office. Everyone was doing something to catch Cunanan. All other work of the Minnesota FTF had been put on hold or shipped out to other offices. Everyone was on a phone line, or searching and evaluating pages of information that sat in deep stacks everywhere.

"You see the newspaper?" Gilkerson asked cynically as Lee walked into the office.

"Yeah," he held it up and growled as he walked to his desk, digging his scissors out from the cluttered drawer. He cut the article out of the paper and stabbed it with thumbtacks to his bulletin board, right where he could see it every day. He seldom needed motivation to catch bad guys, but this reminder re-fired his adrenalin every time he felt fatigued.

With the article firmly attached to the bulletin board, he walked to the dartboard and grabbed a couple of darts. "Yeah!" he said as he threw the first. "I saw the article," he said with clipped intensity. "And this guy's going down," he said as he threw a second dart, hitting Cunanan dead in the right eye, right where Cunanan shot David Madson.

Lee really thought very little of the psychologists, shrinks and behavioralists whose job it was to profile crooks. Still, he wanted to use every tool available to him, and the FBI did run a Behavioral Science Unit. He called and asked for help.

"We're chasing this guy named Andrew Cunanan. He's a gay guy who came out of San Diego, and I wonder if you can help us try and figure out where he'll go next, and what he'll do," Lee asked.

"No sir, we don't do that," the voice answered.

"What?"

"No, we're set up to help profile unknown killers, from whatever information the agent can find. We really never get involved when the perpetrator is already known to the agent," he said.

"That makes no sense," Lee argued.

"Well, maybe it doesn't, but that is what we do. I am sorry I cannot help you on this one," he said.

"Okay. Well, thanks for your time, I guess," Lee said hanging up, very disappointed. *Makes no sense to me.*

Lee waited for a phone line to open up, and began the mundane work of a cop – talking with yet another agent in another city. Peoria, Illinois, New Haven, Connecticut and Albuquerque, New Mexico all had had sightings. Lee knew that Cunanan could not possibly be in all three places at the same time, but he could be in one of them. He called them all, updated them on current information and had information packets sent immediately.

The America's Most Wanted program had generated numerous calls from Boston, the home of a huge number of gays. Would Cunanan be hiding out there? He meant to find out.

Boston's bustle and Miami's madness

"Lee Urness calling from the Minnesota Fugitive Task Force. Is anyone there handling the Andrew Cunanan case?" Lee asked the secretary who took the call.

"Yeah, Mike Curazza. I'll ring him for you," she said.

"Curazza," Lee heard as the man picked up the phone.

"This is Lee Urness, case agent on the Andrew Cunanan case, file number 88A-MP-47461. Are you handling this in that office?" Lee asked.

"Yeah, I'm your man. You have anything for me?" Curazza asked.

"No, nothing earth-shaking, but a few leads from American's Most Wanted."

"Yeah, we got a few here, too. You know, this area's got a huge gay population and he could easily blend in," Curazza said.

"You need to do what New York's done," Lee answered, and told him about the posters and how Emilio Blasse went to every known gay hangout.

"I'll get it done. Send me your latest posters and we'll get them out," he promised. "What about this gay pride day coming up?"

"The what?"Lee asked.

"Gay pride. They have these picnics and parades and stuff. Tens of thousands of people come. You think he'd show up for one of these?" Curazza asked.

"Could be. He sure could blend in," Lee offered.

"Well, they have these in all major cities. Sounds like an issue for an alert," Curazza suggested.

"Gay pride, huh?" Lee asked, harrumphing cynically. "What they got to be proud of?"

"Beats me, but they make a big deal out of it, and it draws tens of thousands of people, gay and straight," Curazza said.

"Can you beat that?" Lee said, shaking his head.

"Well, we've covered a lot of local leads here already, but we'll keep on working. Send me anything you get," Curazza said.

Curazza had only begun to understand just how many leads Lee would be sending him and that he would be spending hundreds of hours chasing them down, while visiting some of Boston's most notorious gay hangouts.

Big apple on red alert

Lee dialed Emilio Blasse in New York City.

"Emilio, Urness here. How'd the weekend go?" Lee asked.

"Oh, we had a great time," he said, his voice laced with cynicism. "He's gone, thank God." Blasse had been assigned to protect William Norman and his boyfriend all weekend, and despite the risk that Cunanan might show up, it did little to cramp Norman's style.

"Me and my partner sort of hung around them when they went out in public, to bars and dinner. We had a gay time," he laughed.

"No problems?"

"Not with Cunanan. Anyway, him and some guy went on the Queen Elizabeth II. You owe me big time, Mr. Urness," Blasse said.

"You see my guy anywhere?" Lee answered.

"No, but New York City is plastered with Cunanan's poster and the gays have offered a $10,000 reward for his arrest. I say he's not here."

"Well where is he?"

"Don't know, but this was a long weekend. I'm going home to the wife," Blasse answered.

"Okay, but then back on the streets," Lee said, laughing as he hung up. Lee knew he would see little of Kathy until this was over, but he had to chuckle seeing the macho FBI agent Blasse hanging around two gay men all weekend. *Anything to get a bust,* he laughed again.

Lee figured that within a week, all the gay men in America would know Cunanan's face. And for sure, the office received dozens of calls from worried gays wondering if Cunanan would show up in their town for the gay pride celebration. Ironically, though, those thousands of wanted posters now plastered to windows, bulletin boards and telephone poles in Minneapolis and elsewhere began disappearing. *I guess they make great souvenirs,* Lee thought. *I wonder how many of these people would chance a night with Andrew just for the thrill of it?* He sat shaking his head in amazement at this case that continued to take bizarre and unpredictable twists.

Credited

"Lee, Sears calling on line five. Says someone called and claimed they were Cunanan," Vern Lee called to Lee.

"Hello, this is Lee Urness, the case agent in charge on the Cunanan case. You say Andrew Cunanan called you?" Lee asked.

"We got a call from a man who identified himself as Andrew Cunanan this morning. He had Cunanan's social security number and account number, and he said he disputed a late charge on his bill, and that he would go into a store to pay it tomorrow," the caller said.

"That's crazy. Why would he do that?" Lee asked, more of himself than the Sears' employee.

"I have no idea. All I have is a note to call the FBI if we hear from him or he tries to buy something," she said.

"You did the right thing. Thanks. Look, I doubt that this was really him, but just in case, you need to put out an alert to all your payment centers to watch for him. Can you do that?" Lee asked.

"Certainly, right away. Anything else I can do?" she asked.

"No, not really. Just be sure that if your people spot him, they call the local FBI office right away. This guy is a killer, and they should do nothing to try and restrain him, okay?" Lee said.

"Okay, and thanks" she said.

"No, thank you." Lee found it astounding that this would happen. Lee had learned that on Thursday, May 8, someone in New Jersey ran a credit check on Cunanan. It made no sense that Cunanan would be applying for credit, or that he would do this himself. The news about Cunanan had spread nationally, even internationally by that date. It could have been a cop from another jurisdiction – maybe Chicago. It could even have been a news reporter or author posing as Cunanan, trying to dig deeper into his private life to get a scoop.

Lee never learned who made that call to Sears or the earlier one to the credit bureau, but these were classic examples of what cops dealt with in such high profile cases. Someone wanted in on a big case to gain their "15 minutes of fame."

In June, Neiman Marcus reported a similar incident. This time, Lee ordered a reverse toll record from the phone company. The call did not lead to Cunanan, and Lee was unable to determine who had actually made it.

Lee needed to find Cunanan quickly, and anyone with a lead that provided real hope of doing so got his attention, like the caller from Miami.

Sun, sand and a killer

"Lee, line one is Miami FBI," Jeanie Burns yelled above the office clatter.

"Got it," Lee said, pushing the button. "Urness here," he said.

"Keith Evans, from the Miami Fugitive Task Force," Evans said.

"You FBI?" Lee asked.

"Yup, and I been assigned the Cunanan case. I know where he is," he said confidently.

"What?" Evans' boast startled Lee.

"Yup, he's here in Miami and in fact, Miami Beach, South Beach. It's the ideal place for him. It's really jammed down there and people are constantly coming and going. It's packed with gays."

"I don't know that he's ever been there," Lee said, skeptical of what he just heard. "And we have no leads at all in Miami."

"Yup, that makes sense. Whether he's ever been here or not, he's sure to have heard of the place. It's perfect for him. I'm getting in touch with local police and gay hangouts. And the national gay cop organization…"

"The what?"Lee said, even more startled, and so much so that his legs comfortably propped up on Lisa Davis' desk fell to the floor.

"Yup, there certainly is one," Evans chuckled.

"News to me," Lee said, scratching his head.

"Oh I'm not surprised. The FBI is not exactly into the gay thing, but when you work down here, you learn these things," Evans said. "And I'll be meeting with local gays. You have any posters?"

"All I have is what we made up here. I'll VIGIT them to you and you can show them around. As soon as we get something official, I'll send you an original and you can print them down there," Lee suggested.

"No, can't so that."

"What?"

"It's a budget deal. My boss said that Minneapolis can pay for copies," Evans said matter-of-factly.

"How many do you need?" Lee said as he shook his head.

"A lot. At least a thousand."

Lee wrote a note for later.

"You'll have them as soon as we do," Lee said. "You really think he'd be there, huh?"

"Look, it's really the perfect place. He could hide out during the day, hit the beaches and clubs at night; maybe cross dress. Is he into that?" Evans asked.

"Well, he did go to his senior prom in drag."

"So, it's possible. No one would notice, and you know what else?" Evans asked.

"What?"

"The tourist industry wouldn't want anyone to worry about it. This is a huge business down here and they wouldn't want to scare the tourists away, especially the gays," Evans explained.

"Okay. Well, it's your town. You know it best," Lee said. "I'll get those posters off to you. Say, how long you been on the job?"Lee liked the can-do confident spirit of the agent.

"Just about 13 months," he answered proudly.

"Huh? A rookie? They give you the crap detail here, huh?" Lee said, half jesting.

"Hey, I know what I'm doing," Evans answered. "I was a street cop for five years before the FBI."

"Great. No, I'm sure you know what you're doing. Glad to have you on board," Lee said. "I got a stack of calls here. Stay in touch. Let me give you all my numbers and use the pager first; it's the only way you'll get through."

As he hung up, Lee swiveled his chair around toward Lisa and only half looked at the others in the office. He stared off at the ceiling, closing his eyes to help him think more clearly. *Miami. South Beach. Why there? Does it make sense? Where would he go? Who would he see?*

"Lee! You in there?"Lisa Davis said, startling him.

"Huh? Oh, sorry," he laughed. "Hey folks, I gotta go send some pictures to the Miami agent. He thinks Cunanan might be there." Lee headed to the FBI office and sent the photos on to Evans. *Miami? I don't know.*

San Francisco had many more contacts

Agents in several cities had already put in hundreds of hours on the Cunanan case, despite what the *Star Tribune* suggested. Typical, was in San Francisco.

On Monday May 12, Agent Rich Anderson met with Satwar Glennon* who had contacted the local FBI office. Glennon had seen Cunanan in April when he was with Jeff Trail and David Madson. That day, Cunanan bragged he had just closed an area real estate deal and would soon be living on Telegraph Hill or Nob Hill. Cunanan, who drove a new Infinity, acted "hyper," somewhat out of character.

That same day, Anderson talked with travel agent Paul Munson*. Munson confirmed that Cunanan had purchased a one-way ticket from San Diego to Minnesota for April 25. Munson had previously made numerous travel arrangements for Cunanan and William Norman, whom he described as more than willing to accommodate Cunanan. He understood that Cunanan had broken up with Norman following one of their European trips. Munson knew that Norman had been scheduled on a cruise that same day, and would be returning in June. Norman told Munson that Cunanan had severe financial problems.

When Munson saw Cunanan in April, he was alone, and paid for his ticket with a Gold American Express Card. (Munson did not know that Cunanan had begged the card company to extend credit as he had exceeded his $20,000 limit.)

Munson remembered that Cunanan had bought a round trip ticket for David Madson the previous month, and thought it strange that an architect would need someone else to pay his way.

Cunanan told Munson that he had burned his bridges in San Francisco and had tired of the town. He was seeing someone in New York and he also liked Boston.

Munson knew that Cunanan liked the finer things in life, from food to clothes to lodging. He knew him to be well read and mostly sober. Cunanan told him once that he had been treated at the Betty Ford Clinic.

Munson believed that Cunanan had a wife and child somewhere in the San Francisco area.

Later that day, Agent Anderson talked with Mac Famento*, a man who said he had met Cunanan just a month earlier. Famento said that Cunanan had put on 20 pounds and looked fatter than the picture shown on America's Most Wanted. Cunanan and Famento had an Israeli boyfriend in San Diego. They all stayed at the home of a porno star in an apartment near Flicks. The porn star usually walked his two Rotweilers in Balboa Park. Famento felt Cunanan would likely try to contact the porn star, but Famento did not know the name of the man.

"Here's a new challenge," Lee chuckled upon hearing the report. "The FBI does surveillance in a park looking for a porn star with two big dogs who might know our guy. This is certainly developing into a unique case."

Chapter 22 ~ Still most wanted

"Donna Brant on line 3," Jeanie Burns called to Lee.

"Mizz Brant, this is Lee Urness," he answered curtly.

"Look, I'm sorry about the timeliness of our report Saturday, but we really want to help you on this," she apologized. Her staff had been ecstatic about the overwhelming response to the show, and they committed to working on the story for the long haul. From the moment the first show aired, her desk began to pile up with information and requests from local and national media. She knew that to keep AMW's edge, she needed help from someone deep inside the Cunanan case. She chose the top guy, Lee Urness.

"Well, what do you think you can do to help?" Lee asked.

"We can keep on digging, calling on people, looking for Cunanan. We're already being pummeled with media inquiries. But we need your help," she said.

"Oh? What kind of help?"

"We need to know as many details as possible so we can go in the right direction. Like, has the FBI got any solid leads? Have you folks actually spotted him or found a trail of any sort?"

"Last time someone gave out that kind of information Cunanan killed a cemetery worker. Why would I want to talk to you about this?" Lee asked.

"Because I will not do that to you. I will not reveal anything that you want kept quiet. What I will do is take what you give me and run with it, and I will share everything I find with you. We can get a local producer and reporter anywhere in the country within hours. We are fully committed to this story," she said, needing to sell the skeptical cop on her plan.

"Look, I don't talk to newsies as a rule, but I do want to know what you find out. So I'll take a chance. You sound like someone I can trust, but I warn you; screw me over on even the smallest detail and I'll cut you off immediately," he said.

"I understand. No one will ever know that you are my source unless you agree to it. Do we have a deal?" Brant asked.

"Okay, I'll give it a shot."

"Now, are you coming in for this Saturday's show?"

"No. I am not leaving this office unless it's to arrest Andrew Cunanan. But I can send someone down there. You doing a show on this this week then?" he asked.

"Yes, we plan on it, unless you catch him first…"

"Which we hope to do…"

"You have a hot lead?" she asked.

"None other than what your show generated this weekend. So far, none of those panned out, but we're still working some. All I can say is it makes sense to us that he's on the east coast," he added.

"Why?"

"It's just logical. The last thing we know for sure is he killed Reese in south Jersey, and he had been heading south. No one has found anything going north. New York City gays have a big reward out for him and his picture's plastered all over the place. I just don't think it's logical for him to go north. Other than that, I have no evidence of where he is," he explained.

"Okay."

"Well, if he is on the east coast, or no matter where he is, we will find him," Lee asserted.

"And you'll let me know?"

"Sure, right away," Lee said. He wanted all the help he could get and Brant could keep a pair of neutral eyes on what all the newsies were doing and saying.

"Okay. I won't bother you unless it's something important. I promise," Brant said. "But don't you really want to come out here yourself?"

"No, I want to catch Cunanan and I can do that best from here. Now I gotta run. I'll call you if anything important breaks," Lee said.

Donna Brant said good-bye, happy at least that she had won cooperation of the chief investigator on the case.

"Hey Donna, you want to go to lunch?" Evan Marshall said, popping his head into her office.

The short, thin woman felt hunger pains racing across her stomach, but there was yet far too much work to do. "No, I'll catch something later," she said. And she did catch "something" later. Her entire menu during the long weeks ahead included a couple of slices of pizza and a few glasses of wine a week. She lost weight, even though she had little to lose. But Andrew Cunanan had that kind of effect on everyone involved in the case – no sleep, no food, no personal life – even for reporters who chased him.

Some stunning news from Minneapolis

Lee continued to call across the country in-between handling Coleen Rowley's pleas for help with the newsies, sorting through leads and coordinating his own team. Again, every so often he found refuge from the crush of information and noisy chaos in the office by heading out to his van in the parking lot. While there, his pager beeped with a message to call Jon Hermann.

"Jon, Lee here. What's up?"

"Well, I've been going through the MPD's investigation and went to the property room. You'll never guess what I found there," he said without much emotion.

"A box of condoms and K-Y jelly," Lee deadpanned.

"Hardly; more like chains and whips," Hermann laughed. "I found Cunanan's gym bag in the evidence room. They inventoried it, but it looks like nobody did anything with it."

"What?" Lee said, incredulous. "What'd you find in it?"

"Zipped in a pocket was a small blue address book. Lots of phone numbers."

"You gotta be kidding me!" Lee immediately realized that the other address book might not have been Cunanan's and they had been chasing the wrong people for more than a week. "I need that like right now."

"I'll make copies and bring them right over," Hermann answered.

"Good."

"I can't imagine how the MPD missed this," Hermann offered.

"Too concerned about getting the warrant to look at the evidence," Lee said. "Damn!"

"I'll stop over before the day is out. Then I'm going to re-interview all the witnesses. I'll keep you posted," Hermann said.

"Good."

Shortly after, Hermann brought photocopies of the phone book to Lee. Lee sat staring at the copies of the 2" x 3" blue phone book, slowly flipping through the pages. Again, he searched for "Miglin," and again, the name never appeared; and this was actually Cunanan's book. *How the hell did he know Miglin?* Lee had asked himself that question dozens of times, and not finding the name in this book left him frustrated. He wrote a note to call Scott Bakken with the news.

He saw dozens of new names and phone numbers, as well as notes about daily activities and the like. He grabbed a photocopy of the earlier phone book, the one they had been using since the beginning of the chase that had been among Cunanan's affects in San Diego. They had different handwriting. "Unbelievable!" Lee said, sighing deeply. He quickly scanned it to see how many new names appeared; there were many, but none of them were Lee Miglin.

"People, we got the *real* Cunanan phone book here. Let's get to work on it," he said, making copies of the pages and handing them to the three new FBI agents Tremper had sent over. "No grass grows under these. They need to be identified and leads set immediately."

Lee handed off the information and went back to his desk, shaking his head. He knew that the newsies would have a field day with something like this, but it sure would sap their claims that Cunanan had some super-intellectual criminal mind holding sway over the dumb cops. No, this was dumb luck, and very frustrating.

"Lee, Fred Tremper on line 5," Jeanie said.

"How'd you like the article?" Lee snapped as he took the call.

"Just swell. Well, they reported what we told them," he said.

"I know, but..."

"Well you're going to love this. We have a long-standing appointment with Chris Graves to talk about the Fugitive Task Force," he said. "We're going to do that on Thursday morning."

"We don't have time for that!" Lee protested.

"Oh I know, but we gave our word and we have to keep it," Tremper answered.

"No choice?"

"No choice. See you here, all of you, at 10:00 a.m.," Tremper said.

"Yeah, see you then," he answered. "I'm just looking forward to it." After he hung up, he threw a glance at the news article hanging on his bulletin board and cursed loud and long. "The hell you say," he finally said, shaking his head.

Lee left the office long after dusk and made the trip home, replaying again the details of the case, hoping for a breakthrough as soon as possible. His stomach burned with hunger. He realized that once again, he had worked through the day without eating, save for more coffee than he normally drank. He reached over to the passenger seat and picked up the muffin he had intended to eat that morning, carefully peeling off the wrapper and breaking off a piece at a time. The crumbs fell at random on his fishing vest, just as the crumbs of information he had about Cunanan fell at his feet.

"Somewhere you hide in the shadows, but you can't hide forever, you SOB," Lee said, as he tuned to the classical music station, letting the soothing sound of violins relax him.

Hot days and nights

Andrew Cunanan relaxed in front of the TV, waiting until dusk before leaving the safety of the Normandy Plaza Hotel. He had monitored the endless news stories of his whereabouts, laughing at the stupid reporters on America's Most Wanted and dumber cops who kept missing him. He imagined a poor unsuspecting slob driving a dark-colored Lexus "who-knows-where" being stopped and frisked, accused of being him. "Maybe he even looks like me," he laughed, secure that no one had the slightest idea where he had hidden these past few days. Still, he saw no value in risking being exposed, at least until he had finished the job for which he had come to Miami.

He went to the Miami Subs shop a block north and ordered supper, leaving as quickly as possible. Back on 71st, he went around the corner and stopped at the news store next to McDonalds. There he bought chips, sodas and a couple of gay magazines.

Now that it was dark, he could head to the beach and enjoy the sound of the surf as he ate his supper. He had already spotted the men who frequented the area, some at the Crystal Court Hotel next door, and others, in his own building. He knew immediately that finding sex would be easy enough. Soon enough a boy would come along who would never ask his name nor offer his own as they fell into each other's arms.

A few weeks earlier, he had dined openly with his friends at California Cuisine, or one of his many favorite Oriental restaurants. He slept with them in the classiest of California hotels. He talked about traveling to Australia with two other gay lovers, moving to San Francisco or living on the French Riviera. He had rough sex with David Madson, and hoped to move in with him once he got to Minneapolis. All of his greatest hopes and dreams had been dashed when Norman "fired" him. His problems were compounded by the ingestion of steroids, the realization that his life as a pretty boy had begun to bottom out, and he was a man with no job, no money and no marketable skills – a true loser. His newly acquired identity as a violent man had already exploded in a bloody binge of murder. Everything had spun out of control.

Cunanan knew his days were numbered. He saw that his cash reserve would quickly disappear, and with but a few gold coins held in reserve, he would soon be without resources. He would have either to kill and rob again, or just end it all. But if he ended it all, no one would ever remember him, making him a total and ultimately pathetic loser. That would not do.

Cunanan fashioned one more death sentence that would forever stitch his name into American folklore – Andrew Cunanan, executioner. Thus would be created a place for him in history and a hope for immortality.

Chapter 23 ~ Leads and mysteries

Lee had armed his Minneapolis agents with Cunanan's real address and phone book on Monday. They had worked it in earnest since then, contacting several people whose names were new to them.

In Las Cruces, New Mexico, Resident Agent Larry Houpt followed up on an earlier lead, sending him to the trailer home of Olive Lindner*. Lee had found her name on a page of the phone book found at Cunanan's San Diego apartment, the one the FBI had been using from the beginning.

Lindner told Houpt that she had no idea why her name would be associated with Andrew Cunanan. Ellen Lindner*, Olive's daughter, likewise had no knowledge of Cunanan, and the only gay person she knew was her uncle, Darcy Phillips*, who lived in San Diego. Darcy, she felt, would be the only person who would know her unlisted phone number.

Later Olive Lindner called Houpt and reported that she had talked with her brother Darcy and he mentioned that he had known Cunanan for a short time earlier that year.

Houpt next talked with Darcy. He had no idea where Cunanan might be at the time. "But," Darcy said, "My address book disappeared during the time I knew him. It was a little one, sort of credit card sized. It had Linda and Ellen's phone numbers in it."

In Minneapolis Lee finally knew the answer to one question – whose phone book they had been using since May 8. He wondered how many other people who had no connection to Cunanan had been needlessly bothered. The idea that hundreds of agent hours had been spent chasing down that bunny trail made him angry. *And the real phone book sat just a few blocks away at the Minneapolis Police Department. Damn!*

Departments working together

On Tuesday, San Diego agents John Hause and Ann Murphy met with Chicago detectives as well as those from Minnesota's Chisago County. San Diego police joined them as they did a follow-up examination of Cunanan's apartment. The entire place had been dusted and latent prints lifted, hoping that by eliminating the known prints, they could find Cunanan's. But the place had far too many prints to make any sense.

Hause wanted copies of everything in the apartment to compare with the reports collected in Minneapolis, Chisago County, Chicago and Pennsville, New Jersey. Included in their search warrant was a request for Cunanan's dental records so that they could establish that he had, indeed, eaten an apple at Miglin's townhouse.

Meanwhile, in New York City, Emilio Blasse learned from the New York City Police Department that they were offering a $1,000 reward to anyone helping to apprehend Cunanan.

That same day, Blasse met Bea Hanson and Christine Quinn of the New York City Gay and Lesbian Anti-Violence Project. Blasse asked for their help which they offered readily. They agreed to distribute Cunanan's photos everywhere in their New York network and they went beyond this; their group offered a $10,000 reward for help in capturing him.

As agents across the country continued to work hundreds of leads, new ones trickled in, and often unsolicited. Not used to the lifestyle of active gays, the cops continuously found themselves confronted by unusual surroundings and relationships. Lee had reminded each agent with whom he worked that they were to make no value judgments about gays and lesbians, and that they had to keep in mind that Cunanan was a killer first and gay man second. His "gayness" mattered only in that it created unique relationships with which the cops were unfamiliar.

"Business" picks up

On Wednesday, May 14, the leads that had exploded the previous weekend now turned into a flood. Agents were following up on their original contacts at the same time that new sightings were being reported. Lee found that already, it had become difficult to keep the names straight.

In New York, Emilio Blasse checked on a report that Cunanan had moved into an apartment in Queens. Supposedly, Cunanan was staying with a man named Vito Ricardo*. But Ricardo had never lived there.

Blasse also interviewed Thomas Matthews*, a student at Columbia University in New York City. Matthews stated he had spent time with Cunanan in April, though he assured Blasse that he had not seen nor heard from Cunanan since then. Matthews promised to call Blasse if Cunanan ever tried to contact him.

Blasse followed up on a call from the manager at the G Lounge on West 19th Street. The manager felt sure that Cunanan had been there that morning, leaving at 11:30 a.m. Blasse canvassed the area, but could find no trace of Cunanan.

In San Francisco, agents met with Laura Koski, a long time friend. She had met Cunanan for lunch at the Zuni Café on Market Street in San Francisco on April 12. While they ate, the waiter had told them about the gay pride celebration in Massachusetts to be held Memorial Day weekend. Cunanan seemed excited about visiting there.

Cunanan had left her at the restaurant and returned to her house late that evening. She believed he had picked up a guy for sex, or perhaps had been picked up.

Koski and her husband believed that Cunanan might try to contact them if he ever came back to San Francisco. She warned Agent Anderson that if police ever cornered Cunanan he would shoot it out with them, and he would never commit suicide.

Koski also knew David Madson, who had told her that he was no longer interested in Cunanan. Cunanan had taken that news hard, she said. Apparently, he had taken it much harder than she imagined.

Agent Anderson then spoke with bartender Salvador Johnson*, who had called the San Francisco FBI. Johnson had known Cunanan for eight or nine years at US Berkeley. Since then they had met off and on, but he saw Cunanan on April 18 and 19, 1997. He noticed that Cunanan had changed. Previously, Cunanan had been fun and charming; now he had turned sober and solemn.

Johnson went to a party with Cunanan at a leather bar. Once there, Cunanan had become rough, grabbing and hurting him. Johnson had to order him to stop.

Johnson believed that Cunanan had snapped, and for several reasons. He thought Cunanan might have HIV and was angry with everyone else, and he had changed his appearance, getting a buzz cut and wearing dumpy clothes. He had put on weight.

Johnson saw that Cunanan felt he was above the rest of society, but in reality, he was a sociopath without remorse for his actions. As for what might happen if police tried to arrest Cunanan, Johnson believed he would view the whole scene as something from a movie, as surreal.

Johnson believed that if Cunanan came back to San Francisco, he would go to the Café Flor, and perhaps, the new Porn Star Café. Cunanan had also told him that he had just bought land in Pacific Heights, and perhaps he might try to go there.

That same day, Lars Betsdorf* called the San Francisco FBI. Betsdorf feared for his own safety. He had also been with Cunanan during that April visit, and they partied together at The Café. Cunanan had been very aggressive, more so than when he saw him in March. Cunanan told him that he was going to move to San Francisco, but he was not sure when. Cunanan had a daughter there, he had said.

Mike Binder*, too, called directly to the San Francisco FBI. He had been a close friend of Jeff Trail's and was very upset. On April 11 or 12, Binder said that he danced and spent time with Cunanan at The Café Bar, and that Cunanan had hung all over him. Finally, Cunanan grabbed Binder's ball cap off his head, and Binder had had enough. He slammed a glass of water down and Cunanan backed off. They had all been drinking heavily that night, and he said Cunanan looked crummy, unlike his normal suave self.

Binder felt that Trail's move to Minneapolis was strange, as though there was more to the story than just a change of scenery. He knew that Trail desperately wanted to be a police officer.

Binder believed Cunanan to be dishonest, a liar who could not be trusted.

Across the country, a call came to the Long Island Police Department. A neighbor near a residence at East Hampton had called with a tip that the cop thought might be useful.

East Hampton, a city founded more than 350 years earlier, had become home to or a refuge of many of America's movers and shakers. It also attracted the artsy crowd, and its website stated that it "...is replete with all the peculiar baggage that comes with runaway egos engaged in the endless dance of social climbing and posturing." Lee thought it sounded like the "San Francisco of the east."

Included among those social climbers and egos was Abner Paulson*, a wealthy Detroit resident who also kept a house at East Hampton. Despite Paulson's wish to stay divorced from the Cunanan case, the neighbor had decided to inform the FBI. During July of 1996, Paulson had invited Andrew Cunanan and William Norman to spend a week with him at his East Hampton residence.

The neighbor worried about Paulson's ties to Cunanan, but even more than that, he worried about Paulson finding out he even made the call to the FBI. Paulson, he knew, wanted to keep his homosexuality private. Into this situation walked a Detroit FBI agent, hopeful that by pulling this string he might somehow find Cunanan on the other end.

Lee studied the teletyped report about Paulson. *How many other men are there like Paulson in Cunanan's life? Did he try to call Paulson, or go see him in Detroit? Did Cunanan go to Paulson's place on Long Island to lay low? Maybe it was a one-week affair? He's had enough of these kinds of relationships.* He waited for the Detroit agent's report.

When the Detroit agent interviewed Paulson, the angry man explained that Cunanan and Norman had attended a party that lasted four days, along with several other gay men. Since the information about Cunanan's murderous spree had become public, Paulson had talked with Norman several times. Paulson believed that Cunanan had fled overseas, most likely to Italy or France.

Later, Paulson's attorney called the agent and told him to leave his client alone; that he had nothing more to say.

Lee read the agent's report and sighed, shrugging his shoulders and throwing the report on his growing stack. For now, he would leave Paulson alone, but not forgotten, not until Cunanan had been captured.

More good information from San Diego

Kurt Demars, Cunanan's San Diego friend, called the local FBI office again on May 14 with additional details. John Hause and Ann Murphy interviewed him.

Cunanan had once bragged that he had bludgeoned a man named Lincoln Aston to death in 1995. Police had arrested, charged and seen convicted Aston's real murderer and never believed that Cunanan had anything to do with it, though he certainly knew its details. William Norman, Cunanan's sugar daddy, had bought Aston's house after the man died, and Cunanan lived with Norman there during 1996.

Demars knew that Cunanan often traveled to New York, and believed that he preferred staying in the Paramount Hotel in Chelsea just above Broadway.

Demars said that Cunanan was a good friend of a San Francisco woman named Laura Koski, and that Cunanan claimed he often confided in her. In San Francisco, Cunanan spent time at Club 181, where the owner had also been a close friend. He also enjoyed the Porn Star Café and the Luna Piena.

Cunanan preferred shopping at upscale stores, especially Nordstroms and Banana Republic. He usually stayed in high-end motels where rooms ran $600 a night or more.

Demars knew that Cunanan had an ex-boyfriend in Minnesota, though he offered no names. He also claimed that Cunanan used to sell drugs.

As Hause and Murphy reported this information to Lee, he felt they were on the right trail. Agents interviewed Ms. Koski and, Lee hoped, that would open up the door of understanding another notch, while shutting the window on Cunanan's opportunity to escape.

Had he ever been married?

Investigators heard from some who knew Cunanan that he had a wife and child. He never did, but he had a woman who was a close friend and this woman trusted him with her child. He often showed that picture to his friends, claiming this was his daughter.

That girl's mother was Elizabeth Cote of Los Angeles. She had known Cunanan since junior high school. Cote previously had been married to Philip Adam Merrill from Pasadena. They both considered Cunanan to be a close friend.

Special Agent Scott Hanley got their story, and it added to the uneven threads being woven into the quilt of Cunanan's life.

"Cunanan served as our best man when Elizabeth and I got married," Merrill explained. "Then he moved in with us." He had lived with the couple from 1988 to 1992. Cunanan had, in fact, stayed overnight at Merrill's house during April of 1995, and sponsored the baptism of one of the couple's children. Merrill had always believed that eventually, Cunanan would come back and live permanently with them (prior to their divorce).

An anguished Maryann Cunanan had called Merrill's house on May 8 looking for Cote, who happened to be there. She talked to the worried mother. Maryann told them that Andrew had been implicated in murder.

Merrill knew that Cunanan loved to trade his company with wealthy people to enjoy their lifestyle. "But I never thought of Andrew as a prostitute, though he would certainly not refuse money if it was offered." He said Andrew had a sense of mystery and was a lazy man who somehow always had money, and who would often disappear for several months at a time.

Cunanan told Merrill that he was bisexual, but really did not care much about sex. "He said he often did not know his sex partners."

Merrill believed that Cunanan had a girlfriend named Kim whom he had met at the University of California at Berkeley. And he knew that Cunanan had lived for a time with a San Francisco woman.

"What do you think about Andrew being involved in murder?" Hanley asked.

"Well, I don't see him with a revenge streak. Maybe if someone had done him wrong he might feel obligated to do something for the sake of his personal honor," Merrill answered.

"What about the cemetery caretaker? Was that about his honor?"

"I just can't imagine him going after that man just to get his truck," he said in disbelief.

"How about guns?"

"I've never seen him with one, but he did like to talk a lot about guns," Merrill answered.

"So why would he kill someone?" Hanley asked.

"Well, I do remember one time in 1991 when he was telling my ex and me about how if he ever had AIDS, or if someone did that to him, he'd go on a five state killing spree and take everyone with him he could. I always thought he was joking," Merrill answered. "I thought he got that from a movie."

Merrill remembered that Cunanan had a scar on his abdomen and believed it came from an appendectomy.

"What about aliases?" the investigator asked.

"Oh, he would use the name DeSilva. Sometimes at parties he called himself Baron Ashkenazy," Merrill laughed. DeSilva was the name of one of America's wealthiest families and friends of the parents of Elizabeth, his former wife.

"Okay. Look, if he tries to contact you, you need to let us know right away," Hanley said.

"Oh yes, I will. Since he knows where I live, he just might try to do that. And he might remember my phone number," Merrill said. "But he was not the type to ask for help. He'd rather take matters into his own hands and not impose on people." Months later, those words must have fallen like lead on Merrill's memory.

Elizabeth had a hard time believing that her old friend could do such terrible things. She had not heard from Andrew since 1996, though she had tried to call him during the previous November. Earlier that year, Cunanan had given her a voice mail phone number, telling her that he planned to move to Mexico. Finally, he had the voice mail disconnected.

"Andrew is extremely vain and very conscious of his looks," Elizabeth said. "He wants the best of everything. His clothes were the most expensive and he grew up around a lot of money." The latter claim only applied to Andrew and his younger sister, Regina, according to Christopher, Andrew's older brother.

Christopher described the family's early life as limited by the meager income of Modesto, their father. During that time, Modesto had served in the U.S. Navy. Following his discharge in the early 1970s, Modesto went back to school and eventually began working as a stockbroker. Maryann Cunanan believed that Modesto earned as much as $300,000 a year before being charged with embezzlement and abandoning the family in 1988, fleeing to the Philippines to avoid prosecution. Andrew benefited from Modesto's high earnings years by being sent to private schools, wearing the finest of clothes and driving his own car.

"When I talked to Maryann she was very upset about the police and news reporters who she said were bothering her," Elizabeth said, discussing the calls she had received from Cunanan's mother. "And I talked to Andrew's sister Gina, who lives in San Francisco. Neither Maryann nor Gina has heard from Andrew."

"Andrew and I are very good friends," she explained to investigators. "I am probably his closest friend. He had thousands of acquaintances, but no other close friends." Such good friends were they, that she and Phillip had taken Cunanan with them on many trips. She knew he had visited Florence, Rome and the Philippines.

"Did you know any of his other friends?" the investigator asked.

"No. I mean I knew he was gay, but I didn't know his gay friends. He lived a very private life," she explained.

"Did you and he ever have a romantic relationship?"

"Oh no. Uh-huh. We were just close friends. We did live together during 1987 and 1988, and then later, when I got married, he lived with Phillip and me in San Francisco," she said. "I even supported him during his first year of college."

"Why did you stop?" he asked.

"He quit school when he ran out of money."

"What else can you tell me about Andrew?" he asked.

"He is a very caring person. He used to take care of my daughter when she was younger," she said. "I just can't believe he would be involved in murder," she said, shaking her head and frowning. "Something must have really altered his life to cause him to do the crimes he's accused of."

"Oh?"

"Well he was raised a Roman Catholic, and often went to church on his own. It's just way out of his frame of mind to go out and kill people," she insisted.

"Did he use drugs or have any weapons that you know about?"

"No. I don't know about that," she said. And she could not think of Cunanan as being a male prostitute, although she knew that he always had many wealthy friends and took care of his image, wearing designer clothes and Giorgio Armani glasses.

"What about aliases?" he asked.

"Well, he used to use the name DeSilva to make restaurant reservations. That is the name of some friends of my parents. But that's the only one," she said.

"Did Andrew ever talk about going on a five state killing spree?" he asked.

"Oh, that? That was just a joke," she said. "I have even said that when we were frustrated about something."

"Well, I want you to contact me right away if Andrew calls you or you see him," Hanley instructed.

But Andrew never called, and it was perhaps lucky that he never showed up at her door. On the day of this interview, Cunanan had killed in three states. Soon he would another. Did he have his final sights set on California?

At the beginning, the only photo available to the FBI was this one, taken from Cunanan's drivers' license and then enlarged.

Here, Cunanan's picture graces a dart board in the task force office. Lee managed to lodge the dart in the center of Cunanan's face.

Eventually, Lee made a composite photo array from several different Cunanan pictures. These showed how different he could look, making it so difficult for citizens to recognize him.

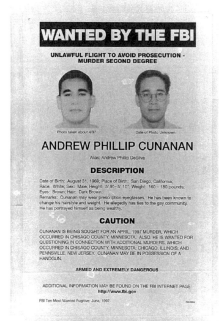

During June, the FBI placed Cunanan on its 10 Most Wanted List. This official FBI poster, placed in public buildings across America and sent to foreign offices, still lacked a clear depiction of him. Many people looked like Andrew Cunanan.

234

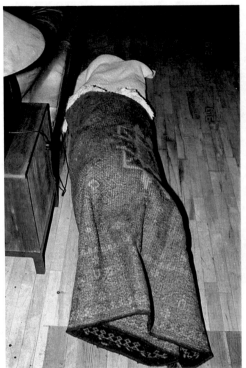

Jeff Trail's blood spattered widely, across the floor, on the door sill, and several feet up the wall. This indicated that he was trying to get away from Cunanan as the latter was pounding him with the hammer. Yet, no one heard a thing.

For two days, Cunanan and Madson stayed inside the apartment with Jeff Trail's body wrapped in a rug.

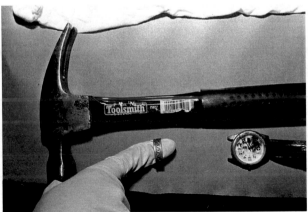

The hammer Cunanan used to bludgeon Trail to death, and Trail's watch and ring, found in the apartment.

Several people identified David Madson's Jeep Cherokee, and recalled seeing two men inside, who matched the description of Cunanan and Madson. Most mentioned the VAIL sticker on the back window.

Two fishermen found David Madson's body laying in brush and small trees near the shoreline of East Rush Lake, near Rush City, Minnesota. Cunanan had shot him three times. Controversy about when this shooting occurred could not be established forensically. Experience investigators believe it occurred on Friday evening, five days after Cunanan murdered Jeff Trail.

Lee Urness sat at his desk inside the Fugitive Task Force office, feet propped up, trying to figure out where Cunanan had fled. A stack of phone calls always sat nearby,
with all phone lines lit. Lee spent most of the days of this manhunt working from this
location, before the FBI opened a task force office down the street, in the FBI's Minneapolis facility.

Lee Urness first became involved with Cunanan when he spotted a notice about possible stolen Red Jeep Cherokee on a police wire. Three days after Cunanan murdered
Lee Miglin, a Chicago Police Officer noticed the Jeep parked just around the corner
from Miglin's home. Police had placed several parking tickets under the wipers. Now
Lee knew for sure that Cunanan had found another "ride."

ESOTA, TUESDAY, FEBRUARY 7, 1956   P ce 5 Cents   EIGHT PAGES

3 Men Shot In Attempt To Rob Store In Garfield

Sheriff, 2 Deputies Escape Injury

In a blazing gun fight early Monday morning, Sheriff Bennie Urness, Deputy Howard Urness and Luther Urness broke up an attempted safe-cracking at the Garfield municipal liquor store.

Deputy Howard Urness sent slugs from his .38 Special crashing into the right shoulders of two of the burglars while a blast from Luther Urness' .12 gauge shotgun dropped the third as he attempted to escape.

The gunfight took place shortly after 4 a. m. after Urness had been alerted by Clarence Gease, whose son-in-law, Jerome Johnson, heard suspicious noises in the liquor store as he passed there on his way to work at the Garfield creamery.

"After I made the phone call," Gease said, "I stood on the corner and watched the store to see if anybody came out. I timed it and it took Urness just ten minutes to get here."

Gease said the sheriff's car had just pulled up in front of the liquor store when he heard a volley of shots.

"I guess they must have started shooting as soon as they saw the lights from Bennie's car," Gease said.

Two of the burglars fired from a side door of the liquor store. The sheriff's car was a scant 50 feet from the door.

"I'm not sure," Howard Urness said, "but I think they fired before we got out of the car."

One of the bullets from the burglars' guns whistled over Bennie Urness' shoulder while another buried itself in the front fender of his car.

Howard Urness began firing immediately and Luther Urness raced for the corner to cut off any escape from the rear of the store.

"I couldn't see them very clearly," Howard Urness said, " so 1 fired at the flames from the muzzle blasts of their guns."

Urness' aim was almost unbelievably accurate, for both gunmen were hit in the right shoulder.

Lee Urness was a fourth generation law enforcement official. His great-grandfather, grandfather, and father all served as Sheriff of Douglas County, in North Central Minnesota. Grandpa Bennie is shown in the top left, pointing to the bullet hole made during a gunfight with robbers. Howard, Lee's father, is shown on the right side of the picture. No police officers were hurt in the exchange, although Howard heard a bullet fly past his ear. Two of the robbers were injured in the exchange. For a small rural Minnesota town, this story made big news.

Lee and Marilyn Miglin lived in an upscale townhome in Chicago's Goldcoast. No one has ever been able to establish a clear link between Cunanan and Miglin, the wealthy building developer. Lee never believed their meeting to be a random event, and had his theories. Otherwise, there was no reason for Cunanan to be in this neighborhood.

Chicago police found Lee Miglin's brutalized body in the Miglin garage, located across the alley behind their house. Miglin liked to "tinker" in the garage, and Mrs. Miglin was away on a business trip. Cunanan may have had knowledge of the garage location, since it made little sense why else he would have found the man working there; unless it was a random meeting.

Cunanan tortured Lee Miglin, tying his feet together with electrical cord, using masking tape on Miglin's head, stabbing him repeatedly with a screw driver, and using a bow saw on his neck. The violence of the scene astounded seasoned homicide investigators.

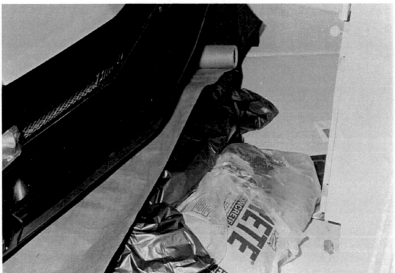

Miglin's body lay in front of a car in the garage. Cunanan had laid it out on black plastic bags, unrolling brown wrapping paper on the man. As if to finalize his brutal attack, Cunanan dropped a bag of cement on Miglin's rib cage, shattering bones and causing excruciating pain.

After hiding out in New York City for several days, Cunanan began driving south, through New Jersey. A radio story warned him that police were tracking him through the car phone signal. In a panic, Cunanan left the freeway and ended up at Finn's Point National Cemetery located inside Ft. Mott State Park.

William Reece's wife found her husband shot to death in the basement of the cemetery's Miegs Lodge. Cunanan had forced Reece downstairs and shot him one time, leaving a trail of blood across the floor. Cunanan murdered Reece because he needed a new escape vehicle, Reece's red pick-up truck.

Cunanan parked Lee Miglin's Lexus outside the garage at the cemetery. He had wrenched free the car's telephone antenna in an attempt to keep police from tracking him. After he murdered Reece, Cunanan left the Lexus and drove away, crossing the Delaware Bridge.

Cunanan checked into the Normandy Plaza Hotel, at South Beach near Miami, Florida. For more than two months he lived here, moving about unnoticed, as FBI agents combed South Beach looking for him.

Lee trusted very few members of the media, or "newsies" as he called them. He made an exception for Donna Brant, an Executive Producer at "America's Most Wanted," the TV program dedicated to catching fugitives – like Cunanan. Brant produced several features about Cunanan, and nearly made herself sick from the hours she spent working on the productions.

FBI Agent Kevin Rickett worked as a co-case manager alongside Lee, almost from the start. Lee loved Rickett's ability to handle the constant flow of FBI paperwork, and Rickett's dedication to catching Cunanan. Here the two officers are seen just before pasting the word "captured" on Cunanan's wanted poster, after the killer had committed suicide.

243

One day in July, Cunanan took a huge chance. He walked north from the Normandy Hotel, crossed the street, and walked down to the pawn shop, Cash on the Beach, just next to the pizza shop. There he exchanged one of Lee Miglin's $50 gold coins for $190, telling the clerk, Vivian Olivia, that he would be back to redeem it some-day soon. He never returned.

On June 10, Cunanan parked William Reece's red chevy pickup truck in this ramp, just around the corner from the Versace mansion. By then, his money had run out, and he lived in a sailboat docked at 5445 Collins Ave. The boat's owner, however, showed up one day, and Cunanan moved down the beach, to a locked, two-story houseboat.

Cunanan sat in Lummas Park, on a grassy berm, watching the Versace mansion across the street on Ocean Boulevard. Just around 8:30 a.m., he saw Gianni Versace walk through the gates and on up the street. Soon after, he saw Versace return, and followed him across the street, shotting him point blank in the back of the head.

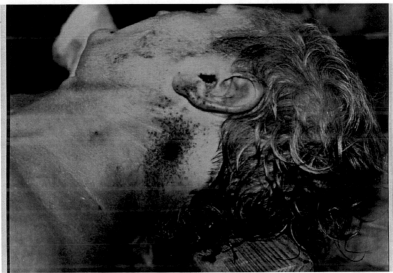

Cunanan shot Gianni Versace in the neck under his left ear, blowing a star pattern into his left cheek as it exited. The sound and sight of a man being shot in broad daylight caught the attention of many witnesses, who watched Cunanan run up the street and around the corner, back to the parking ramp, where he changed clothes and made his getaway.

Versace fell on the steps, his bag of magazines falling under the steel gates. His blood sprayed across several steps, and a heavy pool of blood gathered where his head had lain.

Police arrived at the house just minutes after Cunanan fled, and quickly taped off the crime scene. Gawkers who gathered across the street could easily see Versace's blood as it stained the marble steps. Ocean Boulevard soon took on a circus effect as thousands of curious tourists, and hundreds of reporters passed the scene during the next several days, all of them wondering what happened to Andrew Cunanan, the cold-blooded multiple-murderer.

Cunanan either ran up the boardwalk that sat on the beach just two blocks to the east, or, as police suspect, he simply grabbed a taxi and was dropped off up on Collins Avenue, at this houseboat. Here, the desperate man waited until the inevitable end of the drama.

This is the 40-caliber Taurus pistol that Cunanan used to execute David Madson, William Reece, and Gianni Versace. He reserved the last bullet for himself.

Months later, New Jersey FBI agent Paul Murray destroyed the gun in the presence of a member of Jeff Trail's family. Cunanan had taken the gun from Trail's home the day before he murdered him with a hammer.

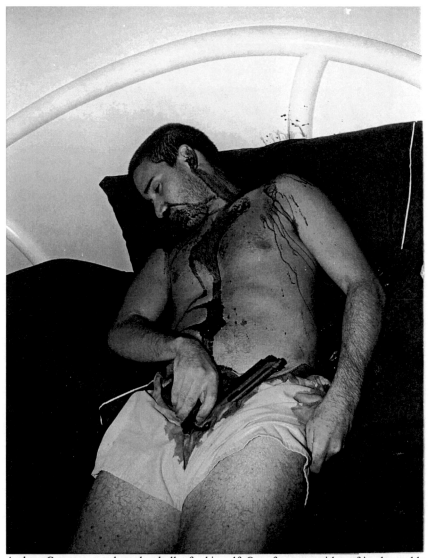

Andrew Cunanan saved one last bullet for himself. Out of money, without friends, unable to contact his family, the FBI had "put him in the bubble," and he had nowhere to go; he had no future.

He fired his last bullet into his mouth, and it lodged in the back of his skull, as it blew out his eardrum. Blood from his nose, mouth, and ear washed down his body, and the gun came to rest on his loin.

"He pled guilty," Lee Urness said, upon hearing the news.

248

When FBI Special Agent Keith Evens told Lee that the man on the boat was Cunanan, Lee walked to the easel and wrote "DRT," Dead Right There!

Lee Urness   Dave Racer

Chapter 24 ~ Help flows from everywhere

Glenda Elison*, A Gordon Communications customer service representative from Los Angeles, thought a recent customer just might be Cunanan. That Wednesday, on her own volition, she called the FBI who contacted Lee. She told Lee that, "this man, who sounded gay, called to order prepaid calling cards. He said he was calling from Palm Springs, but had just been to Minneapolis."

"Oh?"

"Yes, and he said he had been traveling around the country. I don't know. Maybe it's your man. It just seemed too coincidental to me," she said.

"Thank you for calling. Listen, I'm going to have an agent come over and talk to you. Tell him what you told me, and give him the man's name," Lee said. "You said it was Peter Davidson*?"

"That's right. And he said he was going to Chicago and then coming to West Hollywood for the May 18 gay pride celebration."

Lee called the LA FTF office and agent Joseph Schall immediately followed up the lead. Davidson had indeed contacted the company; he was a real person.

Taking careful notes about contacts and locations, Schall contacted The Villa in Palm Springs. He learned that Davidson had stayed there many times and had just checked out on May 14. Henry Charles*, a desk clerk, stated that he knew Davidson and he could not possibly be Cunanan. Davidson was at least 55 years old. Charles had seen Cunanan's picture several times. "No way is Mr. Davidson Andrew Cunanan," he chuckled.

Harold Richter*, General Manager at The Villa, knew Cunanan. He used to tend bar at a San Diego club where Cunanan often partied. "Andrew was the life of the party. Always had lots of money. Very friendly and outgoing."

"Yes, we've heard that. What else?" Schall asked.

"Well," Richter said, rubbing his neck and frowning, "I just cannot believe that Andrew would be involved in a murder, much less multiple murders. It just doesn't fit."

"I can assure you that we have evidence to the contrary, and I urge you and your friends to be careful," Schaal suggested.

"A lot of Andrew's former friends from San Diego, I have heard, have gone into hiding. But I can't believe he'd come back here. Too many people know him," Richter offered.

"So Mr. Richter thinks your guy is just a regular party man, harmless," Schaal said when he called Lee after the interviews.

"Yeah, harmless as a viper," Lee said. "Oh Andy is a nice boy who'd never harm anyone," Lee mocked. "Thanks for your help. I'll watch for your report."

Hertz is Number One...but not at spotting Cunanan

Alberto Pietro* approached the Midland, Texas, International Airport Hertz Renta-Car desk on Tuesday, May 13. The Ciba pharmaceutical representative had come to town to conduct business. Bruce Shano* processed Pietro's order, and as he had trained himself, studied Pietro carefully, making sure to check his driver's license and other ID.

On Wednesday evening, Shano surfed the internet and made a stop at www.amw.com, the website of America's Most Wanted. As he looked at the various crooks AMW was chasing, he closely studied Andrew Cunanan's profile.

On Thursday, Pietro came back to the airport to turn in his car. Shano saw him coming across the lobby and as he drew closer, his brow began to furrow, and his adrenalin pumped. Pietro, he felt sure, was really Andrew Cunanan.

As soon as he could safely and discreetly do so, Shano contacted Allen Haes at AMW and told him what he had seen. Although Haes felt that Shano had confused Pietro's name with that of two brothers, Miguel and Thomas Pedro*, his description certainly matched Cunanan.

Haes contacted Lee Urness.

Within minutes, the Midland FBI office had Cunanan's photos in hand and headed to the airport. They showed Cunanan's photos to Shano and he assured them that the man he saw had, in fact, been Cunanan. In fact, his flight had not yet left the airport.

It took only a few minutes for the FBI agents to find Alberto Pietro, and he, as were they, were struck at how closely he resembled Cunanan. After talking with Ciba officials and checking Pietro's other unique identifiers, including looking for warrants on him, they let him get on the plane.

Lee felt nonplused. By this day, Cunanan had been on several flights and in several airports all at the same time. "Hey, one of these times, it really might be him," he laughed as the Midland agent reported to him.

Not a gay park

On Thursday, May 15, Special Agent Nathan Williams heard from Officer Brian Hartley of the Walnut Creek, California police department. Hartley had received an anonymous tip from a woman who spotted Cunanan in Civic Park. Hartley felt she had been mistaken because Civic Park was not known as a gay hangout, but he knew of a different park that had such a reputation.

Agent Williams set up surveillance at the "real" gay park several days later, but to no avail. It did, however, give the agents a chance to interview a number of gay men who were shown Cunanan's picture. None recognized him.

Late in the evening of May 15, Merrill from Ft. Walton Beach, Florida, called AMW. When the operator heard the news, she immediately paged Lee, who had just gotten home.

"What's up?" he asked.

"Got a hot lead, in Ft. Walton Beach, Florida. A man says he just saw Cunanan, like 20 minutes ago," the operator said.

Lee wrote down the contact number and called immediately. "And tell me," he said, after introducing himself, "what exactly did you see?"

"I saw Andrew Cunanan, the man on America's Most Wanted. He was walking on the beach, maybe just 25 minutes ago," Merrill answered.

"Tell me what he looked like and what he wore," Lee said.

"He had on a navy shirt, white shorts and white hat," Merrill said. His description of Cunanan's body size was wrong.

"Okay, thank you for reporting this. I'll get right on it," Lee said. As he hung up, he pondered the report. *Okay, Florida is possible; anywhere in Florida. But this sounds like someone else. He's not heavy like this guy says.*

Still, it sounded close enough that Lee made the call to a weary Fort Walton Beach Resident Agent. The beach walker, however, never materialized and Merrill provided no additional help.

Back in San Francisco, Agent Anderson talked with Otto Denizen*, one of Jeff Trail's former lovers. Denizen had met Cunanan through Trail and became Cunanan's friend as well.

Denizen went drinking with Cunanan during his San Francisco romp in mid-April. At that time, Cunanan said he was in love with Trail and that he was going to Minneapolis to see him and David Madson. Denizen noticed that for a time, Cunanan dressed like Trail and even grew a goatee like his, as though he wanted to be Trail.

In reality, Cunanan only wanted Trail to shut up and now that he had killed the man, he certainly did not want to look like him any longer.

Please, Andrew, friend, stop this!

KARE 11 TV reporter Bernie Grace, finished with Chicago stories and looking for a scoop, went to work in his own backyard, the Twin Cities. He sought help from his local police sources and talked with gays and lesbians, some of whom were willing to admit they had known or met Cunanan. Along the way, he learned of a Twin Cities' man who had once been Cunanan's live-in lover in San Diego. (His name has never been revealed publicly. He is referred to here as "Alan.")

Grace went to Alan's house and sat talking with him for more than two hours. He pled with him to go on camera and tell his story and if he did, make a plea to Cunanan to stop the killing. Alan feared being outed and worse yet, he feared Andrew. Finally, he agreed to do an on-camera interview under strict conditions. His face and voice had to be altered, and no reference could be made to his place of residence. The background scenes, too, had to be altered to insure that no one, and especially Cunanan, could figure out where he was. With this settled, Grace sent for a camera operator.

The 10:00 p.m. news on May 15, 1997 carried Grace's exclusive story. The news anchor began with this narrative:

"Tonight there's a public plea for alleged serial killer Andrew Cunanan to turn himself in. The plea comes from a man who says he's known Cunanan for several years and has long considered him a personal friend. The two knew each other when they lived in San Diego, and they crossed paths here in the Twin Cities. Tonight, Cunanan's friend reluctantly agreed to talk to us after we agreed not to disclose what state we did our interview, and we would shade his face out for his safety. KARE 11's Bernie Grace has this exclusive report."

"He's not a monster," Grace began. "Andrew, he was the life of the party. We all loved him. Everybody loved Andrew. Andrew was everybody's friend. This man says despite the advice of the FBI not to talk to us, he agreed because Cunanan should know there are people who still care about him."

The camera cut to a face darkened and blurred. The background, as well, had been altered. Had Cunanan actually seen this, he could never have been able to discern where Alan sat while talking.

"Andrew was one of the happiest go lucky nicest sweetest guys I've ever met in my life. I can't believe Andrew is doing this. I'm shocked. He's such a great guy."

A cutaway to the New Jersey crime scene began to roll. Bernie Grace said, "Cunanan's friend knows he's been charged with one murder so far. And suspected in three others. He wants the horror to stop."

"I don't know if you did this or not," Alan said as the camera once again panned his face, "but if you did you need to turn yourself in and talk to somebody. Get some help. Get things cleared up. Everybody wants the killing to stop. I'm scared. I'm scared who's next. I'm sacred that either the police are going to kill him or he's going to hurt himself. And I don't want to see that happen. I've already got one dead friend, I don't need another one."

"That one dead friend was Jeff Trail," Grace broke in," who was lured to this Minneapolis apartment building and murdered almost three weeks ago [tape of Harmony Lofts rolled under all this]. Cunanan's friend says he can't understand why this killing spree started. But as for police speculation that he may be killing because he has AIDS and is out for revenge..."

"I'm not going to sit here and be a part of that and speculate," Alan said, "and Andrew is the only one who knows what happened so he's the only one who can tell us what's going on. We need the answers. There's a lot of us out there who need answers. You're the only one who can give it to us. So come forward and let us know what's going on."

"Not knowing what's going on," Grace explained, "this man has moved from his home and has gone into hiding. He fears for his life and the safety of others who consider themselves good friends of Cunanan."

"My friend's dead," Alan concluded, "and if it was that easy for him [Cunanan] he could be just easily me or any other friends."

Tape footage of San Diego rolled on as Grace finished the segment. "Yet this man says knowing Cunanan, first in San Diego's gay community and believing over the years he's gotten to know him better than most, he's not giving up on his friend."

"I still consider him my friend. I still do. He's never done anything to hurt me. I've never ever, ever in the entire time I've known him known him to be violent or wish anybody ill will," Alan said, disbelieving that his dear friend and former lover could possibly be involved in such a series of events.

"Yet the charges are adding up and longtime friends like that one now in hiding struggle with the Cunanan they know and one that they fear could strike again. And that's why the plea for him to give up. In Minneapolis, Bernie Grace, KARE 11 News."

Alan never had to worry, really. Andrew, his friend, would never again show his face in the Twin Cities, even though his gruesome work was not yet done.

Chapter 25 ~ Media buddies

Just at mid-day on Thursday, after Lee completed his first round of phone calls, he and the other FTF agents drove to the FBI headquarters building a few blocks away. As he got out of his squad car, Lee took a deep breath of the fresh Minnesota spring air, but the air reeked of auto and bus fumes, just as the interview he was about to attend reeked of the foul words of the *Star-Tribune* just a few days earlier.

A few blocks away, Chris Graves headed out the door of the *Star-Tribune*. She had the "joy" of interviewing the task force she had just written about on May 12. Still, she hoped for a good story with at least one major newsbreak.

The agents gathered in a conference room with Fred Tremper. Lee sat at the far end of the room, determined to keep his mouth shut. Before Chris Graves came into the room, they discussed how they would handle the Cunanan case. Lee feared leaks, and they all agreed there would be no comments.

Graves came in and sat down, opened her note pad and turned on her tape recorder. She looked at the dozen people in the room and saw blank stares. *Oh this looks like fun,* she thought. Lee could see she was anxious to get an earful, and he set his jaw not to cooperate.

"So, what can you tell me about the Fugitive Task Force?" she asked. She saw more blank stares.

"What do you want to know?" Tremper asked.

"Your history, statistics, maybe some of the tough cases, that sort of thing," she said.

They grunted out answers reluctantly. Lee fidgeted in his chair, refusing to participate. Graves felt frustration building inside her, but at least she got the outline of a vague story about the task force. It was time to go for the jugular vein.

"All right, now what I really want to know is what is going on with this Andrew Cunanan case?" Graves asked, studying the faces, hoping that blanks stares would be replaced by intense interest and willingness to talk – they were not.

"We are working very hard on it, and we're coordinating with agents all across the country," Tremper answered. "The entire Minnesota FTF is assigned to this case. We are doing no other cases. We're coordinating all the leads from our office. It is going well, and we are going to catch him."

"Well, do you have any idea where he is?" she asked.

"You know, we can't really talk anymore about this case," Tremper answered.

"Can't you tell me anything?" she asked again.

"Not about this case," Tremper answered.

"Well, then, who is the case agent?"Everyone sat mute. "Come on guys," she pleaded. They all pointed at Lee. "Oh, Lee Urness."

"Yes, it is my case," Lee admitted reluctantly, "but we don't have to publicize this." He felt angry about even being at the interview and despite his observation that Graves was a competent and professional reporter, he meant to give her no help.

Graves realized she had wasted her time and closed her notebook. The interview had ended. The agents quickly filed out with not another word. Lee and the others went back to work, satisfied that they had done what the FBI requested – meet with the newsies – while not giving them anything that would hurt their case. Graves went back to the *Star-Tribune,* a frustrated reporter. She had no idea what to write, and the story was delayed for weeks.

Lee and Graves never talked again until July 15, when Cunanan once again exploded in rage at an unsuspecting man in Miami Beach, Florida, a city Graves visited July 16, thanks to Lee Urness.

Don't be overly hospitable

Kelly Cooper* sat in her City Club office in Los Angeles, reading the *Los Angeles Times*. Suddenly, her eyes focused on a story about someone she thought she knew; a picture accompanied the story. She studied the face in the picture and thought she recognized the man identified as Andrew Cunanan.

She went to her files and checked to see if her memory was correct. It was. She called the LAPD to report that Cunanan had done two dinner parties at their facility during 1994 and 1995, and that he had paid up his dues through May 1997. Cunanan had listed his residence as Huntington Beach, California on the membership application. City Club's headquarters was in Dallas, so while Los Angeles FTF agents checked the California address, Dallas FTF members went to the company's headquarters to check their records. Anyone who appeared on Cunanan's guest list needed to be contacted immediately.

When Lee heard this report, he smiled broadly. One of the primary jobs of the FTF was to close down as quickly as possible all potential contacts of the crook. As each one of these contacts sat facing an FBI or FTF agent, Lee knew that his chances of catching Cunanan had increased dramatically. All he needed was that one phone call, that one plea for help. And maybe the partying prostitute would make it to someone on his party guest list.

Cunanan loved to party, whether acting as host at a supper club, or alone with a gay lover in a posh hotel. Rich Anderson realized that, given how much Cunanan traveled in San Francisco, a letter to all the hospitality security officers would net positive results. On May 16, he sent a letter to the San Francisco Hotel/Motel Security Association. He asked that if Cunanan tried to register, that they not interfere with him. He reminded them that Cunanan was unpredictable and violent. He asked them to call the FBI the moment it felt safe to do so. Anderson did not want a retired cop working at hotel security to get in Cunanan's crosshairs.

Easy to start rumors, even on the inside

On that Friday, Connie Husan*, a Twin Cities attorney, called the Minnesota Highway Patrol. The face of Andrew Cunanan had been churning through her memory. She saw him, she thought, speeding and driving erratically going west on I-394, a stretch of road that leads out of Minneapolis. She wondered, could it be possible that he was still in the area?

Husan exited at Minnesota Highway 100, "but Cunanan kept driving west," she said.

The highway patrol referred the call to the FBI, where an Intelligence Analyst wrote down the information and created an EC. Each lead, even the most bizarre, had to be dictated and typed, then entered into the permanent record. When this one was reported, it looked like any other except for one significant exception. In bold capital letters, it stated, "ARMED AND DANGEROUS, WARNING: KNOWN OR SUSPECTED HIV INFECTED PERSON."

Lee had made sure that every lead sent from Minnesota bore these types of warnings, but they never included anything about HIV infection. No evidence of that nature existed, save the speculation of a single Minneapolis police officer. Forever putting to rest this supposition meant waiting until they caught Cunanan and could do a blood test. Yet such speculation provided the media, gays and lesbians, and the general public with the kind of sensationalism that feeds even more speculation just as gas feeds a fire.

"Is he killing people because he's got AIDS? Does he hate gays for doing this to him? Why else would he become so violent?" people asked.

Lee had to consider all possibilities and HIV infection was one, but at that time, it had no basis. It certainly did not belong on an official report.

Steve Gilkerson followed up on the lead, but could get no further information from the woman. He decided the lead led nowhere.

TV Leads

America's Most Wanted had gotten the story right on May 17. They *did* tell the story of Andrew Cunanan's murder of William Reese in Pennsville, New Jersey, and the red pickup truck the cops were trying to chase down. They told how Cunanan had disappeared and gave the phone number for people to call with leads. It went well.

Greg Jones, from the Minnesota FTF, sat in the Washington, D.C. AMW call center and sorted through that night's load, some 20 fresh leads. One struck a chord, and Lee got on it right away.

A Scarborough, Maine caller told about a lady who had disappeared on Mother's Day. She had stopped at a store and when finished with her business, walked outside to her car, got in and disappeared. Police found her dead body later that day dumped in a wooded area a short distance away. The car and murderer(s) remained at large.

The place from which she disappeared sat on the main east coast route to Canada, and the murder had occurred the day after Reese's demise. Lee felt this lead had real potential, that Cunanan could have murdered this lady and long since entered Canada in her car. Also, he remembered the two girls who claimed they had seen Cunanan at a truck stop north of Pennsville on May 9. And Canada was one of the places to which Lee had often thought Cunanan would flee. Maine investigators needed to be alerted to look for the red pickup somewhere near Scarborough.

Sometime before midnight, Lee called the FBI Com Center and learned that Ed DeZeilio, the Resident Agent in Portland, Maine, had responsibility for the area.

"Patch me through to him right away," Lee asked.

"Well don't you think it can wait? I mean, it's almost 1:00 a.m. out there," the dispatcher said.

"Who cares? Get the guy up? That's his job," Lee answered. *Sheesh, it's past midnight here and I'm still working. Give me a break!*

Lee called Ed DeZeilio.

"Yes, I am familiar with the case. They haven't found the killer yet and no one saw him," he answered. "I can give you the phone number of the cop who's running the investigation."

Lee thanked him and called immediately, waking the man out of a sound sleep.

"We have no idea where the car is or who killed her," the sleepy cop said after briefing Lee.

"Okay, I'll send you photos on Monday and maybe you could pass them around. Reese's red Chevy truck might be in the area, and you'll want to look for it." Lee knew for sure that Cunanan, even if he had done the murder, was long gone. It really made no difference if he waited until Monday to send the photos. What mattered was getting cops to search for the truck, and for her car, because Cunanan could be driving it.

He called the Toronto FTF and told the duty agent the story about Scarborough.

"No problem, we'll check and see if the license plate has been typed in, then I'll get back to you," the agent said.

"Well, if you find nothing don't bother to call me back." Lee really did not expect a return call and one never came. If Cunanan had killed the lady and stolen her car, he never went to Canada.

Satisfied that he had done all he could on this call, Lee looked up at the clock – 1:00 a.m. That single call had eaten up an hour. "Whew," he said as he picked through other calls that had come in since then; he wondered when he would get to bed.

Just before 2:00 a.m., Greg Jones forwarded a Boston lead to Lee. The anonymous caller claimed that he had recently met a guy in a rest room at the Boston Central Library and they struck up a "gay" conversation. The caller followed the man out to the parking lot and they walked to his car, a Ford Taurus. At that point, the other man – he now felt sure it was Cunanan – pointed to a number of newspapers in the back seat that bore headlines about Andrew Cunanan.

"See, I am famous," the man said, while pointing at the articles.

The caller immediately changed his mind about leaving with the man, but that night he saw the same face on AMW. He felt certain it was Andrew Cunanan.

Lee thought the call was ridiculous, save for two things: another anonymous caller reported much the same experience in the same city during the same time period, and the detailed descriptions of the man he had seen matched those of the first caller. And there had surfaced a few sightings involving a Ford Taurus. "Sounds crazy, but who knows?" Lee said, setting it on a pile of calls to make later that day. "But it isn't worth getting Mike Curazza out of bed," he grunted.

He might kill me

Neil Stoker* had known Cunanan since 1992 and unlike some of his other longtime friends, he actually felt the man had the ability to murder. So much did he worry about Cunanan's murderous ways that on May 17, he called the Long Beach Police Department to tell them about it.

"You know, we have our Long Beach Gay Pride parade and celebration on May 18. Tomorrow. I'm worried that Andrew might come back for it," he told FBI agent John Hause.

"Why are you worried?" Hause asked.

"I'm afraid he might try to kill me!"

"Why you?"

"Because I know him so well. And besides, he knows where I live and he has my phone number," Stoker explained.

"Okay. Look, we will have officers on the street and make sure there are posters up everywhere. If you even hear from Cunanan you call this number immediately," Hause said, handing him his card. "It's okay to be paranoid about him. None of us really know what he might do next. Just help us find him."

"Of course."

"Do you know any other people he might contact or who were his friends," Ann Murphy, Hause's partner asked, readying her pen and pad. Stoker looked to be the kind that readily spills his guts to protect himself.

Stoker immediately rattled off the names and locations of nine other men whom he believed were Cunanan's friends, lovers and associates. "That's all I can think of now."

Soon after talking with Stoker, John Hause called Lee with a report. And they chatted about other possible ways of tracking him.

"You know, if he's got friends with money, one of them could wire him cash through Western Union. You can check them out," Hause suggested.

"Hadn't thought of that. Good idea," Lee said and wrote a note to call them right away, which he did as soon as he got off the line with Hause.

In 1996, Lee had worked with Western Union to track down Louis "Butch" Buggs. Buggs had celebrated Valentine's Day 1996 by buying his girlfriend Talley a bouquet of flowers. Instead of handing her the flowers with a kiss, the 24-year old man shot her to death and promptly fled from the state.

The Minnesota Fugitive Task Force used Western Union to track him to Mexico. Friends had used the service to transfer money to him. As well, Lee had talked on a daily basis with Buggs' grandparents, who lived in Minneapolis, building trust with them. He knew that Buggs would eventually contact them. Buggs finally made the call, and now all that remained was for international red tape to be cut.

Calls about cases like this could come at any moment and if it did, Lee would drop whatever he was doing and hop a plane to wherever they held the killer to bring back his prey. He wanted to catch that plane to pick up Cunanan, and Western Union could produce the missing piece that would punch his ticket.

Lee gave Western Union all of Cunanan's aliases and they did an immediate search. He told the director of security to search for Cunanan's close friends and acquaintances as well – William Norman, Garth Davidson, Erik Erickson, and family members. He wanted to know as much as he could about anyone close to Cunanan who could have sent Cunanan money in this way.

"I want to know any wire transfer they made in the last six months," he told the man.

His search turned up one transfer from the attorney to a woman in Mexico and one from Cunanan to himself, but it was old information and not at all helpful. Such was the nature of this or any other case, searching out information that may or may not be useful. Still, he had to do it, never knowing which piece of data would trigger the final solution.

"Okay. Appreciate the information."

As for relying on friends and acquaintances to turn Cunanan in, the cops heard from plenty of willing helpers, some who feared being "outed" more than they feared becoming Cunanan's next victim. Lee heard from gays all across the country worried that Cunanan might show up in their town or at their celebrations. He made sure that each gay community had all the posters they needed to well mark their events, and he reminded local police to be aware of the possibility that Cunanan might show. But, Lee felt that Cunanan would never show himself where he was known, especially in broad daylight.

"I'm convinced he's only coming out at night. I doubt that you would have anything to worry about," he said. "And I think he'd avoid large crowds because of the likelihood that odds are someone there would know him. He's not going to take that chance."

Cunanan bided his time in Miami Beach. He never left the city and posed no threat to Neil Stoker or any of his former contacts; they did not fit his plan's design.

Chapter 26 ~ Typical AMW night

Each showing of America's Most Wanted created a bevy of calls; some came immediately, even while the show still aired. Other came days, even weeks later. No matter the quality of the information provided by the call, Lee's office dispatched officers to investigate, any time of the day or night. Each investigation cost a few, or even dozens of hours of police work followed by the omnipresent report.

On that Saturday evening, May 17, AMW faxed Lee several dozen calls.

Louise from Owego, New York saw Cunanan driving a red pickup truck on Route 38. Cunanan wore a baseball cap and drove alone. He kept looking in the rearview mirror. She could see that he was good looking.

An anonymous New York caller saw Cunanan driving a red pickup truck in traffic on May 14 near Billingsackie, just south of Albany. Cunanan wore no cap and had black hair. Five others sighted him in the same area.

Jason, from Whitewater, New York saw Cunanan the previous Friday. Cunanan was heading east alone, hitchhiking and carrying a knapsack. He looked "preppie" and wore a nice shirt and khakis.

An anonymous New York caller told AMW that he knew one of Cunanan's gay friends; he said they were "good" friends. He gave the name and address of the fellow in Utica, New York. The caller felt it likely that Cunanan would go visit this man. When Lee saw this, he wondered how many gay men would be accused by angry former lovers of being one of Cunanan's "guys". It made for a wonderful way to get revenge on somebody.

"Hey, imagine this," Lee said after reading this call. "This poor slob answers the door to two FBI agents. 'Hey, we hear you're one of Andrew Cunanan's lovers.' And the guy never had even told his family that he was gay. Or worse yet, maybe the guy isn't even gay. Imagine what his wife and kids are thinking when those two FBI agents are talking to him." Lee knew that these kinds of leads needed to be handled with discretion.

Elizabeth from Biddeford, Maine had just seen Cunanan at a Shop & Save store on Elm Street. He wore glasses, jeans and a black leather jacket. He had black air and brown eyes and came in alone. She thought he looked odd and pointed him out to someone else in the store.

Catherine, also from Portland, Maine saw Cunanan at 5:30 p.m. crossing Temple Street. Cunanan walked casually, smiling and alone. He wore dark clothes and a baseball cap. She believed he hung out at area bars.

In Pittsfield, Maine a man named Terry went to The Broken Putter near the J.W. Parks Golf Course on Harland Avenue on May 16. He saw Cunanan's (Reese's) red pickup truck parked in the lot, and Cunanan was just hanging out there.

Lori from Manchester, New Hampshire knew that Cunanan had lived in the area for about a month. He had been using the name Mike Kessing*. She had last seen him on Wednesday of that week.

Teresa from Winchester, New Hampshire saw Cunanan at 5:00 p.m. in Pisgah State Park. Cunanan had a shaved head and he rode on a motorcycle with an older gay man.

Maurice from Chicago, Illinois had previously worked at the Unicorn Limited bathhouse. He felt sure he saw Cunanan there two weeks earlier but never told the cops, fearing for his job as a security officer. This one intrigued Lee for two reasons: a security cop who feared telling police about a four-time killer made no sense; if it was true that Cunanan had been at the bathhouse two weeks earlier, it meant around May 3. Miglin had been murdered on that date.

Chad from Columbus, Ohio saw Cunanan on the previous Wednesday. Cunanan drove a maroon pickup truck with New Jersey plates, and had shaved his head.

Another Ohio man, Steve from Painesville, saw Cunanan at a flea market at the Lake County Fairgrounds in the afternoon of May 17. Cunanan drove a red truck with New Jersey plates.

And another Ohio Steve, this one from Youngstown, told AMW that Cunanan had driven a brand new red pickup truck on Highway 680, going east. The man saw him at 4:00 a.m. on Wednesday. Cunanan had very short hair, and that was all he could see of him.

A caller from West Virginia saw Cunanan at the Tomahawk Truck Stop in Colorado Springs, Colorado on the previous Monday. He felt sure that the truck stop would have a receipt bearing Cunanan's name. Cunanan traveled with two other men and used a credit card to buy soda and candy.

Joel from Baron Springs, Michigan heard the phone ring in his house at about 11:00 a.m. that Saturday. He claimed that Cunanan spoke with his girlfriend. Cunanan told her that he had stolen a red pickup truck in New Jersey and needed to park it at her house. She told Cunanan that she did not know him, and he replied, "Yes you do. I'm Cunanan." The girlfriend wrote it off as a joke until she saw AMW that night.

Melanie from Westland, Michigan saw Cunanan walk into Sally's Beauty Supply on the previous Friday. Cunanan asked to purchase a clipper to shave his head. He wore designer clothes and tortoise shell glasses. He came back around 5:30 p.m. the same day and started to pay for the clippers with a credit card, but changed his mind and used cash.

An anonymous male caller from Florida called with startling news. Cunanan had been calling a 16-year old girl, Micky Gatson*, of Noblesville, Indiana. The caller claimed that Cunanan and the girl "used to be tight." Gatson had last seen Cunanan seven months earlier; her mother was pretty angry about Gatson's relationship with this "older man."

A Georgia truck driver named Ray drove westbound on I-10 toward Tallahassee, Florida about three weeks before AMW aired. He saw Cunanan masturbating while driving a red pickup truck. "He obviously wanted someone else to see what he was doing," the driver said. Cunanan had short cropped, brown hair, a beard and moustache.

Joe, from Panama City Beach, Florida saw Cunanan at the Big Easy bar in that town on April 30. Cunanan called himself Brian, had black hair and a southern accent. Cunanan/Brian claimed that basketball was his hobby and he was from the west coast. He drank a lot of beer.

A gay man called from Daytona, Florida. He saw Cunanan at The Back Door on May 8. Cunanan had a slight beard, wore glasses and had short brown hair. Cunanan got violent and the bouncers threw him out of the place. Before he left, Cunanan claimed he owned a business and was from Minnesota. He had just come in from stops in New York, New Jersey and Illinois.

Lindsey called from Jacksonville, Florida. She saw Cunanan hitchhiking along I-95 the prior day. He had a buzz cut, and wore blue jeans.

In Edgewood, Kentucky, June saw Cunanan during the early afternoon the prior Thursday. He wore glasses, dark clothes and had dark hair; he drove a small car. He really looked like a homosexual. She reported it to the Kentucky FBI office as well as AMW.

At 10:30 p.m., Keith called from the Bobby Valentine bar in Stamford, Connecticut. He said that at that very moment he stared at Cunanan. Keith said that Cunanan stared back at him while he was making the call. AMW had been airing on the TV above the bar. When Lee got this call, he immediately called Stamford police to get squads to the bar.

Celine from Huntington, New York saw Cunanan either the previous Thursday or Friday. He drove a red truck and seemed to be going nowhere in particular. He wore sunglasses and had short black hair. He winked at her.

A New York City caller remembered that his friend had talked to Cunanan at The Break, a gay bar in Manhattan, on May 12. Cunanan told the man that he was talking to "the serial killer."

Jeanine saw Cunanan driving a red Nissan pickup truck in Greenwich Village, New York City, on May 12.

Rick saw Cunanan walking in Greenwich Village on Thursday, May 15. Cunanan had shaved his head, and looked almost Mexican. He wore a jean jacket, plaid shirt, light-colored jeans and sneakers.

Sandi from Virginia Beach, Virginia saw Cunanan sometime between Noon and 2:00 p.m. on May 17. Cunanan had a 17-year old girl and an older man with him. They were visiting the J.B. Galleries in Virginia Beach. Cunanan was waiting for a cab.

Robert, a Pennsylvania man, saw Cunanan at about 1:00 p.m. that Saturday at a gas station in Carlyle near I-81. Cunanan had dark brown hair, sunglasses and a scruffy face. He drove a black BMW with New Jersey plates. Cunanan tried to pay for his gas with a credit card, and seemed nervous. The card was rejected. The caller never said how Cunanan paid for his gas.

The previous Friday, Cunanan stopped alone at Newbury's store on Oksmond Street in Sayre, Pennsylvania. Samantha saw him there and called AMW.

John saw Cunanan driving alone in a small red pickup truck with New Jersey tags on Route 248 near Slatington, Pennsylvania on the previous Wednesday. He had a two-day growth of beard and dark hair.

Lena from New York called. On Friday afternoon, May 9, Cunanan talked to her at a rest stop on either Highway 81 or 78 on the Pennsylvania side, just before it crosses into New Jersey. He had a thick moustache and long dark hair. His brown eyes suggested to her that he was stoned. Cunanan approached her and wanted to "fool around," but she turned him away. She thought he had been hitchhiking.

Beth, from northeast Philadelphia, had a husband who worked for Brooks Armored Car service. The husband saw Cunanan talking on a pay phone at an area WAWA store. The husband remembered Cunanan well because the truck carried a lot of money. He felt that Cunanan was studying him as if to rob him.

Lewis from Phoenix, Arizona saw Cunanan on the previous Wednesday at the 307, one of the town's gay bars. Cunanan drove with a man in a brand new Ultima that had Arizona plates. He remembered the first three letters –

MYY, he thought. Cunanan seemed to be having no luck talking to his partner who only spoke Spanish.

Vorda, of Somerset, Pennsylvania, saw Cunanan driving a red pickup truck with New Jersey plates on the previous Thursday. Actually, she really had not seen the driver; she only saw the truck.

Wanda from Shinnston, West Virginia wondered if a doctor named Cunanan in a nearby town might not be related to Andrew.

Perry from Orlando, Florida had crossed paths with Cunanan three times during the previous week at temporary job agencies. He saw Cunanan at Labor Finders, Right Hand Man and Labor Solutions. Cunanan hung around at Zuma Beach and a gay club in downtown Orlando.

Another Orlando caller claimed he spotted Cunanan at the Galleria, a brand new gay bar in town. Another caller claimed that Cunanan was in Orlando on the previous Sunday at Big Lots. Yet another caller felt sure Cunanan had been in Orlando because police had found a dead man wrapped in a blanket in a car; the man had AIDS.

Charles from Brooksville, Florida had been driving south on I-75 at 8:00 a.m. that same day when Cunanan cut him off in traffic. Cunanan drove a red pickup truck with a camper on the back.

Elizabeth, who had just moved to Bloomington, Illinois from Washington, D.C., felt sure she had just seen Cunanan. Unfortunately, she could not remember where or when.

Each AMW lead required that a local FBI or FTF agent make at least one face-to-face call; in some cases, the agent made several visits. Each interviewed required a written report, and usually generated at least two calls – sometimes a dozen – between Lee and the investigator.

Still, though few of the leads resulted in anything useful, Lee felt grateful that AMW continued to air the case. One day, some day, someone would *really* see Cunanan and when they did, Lee had everything in place to grab him.

AMW's switchboard quit taking calls at 1:00 a.m. EDT, giving the Minneapolis agents time to complete their paperwork. A few of the leads had resulted in calls to local jurisdictions; follow up calls back to Minneapolis were pending. Finally, the phones quit ringing.

The FTF members left the Minneapolis FBI office just before 3:00 a.m., exhausted, but with no real hot leads that gave them hope for a score within the next 24 hours. They knew that more calls would come in during the next few days, but for now, all they wanted was a warm bed.

Not having a ball

Lee dug himself out of bed just at 7:30 on Sunday morning, May 18, glad that Kari's first game did not begin until 10:00. His body felt like lead, his head ached. He needed more sleep, and a diversion from Cunanan. Softball provided the diversion, but sleep would have to wait.

Having Greg Jones inside the AMW studio to screen the calls had kept Saturday night from being too crazy. He regretted that "the" call had not been received, and figured there would be more calls that day, most likely during Kari's softball games.

Lee knew that the FTF agents and local police departments would not be doing much on Sunday, unless something big broke. He determined that he would handle all calls himself. He did not want to bother the others.

He laid in bed thinking about the red pick-up truck. *How could it be that no one had seen it, as though it had simply disappeared? Perhaps it really was in the bottom of a Pennsylvania quarry, with or without Andrew Cunanan. Had Cunanan stolen another car? And did he stay on the east coast, or had he left the area or worse yet, somehow slipped out of the country?*

He thought yet again about Cunanan killing a cop. Curt Felt's boyish face played across his mind. He had known Curt since the man had been a child. Then Curt had become a Douglas County Deputy Sheriff. One day, while escorting a prisoner to jail, the crook shot the 23-year old deputy dead. Deputy Felt had no inkling of his fate, nor any warning. Lee knew that death could suddenly come to any cop at any time or place. Any cop who surprised Cunanan ran the risk of being blown away.

So on top of worrying about cops dying and catching Cunanan, Lee took responsibility for other innocents whom he might yet attack and kill. The thought worried him greatly, much more so than any other person he had chased, not the least because Cunanan had killed Reese after Lee got the case.

He needed to snap out of his fixation on Cunanan and become part of Kari's world that day. He hoped for a reprieve from the pager, at least long enough to help the Lakers win the Rosemount, Minnesota softball tournament championship.

As he arrived at the softball fields, he found them jammed full of cars. He had to park 100 yards from where Kari's team would compete, and from there, he could not see the field. Getting out of his van, he adjusted the pager on his belt after slipping into his Laker's jersey and walked quickly to the ballfield. The air already felt warm and humid for such an early spring day.

"Hello coach," a grinning Jessie, one of the players said as he walked up. "Did you catch Cu-na-HAN yet?" she asked, purposely saying the name very slowly and incorrectly. (Jessie asked this question of Lee every time she saw him and after a few weeks, it began to weigh on him.)

"Nope, not yet, but we're working on it," he laughed, tussling her hair.

Elizabeth, the tow-headed blond girl who ran like a deer, scampered alongside Jessie. Lee laughed at her boy-like stride, because he had taught her how to run. She had incredible natural speed, but as he often said to her, "You run like a girl." He had taught her how to pump her arms, lean in as she ran and lift her feet, increasing her speed. Itsy Bitsy, as he called the short girl, was the team's stolen base leader.

"Well, if *you* knew how to run, you could catch him," Itsy Bitsy teased her coach.

"Ah, girls don't know how to run," Lee laughed.

"Okay, let's have a race," Bitsy dared him.

"Oh I'd love to, but I have to go coach first base and besides, I wouldn't want to embarrass you," Lee said.

He loved this give and take with the kids, especially after yet another day from Hell, thanks to Andrew Cunanan.

"Hey, how about some gum?" Carly, Kari's catcher yelled as he came near to the dugout.

"Why? You haven't done anything yet," he teased. Carly played a major role in the success of Kari's pitching as the only girl good enough to catch her flaming fastball. Lee called her "Gumby," because she could force her body into some of the unusual contortions to catch Kari's wilder pitches. She was one of the most athletic and nimble girls, or boys, Lee had ever coached.

As always, Lee had stuffed a huge bag of Double Bubble Gum into his pocket from which he would retrieve a piece to reward one of the girls for a good play.

Lee believed that many of life's lessons could be learned on a softball field. He especially pressed his players to play hard all the time. "Never give up. Never stop trying. Keep working to get better and to win. Then even when you lose, and you will lose now and then, you will know you did your best, and your best will make you better." This thought struck him now as he pondered his long police career and how he had never quit once a chase be-

271

gan. He would not quit now, even though his frustration had reached an all-time high. He remained confident that he would eventually catch Cunanan, but wondered how he could maintain the physical and emotional commitment this chase required. *But I will keep on. I will win*, he told himself.

Paging Dr. Urness

Lee sat in the dugout while Kari waited for the next batter to step up. He watched as she looked over at him. He flashed her the "fast ball" sign. Lee had always given Kari her signs, wanting to make sure that she threw the right pitches in each situation. As good as she was, asking a 10-year old to know when to throw which pitch seemed to him beyond her years.

With the sign filed away in her head, Kari stared in at Carly, her catcher, and in one fluid and perfect motion her arm whipped around in a perfect circle, snapping the ball out of her hand at the perfect release point. A 60-mph fastball crossed the plate seconds later.

"Strike," yelled the umpire.

"Way to go," Lee yelled. He signaled her to throw another fastball.

"Strike two," yelled the umpire as the helpless 12-year old batter looked over at her own coach, fear written on her face.

Kari smiled at Lee. He gave her the signal for a change-up. Kari's arm whipped forward with tremendous velocity, but the ball came out at only 40-mph. The hopeless batter swung long before the ball got there.

"Strike three! You're out!" the umpire said.

Lee and Kari nodded at each other.

As the next batter stepped into the box, Lee's pager went off. The message said to call the FBI ASAP.

"Gotta go answer a page," Lee said to the other coach. "Kari's on her own."

Kari frowned as she saw him leave the dugout.

Lee had no choice but to head out to the van to make the call. He dialed the FBI and had them patch him through to the Miami Police Department.

"Lee Urness here, case agent on the Andrew Cunanan case. Someone called just a few minutes ago."

"Yes, I called. I saw the America's Most Wanted Show last night, and I would like some pictures of Cunanan. Any way you can get me some?" she asked.

"We're doing a new set tomorrow, but I will have the current photos faxed down immediately. Okay?" Lee asked.

"Yes, do it. I'll get it to the street cops and to every shift commander," she said, giving Lee her fax number.

Lee dialed up the Minneapolis FBI Communications Center and had them fax the packet to Miami PD immediately. Once confirmed that the packet had been sent, and leaving nothing to chance, he called her back to make sure the copy was good.

"Yes sir, this is great. Thank you. I'll get it out right away," she promised.

"Thanks a lot. And feel free to call if anything comes up," he said, giving her his pager number.

Lee hurried back to the ballfield. He saw Kari getting ready to throw another pitch, and worried that she had struggled through several batters while he was gone, although the bases were empty. "What's going on?" he asked the coach as he stepped into the dugout.

"Oh, two outs in the third inning. Kari hasn't given up a hit, and we're up 2-0."

"Oh," Lee said, a little disappointed that Kari could do so well without him, but happy for her and the team. Still, when his pager rang again several minutes later, he cursed as he walked to the van.

His pager interrupted him only a few times during the first game, which the Lakers won easily, and in-between games he made several calls to FTF members across the country, updating them, getting updated; trying to stay current.

Around 1:00 p.m. Lee sat on a blanket next to the big cooler he and Kathy always brought to the ballfield. They had filled it with sandwiches, sodas and other treats. Lee munched on a sandwich as his pager sounded. AMW had received a call from a Southwest Airlines flight attendant. She claimed to have just seen Cunanan deplaning in San Francisco. Lee called her.

"Oh yes," Arlene Person* said, "I'm the flight attendant that called America's Most Wanted," she told Lee when he got her on the phone.

"Where are you?" Lee asked.

"Still at the airport."

"And what did you see, exactly?"

"Well, last night I watched the TV and today I saw Cunanan on the plane. We flew from Houston to San Francisco, and we just landed. He is probably still here," she said.

"Can you see him now?"

"No, he's probably in the baggage claim area," she said.

"Tell me what he looked like," Lee said.

"He was very casual. He wore jeans, a short-sleeved shirt, and no glasses. He looked just like the picture from the TV show," Pearson said.

"Where can I reach you later? I'm going to have an FBI agent come and see you," he explained. She gave him the location and Lee made a note to call Rich Anderson. "Okay, I'll call you back if I need anything else."

Lee called the FBI and asked for the number of the San Francisco airport police. "Patch me through," he said. He gave them descriptors and asked them to alert their offices and search the terminal and parking lot areas for Cunanan.

Next, he called Rich Anderson and briefed him on what he had done. "And I need you to go see this stewardess," he added, giving him all the detail. "She'll be there this evening."

An hour later, AMW got another call from San Francisco. A man claimed that Cunanan was at the Palisades National Park in San Francisco at that moment.

"Tell me what he looks like," Lee asked.

"He's wearing jeans and a short sleeved shirt; dark hair, medium build," he said.

"Glasses?"

"No, no glasses."

"Thank you sir," Lee said, taking down his contact information. "Please, do not do anything. I am going to get agents there immediately."

Again, Lee called Rich Anderson and gave him the information and asked him to get the San Francisco Police Department out there right away.

He doubted that Cunanan would travel on a public conveyance like an airplane where he would need to show identification, or wander around in a public park, but Lee could take no risks. He called Southwest Airlines and ordered a ticket manifest for the flight the attendant had identified. He knew that everyone who flew had to use a picture ID, and that meant Cunanan most likely had to use his own name.

When he studied the manifest the next day, it did not contain Cunanan's name, or any of his known aliases. Yet Lee knew those two callers were both sincere, and though he felt frustrated at burning up so much police time chasing those two ghosts, he had done the right thing – no one really knew for sure when and where a crook would turn up.

He went back to the picnic and found that the cooler had been closed and packed away. The girls had filtered back to the ballpark to await their 3:00 p.m. game.

A few more leads from AMW had come that day, but none seemed very promising or pressing until the one at 1:50 p.m.

This could be your guy...and then again...

Lee got a flash call from AMW and ran to the van. Hallie Jarkess*, a clerk at the Race Track Gas Station in Clearwater, Florida claimed someone matching Cunanan's description drove off without paying for their gas. Jarkess had captured the license plate number of the red car and saw that it was from Maine. Lee had the FBI patch him through to the Clearwater Police Department. He filled them in on the details he had, including that the driver apparently also had a girl with him.

The description of the man sounded enough like Cunanan that Lee immediately contacted the FBI Resident Agent and faxed his picture out. "And send someone out there right away to interview the clerk, in person," Lee asked.

They plotted a strategy of how to arrest Cunanan, just in case this was a legitimate sighting. What gave this call credibility was that it was a red car and the Maine license plates matched those of the missing Scarborough woman's car.

TV stations quickly noticed the story. The fact that the car had been owned by a murder victim gave it local play. The station described the incident and the man, possibly Andrew Cunanan, and his accomplice, in some detail. The manager of the gas station told the public that the culprit clearly resembled Cunanan.

Cunanan, hidden away in Miami Beach, watched the TV reports with rapt interest and laughed snidely at the foolishness of the reporters and cops. He had never been to Maine, never murdered a woman and certainly did not drive off from a gas station. That would be dumb.

Later, the gas station manager admitted she had made up the part about Cunanan, although Jarkess had reported exactly what he saw. When shown pictures of Cunanan, though, he knew it was not him. Another false lead and dozens of police man-hours wasted. A week later, police in the Clearwater area caught the two young thugs who had killed the Maine woman and stolen the car. They looked nothing like Andrew Cunanan.

As Lee walked back toward the ballfield, he turned right around and headed back to the car. His pager had rung again; CALL FBI ASAP.

"Urness here," he said when the dispatcher picked up. "What great breakthrough do we have now?"

"Eagan (Minnesota) police called. Some guy says he saw your man at a Burger King this morning," the dispatcher said. "They're checking it out right now."

"Give me the information," Lee said, pulling out his legal pad. His pile of pads had tripled in size just since the previous weekend. At this rate, he felt he personally would use up a few cases of them before he caught Cunanan. Moments later he had Kerry Leplin* on the line.

"Mr. Leplin, the FBI says that you may have seen Andrew Cunanan this morning?"

"Yes sir, at the Eagan Burger King right on Cliff Road," Leplin said.

"Why do you think it was Cunanan?" Lee asked.

"Well, I met him at a gay pride festival last summer and then last night I saw him on America's Most Wanted," Leplin claimed.

"Tell me what he wore and what he looks like," Lee said. But Leplin's description was far off base; save for a vague resemblance to the AMW picture, Leplin certainly had not seen Cunanan.

"Well, thank you sir. You've been a great help, and if you see him again, or he tries to contact you, give me a call right away," Lee said. "Here's my office number. Please write it down."

Finished with the caller, Lee called the Eagan Police Department. "Say, on that sighting of Andrew Cunanan, you can call off your dogs. It's not him," he said. Lee saw that he had filled another legal pad and so, shoved it into the expandable file he kept with him at all times. He noticed that the manila folder that held his case file had become severely dog-eared. "Let's see if you and I can make it through this case," he said to the folder. "Maybe I'll get all wrinkly and worn like you before this is over."

Chapter 27 ~ Let's play ball, please?

Finally, game two began – the tournament championship. Lee knew this was one of the biggest tournaments of the year, and winning it meant a lot to the girls. The other team had a lot of talent and older girls, and Lee knew they would not roll over for the Lakers.

"Let's go girls; this is what it's all about. Now give it your best," he said as the team ran onto the field. *Yes, this is what it is all about. Using all your practiced skills to win the game. Mr. Cunanan, you will lose, and you know it.*

Both teams played hard and the other team actually got to Kari. Lee had to will his body to move by the top of the fourth inning and looked at a scoreboard that showed the Lakers trailing 4-2. As much as he wanted the Lakers to make a comeback, even more so he wanted the friendly easy chair in his living room, where he could sip a Jack Daniels and 7-Up.

No sooner had he taken his position at first base in the top of the fourth inning than his pager beeped. The message said, "CALL FBI ASAP." He waved at one of the fathers who sat in the stands to take his place and made for the van, buried among hundreds of other vehicles 100 yards away.

"What have you got?" he asked the dispatcher.

"We got a call from AMW. They have a hot lead."

Lee called AMW and heard, "We have a guy who says that he is looking at Cunanan right now."

Lee wrote down his name and phone number and immediately called the man. Before he would call local police, he wanted to ensure that the call was legitimate.

"Is this Will Stevens*?" Lee asked as he heard the phone pick up.

"Yes, it is."

"This is Lee Urness, the case agent on the Minnesota Fugitive Task Force. America's Most Wanted called and said you may have seen Andrew Cunanan," Lee said.

"I'm looking at him right now," Stevens said.

"Why do you think it is him?" Lee asked.

"I saw Andrew Cunanan on America's Most Wanted last night and I am absolutely sure it was him. He was leaning against a post just maybe 15 feet away, just outside my store."

"What did he look like? What was he wearing?"

"I'd say he was of medium height, wearing blue shorts, a long-sleeved jean shirt, hiking books and was clean shaven. And he wore glasses, thick prescription glasses," Stevens explained.

"Well thank you for making the call. If we find him in the area, we owe you a lot. And keep your eyes open. If you see him again, call the Boca Raton Police right away," Lee said, "and then call me," he added, giving him the toll-free BCA number.

Lee felt his pulse quicken ever so slightly. *Could it be?* While he waited, he strained his neck to peer around the cars that blocked his vision of the ballfield. No dice.

Within seconds, he had the Boca Raton dispatcher on the line.

"This is Lee Urness, case agent on the Andrew Cunanan chase. He is a four-time murderer and…"

"Who are you?" the dispatcher asked.

"We are chasing a four time murderer named Andrew Cunanan. I am the case agent on the Minnesota Fugitive Task Force. We just received a call from the Boca Mall that Cunanan is standing outside a lady's handbag store at this moment," Lee said.

"That mall is on the edge of town."

"Can you dispatch squads immediately to the mall, to this store?" Lee asked. Lee gave the dispatcher the NCIC number and other descriptors.

The clerk hesitated long enough for Lee to add, "Give me your fax number and I'll have the photo and descriptors faxed to you immediately." Lee called the FBI Com Center on his personal cell phone and had the packet faxed. He went back to the dispatcher. "It should be there in seconds."

"Well, okay. Tell me this again, please."

"The guy claims Andrew Cunanan is standing in front of his store right now at this mall near Jacobson-Meier at 200 Park Real or something like that." Lee gave the dispatcher the clerk's name and location.

"Yes, I know the place," the dispatcher said.

"Send the squads now and on their way out there, make sure they're looking for the red pickup truck as they drive. He could be leaving the place. You might want to call the clerk while the squads are going out," Lee said. He knew that they might have only a few minutes before it would be too late.

"Okay," she said as she put him on hold. "They're on the way. They'll be there in five minutes."

"Call me back when they get there. Here's my number," he said.

Then began the longest five-minute wait he had endured since first getting the case on May 7. *Could this be it? Did we finally get their lucky break?* Still, it made no sense. *Why would Cunanan risk such a thing, being out in public in broad daylight? But was he staying in the Boca Raton area? And where was Boca Raton anyway? What was it close to, that is, places where Cunanan might lay low?*

He felt that if Cunanan really *was* at the mall, they had a chance at getting him. The time from his being paged to the arrival of the squads had to be no more than 10 minutes. It was the best lead yet.

"Urness here," he said, when his cell phone finally rang.

"This is Boca Raton PD."

"Your people at the mall?"Lee asked.

"Yes, they are there. And in the store. No one of that description has been found," the dispatcher said dispassionately.

"Is it busy there?" Lee asked.

"Oh yes. It's a very busy mall"

"Did they check the parking lots for the red truck and did they check the entire mall, every store?"

"Yes sir, I am sure they did," the dispatcher answered. "But they did not spot anyone who looked like him."

"Did you get the fax?" Lee asked.

"Yes sir, and we will distribute it to the supervisors and squads right away. If he's here, we will spot him," she answered.

Lee knew that they would be short-staffed on a Sunday afternoon, and it still seemed illogical that Cunanan would be standing in a mall in broad daylight, but he also knew that crooks are dumb. He worried that the Boca Raton PD might overlook a small detail, and it would be the one that prevented them from finding Cunanan. In any event, whether any part of this current lead made sense was irrelevant.

"Well thank you for your good work," Lee said. "We will be in touch, and please, have the officers call me right away if they find anything at all."

"Will do."

Lee sat back thinking for a moment. He became convinced that the man Stevens had spotted could not have been Cunanan. Cunanan was a night person, and it was illogical for him to be in the middle of a mall during the daytime, given the continuous and voluminous media coverage he had generated.

Lee could not imagine a place in America where Cunanan's face remained unknown.

Then again, Cunanan was a social person who needed to be with people to be happy. He pictured him spending the last several days holed up in a seedy motel room somewhere, unlike the fancy digs he preferred, wiling away his time watching TV, reading newspapers, totally bored, wondering when the door would be smashed open by a SWAT team. *And what about his voracious sexual appetite? Is he doing himself?* From what he had learned about him, that, too seemed unlikely. *Pity the guy who has sex with him and then finds out who he is*, Lee thought, shaking his head.

Lee checked his watch. The whole incident had taken 20 minutes. As he got out of the van, he half expected to see the Lakers players making their way to station wagons and mini-vans, ready to leave after their loss, but he saw no such thing.

He rushed back to the field, hoping that somehow they had gone into extra innings. As he neared the field, he saw Kari throw a blazing fastball toward home plate and heard the umpire yell, "You're out!"

Kari began jumping up and down and the other girls mobbed her. When the excitement stopped, the other coach told him the story.

"It was unbelievable. We got two runners on with two outs. Kari hits a double and ties the game. Then she gets driven in with the go-ahead run! Then in the bottom of the fifth, she strikes out the side. What a game! You should've seen it."

"Yeah, I should have," Lee said, dejected. Kathy saw him and walked over.

"You okay?" she asked.

"You know, this really sucks!" he said. "I got screwed out of this, and we didn't even find the guy anyway."

"Yes, you're right. It sucks," she said. "You have to catch this guy before he destroys your summer, too."

As he drove home, he called Kevin Rickett and told him about the calls and missing the Lakers' victory. "Cunanan is mucking up my life!" he growled. "This has got to end."

It did, but not before Cunanan mucked up his life for several more weeks.

Finally, that chair

Lee got home and made himself a sandwich. Then he found his easy chair and crashed, turning on the TV, but not really seeing it.

Once again, his thoughts went back to Douglas County. He remembered that the sheriff's office phone rang at all hours, just as did his FTF pager. As a teenager, Lee knew his dad could be called out at any hour, but even when no one called, Howard seldom slept through an entire night.

Howard hated burglars. He made it his personal mission to stop them before they did their foul deed. Each night Howard went to bed at 10:00 p.m., leaving the night patrol to one of his two deputies. Still, he usually roused himself around 1:00 a.m. Dressing in his sheriff's uniform, he quietly slipped out of the house and drove to one of the nearby towns to sit and keep watch. When Lee did not have school the next day, he would often get up and tag along.

One of Howard's favorite towns was Brandon, a tiny city of 1000 residents located about 20 minutes north and west of Alexandria. Brandon featured a liquor store, a grocery store and a gas station. High on a hill just on the edge of Brandon sat a tiny white country church, and it was there that the sheriff set up his surveillance.

Surveillance, using the Urness method, meant turning off the lights, rolling down the windows and studying "downtown" Brandon with the binoculars that Howard had taken off an old German officer in France during World War II. Most of the time he spent listening.

"On a quiet night I can hear a car five miles away," Howard told his young protégé. "Listening is better than watching, but you gotta have patience. In law enforcement, patience is one of the greatest virtues."

As Lee remembered that lesson, he almost had to pinch himself. If anything, the Cunanan case had caused him to become reactionary, not patient.

Howard explained that during surveillance, "If you smoke cigarettes, the crook can see the end of a burning cig for miles at night, so you have to cup it and hide it."

As an adult, Lee had done thousands of hours of surveillance, both as a narcotics cop and now, chasing crooks. He often sat in a car blocks from a sting, using a special telephoto lens installed in his van to spy on someone, or he tapped into high-tech eavesdropping equipment he had planted earlier near the target site. Sometimes he rented space next to or across the street from a suspect. Patience was a lesson he had learned well from his father. *But I'm losing it on this one*, he realized.

Lee loved working with his dad, and his dad loved to have him along. Yet, as much as Howard enjoyed his job, he did not want to force it on Lee.

"Don't get into law enforcement," he told him more than once. "Get a job where you don't have to get up in the middle of the night and where you can spend more time with family."

"Ha!" Lee said to himself aloud. "Guess I never followed that advice," but he had never regretted it, and neither did Howard Urness. Lee coveted the picture of his grandfather, Sheriff Bennie Urness, pinning the sheriff's badge on Howard. Lee also had the picture of Howard pinning the badge on him when he was sworn in.

Lee remembered how he got antsy sitting quietly there in the car with his dad. Yet to see how Howard was so committed to protecting the local community from crime, especially crime perpetrated by big city crooks who sometimes plied their craft in the small towns, made a huge impression on him. When it came to doing surveillance, not even sleep took precedence.

At that time, Howard drove an unmarked 1960 Buick. He also provided the sheriff's department with a 1957 Buick that had a stick-shift transmission and could do 90 in second gear. Howard had to pay the costs of operating those cars, with the county reimbursing him at a dime a mile. Lee saw in this that personal sacrifice, and the dedication to do hated paperwork, was a necessary part of the job.

Howard tried to be on his surveillance hill before 2:00 a.m., telling Lee "between 2:00 and 4:00 is prime burglar time. If someone's driving on my roads after 2:00, I want to know what they're doing."

On those occasions when he spotted something going on, he quietly rolled the car down the road that led from the church, turning off his headlights. Howard seldom called for backup; and even if he had, his tube radio had at best a 15-mile radius and it would have done very little.

Most often he found area kids – kids whose parents and grandparents he had long known – breaking in to steal pop or beer. He could usually stop them with a stern warning, sending them home. If they refused to obey, he would take them home – justice enough for most rural kids. The occasional professional burglar met a tougher fate, ending up in the old brick jailhouse back in Alexandria.

Lee smiled at the memories. Howard never had to chase down a crazed killer like Andrew Cunanan, but if he had, Lee could picture him sitting in a car, watching, waiting and listening. He picked up the phone and called his dad in a ritual he tended to repeat when he needed wise counsel from an objective source.

Them Lee relaxed and soon dozed off in the chair.

He awoke in time to hear the 10:00 p.m. news, and saw the latest story about Cunanan. *Soon I'll have you in my sights, you jerk, and then you're mine*, he said. He never heard the weather or sports reports that night, focusing on but one thing: catching Cunanan. He picked up his case file and the note pads he carried with him and once again, read every page looking for something he may have missed. His eyes begged him for sleep, and finally, he headed to the bedroom.

Sleep came quickly, uninterrupted by any calls. Morning, too, came quickly, but with it, no breakthroughs.

Chapter 28 ~ Need a breakthrough

Lee got to the office early Monday. The Cunanan case was now officially 12 days old, and he was no closer to apprehending him than on that first day, save for cutting off most of Cunanan's contacts.

At precisely 7:00 a.m., he called Paul Murray. He had a big issue to discuss with his friend and confidant. He felt he had done everything right in this Cunanan case, but he had hit a wall. The only time he had really gotten close was in New Jersey and Cunanan had slipped through his hands. Since then, the FTF had received dozens of leads, but nothing of value. He needed to regroup, to take the next logical step. That meant climbing the FBI pyramid to its apex – a Top Ten listing, but a decision not made easily.

"You find my pick-up truck yet?" he asked Murray when he got him on the phone.

"Do you have any idea what you've done to me?" Murray asked. Lee could hear that his friend was both agitated and tired.

"What do you mean?"

"Your obsession with that truck is driving me nuts. Last night I couldn't sleep. All I could hear was you asking me, 'did you find my truck yet?' So I got out of bed in the middle of the night, got dressed and drove to the Philly airport. I personally, personally I tell you, checked every parking stall at that airport," Murray went on, getting more excited as he told the story.

"So did you find my truck?" Lee needled him, in fact, really grateful for the sacrifice Murray had made.

"Your truck is nowhere in New Jersey. Of that I am now sure," Murray said.

"How can you be sure?" Lee said, not willing to give up yet.

"We got the choppers and they flew over every inch of woods and the beaches. I wrote to every parking lot in New Jersey and New York City, and they all checked their lots. The FTF agent in Atlantic City personally checked the casino lots. The park rangers checked all the parks. I even checked the flying schools. Your truck just isn't here," Murray said.

"Okay."

"And I didn't find your man either," Murray answered. "But I've been on the phone every day with Thedford and Bakken and anyone else I can raise. I begged San Francisco to get Cunanan's lady friend Elizabeth to go public

I'm doing everything I can," he added. It had become his full-time and only job.

"Good work." Lee changed the subject. "I've got some new posters to send out. I sent Charbonneau to Hennepin County to ask their crime lab to make me a master copy and Fred Tremper said go to Kinko's and print them," Lee explained. "So I have this new, four picture spread of Cunanan. We'll print a ton of copies and send some out to you," Lee added.

That day, he had 5,000 black and white copies printed at a nearby offset print shop. These became his staple wanted poster until they could find even more recent pictures, or until the FBI finally made official posters.

Lee had talked to FBI headquarters early on about getting communications help, but he felt he really did not need them. He knew that winning their help required painstaking hours of paperwork and procedures, and he wanted to focus on fieldwork. He knew that most of the agents at the FBI's D.C. headquarters are on a supervisory career track, and to rise in management they followed a certain promotional routine and that included a stint at HQ.

"When you talk to these agents at HQ, you know they're in a place they are not going to stay," he said to Lisa Davis. "And many of them are not street cops, but they can still really help us out. They've got assets we can use."

Lee could never see himself as an inside agent. He preferred arresting guys and doing investigative work.

"But I hate having to go through channels all the time," Lee complained and did his best to work around procedure whenever he felt he had no choice. Kevin Rickett became his most valuable team member for the sole reason that he knew the paperwork system – what could and could not be done, and he kept Lee balanced.

Better get on with it

"What do you think about me doing a Top Ten request on this case?" Lee asked Murray. Few crooks ever made the elite list. Most commit less serious crimes than Cunanan and other murderers, and almost all are caught fairly quickly.

"It's a real pain in the rear," Murray answered. "I know I'd hate to do one. I'd rather be out chasing the bad guys."

"Well, we've been doing that, but we haven't caught him," Lee reasoned.

"Okay, yeah, I think you probably should. But you guys are really going to be in a paper mess," he said.

"That's why I have Young Rickett. He's my FBI paper expert. If I didn't have him, there is no way I'd do it," Lee said. "And I have to do the Red Notice for Interpol, so I thought I might as well do it all at once."

"Yup, if you have to do it, that's the way to go. I wish you well and," he laughed, "I'll be busy chasing your guy, so don't call me for help."

"I thought you'd fly in to type it all for me," Lee laughed as he hung up.

As soon as he knew Fred Tremper was in his office, Lee drove over to talk with him. He updated him on the weekend's activities and his confident resolve that they would catch Cunanan soon. "But I think we need to go the next step."

"Top Ten?" Tremper asked.

"Yup. We've had it for two weeks now. I think it's time to get Rapid Start, Top Ten, Interpol. All of it," Lee said.

"Well, it's your call," Tremper sighed. "I think it's the right kind of case. It's gotten tough, that's for sure."

"Oh I still guarantee you that I'm going to get that son of a bitch. Sometime in June," Lee said intensely. "He'll screw up. They always do."

"Okay, I say go ahead and get it done. I'll sign off as soon as I get the paperwork," Tremper answered.

Lee went back to the office both pumped and frustrated. He knew that the tip that could end the case could come at any moment, and he felt ready to pursue it, but in the meantime, he had to prepare for the long haul. The idea of doing hours of paperwork nearly gagged him. As he walked into the FTF office, he raised his eyebrows, took a deep breath and called the group together.

"Hey gang, I've decided we have to do a Top Ten filing, and Tremper says go ahead," he told them.

"Damn it Lee," Steve Gilkerson said. "I've been in this company for 30 years and never got involved in a Top Ten and now you're gonna suck me in."

"I got you," Lee laughed. "I think all you guys should do one before you retire. Anyway, Young Rickett, Burnsie and I can do it. You go catch my guy."

Gilkerson threw a dart at Cunanan's face.

"Rickett, you and Jeanie figure out what we need to know and as soon as we can find a moment, we'll get it going," Lee said. It would be Wednesday before they actually began putting the paperwork together, but getting "all our ducks in a row," as Lee told them, would take many hours.

The Top Ten listing would give Lee a tremendous boost. Street agents saw busting a Top Ten Fugitive as a career step, and they would make it their number one priority.

Though the media continued to carry regular reports on the case, it had already begun to lose some its charm with the newsies – coverage had lessened. In time, Lee believed that the reporters would quit saying much at all about it, until Cunanan killed again. Then they would feast on the cops for not having caught him first. Once Cunanan made the Top Ten, media interest would be sparked, and having Cunanan's face hanging in every Post Office and on the FBI internet site would be a great help.

Lee knew that once Cunanan made the Top Ten, the FBI treated it as a first priority case. If Lee needed money, there would be no limit. If he needed help from headquarters, they would drop everything to do what he needed. When he would say Cunanan and Top Ten in the same sentence to a sleepy agent anywhere in the world in the middle of the night, he knew that agent would snap awake. There would be no excuses, just action.

Even the dreaded paperwork that followed every step of the case would get a high priority.

"So, people, let's get going on it," he said to Jeanie Burns and Kevin Rickett.

First, Lee had another round of phone calls to make.

Follow up leads nowhere

He called the Clearwater, Florida police department to get an update on Sunday's gasoline drive off.

"So, did you find my guy?" Lee asked.

"Nope, sorry. In fact, you'll love this. The station manager, the one that was on TV last night telling everyone what she saw – she admitted she never saw the suspect. She was in the storeroom all the time. It was her clerk who actually reported it," he said.

"I guess they all want their day in the sun. Oh well, it's not the first time and it won't be the last," Lee sighed.

"Well the lady who reported it sure thought the guy looked like Cunanan," the officer added.

"Well that happens a lot. By the way, I also called in another one to you guys yesterday. Some anonymous Clearwater caller said he saw the red pickup truck. I don't suppose your people came across my truck?" Lee asked.

"I see the report here, but no; there has been no report about the truck."

"That's what I figured, but thanks for you help," Lee said. "Listen, I have to call Maine about the drive off. It's their car that the lady saw, so thanks a lot and keep your eyes open for my guy."

Lee checked his notes and found the phone number for the Portland Resident Agent with whom he had spoken on Sunday.

"Just thought I'd let you know that the drive off yesterday in Florida was your car, but not my guy," Lee said.

"So I heard."

"At least we found your car for you," Lee laughed softly. "Hey, let me know if you catch your killer." He heard that just a few days later they caught the two men who had done the Maine murder. He took solace in helping out on that case.

"I'm still going to send the photos up to you, if that's all right, and maybe you can show them around," Lee suggested.

"Sure, can do."

"Toronto FTF has alerted all the border crossings, but who knows? He could be hiding in one of your mountain cabins. We really don't know where he is," Lee admitted. "So thanks for your help."

"No problem."

Lee sat back and shook his head. *How many of these will we have to chase down before we catch the real one?*

"Hey people," Lee said, calling out to his Minneapolis team, "we have to watch for these, too." He reminded them about Clearwater and the "wanna-bees" who glom on to big cases. "And I'm sure we'll get more," he said, in what was perhaps his single greatest understatement during those weeks.

"Lee, line 3. This time it's the genuine article," Vern Lee said cynically. "Cunanan's in *Minnesota*."

Lee rolled his eyes before picking up the phone.

"Lee Urness here. Can I help you?"

"Yeah, this is Wanda Witherspoon from America's Most Wanted. We just got a call from someone who says they just spotted Cunanan somewhere in Minnesota," she said.

"Oh really. Where?"

"Is there a place called Marshal? That's where they said they called from."

"Oh yes, in southwestern Minnesota. Well, give me what you got," Lee said, writing it down. The caller had spotted a silver Lincoln with New Jersey plates heading westbound on I-90. The car had exited at Worthington, Minnesota. "Okay, I have it, and thanks a lot," Lee said.

He called the Nobles County Sheriff's Department and gave them the information, then faxed an information packet down.

"Call me as soon as you know anything," Lee said. He had to fight the urge to tell the sheriff to let it go. Cunanan could not be in Minnesota; it made no sense. Yet there was always a remote chance that it could be him, no matter how crazy it sounded.

Lee tried to imagine what it would be like for a rural sheriff who might actually pull that Lincoln over and find Cunanan. The thought of Cunanan opening fire sent shivers down his spine.

When they finally did corner Cunanan, Lee knew that a SWAT team would surround the place where he hid. He visualized dozens of trained officers with M-P 5s, rifles, shotguns and .40 caliber pistols trained on a closed door or a bank of windows as the team leader shouted on his megaphone to Cunanan, trying to get him to surrender peaceably. Lee chuckled at this vision and compared it with how these things had been done in rural Douglas County, long before someone invented the acronym, "SWAT."

Peaceful or violent ending?

Just after Lee had become a sworn deputy at the age of 21, a call came into the Douglas County Sheriff's office reporting that a crazed man was standing in a field alongside a county road threatening people with a gun.

Sheriff Howard Urness, Lee and another deputy jumped into the old Buick squad car and sped to the farm where the man had been spotted. It sat out on a sparsely populated rural road that ran past a long string of 160-acre farms.

Howard parked a quarter mile from where he had been told the gunman was holding forth, and the three cops walked slowly and cautiously toward the driveway into the field. There they saw the "crazy" man, a local doctor who owned the farmland. He stood on the field side of a barbwire fence, waving a .357 magnum pistol in the air and screaming at them.

Lee drew his own .357 and held it ready. The other deputy carried his shotgun, ready to fire at the least provocation. As they drew nearer, though, Howard left his gun holstered. He walked slowly toward the doctor, his eyes focused on the man's eyes.

"Why in hell do you have that gun?" Howard asked, stopping about 10 feet from the doctor.

"The government is trying to take my land, and I'm not giving it to them. They can do anything they want to me, but they aren't getting my land!" he screamed.

"Come on now, this is not the way to handle it," Howard said, stepping closer. The doctor raised the gun slightly, his hand on the trigger. Lee's arm tensed, preparing to swing up and sight in on the man's head. The other deputy raised his shotgun slightly.

"And my kids. They don't care about the farm. They want me to just sell the place," he said, tears forming in his eyes. "Don't you see? I can't let that happen."

"Come on now, you have to stop this," Howard said. "You're a doctor. Hire a lawyer…"

"Damn lawyers! They just want my money!" he screamed.

"Doc, come on now. You have to stop. Now give me the gun," Howard pleaded, holding out his hand as he drew within a yard of the man, never breaking eye contact.

"Okay sheriff," he said. "But you tell that kid to quit pointing his gun at me, I'm afraid he might hit me," the doctor finally said, nodding toward Lee.

"Okay son, you can lower the gun now," Howard told Lee. Lee holstered his gun.

The doctor handed his gun to Howard and walked with him to the squad car, his head bent in shame.

"Oh," the doctor said as he prepared to get into the back seat, "I better give you this." He reached down and pulled a hunting knife out of his boot and handed it to Howard. Then he climbed into the back seat without further incident.

Lee shook his head as he remembered that situation. *Man, how'd we ever keep the peace without shooting people? If that poor doc was Cunanan, I doubt he'd still be alive. But, then, if it was Cunanan, I doubt that he would have laid down the gun.*

The ringing of a phone jarred him back to reality.

Not your guy

"Lee, line 5. Nobles County," Jeanie Burns said.

"Urness here."

"Sorry, we found the car and it's not your guy," the deputy said.

"No problem. I really didn't think it would be, but thanks a lot. You never know when the real call comes in," Lee said.

"I wish you well."

Lee ached to get out of the office and talk to someone, anyone, associated with the chase. Sitting there at his desk or in the car when he needed a break, made him ever more anxious. He hated the feeling that he could not look Cunanan's friends in the eye as they talked, or commiserate with Cunanan's family.

Instead of grabbing his jacket and heading out to do interviews, he headed for the van. He had more phone calls to make.

"Hey Murray, Urness here.

"No, I didn't find your truck," he said before Lee could ask it. "I need your help on something," Murray added.

"Okay."

"Investigators out at Finns Point found that some government drafts were missing out of a check book Reese kept at the caretaker's house. They were issued out of Gelco Finance there in Minnesota. Will you call and see what they can do?" Murray asked.

"Got it. Do you know the denominations or draft numbers or anything?" Lee asked. There were two: one for $1,200 and one for S5. "I'll ask Gelco to flag them if anyone tries to cash them." Lee discovered later that day that neither of the checks had been cashed.

"Say, we got a latent print off the Lexus," Murray added.

"*A* print?"

"Yes, just the one. But you'll never guess which print?" Murray teased.

"Okay, fill me in."

"The middle finger of his left hand," Murray chuckled.

"Figures."

"I'll keep you posted," Murray said.

"I'll do the same," Lee said, and they hung up. Then Lee made his other calls: to New York, Boston, Miami, Chicago, San Diego, Los Angeles and San Francisco. He chatted with Coleen Rowley about what the media was saying. He reported to his FBI and BCA bosses. FBI officials in Washington,

D.C. had taken a keen interest in the case, creating more phone calls and the longer this went on, the more they wanted to know. *Well, all the better. We should get our Top Ten and Rapid Start approved right away. I guess that's one way to cut through red tape.*

Wisconsin: the next sighting

Ellen Renstrom* stood behind her teller's window at the Security Bank on Wisconsin Avenue in Milwaukee at 1:15 on Monday. "Next," she said.

"I'd like to cash this Visa Traveler's Check," a male customer said.

"Are you a customer here?" Renstrom asked.

"Well, no, but this is a Visa check. It should be good anywhere," he said.

Ceil Kroll*, another bank clerk, overhead the conversation and glanced at the customer. Then she looked again, thinking he looked familiar.

"It is our policy that we only cash these for our customers. I am sorry, sir," Renstrom said firmly.

"What am I supposed to do?"

"You could try Bank One or First Bank. I'm sure they will help you," Renstrom said. She and Kroll watched the man leave.

"He look familiar to you?"Kroll asked.

"Yes, he does. But why?"

"Maybe it's *him*," Kroll said, pointing to a newspaper article from the prior day. "That Cunanan fellow."

"You know," Renstrom said, studying the photo, "you could be right."

They notified Milwaukee police. Lee immediately faxed Cunanan's photos over, and the police took them with them to the bank. They showed the photos to Kroll and Renstrom. "It sure does look like the man we saw," they said.

Police reviewed the bank surveillance tapes with the two tellers. Though there was a resemblance, the customer's male pattern baldness immediately ruled him out. Despite knowing for certain that it was not Cunanan, the cops made copies of the photo from the surveillance tape for the record.

Chapter 29 ~ One day flows into the next

The days had been a blur since Lee got the case on May 7. Nothing about this case felt normal.

Tuesday came as fast as Monday fled, and the routine was the same. More leads turned up. They were all wrong.

Tom from Broward County, Florida, called America's Most Wanted that day. They immediately referred the call to Lee. Tom believed he saw Cunanan at the Ft. Lauderdale airport on May 15, 1997. Cunanan acted nervous and wanted to get to South Beach as quickly as he could. This report required contact with the Ft. Lauderdale airport, distribution of Cunanan photos and a request for all airlines with service to Miami Beach to check their passenger manifests. Neither Cunanan's name, nor any of his aliases, turned up.

In the Saugerties, New York area, Heather, a 15-year old high school girl spotted a man in a red pickup truck that had pulled over to talk with a man on the street. She thought, four days later, that the driver was Cunanan. She overhead Cunanan asking the man for directions to Woodstock, New York.

Lee contacted the R.A. and asked her to track it down. FBI Agent Lisa Massaroni located the man to whom Cunanan had spoken, and he confirmed the event. He said he had been out walking his dog when Cunanan stopped and asked directions, which he readily gave. That night he read an article about Cunanan and felt sure it had been him earlier that day.

The man gave Massaroni a good description of the truck. Together, the Saugerties Police Department and FBI issued an alert about the truck and Cunanan.

Meanwhile, Massaroni contacted Paul Murray and asked him what he thought. Murray informed her that Reese's truck did not have a white cab, but it *did* have New Jersey plates. He also told her that Cunanan had put on weight since the photo had been taken.

Given what facts she had gathered, Massaroni believed she had an unconfirmed Cunanan sighting. It did not surprise Lee.

Lee marveled at how people reacted to the AMW stories. No one outside of his office knew how many times already Cunanan had been spotted in several different cities at the same time by people absolutely convinced it really was him. Lee found that even he had started seeing look-alikes when he went into a store or gas station.

That Tuesday, Lee convened a conference call with the case agents in 10 FBI divisions. During the one-hour call they talked about everything they knew, their progress and the lack thereof. They agreed that they were running out of good leads. Everyone associated with Cunanan had been talked to in person, and he had not tried to contact any of them.

The agents discussed those potential Cunanan contacts who needed to be closely watched, especially two on the west coast.

Lee went down his checklist of questions, and as always, concluded by asking, "What have I missed?" The call ended.

He looked at his watch. It was past 1:30, and his stomach growled.

Among other things that had changed since Lee got the case was that his whole eating schedule had been thrown off. Lee liked to eat, but this chase gave him no time for it and, in fact, he had not gone out for lunch once since he got the case.

"Hey Gilkerson. Come on, let's go to Cuzzy's," he said, determined to at least get a good lunch that day. One meal at Cuzzy's could fill him for the rest of the day.

They came in through the back door, walked down a narrow hallway that led past the restrooms and found a table near the back of the restaurant.

"Hey Lee," shouted Mike the cook from the kitchen. "How's it goin?"

"Oh pretty good," he lied. "You have anything good to eat for a change?"

"Anything you want," Mike laughed. "I, the head chef, can make anything."

"You close to catching that Cunanan guy yet?" John Lee saw him and walked over. "I can't see how you have time to sit here and screw around when this guy's on the loose," he said, laughing as he slapped Lee on the back.

"Hey, this is my first meal since May 7!" Lee protested. "Give a guy a break."

"Seriously, you close to nabbing him?" the restaurateur asked.

"Yeah, any moment," Lee answered.

He and Gilkerson tried to talk, but Lee's pager kept going off. He spent most of his time in the restaurant using Cuzzy's wall phone hung behind the bar. During one such call, he felt his eyes surveying Cuzzy's patrons. There, right in front of him at the end of the bar sat Andrew Cunanan. He looked again. *Boy, that sure looks like him*, he said. He tried not to stare.

Hanging up the phone, he walked back to his table and sat down, his back to the bar.

"Hey, look at the guy on the end of the bar closest to us," Lee said to Gilkerson.

"Yeah, what about him?"

"Look at him closer. Is that our man?" he asked, wanting to turn around but fearing he might frighten Cunanan away.

Gilkerson studied him from across the restaurant, looking up and down his profile, and staring more closely as the man turned his face to take a bite of his sandwich.

"Man, you might be right. He sure looks like our guy," Gilkerson said as he pulled Cunanan's picture out of his shirt pocket and studied it.

Lee looked at his own copy of the picture and then went back to the phone while Gilkerson walked toward the front of the restaurant, all the time keeping his eyes on the man's back.

"Excuse me sir," Lee said as he walked up next to the man. He showed his badge. "May I see some ID?"

"Ah, sure, what is this about?" he asked as he reached for his wallet, pulling it out and opening it so Lee could see his driver's license.

"You just look like someone," Lee said, staring at the photo ID card. He shook his head slightly and Gilkerson went back to his seat.

"Sorry to bother you," Lee said. "Enjoy your meal."

Just as he started back to his seat, CNN headline news carried yet another story about Andrew Cunanan. The restaurant went quiet as everyone watched the report.

"When you gonna catch that guy?" the bartender asked Lee once the story had ended.

"Soon, I'm sure. Real soon," Lee answered.

The Cunanan look-alike at the bar looked at Lee and then realized what had just happened. He paid his bill and left, shaking his head on the way out.

"No wonder we keep getting these crazy calls," Lee said. "Even to me everybody looks like Cunanan."

His pager went off. CALL FBI URGENT.

"Here we go again," he said, as they left the restaurant and made the call on the way. "They spotted him where?" he asked.

Another hot lead

An AMW caller from Muncie, Indiana saw Cunanan at a gas station just southwest of Muncie. The anonymous caller said Cunanan drove a red Ford Taurus with Iowa plates, and he had written down the numbers.

Lee called the Resident Agent for Muncie who immediately sent out the alert.

As Lee pulled up outside the FTF office he said, "Well, now he's in Indiana." He shook his head, rolled his eyes and the two men got out of the car.

An hour later, the Muncie agent called back.

"It's not your guy. The car's registered to an Illinois company, and they knew it was out there. We're going to find the car and talk to the driver, but I doubt it's Cunanan."

"Thanks. Hey, it doesn't sound too logical to me, so just send me an EC on it. No need to call back unless you get lucky," Lee said. "Luck," Lee grumbled to himself. "Cunanan's had it all."

Lee looked at a callback note from an Oakland, California agent. It said, "Angry mother," and bore the agent's name.

"Lee Urness here, Minnesota FTF. You called?"

"Yeah. Say, I followed up a lead you sent me and interviewed this young male. He was living at his parents' house and his mother was pretty shocked that he would know these gays. Could you call her for me?" the agent explained.

"Yeah. Okay. Fine," he said, tripping across an unintended consequence. He had called mothers before and shocked them with the news that their saintly son was a murderer or rapist, but never gay.

"Ma'am, this is Lee Urness with the FBI task force in Minneapolis. Our Oakland agent said you wanted to talk to me," he said.

"I just wanted to let you know that you really messed up my life. I knew nothing about Alan running around with those homosexuals…"

"I'm sorry, ma'am, but his name turned up in a private phone book and that's why we called looking for him," Lee explained.

"Oh I know. I did finally get an answer from him. And he says he's gay. But it was a total shock. His dad is very angry."

"I can understand that."

"Well, I wanted to ask you how you'd react if you found out your son was gay this way?" she asked.

"I'm not sure that is relevant. I'm really sorry, but it was really important for us to follow up," Lee answered. He felt very uncomfortable.

"Well that's the strange thing. Alan says he doesn't even know who this Cunanan fellow is. He says he never met him. He doesn't know how he got into his address book," she explained.

"Well, I'm sure I don't know. But I am sorry. I didn't mean to bother you," Lee said, trying to get off the line. This was not getting him closer to catching Cunanan. And he certainly did not want to explain that Alan's name might have been in the wrong phone book, not Cunanan's own book.

"No, you don't have to feel sorry," she said. "I know you are doing your job."

Lee checked the phone books after saying goodbye. This fellow had been in the first phone book, the one found in Cunanan's apartment that was not his. Still, most of the people in that address book had run across Cunanan. After they found the real guy who owned that phone book, they learned that he had met Cunanan at a party, but he claimed they had only been introduced and that was that. He had no idea how Cunanan had gotten the phone book. Lee talked to John Hause about this. Hause said that as they asked around, trying to find out who owned the book, most of the people they talked to did not want to admit they knew Cunanan.

This had become another strange twist – calming down a shocked mother dismayed at her son's sexual preference. He wondered how many other parents, siblings and friends were shocked to find out the truth. Jeff Trail had tried to keep it secret, but that myth had exploded in Cunanan's bloody rampage.

Lee also complained to Hause about how he had gotten no help from the FBI's Behavioral Science Unit days earlier.

"Oh, you mean BSU? Yeah, that's right, though. They just profile unknown killers and such. I have heard from a local psychic, though. It's hard to believe, but he has helped us in the past," Hause said.

Lee called the man. *What the hell can it hurt?*

"So, you have some sense about Andrew Cunanan?" he asked.

"Oh yes. Let me tell you. Andrew Cunanan is bad and crazy. He used a gun to kill. He has nothing to lose and needs attention. He will be caught in a 'Ju' month," he said.

"What do you mean by that?" Lee asked.

"A Ju month? Oh, like June or July."

"I see," Lee said, rubbing his chin. "Anything else?"

"Yes. He uses different modes of transportation. He is clean-shaven and has short hair. Even his own mother would not recognize him now. And he's on the east coast," the psychic said, concluding his "sense" about Cunanan. Lee had written down each thing the man said.

"Okay, well thanks for your help," Lee said and they said good-bye.

"Hey," Lee joked to Rickett, "the FBI needs to hire some of these psychics for the BSU. Oh well, it takes all kinds."

Before things quieted down that day, Lee got another hot lead, this time from Baltimore. The FBI office reported that a caller saw Cunanan driving an old dark blue-green van with Pennsylvania plates. The caller said Cunanan had dressed as a female. Lee dispensed with it quickly.

Maybe Cunanan *did* dress as a female, though nothing found weeks later in his Normandy Plaza Hotel room in Miami proved it. Lee wondered just how bizarre it would get before this case was finally settled.

Why not like this one?

Late that night, after all the others had gone home, the office actually quieted down. No phones rang, the fax sat quiet and the pager hung mute on Lee's belt. He fidgeted with things on his desk; scraps of paper, notes, paper clips, used staples, shuffling them around just to try to bring some order to his chaotic life. He spotted a note that now seemed months old, though it had been only a few weeks since he first wrote it.

He had written the name "Sam Cotter*" on a slip of paper, and scrawled a couple of phone numbers near it. He recognized those numbers as Cotter's family members.

Sam, an African-American, had been playing cards with his friends one Thursday night, just a few weeks earlier. During a dispute, he pulled out a gun, shot and killed one of the players. Then he disappeared.

Apple Valley police called the Minnesota FTF on Friday morning and Lee took the call. They wanted help capturing the shooter.

Within hours, Lee learned that Cotter had quite a lot of family members in the Twin Cities. His mother and stepfather lived together in North Minneapolis with a few of his siblings, and others lived nearby. He even had aunts and uncles in town.

Once Lee had gathered all the names and locations, he and three other teams simultaneously hit four houses, hoping to find Sam hiding out. The other three hits revealed nothing.

Lee went to the parents' house and as soon as he entered, he sensed utter hatred.

"We aren't helping you at all. No sir," they told him.

"Fine, but we're going to keep talking with you until we get him. Tell you what, I'll come back later and we can talk again," he said, handing the mother his card, "unless you want to talk before then."

"You can forget that. We don't like white cops," the stepfather said.

"You think it over, and then I'll be back," Lee said as he and his partner walked out the door.

Lee went back at 6:00 p.m. "I am done today checking houses for your son," Lee said. "Now I want some straight talk with you."

"We don't trust white cops," the stepfather said again.

"Yeah, I've been beat up by your kind," the grandfather added.

"Why we should trust you?" the mother asked.

"Look, all I want to do is find Sam before he hurts someone else, or he gets hurt. My job is to find and arrest him, not hurt him. But I can't say that for any other officer who might find him first, because he's wanted for murder with a gun. You convince him to come in, and I will guarantee you that nothing will happen," Lee said. He talked softly and patiently, trying to win their trust. He saw that they were people with a good heart.

"Well, we haven't heard from him anyway," the mother said.

"Well, I'll start fresh in the morning and I have a bunch of places to check where I think he might be," Lee said as he stood to leave. "You know he should turn himself in. The cops are looking for him and they know he may have a gun. You and I don't want anything to happen to him. Now I'm not going home yet, and I have some places to check tonight. It would be better for me to find him instead of a street cop. By 9:00 I have to hear from you," Lee said as he walked out the door. He watched their every reaction. They were confused and worried, just as he hoped. He felt confident that soon they would want to help.

Lee and his partner headed back to the office. At just before 9:00 the phone rang.

"We talked to Sam and he said he'll turn himself in to you. He'll be standing at Hennepin County Medical Center at 9:30. You can meet him there and he'll leave with you. We don't want any trouble," the mother said.

"Thank you ma'am. We'll go there right away and I can assure you that unless he does something stupid, nothing will happen to him," Lee said as he put on his jacket.

They arrived at HCMC within minutes and stood outside in the cold winter air, watching and waiting, one on each end of the sidewalk. Sam never showed. After 10:00 p.m., Lee went to his car and called the family.

"Mrs. Cotter, this is agent Urness. Sam never showed. Where is he?"

"Oh my Lord. I don't know. He said he'd be there."

"Okay, well I'm coming over to talk with you again," Lee said.

Lee pulled up just before 11:00 p.m. and stayed with the family until past 1 a.m.

"So I'm a white cop. What have you got against me? My dad was a sheriff, and he said it didn't matter who you were or what color you were. He taught me to treat everyone with respect," Lee said, warming to the family.

Soon the mother made coffee, and their talk became friendlier. He picked up vital facts about Sam that he hoped would help him find the young man more quickly. And he felt he had won the family's trust.

"Well, I have to go home," Lee said, stretching out his legs as he stood to leave. He wrapped his jacket around him. "Remember now, I have to hear something by 9:00 a.m. or I am going to some other houses to find him, but I will find him tomorrow. You call me at the office. And I have to know where we'll be meeting," Lee said to friendlier faces.

Lee made sure to hit the office before 9:00 a.m. that Saturday. He had already devised his next step if Sam or the family failed to cooperate. He knew it would mean stepping up the pressure on them, and he hoped it would not come to that.

"Agent Urness," he said as the phone rang at 9:00.

"Officer, this is Mrs. Cotter. I talked to him all night and he is ready to surrender. He'll be ready in a half hour," she said.

"Wow, I don't know if I can get there that fast."

"Well, you better get going. He's in the right frame of mind now."

"Okay, well where is he?" Lee asked. She gave him a north Minneapolis address. "Ah, yes, that's a place we were going to check today."

"The whole family is here with him in the basement."

"Are there any guns?" Lee asked.

"No."

"Okay. I'm on my way," he said. He called his partner for back up, but he was at home in Newport, another 30 miles from the site. "Never mind," Lee said, and headed out alone.

He drove to the north Minneapolis apartment building where the family lived. He noticed a few guys standing down the street who studied his every move and it made him uneasy. Yet, he had not called the Minneapolis PD, respecting the family's request. Instead, he called the BCA. "Give me five minutes. If you haven't heard from me, call out the Minneapolis squads."

Lee walked to the front door of the apartment building and pushed the buzzer to let them know he had arrived. In a moment, a pair of bright white eyes set into a dark ebony face greeted him as the door opened. Those eyes of a 13-year old black boy radiated hatred for the white cop who dared come and mess with his big brother.

"Good morning. I'm here for Sam," he said. The boy led him to the basement apartment. He saw the entire family assembled in the kitchen in a prayer circle, including Sam. Sam's mother walked to Lee.

"Can we have about five more minutes to pray together with him?" the mother pleaded.

"Sure," Lee said, and went in the other room to wait, along with two of Sam's teenage male relatives. Everything looked under control and relaxed. He called the BCA again, and said, "Listen, it looks okay here, but I will call you back in five minutes. If you don't hear from me, send the squads." The youths with him stayed silent, and Lee felt their distrust and animosity.

Finally, they took him back into the room. He saw Sam waiting for him.

"Hi Sam. Do you have any weapons?" Lee asked as he approached him.

"No sir," the sad young man said.

Lee cuffed and searched him without incident.

"Okay, let's go," Lee said, turning Sam toward the stairway.

"We want to come along," the mother said as she stood in front of the whole group of family members.

"All of you?" Lee asked.

"Yes sir," she said, unsmiling but certain.

"Okay," he agreed and took Sam out to his van, sliding him into the back seat. The stepfather rode along with Lee while the rest of the family followed behind, and Lee let the BCA know that he was proceeding to the lockup, "without incident."

The Cotter arrest had uneventful. It was the perfect situation where Lee had asked the right questions and pushed the right buttons with the right people, good people truly broken by their son's crime and sorry for it. He had laid on just enough pressure and worked hard to win their support.

The whole plan depended on Sam eventually turning to his family and friends, a long established pattern that Lee had come to expect.

He had never chased a crook who had not eventually called someone for help, that is, until he chased Andrew Cunanan. As Lee sat in the FTF office, he realized that Cunanan had not called anyone, and he worried that he never would. "Then I'm screwed," he said, picking up a dart and throwing it at Cunanan's picture.

Not much about this chase fit the "well-established" patterns on which Lee relied. Cunanan meant to defy the odds to remain at large, until he could design his final murder and forever stitch himself into America's criminal history.

Chapter 30 ~ Top Ten filed

By midnight on Wednesday, May 21, Lee felt covered by paperwork. He, Kevin Rickett and Jeanie Burns spent most of the day putting together all the background information for the Top Ten filing.

Lee had notified Interpol early on in the case, but not officially. To win their total assistance meant complying with their paperwork requirements, the filing of a Red Notice and Diffusion Notice. The data needed to complete these filings lined up with that of the Top Ten, but still created its own paper requirements.

Lee also requested that the FBI install their Rapid Start program for use in this case. Lee loved gadgets and computers, and software that worked. With Rapid Start, he felt he would have a real advantage. The program allowed the linking of names, dates, places and times, and would give him ready access to contacts all across the country. If someone called him about a name, at the press of a button he could find out everything on file about the person.

Agents and officers from every jurisdiction regularly called Lee, wondering about leads. With Rapid Start, in an instant he could know whether that person had previously been contacted or if it was new, saving the investigator much time and frustration. As well, if something new turned up, Lee would know it immediately. The FBI installed Rapid Start on May 27.

In between tracking down data and filling in forms, Lee handled a continuous stream of calls. He received and called out new leads, followed up on old leads and talked with agents from New Jersey to San Francisco. His list of Cunanan contacts had grown to more than 200 names already, and he struggled to keep them straight in his mind. His "portable file cabinet," a black leather case, had already grown fat with notes, official reports, lists and his case file. He kept that list of names handy, updating it daily; to make sure he had the latest information for any cop who might call with an inquiry.

A waitress at the Rex Café in San Francisco called the FBI with astounding and potentially critical information. She said that Cunanan had been there on May 19th. Furthermore, she said that Cunanan often dined with Laura Koski and Will Evert. Agent Anderson showed her Cunanan's pictures and she determined that, in fact, it had not been Cunanan there that day, but she knew that the other two were his friends.

Anderson had already interviewed Koski and Evert. They had assured him that they would call immediately if Cunanan tried to contact them. Now it appeared remotely possible that they had reneged on the deal, and in the process, Cunanan may have slipped through his hands.

Anderson then set out immediately to interview Koski and Evert. But neither of them, nor Cunanan, had been at the Rex on May 19.

"Figures," Lee answered when Anderson gave him the report. "Oh well. Maybe next time," he chuckled. "And thanks for the good work."

Lisa Davis took a call from Sgt. Norman Hill of the Boston Police Department. Hill had heard rumors that Cunanan might show up at the Boston Gay Pride celebration during June 1-8. Davis contacted Mike Curazza, the Boston FBI agent and Curazza asked for extra copies of the Cunanan photos and warrants. Curazza planned to meet with Sgt. Hill and then set up meetings with leaders in the gay community. Agents in dozens of towns were doing the same thing, and in so doing, further shutting down Cunanan's access to his closest circle of friends.

The clock showed midnight before Lee, Kevin and Jeanie could finally stand and stretch; all the Top Ten paperwork had been completed. Lee saw how complicated it had been just getting to that point, and knew that once Cunanan made the Top Ten list, the paperwork increased. But the additional exposure and attention drawn to the case, he felt, would be worth it all.

The next day, Lee wrote a formal request to the Bureau of Diplomatic Security in Washington, D.C. to get a copy of Cunanan's passport. Thus, another piece of the puzzle fit into the ever-growing picture of how he planned to stop the man. But Cunanan held the last piece of the puzzle and meant to do so until he finished its deathly design.

Miglin friend shaken

In San Luis Obispo, California, Gail Lynstrom* found herself trembling from unexplainable fear. She had been a good friend of Lee Miglin's when the man lived in California nearly 20 years earlier, and had followed his murder case with close attention. A friend of hers kept her posted with clipped articles from the *Chicago Tribune*.

On May 23, she happened to be walking down the sidewalk when a sense of fear and trepidation overtook her. She could not identify a reason, but spotted a man standing in the door of a barbershop several feet ahead. She shuddered when she saw him, even though she did not recognize him.

Two days later, Lynstrom opened her mail and found yet another article about Miglin and with it, a black and white photo of Andrew Cunanan. Immediately she felt sure that was the man she had seen two days earlier, and she reported it to the police.

Despite her strong feeling of dread, when she saw a picture of Cunanan, she could only say, "I never saw the face of the man in the door, just his profile. But I know what I felt."

What she "felt" and what the barbershop owner could confirm resulted in a negative report and several more hours of FBI time.

Beware look-alikes

Dozens of men found their lives disrupted when earnest citizens felt sure they had spotted Andrew Cunanan. The killer's ability to change his appearance also served to point to many look-alikes.

Hair stylist Rhonda Timmers* saw one of these. She walked to the front desk and looked at the appointment book at the Hair Cuttery in Jacksonville, Florida. She studied the next name in her column. "Andrew," she called, nodding toward the chairs sitting in the waiting area. An average sized, fairly good-looking man got up and followed her to her chair. He wanted a trim.

"I have never seen you here before," she said, making small talk. "Are you new to the area?"The man was somewhat tanned, so he looked more like a native than a tourist. She hoped to land him as a long time client.

"Yes, I just came to Florida from Minnesota," he said.

"Oh, Minnesota. What brings you here?" she asked.

"Well, I just wanted to come here. But I work at Mozzarella's Café just down the street," Andrew answered. "I live in Ponte Vedra Beach. It's real nice. I really like it."

Timmers finished her work and Andrew paid his bill. "Come back again now, you hear?"She watched him walk away and then called her next appointment.

A few days later, Timmers sat watching America's Most Wanted. She could not believe her eyes. Andrew, the man whose hair she had just cut, looked just like Andrew Cunanan, the murderer. She immediately called 1-800-CRIMETV.

AMW's operator immediately called Lee who, in turn, contacted the Resident Agent, Lee Sinton, in Jacksonville. Sinton went directly to Hair

Cuttery to interview Ms. Timmers. He showed her the pictures of Cunanan and she identified one as the man whose hair she had cut – Andrew.

Sinton headed to Mozzarella's and showed him Cunanan's picture. The manager agreed that one of the photos certainly looked a lot like Andrew, but the last name he had given was Runbeck, not Cunanan. Sinton retrieved Andrew Runbeck's private information and notified Minneapolis right away.

Kevin Rickett quickly retrieved Runbeck's driver's license information and Cunanan's thumbprint and faxed them back to Sinton who went immediately to talk to Runbeck. Meanwhile, a Minneapolis agent went to Woodbury, a St. Paul suburb, to talk to Runbeck's family.

His mother verified that he had, indeed, moved to Florida, but his was not any of the pictures shown to her. "This is not my son, I can assure you," she told the agent.

Her claims would not, however, be enough to clear her son. She called him right away, and he wasted no time calling Agent Sinton, asking him to meet to resolve the identity question. Sinton quickly found that Andrew Runbeck and Andrew Cunanan were two different people, and Runbeck knew nothing about Cunanan. He also never went back to the Cuttery for a haircut.

Runbeck was just one in a long line of Cunanan look-alikes.

Ric Christian* parked his Lexus SC 300 near the office door at the Eden Condominium at Pensacola, Florida on May 23. He had three male guests with him. In a few minutes, Christian and his friends had checked in, not leaving again until May 26.

Kelvin Orbach*, the Reservation Clerk at Eden watched Christian and his friends closely. "I know gay men when I see them," Orbach told himself, perhaps fanaticizing about how he might find a way to crash their party once he got off duty.

Something about one of the men bothered him. He felt he had seen him before, but he could not readily identify the time or place. Then he remembered America's Most Wanted.

When FBI Special Agent Davis Kerry showed him a photo of Cunanan, he felt sure that the murderer had been included in the group, though he had gotten a bit thinner. He noticed Cunanan's – or whoever the man was – glasses. "They are identical," he told Kerry.

Kerry found that Christian lived in New Orleans and immediately notified the New Orleans' FBI office, starting a flurry of activity in their city. After several hours of FBI time had been spent positively identifying Christian as himself, New Orleans notified Agent Kerry and sent a copy of their report to Lee.

"Good work," Lee grunted, wishing he could have been on the street with one of those investigators. Yet he chuckled, thinking about how many more men would be accused of being Cunanan before the chase ended.

Two days later, Gary from Hollywood, Florida, called AMW to report he had just seen Cunanan. Cunanan played pool at Frenchies, a restaurant on Johnson Street. And he had two beautiful French-looking girls with him. Gary said that the girls left before Cunanan did. Lee guessed that Gary had seen yet another Cunanan look-alike, and besides, "what would he be doing with two good-looking French girls?" he asked Lisa Davis. "He doesn't even like girls!"

The second cousin

Late that afternoon, Lee sat pouring over his notes and tried scratching his head with his right hand, but he could hardly raise it. His right arm, hand and shoulder ached. *Now what's this?* he asked himself as he rubbed his forearm.

"Lee, Line 2. Orange County, a deputy sheriff," Steve Gilkerson said.

"Urness here," Lee said as he stuck the phone under his left ear to cradle it.

"This is Orange County Deputy Sheriff Pedro Acevedo*," Lee heard. He wrote the name on a legal pad – it even hurt to write. "I had the weirdest thing happen to me today and thought you should know about it. I went out to do a burglary call and when I got to the house, this guy told me matter-of-factly that he was Cunanan's second cousin. He says he recently talked to him on the phone."

"What?" Lee said, his interest piqued. These were the kinds of leads that often broke a case. A key element necessary to find someone was phone calls to a friend or relative.

"Yup, that is what he said," Acevedo said. "So rather than get into this whole thing with him, I decided to track you down and you should talk to him. He's expecting your call."

"Okay, I'll be glad to," Lee said, fighting the urge to smile. If true, this would be a huge breakthrough. "Give me the contact information. I'll have an FBI agent contact you and you can go back and interview this guy to-gether. And thank you. This is great work and very helpful," Lee added.

"My pleasure," Acevedo said. "Oh, and when it's all over, would you let me know how this turns out? I'd appreciate it."

"You're on." Lee hung up and immediately called the FBI. "Patch me through to the R.A. in Orange County, California," he said.

Within 10 minutes, Special Agent Frank Ceresco* had made his call to Emmett Ottson*, the second cousin, and was on his way to conduct a face-to-face interview. Acevedo met him there. They found a frightened and nervous man.

"Listen, if anybody ever hears about this I will sue you and the FBI and everybody," Ottson threatened.

"You have my guarantee that I'm not going to tell anybody," Ceresco promised. "It stays within the agency."

"Well, on the 20th I got a call from Maryann who was crying and upset. She said she had talked to her son, and he had killed two people. His lover was dying from AIDS and he mercy-killed him. And he killed the second one because of AIDS. And he went to see Miglin in Chicago, and said he'd been Miglin's prostitute." (This claim tipped Lee off that Ottson may have made up the entire story. No one had proven that Miglin was gay, nor that he had any direct link to Cunanan. On the other hand, if Ottson told the truth, it meant a breakthrough.)

Ceresco wrote as fast as Ottson talked. Acevedo studied the man while Ceresco did his work.

"Then Maryann called again and said that if the cops catch Andrew they will shoot him on sight. Then she called again and said he might go to New York or San Diego and the gays will hide him. He said that Miglin started him as a male prostitute and he's coming back to get people who gave him AIDS."

"Are you sure you got all this right?" Ceresco asked.

"Oh, very sure. How could I forget words like these?" Ottson answered.

"Did Mrs. Cunanan call again?" Ceresco asked.

"No, but Andrew did; last Thursday. He said that he's coming to see me. He said that he needs to go into the chapel," he said. Ottson's father had often taken the boys to mass at a local Cathedral, and, "Andrew said he needed to go to church."

"Thursday? The 17th?" Ceresco asked, clarifying his notes.

"Yes, I am sure of it. Then he said something that kind of scared me," Ottson said, his voice dropping.

"What was that?"

"He asked whose blue Mercedes was in my driveway. That was really strange because it's a writer's car who went on a trip, and it's been parked there since the second week of May," Ottson explained.

Ceresco carefully evaluated what Ottson said as he wrote notes. He, too, had studied Ottson, trying to discern if he was competent or just someone looking for attention. He saw a serious, scared and apparently sane man, and so noted it. Acevedo agreed.

"How do you know these dates?" Ceresco asked. Caresco meant to check out all the dates, phone numbers and financial transactions Ottson provided; unlike events viewed through an emotional prism, they can be objectively evaluated. Ceresco hoped every word of Ottson's story was true.

"I wrote them down in my diary," Ottson said.

Ottson's wife sat nearby, watching and listening to everything. Her presence added credibility to her husband's claims. "I asked Marie* to check the dates in her diary and such."

Ceresco finished his questioning and he and Acevedo readied to go. "Mr. Ottson, thank you so much for your help. Please, if Andrew calls again, let us know immediately." He handed his card to the man. "And if Maryann calls, please let us know. Will you do that?"

"Yes sir, but just don't let them know where you got this information," Ottson said, still nervous.

"Don't worry about that. No one outside the agency will know about this," Ceresco assured him once again.

Back at the office, Ceresco called Lee.

"So do you think the guy's credible?" Lee asked. Too much of the story sounded strange.

"Well, he seemed very competent, well-educated and articulate. The house was immaculate and well decorated. He claimed he was in the publishing business and his home sure looks like he has money," Ceresco answered. "Maybe this is a break."

"Could be. Hey, send me your report as soon as you have it ready and no copies to anyone else until this is settled. I'll do reverse tolls on the number and make sure it stays close to the vest," Lee said. "Thanks for your quick work."

Lee sat back and pondered what he had just heard. It sounded hopeful, but in many ways, preposterous. It suggested that Cunanan hid out somewhere in or near Orange County, California. *I can't rule out that he really did go back west, but it still makes no sense.* One option was to set up surveillance at Ottson's house, but that meant tying up agent time, and he hated to do so if the story was false. Even though Ceresco saw Ottson as sincere and sane, it did not mean the story was true. Ceresco suggested that Lee send out a second agent to determine if Ottson was telling the truth.

"Go out and interview him in person. This sounds really, really strange," he asked Special Agent Barbara Javitts*. "Study him carefully, and I need you to see if there are any phones he may have used." Lee had already traced incoming and outgoing long distance calls, and found nothing. He needed to know if Ottson had used payphones or perhaps, called from a motel, bar or restaurant.

"And we got a big problem here; because if word of this leaks out, the cops from where he did the murders will want to follow this lead and I don't want them flying in and bothering the source. Because of the cell phone leak that killed Reese, we will not tell anyone else about this. So we can't do any EC's on this," he explained.

"I can handle that. I can just delay it a few days until we know," Javitts said. "Nobody gets that information until we are ready to release it. Is that a deal?" she asked.

"Perfect, and thanks," Lee said.

Javitts conducted an interview later that day, and like Ceresco, found the man credible. Marie Ottson had written all the information in her own address book, seemingly corroborating what Emmett had said.

Javitts' recorded all the phone numbers and times of the calls. Sitting in the driveway she, like Lee and Ceresco, evaluated what she had just witnessed. She called Lee as soon as she returned to her office.

"I don't know how to call this," Javitts reported to Lee. "He really does seem credible and they were both forthcoming with the information. They reminded me that they never wanted Andrew or the family members to know about this."

"Well, okay," Lee answered, but still extremely skeptical. Years of police work had taught him to be skeptical of every piece of "evidence" until he could prove it to himself. "Let me have those phone numbers," he said. He immediately had them traced.

Once Lee received the trace report from Pacific Bell, he saw that, while there had been some long distance calls, none of them related to the case. Ottson claimed there had been three calls from Maryann as well, but none of them passed an objective test.

Armed with these facts, Lee asked Ceresco to go back out and do one more interview, but Ottson stuck to his story.

Boiling down all the information they had about Ottson and the facts he had presented, facts that the cops had determined to be myths, the FTF determined Ottson was either just another wannabee looking to attach himself to a big case, or maybe just imagined it had happened. True, he was a Cunanan blood relative, but Andrew had never called him.

This all seemed really strange to Lee. That Ottson worked in the publishing industry suggested that, perhaps, he had greatly embellished the story. Perhaps he *had* talked with Maryann, using a different phone, and perhaps Maryann had embellished the story – she *was* an excitable woman whose son had been accused of horrific crimes. Maybe Ottson was planning to write a book about it – a fictional work.

"Let's learn from this," Lee said to his team. "There are going to be more than your usual run-of-the-mill wannabees attaching to this case." Little did he know how prophetic those words were.

He do this?

The first thing Lee did on May 30 was send out an EC (electronic communication) letting all FBI offices know that the Minnesota FTF had Rapid Start installed and that it was up and running. That meant that any office anywhere could check on a name simply by calling Lee's office. At a push of a button, he could tell them if the name was related to Cunanan. One such call came that day, from New York City.

Tragedy had struck the Gerald Levin family on May 30. Levin, the Chief Executive Officer of Time-Warner's media division heard news that his son Jonathan had been brutally tortured and murdered. Jonathan, who had chosen the life of a public school teacher, had become the victim of an unknown, but vicious assailant.

New York Police saw in Jonathan's death a parallel to Lee Miglin's murder and immediately contacted the FBI. They referred the call to Lee Urness.

"What'd you find?" Lee asked Officer Uzcatequi at the NYPD.

"The victim was gagged, and then wrapped with duct tape, like that Chicago guy. The perp used a flick knife to torture him, real slow, on the neck and chest. Then shot him," Uzcatequi said.

"What caliber gun?"

"Like a .22 or .25."

"Nope, not my guy. He's carrying a Taurus .40 caliber," Lee said.

"Maybe he got a new gun?" Uzcatequi suggested.

"Not likely. I just don't think he'd so that," Lee said. Lee had become convinced, in what may have seemed to those not familiar with chasing crooks a strange sort of logic, that Cunanan would never again steal a gun, nor rob someone. Such behavior lay outside his perverted character. Stealing a truck for a ride *was* out of character, but given that, Lee felt that Cunanan had hunkered down somewhere, trying to blend in or wait until the next step in whatever plan he hope to conclude.

"Did he steal anything?" Lee asked.

"Some cash, billfold. Maybe credit cards," Uzcatequi said.

"No. No, I'm sure it's not my guy, but hey, I wish you luck on this," Lee said.

During the weeks of the Cunanan case, and even after, Lee heard from numerous police departments who wondered if Lee's "guy" had murdered in their city. Lee never minded the inquiries, knowing that these were just cops like him, exploring every possibility, and he was glad when he heard nine days later that NYPD captured the two young thugs who had murdered Levin. He had only hoped he could have nailed Cunanan before that.

Chapter 31 ~ May becomes June

During May, the Minnesota FTF had handled more than a thousand leads in the Cunanan case; Lee had reviewed them all, and handled hundreds of them personally.

"Hey Lee, cup of coffee?" Lisa Davis asked. She saw that he looked beat.

"Yeah, that'd be great," he said, the telephone stuck under his left ear, head bent to cradle it against his shoulder.

Davis set Lee's mug down next to the phone. She watched him for a moment, and as she turned away, she could see something was wrong. Lee had grabbed the mug with his left hand and clumsily lifted it to his mouth; he dribbled a bit on his chin. Davis knew he was right-handed.

"Hey, are you all right?" she asked.

"What? Oh, this? I don't know," Lee said as he set the mug down. He rubbed his right forearm. "I guess something's wrong. I don't have any strength in my right hand. And my right shoulder is really aching, too."

"Get it looked at," she said.

Lee stole a half hour to run to the doctor who had treated him for nearly two decades.

"What have you been doing?" the doctor asked as he checked out Lee's right shoulder and forearm. "You've definitely got a bad case of tennis elbow."

"Tell me about it," Lee said. "I don't know, except making hundreds of phone calls a day; at least it seems like it."

"Well those repetitive motions have caused this," the doctor said. "I'll give you a shot of cortisone, but you have to let that shoulder and arm rest."

"I guess I'm going to be a left-handed phone cop for a time," Lee laughed. The cortisone brought instant relief, and he headed back to the office, but it took weeks for the pain to subside.

"Imagine that," he said to Davis as he approached her desk. "More than a quarter century of police work without a physical problem. Then I get it from a damned telephone! I demand hazardous duty pay!"

"Lee, line 3, and I've got a stack of calls here for you," Jeanie Burns said.

"No rest for the wicked," Lee said as he stuck the phone under his left ear. "Gotta find out where they saw Cunanan today."

Of the more than 1,000 Cunanan sightings, perhaps one or two actually *were* him. It made no difference; all the leads had to be pursued. In the same manner, every name or place or phone number mentioned during an interview had to be followed. And many of these led to even more leads. Typical of these kinds of leads was the person who would say, "Well, I heard Andrew talk about a fellow named Allen in Columbus, Ohio."

"Allen who?" the agent asked.

"I don't know. All I know is Allen from Columbus."

"What's he look like?"

"Oh, maybe 25 years old. Average height. Nice looking boy. I have a phone number if that would help," the interviewee would say.

The agent wrote it down, and in doing so discovered someone named George Doe, but no "Allen."

"Oh yes, his name is George, but we call him 'Allen,'" would be the typical response.

Despite such a vague reference to Cunanan, Lee insisted that the "Allens" who were really "Georges" still needed to be contacted. He never backed off his demand that every person Cunanan knew or ever talked to, if possible, would be interviewed. He hoped that one of them would be "the" person whom Cunanan would eventually call.

Dozens of gay community leaders from across the country called Lee to talk about their worries. Their pleas created yet another cultural surprise for the Minnesota cop. They had begun to worry that Cunanan would show up at their "Gay Pride" celebrations, to party or to seek another victim. Lee had never before given any thought to these parades and parties, but given Cunanan's nature knew they might have some basis in fact, except for San Diego.

"You think he'd dare to show up in San Diego?" Lee asked one of the callers. "I doubt it very much."

"Well, we're very concerned and we want to know what to do," the caller said.

"But we will need your help, understood?" Lee said, after reassuring them that the police would protect them. "The police gave you Wanted Posters and if Cunanan sees them up, there's no way he'll show up. And you must be our eyes and ears and call us if you see him anywhere."

Whether Lee's comments created comfort or fanned fear, he cared little. He needed all the help he could get to find Cunanan, whether from leisurely lesbians or garrulous gay men, it made no matter to him.

Still, May had passed and Cunanan still ran free. Lee remained confident that Cunanan would soon be in a cell somewhere, but the fact the chase had lasted even this long grated on him. FBI and FTF agents, police and sheriff departments, rangers, highway patrolmen – law enforcement of every type – had chased down thousands of leads. There had been no near catches since May 9.

"Where are you?" Lee asked, as he studied Cunanan's dart-speared likeness that hung on the office dartboard.

Get this book

"Hey Paul, you find my truck yet?" Lee asked as he heard Paul Murray pick up the next morning.

"No, I haven't," Murray answered once again. "But I'm not stopping until I do."

"Listen, I know we've talked to everyone Cunanan ever knew," he started to say, but the phone fell off his ear, bouncing noisily on his desk. "Sorry," he said, as he stuck it back under his left ear.

"What the hell was that?" Murray asked. "Gunfire?"

"Ah, no," Lee said, and told him about his tennis elbow.

"You wimp!" Murray teased. "Telephone took you down. What a riot!"

"Hey, it's tough duty, but someone's got to do it."

"Now you were saying?" Murray continued.

"Not a single person he knows has heard from him, and I think I understand him pretty well. But I can't see where he is, where he would go. What are we missing?" Lee asked. He and Murray talked in this way nearly every day.

"I found something that might help," Murray said.

"Oh yeah?"

"Yeah. I was talking with some gays out here and they told me to get a copy of the DAMRON book. You ever hear of it?" Murray asked.

"Can't say that I have."

"Well, it lists more than 5,000 gay-friendly businesses…"

"Now that's something I'd be likely to have around," Lee laughed.

"I bet you would," Murray laughed with him. "Anyway, I went and got one. All our offices should have it."

"Tell me about it," Lee said.

"You can look up a club or bar, even restaurants and lodging in just about any town in America; even foreign countries. Like in Minneapolis, you can go to Bryant Lake Bowl or buy a book at A Brother's Touch," Murray said.

"I'll be sure to run right out there," Lee chuckled.

"Where the heck is Brainerd? Is that near where you used to live?" Murray asked.

"It's in the center of the state. Not that far from Alexandria. Why?"

"Well, you and your buddy could go do a bed and breakfast at the Hallett House," he suggested.

"Okay, I get the picture. We'll get a copy," Lee said.

"And let all the other offices know about it," Murray suggested.

"Will do." They continued on, discussing their theories and other ideas. It turned personal.

"Hey, how's your mom doing?" Murray asked. Lee's mother had been moved to a nursing home, and his father now lived alone.

"You know, not so good, and I can't even get away to see her. She's not able to talk on the phone. I talk to my dad by phone, but haven't seen him since April. He's not doing so well, either," Lee said. Cunanan had stolen softball time with Kari, but at least *she* was young. There would be many more future games and tournaments. But his dad and mom were old and ill. Nevertheless, Howard Urness would have told his son that cops had no choice when it came to stopping a bad guy or spending time with a sick parent. "I told you not to become a cop," he would remind him.

"Lee, line 3. A Kansas City agent," Jeanie Burns said.

"Hey, I have to go," Lee said. "We'll get those DAMRON books going, and I'll talk to you later." Lee hung up and then pushed line 3.

The agent reported to Lee that they were about to question a man and woman who said they knew Cunanan quite well. "Names are Randy Molter* and Jamie Peisert*," agent Colvert Roll said. "Sound familiar?"

"Nope," Lee said as he eyed his master list. "But go check it out. Who knows?"

Randy Molter worked for Continental Airlines and said he met Cunanan by phone during November of 1996. He enjoyed their conversation so much that they decided to talk again. Cunanan had asked Molter where to find the hottest Kansas City gay bars and clubs and Molter, also gay, made many suggestions.

So taken was Cunanan with Molter that he flew to Kansas City to party with him, and Peisert. While there, Cunanan paid for everything with cash, and said that he had been born in Guam, but worked in the Los Angeles Post Office. Later, the man and woman flew to Los Angeles to spend time with Cunanan.

"So they say the last time they saw Cunanan was in mid-January," Roll reported to Lee after talking with the couple.

"What do you think?" Lee asked.

"Well, they seem sincere. I felt like they told the truth," Roll said.

"Okay. Let me know if you hear anymore from them. Send me the paperwork and I'll add it to the file," Lee said, staring at his ever-expanding file folders. "I'm going to need a friggin' file room before this is over," he grunted to no one in particular.

"Lee!" Jeanie Burns said, pointing at the Swear Can. "That'll be a dollar, please."

"What?" he said, looking over at her like a deer caught in someone's headlights. "I said 'friggin.'"

"You sure?"

"Damn right," he said, tossing her a quarter.

"Hey Lisa, can you get us one of these?" he asked, handing her a note about the DAMRON book. He explained it to her. "We need to contact everyone in here," he added.

"Okay. Maybe we can get the publisher to give us a database on this list. It would make it easier for us to do the contact work," she suggested.

"Great idea. Take care of it, will you?"

Lisa contacted DAMRON's publishers who explained that they did not have their list in a database, but promised to do so as quickly as possible. "They'll be sending it to us," Lisa told Lee later on.

Lee knew that getting Cunanan's face in front of everyone with whom he might come in contact was part of the plan. The more people who recognized him, the more his window for escape closed down.

Twiddling thumbs make for boredom

Lee hated two things equally: early mornings and having nothing to do. And things had begun to slow down. Calls come in sporadically, sometimes hours apart. Since Lee's job consisted of keeping everything together while leaving the investigation to others, he had no choice but to sit by the phone each day, hoping for a break.

The good news, though, was that he no longer had to get to the office at the break of dawn, which for him meant before 7:00 a.m. He returned to his old routine of leaving after 8:30, avoiding rush hour traffic. As he drove up I-35W, he listened carefully to his police radios, begging them to scream out some sort of criminal emergency. If he was lucky, it would be close by and he could get in on some action, maybe arrest a bad guy or break down a door.

319

Lee knew that for some reason, not much crime happened during rush hour. And he never got such a call during the time of this investigation.

On June 5, Erik Erickson contacted the San Diego FTF. More of Cunanan's bills had come to the apartment. San Diego immediately forwarded copies to the Minnesota FTF, and Lee assigned them out to agents in the office. With luck, they might find that he had used a credit card somewhere, but there would be no such luck, just more details to chase.

Lee felt jealous of the cops and agents he dispatched all around the country while he sat waiting for their reports. Yet here he had to sit, waiting for others to do the "fun" work.

He imagined what John Hause could be thinking about as he and Ann Murphy drove out to talk to one of Cunanan's former lovers. *Will the guy be hostile? If so, how will I handle it? I know he knows Cunanan, but what if he denies it? How will I catch him in the lie? What if no one knows this guy is gay, and his family puts it together with my visit? Will I have to handle an emotional family situation here? Would this guy use violence against me?*

Hause had told Lee how glad he was that Ann Murphy went with him when they called on gay establishments or interviewed Cunanan's gay friends. "She's a beautiful woman, and I'm a single guy. The gays leave me alone when they see me with her," Hause had said.

Just thinking about Hause's "good fortune," while he sat there waiting for the phone to ring raised Lee's blood pressure. All he could do was grab a dart and throw it at Cunanan's face.

On one such day, Lee found a good reason to leave the office. He dug through his stacks of notes and found a fax copy Paul Murray had sent him several days earlier. The real estate listing of a South Minneapolis house had a map drawn on the back, and it had been found in Miglin's Lexus. The rough handwritten map showed a route up I-35 to Duluth and another, heading east on I-94 to Chicago. When he first got it, Lee had believed David Madson drew it, and figured it pointed to Madson's parents' home in Barron, Wisconsin. As he sat looking at it on this day, he had a different idea.

What if someone else drew this map for Cunanan? What if Cunanan actually killed Madson on that Tuesday night and then headed back to the freeway? He's not from around here, so he asks someone to draw him a map. Maybe he stopped at the Tank and Tackle there on the highway. And he asks the guy how to get to Chicago, and hands him this real estate listing. So the guy draws him a map, like "here, this freeway goes north and south, like to Duluth and Minneapolis. Then if you take this I-94 east through Wisconsin."

Lee pondered this some more. *If this happened, that explains why there was a Chicago parking ticket in the Jeep from Wednesday. Cunanan went there Wednesday, and never came back to Minnesota. And it might explain how he met Miglin.*

Several Minnesotans claimed they saw Cunanan on Friday, traveling with another man in a red Jeep with a Vail sticker on the back. Those claims made it seem likely that, as Jon Hermann believed, Cunanan had killed Madson late Friday. (Months later, a forensic scientist evaluated the growth of worms in Madson's body and decided that his death most likely occurred on Tuesday or Wednesday. Hermann continues to strongly disagree with her conclusions.)

Lee had to assume that the map had significant value, and needed to be researched. If he could determine who had drawn it and talk with that person, it might help trace Cunanan's flight from Minnesota. Getting that kind of information could help Paul Murray or the Chicago Police finally to get their warrant.

Lee called Ally Pearson*, the realtor whose name was listed on the flyer and went to see her. "My name is Lee Urness, and I am with the FBI's Fugitive Task Force. I need to talk to you this morning, if possible." He never gave her a chance to answer his questions over the phone. To do so would have meant being glued to his chair, but also, he never interviewed people on the phone. He wanted a face-to-face meeting.

"Is this a house you had listed?" he asked Pearson when they met sometime later that day. He showed her the flyer. Just driving somewhere to ask a question felt good.

"Yes, it is one of mine," she said. "Does this have something to do with that Andrew Cunanan case?"

"Why do you ask?"

"Well, you're from this fugitive task force, and the story's been all over the news."

"Do you know the name Andrew Cunanan?" he asked.

"No, I do not," Pearson said. "And as far as I know, he never came to see this house."

"How about David Madson? Did you know him?" he asked.

"No, him neither. I never talked to either one," she said.

"Let me show you some photos," he began to say.

"I saw them on the news," she said.

"Well, I want you to look at the photos," he insisted. She did not recognize the photos.

"What about other realtors? I mean, someone else might have shown him the house," Lee said.

"Well we keep a log of everyone who comes through the place," she said, getting her book. They studied the names together. Neither Andrew Cunanan nor David Madson appeared on the log.

"Well, thanks for taking time with me," Lee said, as he put his photo lineup back into his case file. "If you think of anything, please give me a call," he said, handing her his card, but she never called.

Lee drove back to the FTF office, disappointed that the lead had led nowhere, but feeling good about being out. He kept driving and headed to Cuzzy's for a burger.

"Hey Lee," Mike the cook yelled when he walked in, "you catch that guy yet?"

Lee shook his head, sat down, opened a menu and stared at it. Even his pager left him alone that hour. At least chewing on a burger gave him time to think, and what he thought was that he had no idea where Cunanan hid.

This could really be him!

"This is Jake Berndt*, the manager of the restaurant at Wolona Hotel at Yosemite National Park. Last night I was sure I saw Andrew Cunanan in here with another man. My manager saw him, too," Berndt told Kevin Rickett on Friday afternoon, June 6.

Berndt had also notified the Park Rangers who determined that the two men had checked into the hotel the previous day. "The rangers are out in the park looking for the two men right now," Rickett told Lee after he got off the phone. "And they're watching the cabin."

"This sounds like your guy," Jeanie Burns said when she heard the details.

"Well, could be," Lee answered. "But I just don't think he's out west." But the description of one of the men sounded very much like Cunanan. Lee knew better than to discourage any real possible sighting, especially with this man who had eluded his clutch for so long already. He contacted the Sacramento FBI office and asked for assistance. Though it would take the agents more than an hour to get to Yosemite, other agents began collecting information about the San Francisco man whose credit card had been used to check in, the one who looked like Cunanan.

While he awaited a return call from Yosemite, Lee took several other calls. Each one required several follow up calls and more paperwork.

An employee at the Lagoon Theater in Minneapolis had talked about Cunanan with his manager. He claimed that he knew Cunanan, and believed he would head for Washington. The manager's former roommate had been murdered, the caller said, though not by Cunanan.

"I don't know if he'll be any help, though. He doesn't trust the cops," the caller said. The caller was right; the manager offered no help.

Agent Jay Hardy followed up on a very unique lead, once again, of the type that sometimes turned out to be the case-breaker. Someone had claimed that Domino's Pizza had delivered to Cunanan. Lee knew that crooks made dumb mistakes, even crooks allegedly with 160 IQs. Unfortunately, after Domino's chief of security ran a check of all deliveries since April 20, he could not find one to Cunanan.

Dozens of other calls occupied Lee and his team while they awaited news of the Yosemite search. Lee had grown accustomed to waiting for a clarifying response on Cunanan sightings; he had developed great patience. This one gnawed at him a bit more, given that it seemed such a ripe possibility.

"Hey, I'm going over to the BCA and get some things done," Lee said around 4:30 p.m. "Page me when you hear from these Yosemite guys."

"Well, maybe I shouldn't send out any of these leads, huh?" Jeanie said through a cynical smile as he began to head out the door.

"What?"

"Well, it sounds like you're going to get him," she said.

"Ah, no, we keep sending them," Lee said. "We're not done until he's in a jail somewhere."

Lee finished his business at BCA and returned to the office. Sacramento had still not called.

In Yosemite, Park Rangers continued to search for the men while the FBI watched the cabin, waiting for them to return. No one saw anything useful.

Lee got tired of waiting and headed home. As he pulled into the driveway, he saw his 16-year old son Matt coming out of the garage. He waved at him; Matt waited until he got out of the car.

"Hey, what are you up to?" Lee asked. It felt good to see his son, since on most nights Matt had already gone to bed by the time Lee got home. And Lee left the house in the morning long before any of the children got out of bed.

"Hi dad," Matt said, unable to hide his frustration. Kathy had just told him once again to be patient, that eventually they would get to the lake cabin.

"Something bothering you?" Lee asked.

"Well, I hoped maybe we'd be able to go fishing at least *once* this summer." Matt had gone with the Urness family to their lake cabin since before he could walk. But at that point, during the summer of 1997, the only fish for which Lee trolled was Andrew Cunanan.

"Matt, you know I have to catch this guy," Lee said. "I'm doing the best I can. But I'll tell you what, the first free weekend we're heading north." He smiled, hoping Matt would give him a break and join in his hope.

"Sure dad," Matt answered. Actually, he knew that it was true, because fishing with the family was a ritual for all of them. "I know. Hey, you want to shoot a few buckets?"

"Can't. I've got a few calls to make," Lee said, walking into the house. He saw that the dishes had been done and put away. Kathy told him that if he was hungry, there were leftovers in the refrigerator. It had been weeks since the family sat down and ate a meal together.

Around 9:00 p.m., he could wait no longer and called Sacramento FBI. "What is going on?" he asked. Thoughts of fishing and lake cabins had taken flight.

"Your guy hasn't come back to the cabin. They're still watching for him," the squad supervisor said. "I'll call you as soon as we have something."

Soon after, the two unsuspecting men walked up the path toward the cabin, laughing, enjoying their mini-vacation and ready for the next few hours alone in the seclusion of their cabin. FBI agents saw them coming. The sun hung low in the western sky; it still gave them enough light to clearly see their faces. The agents compared Cunanan's picture to the face of the man whom they suspected.

"It sure looks like him," said one of the agents. Quickly, the agents surrounded the two startled men and ordered them to the ground. They complied immediately and the agents quickly cuffed them. The officers' hopes ran high. In a few minutes, their hopes were dashed.

"Um, sorry to report this, but this was not Cunanan," the FBI superintendent reported to Lee several minutes later.

"Okay," Lee answered, frustration creasing his face.

"Boy, it is unbelievable, though. Our guys said the man looked exactly like your guy," the superintendent said. "But he's not, I guess."

"Well, now those two guys can *really* have a good time with a lifetime of bedtime stories to tell," Lee laughed. "Thanks for your good work. Maybe next time."

Lee wondered how many more leads like this the cops would chase. He had never before chased a guy who looked like so many other people. Well, next time. *Maybe next time we won't have to scare the hell out of some innocent guy.* Maybe not.

Chapter 32 ~ Making music together

Heidi Keller* had watched America's Most Wanted on Saturday night. She had studied the picture of Andrew Cunanan and all weekend, thought about what she had seen. Then she made a decision. She picked up the phone and called the hotline. The 14-year old from tiny Alberville, Alabama, had exciting news. She could not wait to tell the operator her story.

"Friday night I went to this concert here in town and saw Andrew Cunanan," she said.

"Do you mean on June 6?" the operator asked.

"Yes."

The operator wrote down the name of the concert, time and place. "And what did you see?" she asked.

"Andrew Cunanan! *I saw Andrew Cunanan!*" she said.

"Tell me about it."

"Well, I heard this man bragging to his friends with him about having killed someone. He said he did it in New Jersey, like Penns...something; like that," she said.

"Pennsville?" the operator asked, checking her information sheets.

"Yes, that's it. Pennsville. He said he killed somewhere there," she asserted.

"And why do you think it was Andrew Cunanan?"

"Well, the idea that someone would say they killed someone scared me, but it also sounded exciting, so I turned around and looked at him. I looked right at him, and that is the same face I saw on the TV show."

The operator took the rest of Heidi's information and immediately contacted Lee. Lee contacted the Resident Agent in Gadsen, Alabama, F.W. Langdon.

Langdon immediately drove to the Keller's house. Heidi's mother and aunt joined them as they talked about what happened.

"Miss Keller," Langdon began. "Let me show you this fax here that I got from America's Most Wanted. You see there?" he said, pointing to her name, "It says that you called the show."

"Yes sir, I did," Heidi answered.

"Now you say you heard someone at a concert say he had killed a man in Pennsville, New Jersey?"

"I ah..." Keller stuttered and stammered. She looked at her mother and aunt. "I am sorry sir. I made it all up."

"Heidi!" her mother yelled.

"I'm sorry. Did you say you made it all up?" Langdon asked.

"Ah, yes sir. I did."

"Why would you do that?" the agent asked.

"I just wanted to see what would happen," she admitted. "I had no idea the FBI would come to my door, really I didn't. I am awful sorry..."

"Well, filing a false report is a serious offense, young lady," Langdon explained as he shook his finger at her and squinted through serious eyes. He saw this as a teaching moment, not an arresting moment, but wanted to leave no doubt in the teenager's mind as to the seriousness of her actions.

"I'm real sorry, sir. Real sorry. I will never do this again," she said, looking more like a sad Beagle than the energetic teenage girl he had first seen when he came into the house.

After he left the house, he called Lee and explained what had happened.

"She needs a good spanking," Lee said, exasperated by the waste of time and resources.

"Oh I think her momma's gonna take care of that," Langdon laughed. "You can count on it."

Drink it in

Wilma Raymond* had walked through the door at Joseph's Town and Country, a Sacramento, California gay nightclub, at 8:00 p.m. on a late May evening. Some time around 9:30, Anthony, the heavy-set Hawaiian bartender, introduced her to a suave, dark-skinned fellow. The fellow, whose name she later recalled as Andrew something, preferred to be called Andy. After that night, she never saw him again.

On June 7, she watched America's Most Wanted. "My God! It's him!" she said, spying Andrew Cunanan's picture. She called America's Most Wanted on the following Thursday.

"Thanks for the lead," Lee said after chatting with the AMW operator. He read it carefully. "Doubtful," he said, while dialing the Sacramento FBI office.

"Lee Urness here, case agent on the Andrew Cunanan case, file number 88A-MP-47461," he said.

"Yes sir, how can I help?" he heard from agent LuAnna Harmon.

Lee laid out the details, as he had several dozen other times since May 7. He held out little hope of any meaningful results.

Harmon contacted Raymond. Raymond felt sure the photos of Cunanan Harmon showed her looked just like the Andy she had met. The interview led to secondary interviews of five others.

Tom Jefferson*, a bartender at Joseph's, remembered someone who looked like the photos of Andrew Cunanan. "But so do a lot of people who come in here. This is a low key club, a perfect place for a guy to come and blend in."

The club's manager did not recognize Cunanan, but readily agreed to hang the wanted posters in his club.

Luke Tunnie*, who frequented the gay club, knew Cunanan, in fact, claiming that he had grown up with his parents in New York. But he had only seen Andrew once, and that was in the early 1980s. He had heard that Cunanan's father was a financial broker who had moved to the Philippines.

Harmon received a call from bartender Roger Babcock* at the Wreck Room, another Sacramento gay bar. Babcock felt certain that Cunanan had come to the club at about 10:00 p.m. the previous night.

Lee read the reports, but shook his head. It made no sense, given what they knew. He told Harmon to keep on looking and to call him if anything solid turned up, but nothing ever did.

In the hotel, now!

A front desk clerk at the upscale Chateau Marmont Hotel in Hollywood, California, looked up from his work. He saw a man crossing the lobby whose visage startled him. The man wore a baseball cap, wig, light-colored T-shirt and cream-colored shorts. The man listened to music through earphones connected to a Sony walkman that hung on his belt. He appeared to be going nowhere and unworried about anything.

The clerk had seen America's Most Wanted and the man he saw in the lobby looked exactly like Andrew Cunanan. He immediately called the 800-CRIME-TV hotline. AMW immediately paged Lee and within a few minutes, Lee had dialed the hotel's number.

"He's here right now, too," the clerk said. He sounded very nervous and worried. "He's in the alcove here."

Lee knew that Cunanan loved hotels like this. His financial records showed he had stayed there previously. If he had somehow made his way back to California, he could be disguised and looking for one of his friends. "You just stay where you are. We will send the squads," Lee told the clerk.

Within minutes, Los Angeles police and FBI cars surrounded the hotel and officers began their search. The startled wigged man had disappeared. Police fanned out, checking out nearby parks, stores, hotels – anywhere the man might have gone – but they never found him, or the wig. Dozens of police and FBI hours had been burned, but to no avail, because Cunanan sat in a hotel 2,800 miles away in south Florida, though another caller felt sure he was in Virginia, using an alias.

On June 9, Lee set a lead in Raphine, Virginia where an employee of White's Truck Stop felt sure that Cunanan had stayed on May 27. Tammie Conner* remembered that the man came into the truck stop with a Presbyterian minister, Pastor Karl Billing* of Steeles Tavern, a small town near Raphine. The man called himself Clem Dickie*.

Dickie had been hitchhiking on Route 11 near I-81 when he wandered into Midway Machine and Parts. Dickie asked Sally Lawrence*, an employee at Midway, if the company was hiring anyone. He said he had just come into town and needed work. Lawrence told him several times that there was no work available, and finally referred him to Mt. Caramel Presbyterian.

Dickie called Pastor Billing who drove to meet the man. Dickie told Billing that he had been in a motorcycle accident, and that his bike was being repaired at Midway Machine. His wife had died, Dickie said, and he had many injuries from his accident. He needed a job, a place to stay and food. He lived in Charleston, West Virginia.

Billing took Dickie to White's Truck Stop and made sure that all the expenses would be paid by the church. Dickie checked out on May 28.

Agent Paul Hunt went to each location and took a statement, showed the photo lineup and wrote his report. He received handwriting samples from Dickie's signature on the truck top guest checks and a lead was set in Charleston. The FBI meant to be sure that Clem Dickie was not Andrew Cunanan. And he was not.

The next day, an anonymous caller contacted New York police. He had seen Cunanan check into Room 4701 at the Millennium Hotel on West 44th Street. Agent Blasse made a preliminary call to the hotel and identified the registrant as allegedly an employee of Walt Disney Company, from Florida.

Armed with this information, Blasse made a pretext call to the hotel and showed Cunanan's photo around. No one recognized him and they felt certain that the 4701 tenant was not Cunanan. Further investigation revealed that the man really was in town on Disney business. "The caller was misinformed," Blasse reported later.

It was too bad that Blasse had not heard that Cunanan wiled away his time in room 322 of a weathered Miami Beach hotel room. That was the lead all the agents sought, but never found until it was far too late.

Parked for good

At his Normandy Plaza Hotel hideaway, Andrew Cunanan enjoyed anonymity. Clerks at the half-star inn ignored him and asked no questions. Area residents and vacationers staying in the nearby hotels cared about the beach and relaxation, not a murderer on the loose. He had been careful not to get into trouble, and disguised himself with sunglasses and a baseball cap whenever he ventured outside. As in New York City, he blended in.

Cunanan had to preserve his cash, but finding food was no problem. Within a block of the Normandy Plaza Hotel, he could choose from Subway, Denny's, IHOP or McDonalds. He could eat at Olivo's Café directly across the street or on either side of it, the Las Vegas Cuban restaurant or Sapori's for Italian food. Next to McDonalds on 71st he could pick up a newspaper or magazine at Andy's News and Gift Shop, and go next door for a burger at a sports bar. He could walk 100 feet west and grab a pizza at Miami Beach Pizza that sat next to a pawnshop. If he crossed over on 71st, he could catch a sandwich at Jill's Café.

He could walk north to get classic coffee drinks and pastries at Buenos Aires or walk a few feet further and catch take-out at Miami Subs. Whatever he bought to eat, he could sit safely among the pine trees and homeless people in the park at North Beach on 72nd and Collins. Or he could walk 100 feet further east and sit on the beach.

Just north of the park sat a Walgreen's Pharmacy and near to it, a public library branch. The library offered ample anonymity to literate homeless people and residents, or tourists who were killing time.

He could safely park Reese's pickup truck at the block-square, free municipal lot across the street from the park, just a block north of the Normandy Plaza Hotel. The NCIC listed it as stolen, but not with a South Carolina plate on it. Until police caught on, he had no reason to fear it would be discovered.

His room at the Normandy Plaza Hotel had a small TV, and a sink, stove and refrigerator. To save food money and reduce exposure, he could walk a block south and pick up groceries at the Publix supermarket, making his own meals in the security of his room.

He could walk out the back door of the Normandy Plaza Hotel without being noticed, through the grassy back yard and out onto the beach. Looking north or south, all he could see was sand and an endless line of hotels and condominiums that sat close to the beach. No one would bother him on that beach, day or night.

Few Miami Beach squad cars patrolled the area and those that did had no reason to look for him. Unless they frequented gay establishments where FBI Agent Keith Evans had distributed his picture, they would have paid him no attention.

He dressed in tank tops or muscle shirts, shorts and sandals, looking just like any other Miami Beach resident or tourist. The cops would have no reason to bother him unless he did something stupid. If his money held out, he could stay at the Normandy Plaza Hotel forever, or until finally, one of the Normandy Plaza Hotel clerks watched America's Most Wanted.

Partiers at Twist, a gay club on 11th and Washington in South Beach, claimed they saw him on a couple of occasions early in June. One man insisted that Cunanan danced with him and, while doing so, had his hands all over him. They ended their dance with a kiss.

Just as near the Normandy Plaza Hotel, in the midst of throbbing music and packed confines of South Beach's gay clubs and bars, Cunanan could blend in. Though Evans had warned them, letting patrons know that a gay murderer could visit their establishment at any time would be bad for business. If Cunanan visited the clubs, no one reported it until after July 15.

On June 10, however, Cunanan did drive the pickup south on Collins and parked it on floor 3B of the 13th Street Garage. He never again moved it.

Chapter 33 ~ Not the kind of study he had in mind

New York Special Agent Emilio Blasse received a call on June 11 from NYPD Sergeant Al Reghanardt. The Manhattan cop claimed that he had Cunanan in custody thanks to a tip from Bill Donaldson* who had seen the June 7 viewing of America's Most Wanted.

Blasse reported this to Lee as he headed out the door. "I'm on my way to lock-up now, and I'll let you know right away," he said.

He sped to the lockup, but it took only a quick glance to know that the man was not Cunanan, but a guy who had just registered for college classes.

NYPD had done a thorough job of booking the student, fingerprinting him and running the prints against their database while he sat in a holding cell. As with Cunanan, there was no match because the man had never before been arrested.

After consultation with Sgt. Reghanardt and three other NYPD officers, Blasse could officially state that the student was not Cunanan.

Before releasing the man, NYPD apologized and showed the student that they had purged the booking form. "You are free to go," they said.

"There's a lesson he never planned to learn," Lee said after Blasse phoned in his report. "Never look like a killer on the run."

Now Top 10

Lee had received word early during the week of June 9 that Cunanan would be added to the FBI's Top Ten list on June 12 as "Top Ten Fugitive Number 449." He knew it meant a media bump, which he needed badly, and it would also give him a tremendous advantage in wining the support of investigators. The FBI's $20,000 reward gave people more incentive to watch for Cunanan, even though it also meant receiving bogus leads.

Every FBI agent and street cop desired to arrest a Top Ten crook. Besides the good feeling generated by every arrest, the letter in the agent's file certainly would not hurt his or her career. As well, with the Top Ten label, Lee would have an unlimited budget and the total attention of FBI Headquarters. At least, that is what he thought.

The Top Ten designation came with official FBI Wanted Posters, and they would be sent to Post Offices and other federal buildings everywhere. Lee had already received identification cards as a result of the "Identification

Order" he and Rickett had filed on May 21. These cards bore the Cunanan picture from his driver's license, his thumbprint and descriptors. He had each of these cards laminated. The FBI sent the I/O's to each state bureau and asked them to run the thumbprints against their records. Other copies were sent to post offices and other federal sites for posting.

The actual wanted posters appealed to the broad audience of all citizens, but before they could be sent out, they had to be printed. Lee soon learned that while the FBI could hurry up getting the felon onto the Top Ten once an opening appeared, getting the printer to print the posters could take weeks.

"I get it," he said one day while talking to an agent at FBI headquarters, "you've got one guy who prints all the posters. And he's swamped."

"Something like that," he heard.

"Hey Murray," he said to Paul Murray one day while he was still waiting for the posters, "where do you think my guy is?" he asked.

"Damned if I know," he answered.

"I have this bad dream that he's laying at the bottom of one of those Pennsylvania quarries, like you said," Lee said.

"You could be right."

"Or maybe he drove deep into the woods somewhere out of sight, and did himself. You find my truck yet?" Lee asked.

"I told you it's not in New Jersey," Murray answered.

Steve Gilkerson overheard Lee talking to Murray. "You think it's bad now," Gilkerson said when Lee got off the phone. "I told you not to do a Top Ten. When he's on that, he's yours until you catch him. If he's in one of those quarries, you'll go to your death bed and this will still be your case," he said, laughing heartily.

Lee knew that Gilkerson was right, but he also knew that it had been the right decision. Now the day loomed just ahead.

Before the media found out, he wanted to talk to every officer involved with the case. On June 11, he conducted a conference call – all involved agents.

"So tomorrow we announce the Top Ten. It ought to buy us some media exposure," Lee said. "As you know, except for America's Most Wanted, not much has happened.

"So here's what I want you to do. Cunanan may try to contact one of his closest friends. There are 16 people on that list," he said, and rattled off their names. He could hear the other agents grunt their recognition. "We need to go out today and talk to everyone of them. And for you west coast guys, what do you think about keeping an eye on Gary Elly and Garth Davidson?"

"We can do that," Scott Anderson answered.

"Same here," John Hause said.

With that bit of business done, he called Coleen Rowley. She had already begun coordinating press conferences with FBI headquarters, offices in other jurisdictions and in Minneapolis. Lee continued to insist that his name be kept out of the news.

On the morning of June 12, the media trudged up to the eleventh floor of FBI headquarters in Minneapolis. The Special Agent in Charge, Roger Wheeler, handled the statement. Behind him stood Coleen Rowley. Lee stood off to the side, back in a corner, trying to blend into the plain wall. He felt glad that Chris Graves had not come to the press conference because surely, she would have identified him as the case agent.

With the Top Ten announcement done, Lee headed back to the FTF office.

Lee had heard that even mentioning the words "Top Ten" to a cop or FBI agent broke down resistance and reluctance to act. Soon after Cunanan made the exclusive club, he found out both its strengths and weaknesses.

Lee learned that a former San Diego lover of Cunanan's, a Naval medical doctor, had been transferred by the navy to Japan. Maryann Cunanan told John Hause that once during the early 1990s, Andrew had gotten angry with her and threw her on the floor, hurting her shoulder. Andrew took her to the hospital where this doctor-lover worked, and received discreet treatment for her injuries. Andrew told Maryann to tell the doctor that she was his housekeeper.

Lee pondered the question, *did Cunanan try to flee to Japan, or would he go to the Philippines where his dad lived? And who else did he know that we may have missed?* This doctor/lover could prove helpful in answering the questions.

Lee contacted the Legal Attaché – LEGAT – in Japan and asked him to interview the doctor, reminding him that Cunanan was a Top Ten case.

"Well, you have to understand that the FBI really doesn't like to mess with U.S. military personnel," the LEGAT said.

"Hey, I don't care about the military on this. We're looking for a murderer. I need you to get out there and interview this guy," Lee said.

"No, I just can't do that. You're going to have to go through channels," the LEGAT said.

335

"Okay, fine. We'll talk again," Lee said, hanging up.

He made one phone call to FBI Headquarters and explained the situation. Within hours of that call, Lee received back the LEGAT's telephone report.

The doctor had no useful information about how to locate Cunanan. The reaction time of the LEGAT, once Lee got his attention, told him that the system worked. The Top Ten was well worth the effort.

All talked out

By that time, Lee felt they had spoken to everyone Cunanan ever knew. Despite the frustration that they had not caught him, Lee felt they had shut down his options and left him no room to move. Soon he would call one of those names on the list and then within minutes, Lee would have a SWAT team there, ready to put the handcuffs on him.

The media played the Top Ten story as a major news event in many markets, but not out east, and most certainly not in the *Miami Herald*; not a single Cunanan story appeared on its pages in June. This fact must have both frustrated and pleased Cunanan, who seemed vitally interested in any story that contained his name. He laughed at the media as he wiled away his hours in the Normandy Plaza Hotel in South Beach, under the nose of *Herald* reporters who paid him no attention.

Miami FBI agent Keith Evans had worked hard to get Cunanan's picture into the area's gay establishments. Just after the Ten Most Wanted announcement, Lee sent Evans more than 3,000 of his homemade wanted posters for distribution in the Miami area. Evans had told Lee on May 12 that he suspected Cunanan could be in South Beach; and he was, though neither man really knew it. The delicate political balance between protecting the citizens and upsetting the tourist trade may have contributed to the muting of a Cunanan scare in that resort town, unlike the sheer panic Cunanan-thoughts gave to gay activists in other cities.

Thus it would remain in Miami Beach until the day one of their stars was shot dead on his doorstep. Then it became the central story of the life of party-town USA.

Ride along killer

Matt, from Pittsburgh, claimed that his brother Mark had recently met Cunanan. Mark had spotted Cunanan walking along a highway and picked him up, just 10 days earlier. Mark thought the man looked a lot like Cunanan, and noticed that he had a gun butt sticking out of his belt. Cunanan offered to pay Mark for a ride to Cleveland, to which he had agreed. He had rented a car for that purpose and planned to pick him up the next day. But when he started thinking about the AMW show he watched the prior weekend, he quickly changed his mind, so he told his brother Matt. Matt decided to call AMW and report it.

"Sounds pretty strange," Lee said, but still placed a call to the Pittsburgh FBI office.

Matt, who had been a police informant, believed that Cunanan was a man on the run. Cunanan had told Mark that he had trouble in St. Paul and in New Jersey.

Matt said that Cunanan had been staying at an apartment in the Mount Oliver section of Pittsburgh, where he lived on the first floor. Cunanan would be waiting there the next day for Mark to pick him up.

A squad of police drove to the pick-up site the next day. They saw no one who even remotely resembled Andrew Cunanan. In fact, everyone they saw on the street was African-American.

As they questioned the apartment dwellers in the building where Cunanan supposedly stayed, they learned that no one ever remembered *any* white man living there. Neither had any other residents of the adjacent buildings seen a white man, save one rather sheepish, diminutive white fellow across the street – who was not Andrew Cunanan, but was very surprised to be questioned. As Lee had suspected, this sighting was just another red herring.

Too much bourbon on this guy's street?

Lee forced his eyes to open at 4:30 a.m., Saturday, June 14. Kari had a major softball tournament that weekend, and he had set himself to be there. Cunanan had officially been added to the Top Ten Most Wanted list, but new leads only dribbled in. Lee knew there would be no America's Most Wanted that night, so he hoped for a quiet day.

The Laker's first game at the Mankato Peppers Tournament was set for 8:00 a.m. It meant a nearly 60-mile drive just to get to the field in the south-central town of Mankato, Minnesota. They would be competing against some of the best teams in the state.

The Urness family left home at 5:30 a.m., but as usual during the past several weeks, Lee drove separately.

Pulling into the parking lot at the ballfield, he found a spot in the front row. From there he could clearly see the softball field.

Lee got out of the car, snuffed out his cigarette on the ground, and stretched. He felt exhausted, but also exhilarated at the idea of taking a trip out of town, even if not too far away. The cool breeze of the early morning caressed his face, but he could feel the warm moist air building. The day could get uncomfortable. The idyllic park setting seemed almost storybook to him, sitting as it did on the banks of the Minnesota River, surrounded by trees. He took a deep breath.

"What a perfect day for softball," he said as he approached the Laker's girls who were storing their equipment away.

"Did you catch CunaHAN yet?" a grinning Jessie asked.

"No, no we didn't," he said. "Did you learn how to run yet?" he asked. As frustrating as it was that Cunanan still ran free, Lee enjoyed Jessie's teasing, and loved to give it back to her. "Come on, let's get warmed up," Lee said, noticing that it was just past 7:00 a.m.

Thankfully, he got through the first game without interruption. They won easily. In between games, Lee decided against calling any other agents. As a practice, he tried leaving his peers alone on weekends, even though he demanded of himself that he was always available.

The next game started at 10:00. At 10:53, while he sat in the dugout calling pitches for Kari, his pager beeped. He saw the message: CALL FBI ASAP.

Back in his van, he called the FBI who then patched him through to a woman from Coates, Minnesota, a small town southeast of the Twin Cities.

"I just saw someone who looks like that Andrew Cunanan fellow," she said.

"I see. Tell me about it," Lee sad.

"Well, I was driving down Highway 52 and I saw him driving a tan Ford Falcon. I wrote down the license plate number," she said, rattling it off from her notes. "It's a Pennsylvania plate," she said.

"Thank you very much for your help," Lee said, after taking down all the details. "Please stay near a phone in case we need to call you back."

He called the Minnesota Highway Patrol and gave them the information. "And be sure to notify the Rochester police department," he urged them.

Rochester, home of the Mayo Clinic, was the largest city south of Coates on the route the Falcon traveled.

Next, he called the Philadelphia FBI office and asked them to run the license plate and see if they could make a contact.

As he made calls and waited for responses, he watched the Lakers' game.

"We got your car," the Philly office told him a few minutes later. "It is a Ford Falcon, and the family that owns it is traveling in Minnesota. I doubt that it's your guy," he heard.

"Okay. Thanks for your help," he said. As he expected, Cunanan was nowhere near Coates, Minnesota.

He walked back to the dugout.

"How we doing, Little Bear?" he asked Kari.

"We're up 6-1," she smiled. They won the game.

One more game and a high-speed run to Minneapolis

At 2:15 p.m., Lee chugged his lanky body out to the first base coach's box. The afternoon sun burned his neck, and the humid air made him feel clammy. Still, there was nowhere else he would rather be at that moment, except maybe visiting a shackled Andrew Cunanan in a prison somewhere – anywhere.

At 2:17 p.m., his pager rang. He saw the message, "Call Alicia at America's Most Wanted." He signaled to one of the fathers to take his place, and jogged to his van.

"Lee Urness here," he said as Alicia answered the phone.

"We have a tip that a guy dated Cunanan last night in New Orleans," she said.

"No kidding," Lee said. "Did the guy leave a name and number?" *This would get us within hours of Cunanan,* Lee thought.

"Oh yes. Are you ready?"

"Yes," he said, picking up a note pad, and actually surprised that the fellow had left his name. He wrote down Chuck Loomis* and the phone number. "Thanks for your good work," Lee said.

He stared at his pad as he tried to think this through. *New Orleans is not so far from the east coast. I'll bet there's a lot of gay activity down there. He could easily drive there. No toll roads. Well, it might be.*

"Mr. Loomis, this is Lee Urness with the FBI Fugitive Task Force. We received information that you may have spent time with Andrew Cunanan recently," Lee said.

"Yes sir, I was with Andrew last night," he said. Lee heard no nervousness or confusion in the man's answers as he collected general information from him.

"How do you know it was Andrew?" Lee asked.

"Well, I met him in 1992 in San Diego at a bar called Numbers. I certainly would know it was him if I saw him. Absolutely it was Andrew," Loomis insisted.

"And you were with him last night?" Lee asked again.

"Oh yes, we spent several hours together."

"Okay, I'm going to call an FBI agent there in New Orleans. He will come to talk with you. Just sit tight there for a while," Lee instructed Loomis.

"I will."

Lee checked his watch. During the 13 minutes they had talked, he had heard nothing in the man's voice that gave him reason to discount anything he had said. *Well, it could* be, he had to tell himself.

Lee asked Minneapolis to connect him to the New Orleans FBI office. He noted the time as 2:40.

"FBI, Allison Paulson* speaking," he heard.

"Miss Paulson, this is Lee Urness, case agent on a Top Ten case, calling from Minneapolis. We have a potential sighting in New Orleans and I need to speak to someone on your Fugitive Task Force right away," he said. Lee knew that on Saturdays it often took a good deal of time to find an agent.

"I will have somebody get right back to you," she aid.

At 2:51, Lee's cell phone rang.

"Urness here," he said.

"This is Special Agent Brad Michael, New Orleans Fugitive Task Force, returning your call. You mentioned a Top Ten case?"

Lee almost chuckled at how much urgency those two words – Top Ten – added to his request.

"We may have had a sighting of Andrew Cunanan there in your town," Lee said. "I'm the case agent on this one."

"Tell me what you have," Michael said.

Lee gave him the details relayed to him by Chuck Loomis a few minutes earlier.

"He dated the guy?" Michael asked.

"That's what he said. Now, it seems logical to me that Cunanan could be there. That's the good news. But the bad news is, I never heard this guy's name before. We've been all over Cunanan's records for five weeks, and Loomis's name has never come up. And it bothers me about this. So I'm going to fly back to the office in Minneapolis and pull up Rapid Start and go thru everything I have," Lee said.

"That's good. But why would a guy lie about something like this?" Michael asked. "To claim he dated the guy, spent hours with him, and it would be a lie?"

"Well, there's a reward with the Top Ten. Like $20,000. That would be the only reason, I would think," Lee reasoned.

"I will call him immediately and call you back when I get things figured out," Michael said.

Lee went back to the softball field. He had watched the girls take the field again, so found the coach and told him he had to leave the game.

"Well we're ahead 8-0, and it's the last game of the day," he heard.

He found Kathy and let her know he was leaving, and then ran to his van. *Who knows? It could be him.*

Check it out

What Brad Michael heard from Chuck Loomis astounded him.

"Well sir," Loomis began, "yesterday I got a call from Andrew…"

"Andrew? Do you mean Andrew Cunanan?" Michael asked.

"Yes sir."

"How did you know it was Andrew Cunanan?"

"Well, I met him in 1992. He and I were both working as prostitutes in California and we've stayed in touch ever since," Loomis explained.

"What time did you receive that call?"

"About 10:00 a.m. He left a voice message for me," Loomis said.

"And so what happened?" Michael asked, recording the details on his notepad.

"Andrew asked me to meet him at the Clover Grill at about 10:30 p.m. You know the Clover?" Loomis asked.

"Well, I've never been there, but I know of it. In the French Quarter?" Michael asked.

"Yes sir. A nice place, and very popular with gays. So I met him there. He said he had come here from Florida. Then we went to two other gay night clubs in the Quarter, and then took a cab to the Sheraton New Orleans on Canal Street," Loomis said, smiling as he remembered the evening.

"And then what did you do?" Michael asked.

"Well, Andrew said he had a prostitution date with a man at the hotel – room 3204 he said. A guy in his 40s."

"Did he mention the date's name?"

"No. He just got dressed and left for work," Loomis answered, giggling a little.

341

"Did you go with him or wait for him?" Michael asked.

"Oh I left. I took a cab home. Andrew wanted to get together again on Saturday..."

"You mean the fourteenth? Today?"

"Yes."

"And did you?" Michael asked.

"Oh no, not when I heard about him. A friend called me and said that Andrew was wanted for murder," Loomis went on.

"Who called? The name, please," Michael said.

"Sidney Courtland*. Sidney is a woman," he explained.

"And then what did you do?" Michael asked. One thing he liked about Loomis' answers were that he had given him many ways to verify his story and more than that, a hope that Cunanan was still somewhere in New Orleans. If he was, Michael felt confident they would find him quickly.

"I changed my voice mail to try and lure him into calling me, but later I changed it, when I learned how serious the accusations against him are," Loomis said.

"And did he call you again?"

"No, thank goodness. He never did," Loomis added, expressing relief.

"Anything else?" Michael asked.

"Well," Loomis thought, rubbing his chin. "Yes. Andrew said he was HIV positive and taking AZT."

"Really?" Michael said, writing it down. If this fact was true, it opened up immense possibilities to track Cunanan, and anticipate his next stop, as soon as he needed more AZT.

"Yes sir. Oh, he said he drove here in a Ford Probe that a prostitution client in Florida gave him," Loomis said.

"Now I am going to show you some photos," Michael said, laying a photo lineup in front of him. Lee had faxed it down earlier that day. "Do any of these look like the man you were with yesterday?"

He pointed at Andrew Cunanan.

"Are you sure?"

"Oh yes. I know him well, and this is him," Loomis said.

Michael left the interview perplexed. Loomis's confidence and quick answers impressed him. Still, he had a funny feeling about what he had heard. He headed to the office to call Lee, and to plan his evening.

Working and driving

Lee tore back to Minneapolis, 90 miles away, as fast as he could without turning on his siren. He drove straight to the task force office. Driving wasted time, but Lee always tried to use the time the best he could. He worked his mind and his cell phone. *How could this guy's name not be in any records? Did we overlook him? How could he slip through the cracks? But it seems too far-fetched. Cunanan's story's been told dozens of times every day. Why could a guy take a chance without calling the cops?*

As he came close to Minneapolis, he called Kevin Rickett to see if he remembered the name or anything like it.

"No, Loomis doesn't sound familiar to me, but who knows?" Rickett said. "Maybe we caught a break."

He called Paul Murray.

"Paul…"

"No, your truck is not here," Paul said.

"Okay. Say, I got a call from New Orleans and I want to run it past you, to see what you think," Lee said.

"Where are you?" Paul said, hearing the noise in the background.

"Driving to the office. I was at a softball tournament and got the call."

"Yeah, you get no life when you're chasing a bad guy," Paul chuckled.

"So I got this hot call," he said, explaining the details. "Did you ever hear the name?"

"No, doesn't sound familiar."

"What do you think? Is it legit?" Lee asked.

"It could be. You never know, but the name is not in my list. But what would be the motive in making up such a story?" Paul asked.

"I don't know."

"Well, you gotta chase it down," Paul said. "Say, I talked with a psychologist here who had some ideas." Murray knew about Lee's failed effort to get the FBI Behavioral Science Unit's help.

"What'd he say?"

"He says that Cunanan will never commit suicide. Instead, he'd shoot it out," Murray said.

"Great, that's what we need."

"At least the shrink is pretty sure he's still alive…"

"And driving my red truck in New Jersey," Lee teased.

343

"Nope, he's not here. Hey, you'll catch the guy," Murray said. "Just keep on swinging. Hey, maybe this is him in New Orleans."

"Could be. I'll catch you later," Lee said.

Lee called John Hause in San Diego. Hause had never heard of Loomis either, but agreed to check it out.

Back in the office, he checked Rapid Start. The name, Loomis, did not appear on his list. Then just past 7:00, Brad Michael called him. Michael reported on the interview and added, "I don't get it. It doesn't sound right to me."

"Yeah, if he hung around Cunanan, I would think I'd have it in the data base by now," Lee said, "and he doesn't show up anywhere."

"I just don't really know what to do," Michael said. "But we're going out to hit the bars with him. He's going to show us around. We're going to make a discreet canvass of the nightspots. We're going to go everywhere. It's a Top Ten and we're going to flood the place."

"Gee, have a nice evening," Lee laughed.

"You're gonna owe me on this."

"Stand in line. I owe a lot of people," Lee laughed harder. Satisfied that that he would hear nothing more that night, Lee headed home. After all, there were at least two more softball games on Sunday and he hoped for some rest.

In New Orleans, Brad Michael organized a search of all the clubs. They made no pretense of their purposes, making sure that everyone knew they were the cops. They showed everyone the posters and gave them away to anyone who would take one. No one identified Andrew Cunanan, except for Chuck Loomis, his alleged lover of just 24 hours earlier.

Lee rested well that night, fairly confident that Loomis would not prove true, though still troubled by why he would tell such a story.

When Michaels called Lee again on Sunday with his report, it had been as Lee expected – no sighting of Andrew Cunanan.

"This just doesn't feel right," Michael said. "I think he's lying. But he insists it's all true."

"I hear you," Lee said. "What'll you do?"

"Well, stay on it I guess. I'll call you tomorrow."

Lee watched almost the entire tournament that day. The Lakers easily won the championship trophy.

Since the day in ninth grade when he scored 54 points in a varsity high school basketball game, Lee always enjoyed winning. It was how he competed as an athlete, it was how he trained his softball team, and it was what he expected as a cop. How to beat Cunanan, though, still eluded him. In high school and college, to win meant working harder on conditioning and shooting, repeating his shots and studying the game. Chasing Cunanan meant contemplating, visualizing, mentally repeating each step in the investigation. This he did as he laid back in his easy chair late that Sunday night before his fatigue sent him into deep sleep.

Chapter 34 ~ Too slow, also bad

Lee began to worry that with the slowdown in media attention, the public would forget about Cunanan. He knew that Cunanan's picture hung on the walls of gay-oriented businesses, clubs and bars all across the nation. Confirmation of this came from the oddest places. So when an official in a small town in Idaho called and asked for Cunanan posters, it pleased Lee.

"You know," the official said, "we have some, well, odd people living near town. Kind of loners – outsiders. And they're, well, *different,* if you know what I mean. So we thought maybe we should get some of those signs."

"You'll have them tomorrow," Lee said. He doubted that Cunanan would ever party with guys near a remote Idaho town, but the fact that such calls came to him meant that his plan worked. Even in small towns, people had become aware of Cunanan. The risk, however, was that they would soon forget.

As soon as FBI headquarters finally printed the Wanted Posters they had been hanging in post offices and at police stations everywhere, and Lee hoped that would help. America's Most Wanted meant to keep the story alive until the cops caught Cunanan. That still was not enough to please Lee. He called Coleen Rowley.

"Coleen, Lee here. Got a minute?" he asked.

"Sure, what's new?"

"Nothing, and that's what bothers me. My guy is holed up somewhere. He's not moving, at least in the daytime, and the leads are slowing down. I want to do something to get the media's attention," Lee said.

"Like what?"

"Well, maybe it's time for me to come out of the closet," he said chuckling.

"What?" Rowley asked.

"No, no. I mean out of the closet as the Case Agent. You know, do a press conference," he said.

Since mid-June, Rowley had been working for Mike Waldner, the Acting Special Agent in Charge at the Minneapolis Division. Waldner did not like making media statements, not since FBI Director Louis Freeh had clamped down on public comments by SACs. The SACs feared that making a mistake could result in a letter in their file that could hurt future promotions in the "company." Since the Cunanan case had originated in Minneapolis, nearly all

347

media statements came from Rowley, and the FBI had pretty much left her alone to use her best judgment. She worried little about making a misstatement, but she also knew that Waldner would not want to risk a press conference with Lee.

"No, I don't think this will fly. Just keep on doing your job, or maybe, let America's Most Wanted come out to do a story," Rowley suggested.

"Nuts," Lee said. "No, I don't want to tell them too much. Donna Brant's been after me since day one, and I don't want to do that."

Without Lee's knowledge, Brant had made a formal request to the FBI to do a live interview with him. That interview happened on the most remarkable day of Lee's professional life.

C's close friend

On June 17, Paul Murray contacted Lee about a picture he had found in Lee Miglin's Lexus. It showed a man standing in front of a pickup truck that bore a California license plate. Running the plate through the California system had led them to Thomas Robinson.

Robinson confirmed that indeed, he was the man in the picture. He added that he and Cunanan had been close friends and lovers, and that Andrew asked for that picture to take with him when he left San Diego. Robinson had made no additional prints, and had the negative in his apartment.

"This proves the link between Cunanan and Miglin," Murray said. Before this confirmation, Murray had to assume that the picture could also have belonged to Lee Miglin. "Maybe not enough for a warrant on the Reese murder, but still, a good piece of work."

"All right," Lee said. "Send me a copy, and I'll call Murphy and Hause and send them out to see the man again. Robinson was in Cunanan's phone book."

"Did you check out the real estate deal?" Murray asked, referring to the map he had found in the Lexus drawn on the back of a real estate listing.

"Yup. I actually got to go out and do the interview," Lee said, knowing that Murray understood how he hated being stuck behind a desk. "It led nowhere. But thanks for sending it on. At least it got me out of the office."

Crescent City follow up

"Have a good weekend?" Lee teased Brad Michael, the New Orleans' agent, when he called on Monday.

"Oh just terrific," he said. "We plastered the town with posters, talked to everybody we could, went to every gay club and bar." Loomis had worked with them until past 1:00 a.m. on Sunday morning. "We got nothing. I still say he's lying, but he says he's telling the truth. We'll keep working on him."

New Orleans police had identified the occupant of room 3204 as a man from Pensacola, Florida – Lenny Daniels*. That fact seemed significant to Lee, given that he felt sure Cunanan hid somewhere on the east coast. Maybe he had been in Florida with Daniels? Perhaps they traveled together to New Orleans? Michael had contacted the Duty Agent in Pensacola and an immediate search for Leonard had begun.

"But the guy told a good story and claims its all true," Michael said.

"Will he take a lie detector test?" Lee asked.

"Let me try."

On June 18, Loomis did take a lie detector test. He flunked – badly. According to the test, he had made up the whole story.

"I don't care what the test says," Loomis asserted when Michael confronted him with the results. "It's all true." He set his chin.

"Mr. Loomis, come on. Spare us all here. Nothing checks out, and you flunked the test," Michael said.

Finally, a few days later, Loomis confessed. He had fabricated everything. "I'm not even gay," he finally admitted, but never did come up with a sensible reason for his deceptive story.

"He made it all up," Michael reported to Lee, sighing deeply. Hundreds of police hours had been expended trying to verify Loomis's story, and warning the gay community. "Well, at least there isn't a gay man around here who hasn't seen Cunanan's picture," Michael chuckled.

"I hope you guys stick it to the son-of-a-bitch," Lee said, as he pulled his billfold out. "What a waste."

"We're going to see the U.S. Attorney and try to get him charged."

"Why did he do it?"

"I can't imagine. Just to get noticed or something," Michael said.

"Well good work. Maybe next time," Lee said, saying good-bye.

Lee spun his chair around and walked to Jeanie Burn's desk. He dropped $2.00 into the Swear Can. "I might as well pay in advance," he sighed.

After venting, Lee went back to his desk and sat down, swinging his legs up on Lisa's desk. His mind went to Lake Ida. He realized that he never would have found the drowned man in that lake if, on every day, fishermen would have sent him from one end of the lake to the other, spotting the victim in numerous different places at the same time. That, however, was all that he felt he was doing in this Cunanan chase. The faster and more deeply they searched, the more they seemed to get behind. "It's like getting a flat tire during a chase," Lee grunted, as his mind went back to Douglas County.

Flat out chase

Just after he became a Douglas County Deputy, he and Keith Nelson, another young deputy, set out at 1:30 a.m. to do "some burglar huntin'." After they had finished their western tour of Garfield, Brandon and Evansville they drove east on Highway 52.

That night they paid special attention to anything that looked unusual. Minneapolis had sent a teletype informing them of a couple of professional burglars who had been seen heading their direction.

At about 2:00 a.m. they saw a pair of headlights coming toward them. Instinctively, Lee noted the license plate number of the big sedan as it flew past them. Lee grabbed the microphone off the dash and called the dispatcher. "This is Lee Urness. I need you to check on a license plate for me." He read off the numbers.

"Hey, I just saw that on the teletype today. It's on a burglar call out of Minneapolis," the dispatcher said.

"Cripes!" Lee said. "Hey, let's go," he told Keith. He turned the headlights off and swung the squad car around. "We'll head up to the freeway and get there before him."

Lee hit the accelerator and the engine roared.

Bam!

"What the hell?" Lee said.

"Sounds like we blew a tire," Keith said, as the two men got out of the car.

"Toss me the lug wrench and start jacking the car," Lee said, noticing the flat left front tire.

Before Keith had the jack out of the trunk, Lee had started to remove the lug nuts. He looked up to his left at the front bumper as he felt the car being jacked up, but Keith was nowhere to be seen. Yet he could hear him grunt as he pushed the jack handle up and down.

Lee stood up and saw Keith pumping the jack handle as fast as he could – on the right rear bumper.

"What are you doing?" Lee said, as he began laughing.

"Oh..." Keith said, recognizing the mistake. "I, ah, well..." and he started laughing.

They howled in laughter. The crooks drove away. All they could do was radio ahead, hoping a cop somewhere down the line spotted the bad guys.

Chasing Cunanan reminded Lee of that flat tire. "You do everything right and just when you think you got him, a nail in the road blows your tire and you watch him drive away."

Cunanan schooling the FBI?

Late Monday, June 16, the Minnesota FTF office heard from a registrar at the University of Colorado in Boulder. Sal Wesley* saw the June 7 segment of America's Most Wanted and the face of Andrew Cunanan had burned into his memory.

On June 12, a man had walked into Wesley's office. He claimed to be Caesar Diego*, a Columbian student with a student visa. Wesley could not purge his mind of Diego's face, and felt certain he was Andrew Cunanan. Further needling Wesley was Diego's demand that he be allowed to take three semester's worth of management courses in one semester. "He said he was in a hurry," Wesley told FBI Special Agent Jeffrey Snow.

When Diego returned on June 16 to help another student register, Wesley eyed him carefully. "I excused myself for a moment and when to find Kelly, one of my co-workers, to get a good look at him. And when he left, I asked her what she thought. She said she had also seen America's Most Wanted and was sure that Diego was Cunanan."

Snow reported that he would do an immediate follow-up on this sighting, and began contacting other federal offices for assistance. This meant contacting the Social Security Office to run a check on the validity of Diego's SSN, plus face-to-face interviews with the man.

Finally, on Thursday, Diego produced enough evidence to convince the FBI that he was, indeed, a Columbian, not a Cunanan. Another look-alike could get on with his life.

"A. Cunanan" to rent a car in San Juan

Helen Naime* worked as a phone clerk for Dollar-Rent-A-Car at their American headquarters. She also watched America's Most Wanted.

Naime saw the June 7 AMW show and what she saw astonished her. Someone named "A. Cunanan" had reserved a car at the San Juan, Puerto Rico location just a few days earlier. She immediately called AMW. They contacted Lee.

Lee immediately contacted the FBI in San Juan and agent Ivan Vitousek headed to the airport. Lee never believed this was "his" A. Cunanan, but the lead had to be followed.

This lead, however, gave Lee an important insight. When a car rental clerk calls in a lead, there had to be a strong reason, and the reason was that the efforts of the FTF were paying off.

Vitousek looked at the auto rental records. There he saw for himself that "A. Cunanan" had, indeed, reserved a car for June 12, but he never showed. Vitousek found what appeared at first blush to be good and useful news – an address and credit card number.

No one took the time to quantify how many men were named A. Cunanan, but this car-rental-A.-Cunanan was a salesman who lived in Atlanta, Georgia. He had nothing to do with the killer Cunanan.

Well, then, how about Oklahoma City?

A series of sightings erupted in Oklahoma City after Lamont Benjamin* reported to the local FBI office that Cunanan had been in his laundromat. Benjamin told the FBI that a man matching Cunanan's description had used the laundromat on more than one occasion, in fact, just recently. And the man "sure looks like Cunanan, and he even drives a red Chevy pick-up with New Jersey plates."

"Why would he be there?" Lee asked when the FBI agent called him with the report. "It's not on the way to anywhere he would go." Lee ran Rapid Start and not a single Okalahoma address appeared, nor any nearby area.

When Oklahoma City media published news about the laundromat incident, Lee heard about scores of other sightings. Area residents began seeing Cunanan everywhere; some 500 sightings were eventually reported.

As a result, Special Agent Dylan Burns organized and conducted a neighborhood canvass. The canvass involved several FBI agents who contacted both individuals and establishments where Cunanan had been "sighted," or the types of places he would most likely frequent.

On June 16, Hal Johnson* claimed he picked up a man who had been walking northbound on the interstate near mile marker 29. He noticed that the man's dark blue Bronco had a flat tire. Johnson drove the man to a phone booth near Ardmore, Oklahoma. There, Johnson called a tire repair company to fix the tire for the man, who he later came to believe was Andrew Cunanan.

Keith Overgaard* reported that he had seen someone who looked like Cunanan at the Kingswood Square Apartments during the previous few days. Harry Michelson* believed that Cunanan had spent time at True Loves, a Portland gay bar. Carl James* felt certain he saw Cunanan at Sam's liquor Store during June.

Scott Carson* believed he saw Cunanan at the Boulder Ridge Apartments in Tulsa, and that he drove a white Nissan Maxima. That same day, Terry Lenz* saw Cunanan at the Habana Inn, a gay hotel, in Oklahoma City. Lenz said that Cunanan was staying in the hotel there and mingling with men at the Saddle Tramps bar.

Two men at a Phillips Gas station felt sure they watched Cunanan pump gas between 4-5:00 p.m. on July 6 at a station near Oklahoma City. Cunanan used the restroom and as he came out, one of the men spoke briefly to him. They watched Cunanan drive off in a pickup truck headed toward Dallas, Texas. *The Oklahoman* had carried a feature story on Cunanan that same day and the men recognized him from his picture in the newspaper.

On July 8, Sarah Rose* stopped at the Git-n-Go gas station in Oklahoma City. As she stood in line, she noticed the man just ahead of her. She studied his face and appearance. She felt sure it was Cunanan. She reminded the FBI that the store had a video surveillance unit.

Also on July 8, Amy Gaston* told the FBI of her last visit to the Thunderbird Entertainment Center in Oklahoma City. On July 5, she visited the place to play bingo. A man who called himself Don sat across from her. Don had a woman named Jackie with him, and they later departed in a Lincoln Town Car. Gaston had written down the license plate number, so sure was she that Don was really Cunanan. She never mentioned why she waited three days to report the sighting.

Lee finally asked the Oklahoma City FBI office to send out a different agent to do a re-interview. This time, Benjamin, who acknowledged that he was gay, admitted that he was "no longer sure" that Cunanan had been there. "Maybe I read about it in the papers or something," he told the agent, "or I confused him with another guy."

But Cunanan was not in Oklahoma; neither was he in Albuquerque, New Mexico. Lee took a call from a Lutheran church in Albuquerque. The caller insisted, "Cunanan was in church here last Sunday."

Not likely, Lee thought. *He's Catholic, and he's not going to church.* Lee sent an agent out to check on the lead, but expected nothing. However, as in Oklahoma City (and elsewhere), once the hint that Cunanan had come to town surfaced, other sightings followed, all leading to the same end. Cunanan never went to New Mexico, though a well-meaning car rental clerk felt sure he was about to visit Puerto Rico.

Checking all rentals

On June 18, Lee received a report from Paul Murray. Murray had requested all major car rental companies to search their records for any attempts by Cunanan to rent from them. As well, he ran all of Cunanan's aliases and threw in William Norman and William Reese. All searches came up negative. Reason told Lee that Cunanan still had that red pickup truck, but he had no clue where it would be. Of one thing he was certain; Paul Murray was a hell of a cop.

"I'm sending a long list of things to HQ today," Murray told Lee the next morning, referring to the FBI crime lab in Washington, D.C. "These are items found at the cemetery and in the Lexus. I'm asking the lab to run every conceivable test. Maybe we'll find a set of prints," he said.

"Great work. Let me know when you hear back," Lee asked. "And ask them to send me a copy of the results, too." Finding a full set of prints remained elusive, but once Lee had them on file, it could be the element that broke the case. But Lee never did get that full set of prints, not until weeks later, when they were lifted off Cunanan's corpse.

A bad payday

On June 20, The West Palm Beach Police Department received a tip that Cunanan had been working construction in their town using the name Hal Kendal*. The informant said that Kendal would be picking up his paycheck that day at 3:00 p.m. and that he had been telling co-workers that be planned to leave for California that same afternoon.

Special Agent Steve Burdelski and his partner drove to the construction office and asked for permission to show Cunanan's picture around. Two office workers felt that Cunanan and Kendal could be the same person.

Subsequently, the agents, along with two detectives from the West Palm Beach Police Department set up surveillance near the office, allowing Kendal to enter the facility at about 3:00 p.m. Once inside, the cops surrounded the man and explained why they wanted to talk to him. The startled man put up no argument, save trying to explain that he really was, indeed, Hal Kendal, not Andrew Cunanan. He agreed to go to the police station to be fingerprinted, and as a precaution, police handcuffed him.

At the police station, officers rolled Kendal's two thumbs and compared them with the copy Lee had provided them of Cunanan's thumbprint. The police drove the cooperative and relieved man back to his truck by 3:40 p.m. Kendal never forgot that June 20 payday.

Earlier that day, Stella Grace* had contacted Paul Murray in New Jersey. She wanted Murray to know that she had for certain spotted Cunanan driving south on I-295 on May 10. She remembered that Cunanan drove as if he was drunk.

So convinced was Grace that she had seen Cunanan that day, she had stopped at a nearby McDonalds and called 911, but the operator seemed to know nothing about the Pennsville murder. She had even written down the license plate number, but still could get no help.

Next, she had called the Pennsylvania State Police only to learn that the 911 office never passed the information on to them. Grace had lost respect for the emergency service system.

As soon as Murray got the call, he ran the license plate number. It belonged to a Loveladies, New Jersey man and was attached to a 1986 Chrysler Laser. He still had his car at home and without hesitation, allowed Murray to see it.

That the 911 operator had no knowledge of the Reese murder did seem troublesome and perplexing to Lee. In Minnesota, Cunanan's four murders dominated his every waking hour; near the murder scene, a big-city police department seemed not to much pay attention.

Lee knew that he needed police cooperation to catch Cunanan, but even more so, he needed the Stella Grace's of the world to watch for the killer, and to call, no matter how crazy their lead might be.

Chapter 35 ~ Going it alone

The media bump from the Ten Most Wanted press conference died down within days. Leads came across Lee's desk on a regular basis, but had slowed to several a day.

America's Most Wanted had aired the Cunanan story three times: on May 10, May 16 and June 7. Each time it sparked activity. Lee had heard from Donna Brant that they planned to air another segment on June 21, and she wanted the most up-to-date information.

"Which is that he is now Ten Most Wanted," Lee said.

"That's it?" Brant asked.

"Pretty much."

"Do you have any idea where he is?" she asked.

"Only in general terms. We have leads all over the country, but east coast somewhere still seems the most likely. He could be anywhere from Boston to Miami, although we've had almost no leads in Miami," Lee said.

"Well, let's see what we can do to generate some leads. Maybe we'll get lucky," Brant said.

"Sounds good to me," Lee said. "Hey, I think I'm going to do this one alone, at my house. My people are really tired and could use a night off."

"We can do that, if you can set up a fax and give us a hotline."

So on Friday, June 20, Lee told his weary FTF team members to try to get some rest the next day. "But if I get a hot one, be ready to come in," he warned them.

Lisa, his 17-year old, saw him as he came home late that evening. She held the cordless telephone to her ear, talking to one of her friends as she filed her nails. She said "hello" to Lee by raising her eyebrows and then scowling as she saw him staring at the phone.

"Just a minute," Lisa said to her friend. Then she looked at Lee. "You're not getting the phone tonight," she said, scowling at him.

"Ha!" he laughed. "Well, maybe we'll get lucky and no one will call. Besides, that's why I got the extra phone line." Lee knew that his family fully supported him and understood the critical nature of this case, but it had begun to wear on all of them.

"I hope you catch this guy soon so we can have our life back," Lisa said as she walked out of the room. "Huh?" she said into the phone. "Oh, nothing. Just my dad. I told him he couldn't use the phone tonight."

Lee had wished "the" call came that night, but no calls came, giving him some relief; and he would need all his energy for the next evening.

Saturday afternoon, when Lee came home earlier than usual, Kathy wondered what was going on.

"Oh, I decided to do AMW alone tonight, from home," Lee said as he began to clear off the breakfast bar. "I thought I could put the small TV here and use the cell phone and the cordless, and the new line we put in."

"Suit yourself," Kathy said. "I hope you can handle all the calls."

"Well, June 7th didn't produce many. I think I can do it," he said. "Hey, you can help. Just sit here and be my assistant."

Kathy smiled and walked out of the room.

Lee followed up on calls, tuned up the agents in other cities, and made himself a sandwich as he waited for 8:00 p.m. As the time approached, he settled in at the breakfast bar. Kathy walked though the kitchen.

"You can sit here, at the table," Lee said.

"No thanks. I'm off to bed. You have a good night," Kathy said cheerfully. She really meant it. The Cunanan case had totally disrupted her family life like none other. Nothing would please her more than to have Lee catch Cunanan that same night.

Lee wished Kathy would have stayed, but only for companionship. He had always tried to keep her out of his police work.

Lee opened the kitchen window and slid open the door that led to the deck. He felt the warm breeze of an ideal Minnesota summer evening. The air was fresh, sky perfectly clear and even the cardinals were busy feeding. Everything was perfect for a relaxing evening at home, at least for his neighbors. He had work to do.

The program began and the segment was good. Calls filtered in slowly – less than 20 that night.

He recorded each new call on a pro forma lead sheet he had created. It contained all the boilerplate information about the Cunanan case, and a place to write the new information. These sheets would serve his needs until Jeanie could type them up the next business day.

The few hot calls, though, required far more work than just writing down information. A man in Tulsa, Oklahoma believed he saw Cunanan at an apartment building. A York, Pennsylvania man felt "nervous and sure" that he had seen Cunanan that day. Another man said Cunanan sat at the Casablanca Bar in Long Island, New York.

Each lead demanded an initial contact call, calls to police jurisdictions, faxing of information packets and several follow-up calls. The computer tied up one phone line as it received faxes. Lee worked the other two phones simultaneously, calling out on one and receiving calls on the other, juggling them as he consumed a constant stream of hot coffee. After three hours of constant activity, Lee felt as though he was going crazy. It became unmanageable. It continued until midnight.

He had given a break to his co-workers, but paid a personal price for it. By the time he crawled into bed, it was past 2:00 a.m., but the combination of unbridled activity and caffeine robbed him of sleep. And Cunanan still ran free.

Where's my posters?

Lee had counted on the FBI to spread Cunanan's picture to every federal building in the world once they had printed their official wanted posters. But nearly three weeks had expired and he still had no official posters. He complained about this one morning as he talked with Paul Murray.

"Hey, I asked FBI headquarters for some wanted posters," Lee said.

"What'd they say?" Paul asked.

"The guy said, 'They're down at the printers,' so I asked them where the hell are the printers? He said, 'It's here.' I mean, it's like the third week now, you know, so I asked, how slow are they? It would be nice to get some official posters. And he says, 'Well, it's at the printers and we'll get you wanted posters," Lee said, getting more disgusted at each word.

"And so," Murray said, laughing at his friend's frustration.

"So I had made my own posters weeks ago, but I still didn't have the official posters. Then I did some research and found that at the FBI you have some old grey-haired guy with one of those green visors on; he sits down in a dark room and has an old hand cranked press and works until his arm gets tired. And so it takes him forever," Lee said.

Murray roared in laughter. "You just might be right!"

Of course, Lee knew that the FBI had thousands of these requests and everybody wanted their case to be a priority. So he knew he had to stand in line and be patient because all paperwork takes time. The paper pushers knew this and accepted it, but not street cops. And a few days later, those marvelous posters appeared, everywhere, even in Miami Beach.

Cunanan stayed here?

Scott Bakken and Terry Thedford had wanted to meet with Marilyn Miglin, but despite the fact that she had talked with Chicago police, she refused the feds. They wanted her to look at the photos Paul Murray had found in the Lexus.

Finally, though, Duke Miglin, accompanied by Miglin's personal secretary, agreed to meet. They chose the offices of Beitler-Miglin, high up in one of the high rises the company owned.

"This is their building?" Thedford said, in amazement.

"Yes, and they own the one next door, too," Bakken said. Both men saw evidence of how influential Miglin had been.

"We wanted to show you these photos that were found in Mr. Miglin's car," Bakken said, handing them across. One of them showed Thomas Robinson standing in front of his truck. "Do you recognize any of these individuals?"

Neither of them recognized anyone in the photos, but they did recognize the Lexus. Miglin explained that his father almost exclusively drove that car, save the times Duke visited Chicago.

During the Miglin interview, the FTF received a call from Delia Jarmine*, a housekeeper at Accommodations America, a Lombard, Illinois extended stay inn. Finished with Duke and the secretary, the agents went to see Jarmine.

Jarmine remembered cleaning one of their units for a man named Tom Roberts*, a Los Angeles resident, who stayed at their place for two months from August to September of 1996. Roberts had claimed to be an actor, and Jarmine believed him to be about 45 years old. A man lived with Roberts who told Jarmine that he was from San Diego. She felt sure that both men were gay.

The man, whom Jarmine now believed had been Andrew Cunanan, had stayed around the apartment during the day while Roberts went off to work. Cunanan moved out of the apartment two days before Roberts did. Cunanan told Jarmine that he planned to move back to San Diego.

Thedford and Bakken showed her a photo lineup from which she identified Cunanan. They then set leads in Los Angeles to locate and interview Roberts.

Lee read their reports and checked Roberts' name against his Rapid Start list. It appeared nowhere. This meant either that he had slipped through the cracks, or it was just another look-alike sighting. Still, that the system had produced this result made him smile; it meant closing the window on Cunanan one more notch.

While Chicago's FTF worked with Jarmine, Diane Benning, David Madson's sister, contacted the FBI office near her Hartland, Wisconsin home. She had found a shoebox full of Madson's possessions that she felt would be helpful in the chase of Cunanan.

Benning believed that Cunanan would likely dress as a woman. She claimed that Cunanan had mentioned it in references in the letters he wrote to her brother. Benning also claimed that she had personal knowledge that Cunanan had been a cross-dresser.

Lee had considered cross-dressing as a possibility. Cunanan had gone to his senior prom in drag. Had Lee known that Cunanan had purchased a girdle at the Walgreen store on Collins Avenue a few days earlier, he might have been very concerned. That purchase surfaced more than two weeks later, once police found where Cunanan had been hiding.

Cunanan look-alike collared

On July 2, Steve Gilkerson of the Minnesota FTF returned the call of Wisconsin Special Agent David Fitzgerald. Fitzgerald had been in contact with the Buffalo County Sheriff in Alma, Wisconsin, who had processed a prisoner the previous night who refused to give up much information. The sheriff worried that the man, who called himself John Thomas*, might actually be Andrew Cunanan.

The sheriff had rolled fingerprints of Thomas and sent them to FBI headquarters for processing, but the quality of the prints rendered them useless. Thomas had told the sheriff only that he had come from Albuquerque, New Mexico and Minneapolis, and that he had been upset with something that happened at the Minneapolis gay pride celebration. He said he planned to move on to Indiana.

Fitzgerald had Thomas recontacted so that the prints could be re-rolled. He also concluded that Thomas looked nothing like Cunanan. Still, he sent the prints to FBI headquarters for processing. This time they hit a match at FBI headquarters, and the man's name was not Thomas, nor was it Cunanan.

Fitzgerald learned that the prints matched a man named Frank Timons*. He ran a NCIC check on Timons that came up negative.

Timons, aka Thomas, had no idea that even remotely looking like Cunanan could get him in so much potential trouble and had a lot of explaining to do concerning why he had lied about his name.

When Lee heard about the incident, it bolstered his confidence that police officers everywhere continued to chase down every lead, and that soon, one of them really would be Cunanan.

Later that day, Lee and every other FBI office received a lengthy communication from Paul Murray. In it, he replayed his entire investigation to date. Just as importantly, he advised each FBI office to get a copy of the DAMRON book so that agents could contact each organization that catered to gays and lesbians. Murray recommended walk-in interviews and distributing Wanted Posters at each location.

Chapter 36 ~ No independence of mind on this day

July 4 fell on a Friday. At most any other time in Lee's career, it meant a long weekend, a trip to the cabin up north, or a family trip to an out of town softball tournament. And Kari did have a weekend tournament scheduled. Lee, however, could not leave town. He had already missed at least four trips to his cabin in northern Minnesota. All vacations for Task Force members had been cancelled on May 7, until they apprehended Cunanan.

With any luck, he hoped he could at least have this single day away from the case with time to get some things done around the house.

Within minutes of getting out of bed, he sat staring at the newspaper. He never saw the words. He lit a cigarette, but most of it burned away without him taking a drag. His coffee got cold before he drained the cup. His body sat in the kitchen, but his mind was elsewhere, everywhere and nowhere.

He fought off the edgy unease he felt. Sixty-one days earlier Cunanan had killed Lee Miglin. He stole cash. Lee estimated Cunanan had 60 days to spend that money, and once spent, desperation would set in. Cunanan *had* to make a move. The time had come.

No matter what Lee did on that "day off," his mind gravitated to Cunanan. His wife Kathy had given up trying to talk to him: he never heard her.

Late that afternoon he sat outside. Kari and one of her girlfriends fooled around nearby. He tried to watch, to enjoy, but soon his mind began churning.

Where is he?

Did he flee the country? No. He needs an ID. He left his wallet behind. And he has no money. If he could get money, where could he go legally? Bermuda. The Caribbean. No. They all know about him.

Where is he living? Has he found some guy to live with? But wouldn't the guy know C is a Top Ten? No, nobody's that crazy. And he has no money to pay his way. Nobody would just harbor him; they'd be afraid of being victim number five.

Same with sex. Yeah, he's got a huge sex drive. But that was the old Cunanan. Would the new Cunanan take the risk of finding a guy? No, I don't think so. But what do I know about gays? Still, he's not the same guy he was before.

Maybe he found a hillbilly somewhere out in the woods. He killed the guy and moved into his shack. But, no. C hates roughing it. He needs TV, movies, radio, stereos, magazines, books. None of that would be in a hillbilly's shack.

If he's broke, what does he do? He's no robber or thief. Who does he go to to beg for help? And who would dare give it to him?

So where is he?

He's a big city guy. He does nothing in the daylight, but he was always a night person anyway. He's got to be living alone in some cheap hotel somewhere, a place where the clerks are used to anonymous guests and where they never ask questions. But I've been in lots of seedy hotels doing drug busts. Newspapers and "National Inquirer" and things like that are always lying around, and the TV is always on. But why didn't the clerk recognize him? His picture is everywhere! Doesn't the clerk watch America's Most Wanted?

So he must be in a big city. But has he stayed in one place or is he moving around? The license plate is hot. Every cop in America is looking for that truck. I ran the NCIC check on the plate and there hasn't been one sighting anywhere since he stole it.

Okay, then he's stashed it someplace and he's not driving it. Did he park it in a big city garage somewhere? But no one's reported it. But he must have. Where would he get the money to get it out of hock? It's just another dead end. I don't think he's driving the pickup anymore, and he's not a car thief.

Did he sell the truck? No. He doesn't have the title. Not even to a chop shop. For sure they would have seen him and cashed in the reward. I bet he's abandoned the truck. What'd he do with the Lexus? That was a hot car. He killed for a ride. Will he kill for a ride again? Not if he's in a big city.

How about Boston? I've got a lot of sightings there. Miami? That's what Evans thinks, but I've got hardly any Florida sightings.

This is summertime. Millions of people are out and about, and they go to parks and forests. If he's there, wouldn't somebody have seen him? Then again, did he lose himself in the crowds?

What have I missed? We've talked to everyone he ever knew, and no one has heard from him. I don't think he's called anyone. But now that he's out of money, maybe he'll call? But I have his phone book.

What can I do with the newsies to get more coverage? I can't trust them so there's not going to be a press conference.

I wonder how my mom is doing? I haven't seen her all summer. How's she dealing with the nursing home? I haven't seen dad, either. Sure do enjoy talking to him on the phone at least. I need to go up there, but I can't. What if something happened to one of them? Would I even get to go? Damn that Cunanan!

Is he lying dead in a quarry? Am I stuck with this case the rest of my life? Naw. He's too chicken to do suicide, and besides, who'd care or remember.

Okay then, where is he?

"*Lee!*" Kathy yelled. "*Lee!!*"

"What?" he said, turning to look up at his wife.

"Kari is trying to talk to you. Do you even hear her?"

"She's what?" he said, turning and seeing Kari standing there, looking frustrated. He fought the desire to sink back into his meditation.

"Oh, yeah. Little Bear, what did you want?" he asked, almost in a trance.

"I *said*, are you going to the tournament tomorrow?" the 10-year old asked.

"No, I can't," he said sadly. "I'm really sorry, but until we catch this guy..." Kari walked away, her head hanging.

"Until you catch this guy you ought to go rent a room in town. You're no good here," Kathy said, following her disappointed daughter.

"Wait, I'm sorry, it's just that..." Lee saw it was no use. The case ate at him like alcohol to the alcoholic. "This'll be over soon, and..."

Ah. *If he is in Miami, why is he there...*

Chapter 37 ~ He knew it would end, eventually

Lee imagined confronting Cunanan in his cell hours after an arrest, listening in as the FBI's best interrogator pried open the killer's psyche. He had given much thought to this, wanting to be ready the moment a cop reported arresting Cunanan.

Lee held the only warrant so he called the shots. He planned to have the U.S. Marshals immediately sequester Cunanan from local cops and prosecutors. He wanted the expert interrogator to get the first shot. That way, he figured they would get the most information possible before Cunanan "lawyered up" – quit talking. Yet, at the bottom of it all, Lee cared little if a cop shot Cunanan, *before* the commission of another murder – "Dead Right There!" Lee's job meant stopping him, not prosecuting him.

Catching Cunanan, though, might reveal the link, if any, between him and Lee Miglin. But Lee's job was simple – to apprehend or stop Cunanan. Homicide detectives and prosecutors could deal with the rest.

Paul Murray had told Lee that the debate had already begun among prosecutors in three states about who would get first dibs on Cunanan. If New Jersey won that fight, Cunanan could be tried in federal court and face the death penalty.

Lee could speculate all he wanted, but Cunanan chose to frustrate all the prosecutors, cops and reporters. He had decided to face death by his own design. He would be immortalized in history. Immortalization was his only hope, because hell lay just beyond the door of his hotel room.

A little spending money

On July 7, a nervous gay man in Sacramento contacted the FBI. He claimed to be a regular patron of The Townhouse, a Sacramento bar that was one of Cunanan's favorites. The man said someone had put a Cunanan Wanted Poster on his windshield and it reminded him that Cunanan came to the club nearly every weekend, though the man had not seen him the previous weekend.

The Sacramento man had nothing about which to worry. Cunanan still hid away in Miami Beach. There would be no trip to Sacramento or anywhere else; he had run out of money.

Cunanan's empty pockets left him but one option and that meant leaving the safety of his Normandy Plaza Hotel room during the daytime.

His simple hotel room shared but a few things with the five star hotels he preferred. It had a bed, a bathroom and a door to shut out the world. Tolerating his abysmal surroundings further reinforced his fall into ignominy. Within a short walk of his rundown hotel sat exotic and expensive condominiums and hostelries such as he had frequented during much of his adult life. Now, high living, scores of friends and unfettered partying had ended in isolation in a crummy third floor room. Even the view of the Atlantic Ocean could not salve his savage spirit.

The hot Miami sun beat on the walls of his room. He felt clammy and nervous. As he re-read one of the library books he had stolen, or one of the pornographic magazines that lay around his room; as he lay on his bed or tried to refresh himself in the shower; as he watched the tiny 13" TV, watching for the next story about him; he knew that at any moment a FBI or police SWAT team could break down his door.

He had successfully hidden his existence for nearly two months, but today he had to take a risk. He could not wait until night to venture outside. He could not wait to make a food run or sit out on the beach under the dark, starlit skies.

He pulled on a non-descript T-shirt and a pair of dark shorts so that he could look like one of the thousands of tourists that cruised the area. He pulled a white baseball cap unto his head and grabbed his sunglasses. Though a civilian might see him, few cops patrolled the area, concentrating more at South Beach.

He had spotted a pawnshop on 71st Street, just a block away, next door to a pizza shop near Harding Avenue. It sat a few doors west of McDonalds and the newsstand where he bought his newspapers and magazines.

He left the Normandy Plaza Hotel and walked 100 feet north and crossed the street. He walked a block west to the pawn shop, Cash on the Beach. He carried one of the $50 gold coins he had stolen from Lee Miglin. With any luck, he could consummate his deadly plan before he needed any more money.

He rang the doorbell outside of the pawnshop. A buzzer sounded and he walked in, seeing a stark, empty lobby area and straight ahead, a bulletproof glass window that sat atop a counter and stretched the entire 15 foot width of the room.

"Can I help you?" Vivian Olivia asked from behind the plate glass window as Cunanan walked toward her.

"Yes, I have this gold coin," he said to her through the stainless steel speaker grid set in the window. He reached into his pocket and pulled out the gold coin, saying, "and I wonder what I could get for it?" He slid it under the thick bulletproof glass. He fought to remain calm and avoid looking over his shoulder or at the security camera.

Olivia picked up the coin and studied it carefully, then threw a glance at Cunanan. He looked just like any of the other men who frequented her place. There had been no police alert about stolen gold coins, and this *was* a valuable piece of property. She knew nothing about Andrew Cunanan or his murderous ways.

"I can give you $190," she said.

"Why can you give me so little when it cost me so much?" he asked.

Olivia explained how gold prices fluctuated. He accepted. He found himself in no position to argue.

"Okay, I will need you to fill out this form," she said, sliding a pen and a blank form to him.

He studied it briefly and began filling in the blanks. He wrote, "Andrew Phillip Cunanan," under "Name." He wrote his social security number, height and weight, and wrote "Normandy Plaza Hotel" as his address. He slid the form back to her.

"I will need some identification," she said.

He slid his passport to her. She looked at his picture and name, checked his social security number and glanced up again at him. The passport picture matched.

"I will need your thumbprint," she said, pointing at the spot where to roll his thumb. She opened the black inkpad and nodded at it.

Cunanan rolled his thumb on the inkpad and then on the form, sliding it back to Olivia, fighting the urge to run.

"Here you are," Olivia said, sliding $190 in cash under the glass. "Thank you very much."

"And thank you. I will be back within a month to buy it back," he said, shoving the cash into his pocket. He turned and left, walking quickly back to McDonalds. Within minutes, he was back in the safety of his hotel room.

Olivia placed the document in her sales drawer after removing a copy to mail to local police as the law required. She had no idea that she had just done business with a killer. All she knew was her obligation to comply with Miami Beach ordinances.

Family members provide good aid

In most cases where the FTF chased a crook, family members of the crook's victims wanted to help. Their help often proved valuable, and such was the case when Sally Davis, Jeff Trail's sister, contacted the Chicago FTF office on July 8.

Davis had compiled a list of Jeff's friends, and she believed some of them might also know Cunanan. Davis had given this list to Minneapolis police, but that office had not shared it with other agencies.

Davis told Terry Thedford that though she never met Cunanan, she felt sure her sister Lisa had met him. Davis provided Thedford with Lisa's phone number.

Soon, Lee had several more names to run through his Rapid Start program. And although none of the names proved helpful, he welcomed the involvement of the Madson and Trail families. The interaction of Jeff Trail and David Madson within various circles of gay men had opened up many possibilities. The fact that no such common contact existed with the friends and family of Lee Miglin and William Reese indicated to Lee that both murders really were random; they had nothing to do with Cunanan's gay lifestyle. Furthermore, knowing all the Miglin and Reese associates would provide no help; the FTF needed to focus on gay communities.

Dumb luck prevails

On July 10, Cunanan's pawn ticket sat amongst a huge stack of the same on the desk of Miami Beach Police Sgt. Lorenzo Han. Han served as the pawnshop investigator for the city. He checked all the pawn reports each workday, at least when he was in the office. On July 10, though, he sat doing surveillance at a pawnshop far removed from Cash on the Beach. Robert Taylor, a Public Safety Officer, thumbed through the reports for him.

Taylor saw a pawn slip for a rare gold coin. Even though no specific alert existed for that coin, routine caused Taylor to flag the pawn slip, which he added to a small stack of similar items and placed back on Sgt. Han's desk. Taylor filed the balance of the reports.

On July 11, Han attended an investigator's workshop. Han's regularly scheduled days off were July 12-14. On July 15, just as he returned to work, he was called to assist in a murder at 1116 Ocean Drive. Sgt. Han never saw the Cunanan pawn slip until the killer had murdered once again.

Welcome back home

On July 10, Gianni Versace and his long-time partner Antonio D'Amico flew from New York City to Miami, returning to the luxury of his mansion at 1116 Ocean Drive in South Beach. The three-story finished coral rock structure sat behind a concrete wall upon which was erected a black wrought iron fence. The fence was separated from the sidewalk on two sides by lush bushes, palm trees and colorful flowerbeds. The front of the house was accessed through a green wrought iron gate that sat atop a landing reachable by climbing five marble steps. Versace kept the gate locked when he was inside.

The two rich men had been faithful lovers for 14 years, though they occasionally hired male prostitutes for sexual variety. They trusted the choosing of their prostitutes to South Beach resident Carl Jimenez*, who screened the prospects at the nearby Palace Grill. Once chosen, Jimenez delivered the courtesan to the back door of the mansion, a dark wood double door that opened onto an alley (Ocean Court). The door sat several feet north of a double garage in the otherwise plain, three-story back of the house. Inside that door sat a beautiful open court.

On the north side, the house abutted the parking lot of an old hotel that would soon undergo massive renovation. A chain link fence abutted the wrought iron and brick wall at the edge of the property on Ocean Drive.

The mansion's video cameras were trained on the front gate and surrounding sidewalks. On July 15, those cameras were not operating.

Versace enjoyed the privacy and safety offered by the high walls of the mansion.

He had a reputation for throwing lavish parties at his New York City and Miami Beach residences. It was in 1991 at such a party in San Francisco that Andrew Cunanan, then a 21-year old "A" list prostitute, had a chance meeting with the icon. Cunanan attended the party with Gary Elly, a wealthy San Francisco attorney and close friend. Elly claimed that Versace recognized Cunanan from an earlier meeting. Versace's family and friends later denied that any previous relationship existed between the two men. Yet, Versace would be the ideal type of date for which Cunanan would have trolled during his earlier days.

Versace's mansion sat within walking distance of nearly a dozen gay clubs and bars, as well as upscale shops and restaurants. Several exotic establishments catering to either gender, or just voyeuristic men, fronted Washington and Lincoln Avenues or their side streets.

Gianni Versace's second cousin, Domenico "Nico" Versace, lived several blocks from the Versace mansion. He worked as a model at an agency three blocks south of the mansion on Ocean Drive. Nico had no idea that Gianni had come to South Beach on July 10. Cunanan, however, somehow found out. Once he knew, he thread the needle for the final stitches in his simply designed death plot.

Fled to Mexico?

On July 11, Jimmy White* sat in a Hennepin County (Minneapolis area) jail cell. White told the guard he needed to talk to someone about Andrew Cunanan; he claimed he knew him, and that they had recently spent time together.

"I even know where he is right now," he told the jailer.

Local cops had caught White after he returned from Sonora, Mexico, where he had been doing drug business. He said he had seen Cunanan in Sonora.

"That's right," White claimed. "He's in Sonora right now, but he's dyed his hair red. But you'll have trouble catching him."

"Why's that?" the curious cop asked.

"Because he made a deal with the Federales to avoid capture," White claimed.

Lee sat scrutinizing notes he had taken about White's saga and decided the man had seen too many movies. Lee had cornered many crooks in Mexico, and knew how hard it was to win the help of Mexican authorities, so White was right about that. But not only did Jimmy White's name not appear on the Rapid Start list, the whole incident seemed bizarre. Lee remained convinced that Cunanan had stayed on the east coast. Still, Lee contacted the Mexican LEGAT to follow-up on the reported sighting and, once again, wondered why people like White felt motivated to create fables.

New digs floated

Cunanan had less than $50 left and a bill due at the Normandy Plaza of $240. Versace had come to town, but would be leaving again on July 16. Cunanan had to move.

Leaving behind his collection of books and magazines, as well as the motel bill, he walked out of the Normandy Plaza Hotel on July 12. He carried his few remaining clothing items in his backpack, nestled into which sat the Taurus pistol. The red Chevy truck sat securely parked at the 13th Street Garage where he had parked it on June 10. He had no money by which to pay to get it out of hock.

Cunanan could join the homeless people who camped out at the park up on 72nd and Collins. A public restroom remained open there and an outdoor shower offered some relief down on the beach. People walking past the park were used to ignoring the bedraggled men and women who lived on those mean streets and beaches. Living outside, though, went totally against his grain. Luxury hotels were no more an option, but sleeping on a beach left much to be desired.

Sometime that evening, Cunanan went to the Miami Subs shop on 72nd and Collins across from the park. He ordered a sandwich, trying not to look suspicious. He had been in the place many times since moving into the Normandy Plaza Hotel, and no one had ever before noticed him.

Behind the counter, Gerald Benjamin had been helping his workers fill orders. He glanced up and saw Cunanan, recognizing the face. As quietly as he could, hoping Cunanan would not see him, Benjamin went to the phone and dialed the Miami Beach Police Department.

"Hello, I am calling from Miami Subs at 72nd and Collins," he said. "There is a man standing here right now, right in front of the counter who I know I saw on America's Most Wanted."

"Are you sure?" the receptionist asked.

"Yes. Positive."

"Who is the man?" the receptionist asked.

"Well, I'm not sure," Benjamin answered.

"When did you see him? I mean, which show?" she asked.

"I'm not sure. Sometime in the last few weeks. But I know I saw him there. He's waiting for his order now. You need to hurry," he urged. Hanging up, Benjamin tried hard not to stare at Cunanan as he continued to ponder the face.

The police dispatcher immediately put out a call. There were 24 calls already in the police pipeline, but she felt the urgency in the caller's voice and decided to move this call to the top of the list.

Eight minutes later, police cars pulled up at Miami Subs. Cunanan watched from a distance. He had left two minutes earlier.

"Is your video working?" the officer asked, nodding toward the surveillance camera on the wall once he had learned that the suspect had left the place.

"Yes sir," Benjamin answered. He retrieved the tape for the officers.

As soon as the officers returned to the police building, they popped the tape into a VCR and sat back, ready to see a fresh shot of someone. Such evidence, they knew, would be indispensable. Instead of seeing Cunanan, though, they saw the Miami Subs workers going about their tasks behind the order counter. The manager, apparently, worried more about being ripped off by employees than being stuck up by a crook. The tape was worthless, and once again, Cunanan's dumb luck had served him well.

After the police left the area, Cunanan headed to the beach and began walking south, ending up at 5445 Collins Avenue. He knew he could no longer risk living at the Normandy Plaza Hotel. There he came to boat moorings bordered by a 200-foot wide canal on the west and Collins on the east. The Atlantic Ocean sat a short block away behind two large hotels – the Imperial House and the Alexander Hotel. Spectacular homes lined the canal's west shores. With ease, a good swimmer could cross the canal to burglarize one of those homes or steal a new car. Cunanan may have pondered this as he broke into the Bristol sailboat parked in Slip 21 at 5445 Collins Avenue.

Inside the sailboat, Cunanan found refuge, even though the hot humid air inside the boat made it hard to breath. Not a single cop had bothered him since he had moved to Miami Beach and he had given them no reason to do so. He had quickly learned that the Normandy Plaza Hotel staff paid very little attention to anyone coming and going, and even if they had known who he was, may not have known what to do about it. But now that he skipped on the rent, soon enough they would complain to the cops. He knew his days of freedom were limited, but he also knew he only needed a short time to finish his plan.

At least the boat owner had been kind enough to leave behind several books that interested Cunanan. It gave him something to do while he waited for the zero hour.

Confident now that he had a place to hide, Cunanan made his way down the beach and over to the 13th Street Garage. He went to the red Chevy pickup truck and left everything he would need the next morning, including a change of clothes. Then he walked a half block east to Lummas Park and south two blocks, finding a perch in the park from where he could scope out his final act. No one noticed him, but he noticed Gianni Versace. Cunanan had cut the pattern, laid out the material and was ready to tie off the last knot. He nervously awaited the morning.

Chapter 38 ~ A new design for Lee's day

On the hot muggy morning of July 15, Lee Urness rose early, wanting to take care of some of his other police duties before heading back to the task force office.

He took a few minutes to study the birds as they ate their breakfast at the feeder on the deck outside his kitchen. He chuckled as he saw them fussing for food. They looked calmer than usual, more secure; then again, it might have been the heat. A brilliantly colored cardinal pecked away at his breakfast as if not noticing the clamor around him. The bird looked almost regal, like a celebrity among commoners, and yet, the other birds seemed not to notice him, as though he blended in. *Cunanan could be sitting in the middle of a love fest and no one would see him. He looks just like all the rest of them.*

He finished the last bite of his muffin, washed it down with coffee and headed toward the door. He put on his gun and holster, then his vest, and reached for his car keys. "Can I take the day off?" he asked, staring at the keys. Their silence gave him his answer.

He deviated from his normal route, stopping to make a call on one of his other active cases. He drove to the Amoco Station on Lyndale Avenue in South Bloomington. The casual pace of his early day felt good, even though he knew it could not last. If fortune smiled on him, in fact, it could be the day they finally cornered Cunanan.

Patterns reestablished

Andrew Cunanan fought off sleep as he sat in Lummas Park, the grassy berm that stretched for several blocks alongside Ocean Drive. A cool ocean breeze rustled the leaves of the stately palm trees that grew in the berm's sandy soil. Just several hundred feet east, soft Atlantic Ocean waves caressed the white sands of Miami Beach. Cunanan watched the Versace mansion that sat directly across the narrow three-lane street. A constant stream of cars crawled north and south on Ocean Drive during all hours of the day and night.

Looking south across Ocean Drive, Cunanan could see dozens of open cafes busy serving breakfasts, or dinner for those who had stayed up all night. Under other circumstances, Cunanan could have spent the night sitting on the front porch of the Clevelander, enjoying a cigar and loud laughter with gay men whom he only knew by their first name. He could have ventured inside for a tryst with one or more of them, especially one of the older men who would pay for sex.

Wait staff at the cafes wove their way around the crowded tables. Tables sat on every available foot of space, even positioned right up to the curb, with only a narrow path allowing the continuous stream of walkers to pass.

Once Cunanan learned that Versace had come to town, he made sure to watch the house from his perch across the street. He had noticed one of Versace's daily patterns that fit perfectly into his deadly design.

Versace seldom mixed with Miami Beach tourists and residents, but he enjoyed walking down Ocean Drive three blocks to the News Café each morning. The open-air café had a book and magazine shop that sold international newspapers and magazines. Versace shopped there regularly.

On July 15, Versace left the mansion sometime before 8:30 a.m. He unlocked the dead bolt on the wrought iron gate that kept curiosity seekers and burglars out of his yard, and walked down the five marble steps to the sidewalk. He left the gates slightly ajar. The hot, muggy July air buffeted his body like the moist heat of a steam room.

Versace crossed Ocean Drive to the west sidewalk that ran next to Lummas Park. As he walked south, he never noticed the man sitting in the grass who studied his every movement. That man felt for the Taurus pistol he carried in his black backpack as his mind played out the detailed plan he had designed.

Versace walked unnoticed by the bustling crowds on the east side of Ocean Drive. At East 8th Street, he crossed Ocean Drive and went directly into the News Café bookstore. He searched the bins for his favorite Italian newspapers, and added a few magazines to his order, then paid his bill and left.

No one bothered Versace as he walked out carrying a brown paper bag. He looked like any number of the rich middle-aged men who frequent the bustling streets of South Beach. Though his visage had played on TV screens across the world, and though he was one of a handful of worldwide designer celebrities, at South Beach people left him alone, or paid no attention. In the same manner, though Cunanan's face had played across millions of TV screens and hundreds of articles told his murderous story, at South Beach, he was a faceless entity and no one had paid him any attention.

Versace walked north again, making his way through the crowded sidewalks of the three block long string of outdoor cafes. Up ahead he saw his mansion. Cunanan watched him from afar, as his stomach grew more nervous.

Witnesses gathering

Lazaro Quintana walked east past 13th and Collins, just before 8:30 a.m. He noticed Miami Beach Police Officers Tony Lammachio and Armando Torres working a traffic accident at the intersection.

Quintana arrived at the Versace mansion just minutes after Versace had left. He had a 9:00 a.m. tennis date with his good friend, Versace's partner, Antonio D'Amico. Thomas Troutmen, the Versace mansion's manager, opened the door to him and ushered him into the house.

Troutmen went upstairs and awakened D'Amico. D'Amico dressed quickly and, as he walked down the hall, noticed that Versace was not in his bedroom. D'Amico met Quintana downstairs and the two men began to share breakfast.

Merisha Colakovic dropped her daughter off at Fisher-Feinberg Elementary School. She crossed Ocean Drive on 13th Street in front of the Cardozo Hotel. Silvo DeCunha and a crew of others were remodeling the old hostelry.

Colakovic walked south on the west sidewalk. At 12th Street she crossed back to the east sidewalk and continued walking south. Looking ahead, she could see Gianni Versace two blocks away, but she meant not to bother him as they walked toward each other.

Amad Romero met his friend Romeo Jacques at 13th and Ocean Drive and the two men walked south on the west sidewalk. Romero worked at the All Star Café at 960 Ocean Drive and Jacques had just parked his car in the 13th Street Ramp. They planned to spend the morning together before Romero reported for work.

Evan Gertz' daily routine found him in Lummas Park near 15th Street. He began walking back toward 11th Street, as he did each morning. As Gertz and his dog came close to 11th Street, they both noticed a man sitting in the grass at Lummas Park. The man wore a dark baseball cap and sunglasses. Gertz saw that the man seemed focused on something across the street. Gertz' dog began straining at his chain while barking at the man, frustrating Gertz. Gertz struggled with the dog as he crossed Ocean Drive toward 11th Street and never noticed Versace coming toward him. He did notice that the man, who

379

had been sitting in the grass at the park, the man his dog did not like, now followed several steps behind him. Still fighting to control his dog, Gertz nearly bumped into Versace. Then he continued on around the corner.

Up on 12th Street, working his way toward Ocean Drive, Clemmie Smith drove a BFI garbage truck. Willie Hicks and Rosell Neloms worked the back of the truck.

At 8:45 a.m., Colakovic stood a dozen feet away from Versace as put his foot up on the first step of the landing. She, Romero and Jacques noticed a man walk up behind Versace. The two men saw them speak briefly and, for an instant, fight over a black fanny pack. Officers later found that Versace had nearly $1,200 in cash on him.

The witnesses looked in horror as the man, with steely cold indifference, raised the Taurus pistol and fired one shot. A .40 caliber slug ripped through Versace's head just below his right ear, blowing a star pattern into his right check as it exited. He fell forward onto the steps.

Gertz heard the shot and quickly came back around the corner. Victor Montenegro had been repairing a parking meter between 10th and 11th streets on Ocean Drive. He, too, heard a gun shot and looked up, joining the other witnesses as they saw the killer shoot again. This time the slug blew into Versace's head just below the left ear, breaking the cranium bone, but stopping just below the skin.

As blood and brain tissue freely oozed from Versace's face and skull, pooling on the white marble steps, the man all these people had seen, Andrew Cunanan, calmly walked north. He had just achieved immortality, his name forever linked to Gianni Versace. His deadly design completed, all that remained was his exit plan.

Shock begins setting in

When Antonio D'Amico heard the shots he ran to the window as Quintana ran to the interior courtyard. "No, no!" shouted D'Amico as the two men ran to the door. Throwing it open, D'Amico ran to his fallen lover's side. Quintana saw Colakovic on the sidewalk and yelled, "Who did this?"

Colakovic pointed north. Her fear drove her to sobbing. She, along with the other witnesses, felt sure that a professional hit man had just shot Versace. They were wrong. Versace had been shot by a coward, a nothing who never achieved anything lasting, save the destruction of the lives of others.

380

"You bastard!" Quintana yelled as he ran down the stairs and started following Cunanan up the street.

Cunanan walked north and then turned west on 12th Street past Clemmie Smith and his BFI garbage truck. He cut across the street to the alley – Ocean Court, and began running north. Quintana pursued him.

Silvo DeCunha had heard the shots coming from down on Ocean Drive, and turned to see Quintana chase Cunanan to the 13th Street parking garage. He watched as Cunanan turned and pointed the Taurus at Quintana. Quintana cut off his chase. Instead, Quintana ran to 13th and Collins, a half block west, and told Officer Lammachio what he had just witnessed.

Cunanan ran inside the parking ramp and climbed the stairs to level 3B. On July 10, he had parked William Reese's red truck there. He made directly for it. Throwing open the truck passenger door, he tore his backpack off, placing it inside the truck. He removed his grey tank top, black T-shirt and pants, and threw them on the ground. He heard a siren as he began pulling on clean clothes.

Thinking that the cops knew where he was, he quickly finished dressing, grabbed the Taurus and headed up to the top floor of the parking ramp. That siren had come from a cop who was responding to a traffic violation, but Cunanan had no way of knowing.

As Officer Lammachio made his way down 13th Street to the entrance of the parking ramp, he radioed for back up. He told the dispatcher that the shooter might be hiding in the ramp. Several cops responded immediately.

Cunanan, up on the top level of the ramp, ran to the Southeast corner from where he could see Lummas Park. He ran to the Northeast corner, then to the Southwest corner, from where he could see the auto accident. He could see Officer Lammachio calling for help and then running toward the ramp. Cunanan went to the Northwest corner and saw that the street was clear. Meanwhile, a few cops had begun to arrive at the ramp, and at least one looked up and saw a man in a red T-shirt up on the roof.

Cunanan ran five stories down the Northwest stairwell and out into a parking lot. From there he ran west 50 feet to Collins and began walking north. A long train of palm trees hid him from the view of anyone above him.

Some police officers believe Cunanan hailed a cab, being dropped off somewhere near 52nd Street. A later check of all taxi pick-ups and drop-offs proved nothing about this theory. Miami Beach Police Sgt. Gary Schiaffo believed Cunanan made his way north a few blocks and then east, to the beach. Once again, Cunanan would have blended into the crowd. He had discarded the backpack and wore a completely different outfit, leaving his murderous costume behind in the parking ramp. Schiaffo believed that Cunanan made his way north, walking on the white sands of Miami Beach that stretch unending for more than 10 miles on the east and west coasts of the island community.

Cunanan had one small claim to athleticism during his high school days. He had been an average long distance runner. Though 10 years of debauchery had taken its toll on his body, walking or jogging on the beaches to 53rd Street, 3½ miles north, would be no great obstacle. Anyone who saw him would think he was just another among dozens who made the same route day after day. And running up the beach meant that bloodhounds could never pick up his scent.

Cunanan saw that no one pursued him. The dozens of cops who had converged on the parking ramp and the crime scene concentrated their search efforts in the immediate area. Once again, Cunanan escaped apprehension by mere minutes.

At 53rd Street, Cunanan cut back to Collins Avenue, now just a short block from the Ocean. He crossed the eight-lane road and walked to the canal, along which were moored a few dozen boats of various sizes. Looking south two blocks he could see a long, white yacht tied to its moorings. Next to it sat a huge blue two-story houseboat. Smaller boats sat tied to the moorings just above 54th Street. He went directly to the one tied at 5445 Collins, in Slip 21, the old Bristol sailboat. He opened the top hatch, which he had freed three days earlier, and crawled inside. No one saw him. He waited, but no one came.

Cunanan had no place to go, no way to get there and no money to buy his safety. The Fugitive Task Force had closed down his window of escape, and his murder of Versace had sealed it shut. For two months, Cunanan had lived among the gays and lesbians of South Beach. No one noticed. No one cared. Then he killed Gianni Versace and everyone cared.

Frantic search explodes in media spotlight

At 8:46 a.m., Miami Beach Police Officer Paul Marcus received a call that a shooting with injuries had occurred somewhere in the 1100 block of Ocean Drive. He notified Detectives Paul Scrimshaw, Dale Twist and Mike Jaccarino as he raced to the scene.

Police immediately set up a crime scene parameter alongside the east sidewalk, and a second across the street at the curb of the west sidewalk. They diverted traffic to Collins Avenue.

Officer Marcus notified both the Florida Department of Law Enforcement and the FBI, asking them for assistance. No one knew it was Cunanan who had done the killing, but they all knew that Gianni Versace was a celebrity with a huge following. They had no idea how huge until just two hours later when Lummas Park filled with reporters.

Within hours, 119 Miami Beach Police Officers – about one-third of their sworn strength – would be joined by 32 FBI agents and nine agents from the Florida Department of Law Enforcement, all trying to catch Versace's murderer. None of them were successful.

Truck found

Officer Lammachio and several other officers responded quickly to the 13th Street ramp. Within 10 minutes, police officers were posted at all door-ways and exits. They could see in every direction. Unfortunately, Cunanan had already slipped away down the back stairs.

The officers began a slow, careful search of the parking ramp, not knowing whether the killer still hid behind a car, ready for a shoot out, or if he had fled. Car by car, floor by floor, they worked their way up the ramp.

Officer Marilynn Tepperberg began walking slowly down the inside row of 11 vehicles parked on level 3B. She looked left and right between the cars, her senses on edge, hoping and yet not hoping to spot Versace's killer. As she walked around the end of a red Chevy pick-up truck, she saw something lying on the floor next to the passenger door. Walking closer she saw clothes, and they appeared to be bloodstained and hastily discarded.

Tepperberg radioed for help, and within minutes officers Jaccarino and Lammachio had joined her. They cautioned her not to touch a thing as they began to survey the vehicle.

Through the window, they could see a mess of things lying in haphazard fashion throughout the interior of Reese's red truck. A black backpack lay on the seat. Their senses told them they had made a great discovery, even if the demon who had parked that truck had already escaped.

Chapter 39 ~ Pump this!

Lee Urness had just finished pumping his gasoline, and went into the gas station to pour himself a fresh cup of coffee. His pager sounded. Had he been able to keep count, surely this would have been close to 10,000 such pages since May 2. So often had it sounded that he felt no rush to check out the message, just casually lifting it up to read, "CALL KEVIN ASAP."

He paid for his coffee, carefully took a sip to make sure it would not spill and headed for the van. He called Rickett.

"What do you know?" he asked.

"Miami Division called. They had a murder, a guy named Gianni Versace – a famous guy. Murdered in broad daylight in front of his mansion. They're wondering if it could be C," Rickett said, "or maybe a professional."

Lee wrote "Johnny Versatche" on the note pad next to him.

"Yeah, I just looked at the crystal ball and it's really cloudy," Lee said. "What was he shot with?"

"A .45."

"Are you sure it was a .45?" Lee asked.

"Absolutely. A .45 caliber."

"Then it wasn't our guy. He'll never get another gun," Lee said. "Call them back and make sure it was a .45."

"Yeah, I'll do that," Rickett said.

"Look, I'm going over to BCA to drop off some paperwork, then I'll be over. Call me if anything comes up on this," Lee said.

As he drove along, he pondered what Rickett had said. *Well, it could be him, I guess. Right where we thought he was. But wrong gun and what's his motive for killing this Johnny guy?* Twenty minutes later, Lee parked in the BCA parking lot in St. Paul.

His pager sounded: "CALL KEVIN."

"What's new?" Lee asked, expecting to hear the same story he had heard thousands of times during the past 10 weeks – "not our guy."

"Guess what?" Rickett said, but his voice said volumes more.

"Oh no," Lee answered.

"Yup, it's a .40 caliber, not a .45."

"Aw crap. Was he gay?" Lee asked.

"Yup. Openly."

385

"Son-of-a-bitch! Yeah, I bet it's him," Lee said. His mind began racing. "Okay, I'll be over in a little bit. I have to drop off my paperwork and update Nick O'Hara on this."

No golf today

Sgt. George Navarro, supervisor of the homicide division of the Miami Beach Police Department, had just readied himself to hit a long iron on a local golf course. Navarro tried to play golf three times a week, even in the blistering heat and humidity of south Miami. His pager sounded. Never mind that July 15 was his day off. Andrew Cunanan had just woven him into the waft and wail of his deadly design.

Navarro assumed supervision of the case when he arrived at the scene at 11:20 a.m. As he parked his unmarked car and walked toward the mansion, he saw a swarm of media assembled across the street and hundreds of gawkers pushing up close to the police lines.

Navarro quickly checked out the murder scene and then walked inside the mansion. He learned that dozens of Miami Beach cops were canvassing the neighborhood, looking for witnesses and hopefully, spotting Cunanan.

Navarro took his place at the dining room table across from FBI Agent Thomas Farrow and FDLE Agent John Coffey. The three of them set up a Command Post in the Versace dining room and formed a strategy. MBPD and the FDLE agents would process the crime scene while the FBI would pursue leads, but leads flooded in as the rain that fell after God sealed up Noah's ark.

Lee Urness and his crew of far-flung FTF agents had already chased down 2,000 leads. Within a week, that number spiked to more than 2,000 additional leads, and Navarro's cops caught hundreds of them.

Sealing the proof

Agent Keith Evans came to the Versace mansion at about 12:30 p.m. While he and Navarro talked, Officer Jaccarino radioed Navarro.

"We need to check on this truck here," he said. "I've got the VIN (vehicle identification number)."

"Read it off to me," Navarro said and repeated the numbers as Jaccarino gave them. Evans listened carefully, referring to a note pad he carried with him.

"That's our guy," Evan's said. "The VIN matches William Reese's truck."

"Tell me about your guy," Navarro said.

Evans began telling Navarro about the man he had believed as early as May 12 would have hid near South Beach. Navarro had only heard about Cunanan a week earlier when Evans had stopped in with a Wanted Poster. He had no idea Evans had worked the gay community for weeks prior to the murder. And no one in that gay community had seen Cunanan, at least until after the murder when dozens of people suddenly flashed back and felt sure they had been with the killer.

Lee, it is really our guy

Lee Urness sat in his van outside of BCA headquarters in St. Paul. Before going inside, he paged Keith Evans. Then he called home.

"Kathy, turn on CNN now," Lee said. "Cunanan's killed again."

"Oh no!" she cried as she picked up the remote control. "What'd he do?"

"Killed some guy in Miami Beach. Just walked up and shot him," Lee said.

"I see it now," Kathy said as the TV came into focus. "There's a ton of people there already." She saw the crowds forming at the crime scene.

"You and Bear watch it all for me. I got to go," Lee said. Kathy and Kari kept their TV vigil almost non-stop during the next eight days, enthralled by what they saw and knowing how angry it made Lee that this had happened once again.

Lee got out of the car and walked inside, heading straight for Nick O'Hara's office.

"Is the chief in?" Lee asked Blondie, Nick O'Hara's secretary.

"On the phone right now," she said.

"I'll hang around then. Cunanan killed another guy I think," Lee said, hanging his head.

"Oh no, who?"

"Ah, some guy named Johnny Versatche," Lee said, throwing away the name as a nobody.

"What? Oh no! That's terrible!"

"Why? Who's he?"

"He's a big time dress designer. He's got a big mansion down in Miami," Blondie said, still gasping at the news. "Gianni Versace. Wow! He's Italian. An international celebrity. You better go right in and tell the Chief," she said.

Lee walked into O'Hara's office and gave him the news. "We're not really sure yet, but they're checking out the details. But I'm pretty sure it's my guy," Lee said. The feeling of dread had already overwhelmed him.

"Well, I know one thing, you certainly didn't leave a stone unturned. Don't blame yourself," O'Hara said. He told Lee to go catch the guy and not to worry too much about what could not be undone.

Despite O'Hara's words, Lee felt heaviness unlike anything before experienced. Now he had lost two men on his watch. Would there be more?

"Where's Young Rickett?" Lee asked as he called the office. He drove down Washington Avenue toward the task force office and wanted to know the latest developments.

"He's at headquarters. Coleen Rowley's out of town today and he's got to handle the media," Jeanie Burns said.

Lee shook his head at this news. He knew that as crazy as things had been in the past, all records for chaos would be broken within just a few minutes and he really needed Rickett at the FTF office.

"Okay. I'll be there in a minute," he said, as Keith Evans rang in.

"What do you know? Is it my guy?" Lee asked.

"For sure it's Cunanan. We found the pickup truck," Evans said.

"Where?"

"In a parking ramp close to Versace's mansion. It's got the wrong plate. But it's got his personal effects inside," Evans said.

"Oh man." Lee's stomach churned.

Evans mentioned the witness who had tried to follow Cunanan. The man had given police a description. "He looked like our guy, too. He's ID'd the guy."

"Damn!" Lee shouted, and slapped the steering wheel.

"Hey, I gotta go. I'll get back to you with anything else," Evans said, hanging up.

Lee parked the van and nearly ran up the back stairs. He came into the office cursing. "C's killed again. Some dress designer named Versace in Miami."

"Lee!," he heard Jeanie Burns say as he came through the door, "what's the matter?" She pointed at the "Swear Can." He dropped a couple of quarters in and walked to his desk.

Lee called Minneapolis FBI Headquarters to update Rickett, but the line was busy. He tried again. Busy. He tried again. Still busy.

"Jeanie," he said, "how many phone lines do they have at headquarters?"

"Dozens, and they're all busy," she complained. He stomped out of the office and drove to headquarters to update Rickett.

"Lee!" Rickett said as he saw Lee coming down the hall, "I can't even answer the phones fast enough. Rowley's out of town."

"I heard."

"And I can't get them to release it in Miami, that it's Cunanan," Rickett said.

"What? Why's that?"

"I don't know, but it's driving me crazy," he said, getting ready to make another call.

Lee filled him in on what Evans had said.

"Well, I'm sure he's right, but until they release it down there, I can't say anything," Rickett said, frustrated.

He and Rickett formed a plan to contact all the agents and get them on the street right away. They felt it was critical to contact everyone on their hot list immediately.

"Okay, I'll go back over to the task force. At least I can get a phone over there. Keep in contact by pager," Lee said as he headed out the door.

As soon as he could, Lee called Paul Murray. "C's killed again. This time a guy named Gianni Versace, a dress designer, down in Miami."

"Damn it! Son-of-a-bitch!"

"This is the second time someone died on my watch. Maybe it's time to retire," Lee said.

"I'll call Evans."

"No, not now. He's really busy," Lee asked. "I'll call the other agents and get them to hit the list people and get ready for a flood of leads. I'll keep you updated."

He told all the agents the same story and he urged them to get on the street immediately. If ever, now would be the time Cunanan would try to contact someone he knew.

"Talk to everyone again, and I don't care what Miami is saying. This is our guy, and you need to get on the streets and put the fear of God into everyone," Lee told them. "If that son-on-of-bitch calls one of them and we hear about, we're putting his ass in jail! They have to know that."

As much as he hated this latest murder by one of "my guys," he knew the event presented an opportunity.

"Well, I guess we finally figured out where he's been," he said to Lisa Davis. "We're going to get him in Miami. He's not getting out of that town. Miami's got to find him!"

Lee believed the moment he heard that Cunanan had abandoned the pickup truck that he would never leave Miami Beach. He had nothing to drive, no money, and cops from everywhere looking for him.

Checking every angle...again

Lee went to his desk and sat down.

Strewn across his desk and all around him on the floor were stacks. In those stacks were leads, lists, call slips, hand written notes.

He began reviewing each piece of paper. Working from the top to the bottom of each stack, he went over every detail, trying to find what he may have missed.

Since that morning, new names had appeared on his lists. He ran them against Rapid Start, but none matched. Then he ran every Florida lead he had gotten during the past two months. He found 10, and not one from Miami Beach. Other than Keith Evans' early suspicion, which it itself had only been intuition, not a shred of evidence linked Cunanan to South Beach.

Lee sat thinking about all this, not so much to evaluate the quality of his work, but to find if any scrap of paper would now lead him to Cunanan. None existed. All he could say with some certainty was that Evans had been right, and that Cunanan still hid out in Miami Beach.

The slowdown in the pace and the reduced intensity level of recent days had suddenly exploded into frenzy far greater than anything experienced to date. Within minutes of tying Cunanan to Versace, even the FBI Director had gotten personally involved.

Almost immediately, gay and lesbian activists on the east coast became enraged. They believed that the FBI had ignored Cunanan because he was a gay guy killing gays – never mind William Reese or Lee Miglin. They blamed the cops for killing Versace. Yet it was their own brothers, sisters and lovers in South Beach who had looked the other way for two months.

Cunanan had killed Versace, not the cops.

O'Hara's heat

Lee felt the need to update his boss, Nick O'Hara, before the day ended. He headed back to the BCA office.

"The chief will see you right away," Blondie said. O'Hara knew how busy Lee had become since they heard the news about Versace, and he respected Lee's time.

"So, how's it going? You keeping up with things?" O'Hara asked as Lee came into the door. O'Hara nodded toward the chair and Lee sat down. The chief saw that Lee looked exhausted.

Lee related as much as he felt O'Hara needed to know. Before finishing his report, he stood to leave. O'Hara stood up and came around the desk, wanting to encourage him.

"Anything else?" O'Hara asked.

"Yeah, well there is one thing that really pisses me off," Lee said. "I can't understand why in hell the Miami office sat on this information about Cunanan being the suspect. This is my case. They had no right to sit on it."

"They did that?"

"Yes, they did." Lee saw that O'Hara had started to do a slow burn.

"You report here at 7:00 a.m. tomorrow. We'll take care of this," O'Hara said.

"Okay."

"And I want to be updated constantly. Okay?" O'Hara said.

"Of course."

O'Hara stuck out his hand and once again said, "You're doing the right things. Just keep it up."

"Okay. See you in the morning," Lee said. He drove back to the FTF, hoping that something big might have broken and wondering what O'Hara had in mind for the next day.

Nick O'Hara had friends in high places including Bill "Little Bird" Esposito, the Deputy Director of the FBI. O'Hara started his career during the J. Edgar Hoover days, and agents who had a sense or knowledge of the agency's history knew him well – and they respected him. He meant to find out what had gone wrong in Miami and do something about it.

The next morning, Lee sat and listened as O'Hara chewed out the local Miami FBI Acting Special Agent in Charge. From Lee's reports, O'Hara believed that Miami FBI officials had not given Keith Evans much support. But by withholding from the public the fact that Cunanan was the chief suspect in the Versace murder also meant giving the killer an edge. Immediately removing all doubt that he had committed the murder would have made it more difficult for him to hide even for a moment.

Lee knew how much O'Hara loved and respected the FBI. He took great encouragement from listening and watching O'Hara read out those Miami officials.

"There, I think you should get all the help you need," O'Hara said as he hung up the phone.

"Thanks chief," Lee said. "Hey, I have to go catch my killer," Lee said, shaking O'Hara's hand and heading out the door.

In case he calls

By the end of May, Lee had felt the FTF had contacted everyone that Cunanan knew, or at least, that he knew intimately. He had learned that Cunanan knew many men casually, but few were really close to him, and except for his sister Gina, none of the family had much to do with him.

With Versace dead, though, the FBI did a full-court press on the Cunanan family, though the family never knew about it. Armed with a court order, the FBI readied to install taps on the phones of each of Cunanan's siblings and his mother, as well as some of his closest friends. Maybe Cunanan would never call them directly, but there always remained the possibility that somehow, somewhere a caller would drop a piece of information useful to the cops. But these efforts failed to turn up a single piece of information related to the killer.

Chapter 40 ~ Versace's death sent Twin Cities' media flying

Cunanan's string of homicides had begun on a chilly late April night in Minneapolis. Ten weeks later, Cunanan had killed four more times, and the last time in the heat and humidity of Miami's South Beach.

Twin Cities' reporters had started covering the case that afternoon of April 29, when Anne O'Connor followed a police tip to David Madson's apartment. Those reporters had stuck with the story, living and breathing it every day since, and with Versace's murder, their workload exploded both in volume and intensity.

Chris Graves knew nothing about Versace as she drove to work on Tuesday, July 15, content that her baby Emma had been well fed. She made sure to leave behind enough breast milk for the child's feedings until she got home after work. Chris relished the quiet, relaxed moments of nursing her firstborn child, an experience that stood in stark contrast to the stress of meeting newspaper deadlines.

Cunanan was but one story among dozens, but by far the biggest. She knew that Twin Cities' readers had a fascination for stories about defects in human character and they demanded every detail. Cunanan offered an extreme example. Families and friends of the victims wanted closure. Professional curiosity added the final drop of motivation she needed to keep up with breaking news.

That morning, television reporter Bernie Grace headed for KARE TV, Esme Murphy for WCCO TV, and Tom Hauser to KSTP TV. They, too, had been caught up in Cunanan's murderous flight. But soon after William Reese's death, media interest in Cunanan had waned – and May sweeps had ended. The June "Top Ten" announcement had given the story a shot of energy, but it quickly fell off the front pages and lost airtime. The reporters kept in contact with their sources, but until something new broke, they had done all the stories they could. The stories dried up.

Reporters need to write something, too

Somewhat desperate to keep the story alive, but without anything new to report, the *Star-Tribune's* Chris Graves wrote a piece that the newspaper published on July 13 under the headline, "Fugitive hunters use many tools." She had begun working on the story during the week of May 12. The story spoke only briefly about Cunanan for the plain reason that Lee and his fellow agents gave out very little helpful information, and not much had happened for more than two months. To make the story "work," Graves instead wrote about three former Task Force cases that ended with capture of the crooks. After filing the story, she wondered when, if ever, she could write the "real story," the one about Cunanan's capture.

Esme Murphy had, for several weeks, carried with her a sense of fear and foreboding. Convinced that Cunanan eventually would kill again, the story left her with an unshakable feeling of darkness. She prayed that he would be caught before hurting anyone else. Within a few hours, CNN's report of the Versace murder filled her with dread.

"I'll bet that Cunanan guy did it," someone said.

"I'll bet you're right," she told herself. And if he did, she knew she may not have time to pack her bags for a Miami flight.

Became personal quickly

Sitting in the midst of organized chaos that comprises the workspace of a newspaper reporter, Chris Graves saw her editor, Pam Fine, walking quickly toward her. Worry and fear creased her face.

"Could this be him? I mean Andrew Cunanan?" Fine asked.

"Could what be Cunanan?" Graves asked, unaware of the murder.

"Somebody murdered Gianni Versace at his mansion. Just a few minutes ago!"

"Johnny who?"Graves had never heard of the man.

"Versace. Gianni Versace, the internally known dress designer." She explained the sketchy details, adding, "He was at my house for a dinner party once." Fine had also known David Madson and the sense that these two murders were connected already haunted her.

"Well, you can't jump to any conclusions. Why do you think it might be Cunanan?"Graves asked.

"Everybody knows that Versace is gay…"

"Oh? Well that still doesn't mean its Cunanan," Graves said. "Besides, this sounds too Hollywood."

"Well I don't know. See what you can find out."

Graves took the direct approach. She knew that Lee Urness was the Case Agent; maybe he would finally talk to her.

Jeanie Burns took Graves' call and said that someone would get back to her.

"You want to talk to the *Star-Tribune*?" Jeanie asked, handing Lee the note.

"Yeah, right," he said, taking it from her. He studied the name, "Chris Graves," and it clicked. He had been swamped by dozens of reporter inquiries about Versace's shooter's identity and passed them all onto Kevin Rickett. He only handled law enforcement inquiries.

Within minutes of the news of Versace's killing, Coleen Rowley's phone at the FBI had begun ringing constantly. Rowley never answered. She heard the Versace news in the same way as millions of others, on her car radio. She had booked the day in Pierre, South Dakota. "Oh man! I'll bet it's Cunanan," she said, but had no choice but to complete her schedule. Kevin Rickett filled in for her that day.

Lee threw a quick glance at the May 12 *Star-Tribune* article hanging on his bulletin board – "Hunt for suspect lacks strategy," the one that criticized law enforcement for not doing enough to catch Cunanan. He saw Graves' name as the lead byline. "Damn! Why's she calling *me*?" he said. "Maybe she's got a lead or something for me." He called her.

"I saw you called," he said as Graves answered. "What do you know?" he asked.

"I have to know if Cunanan killed Versace," she said. "My editor's all over me on this. Don't blow smoke at me. Tell me what you can, and I'm satisfied with that."

"Yeah, he did it." He let it drop like lead and she felt its impact.

Graves' heart pounded. This was a huge story, if she could get a second source to confirm it.

"Now, do you have anything you can tell me?" Lee asked.

"No, I don't. But I will call you if something breaks," she promised.

"Do that. I gotta go," Lee said, and hung up.

"My source says it's Cunanan," she told Fine as she burst through her office door, "but I can't verify it. Miami Beach police won't say anything. I can only tell you that if my source says it's him, it's him."

"Get your verification," Fine said. "I just *knew* it!"

Across town, Bernie Grace's phone rang.

"Bernie, you gotta get down here now. We're pretty certain that Andrew Cunanan killed Gianni Versace this morning." He heard the excited voice of a former KARE TV colleague, now working for a Miami TV station.

"What do the police say?" Grace asked.

"Nothing! They are saying nothing about Cunanan, but I've got my own sources," he said. "Get on the plane!"

Grace hung up and headed to his program director. "So, I think I ought to go," he concluded after giving him the sketchy details.

"Well, whoever killed him, it's a big story, but if it's Cunanan, we *have* to be there," he said. "Go. Get on a plane and get down there."

Bernie paged his cameraman and headed to the airport. While waiting to change planes in Chicago, he heard the story on CNN.

At the St. *Paul Pioneer* Press, reporter Richard Chin heard the news about Versace's murder. The St. Paul paper had followed the Cunanan case using its Knight-Ridder reporter network, and the *Miami Herald* immediately sent a small army of reporters to the scene. Chin felt he ought to go, too, bringing some sort of local angle to the stories back home.

"Why do you look so happy?" fellow reporter Ruben Rosario asked Chin. Rosario had written a few stories about the case.

"I'm going to Miami to cover the Versace murder," Chin smiled.

Rosario looked at Chin, a man of Asian heritage, with his square face, dark hair and large glasses. He smiled. "You'll be mistaken for Cunanan."

Chin had seen the wanted posters Lee had distributed and knew that Cunanan had a chameleon like appearance, but look like him? "No, I wouldn't worry it." The paper booked Chin to leave on Wednesday.

Esme Murphy and Tom Hauser made the same trip. Competitive pressure would normally be enough to lure them on that airplane, but Versace's alleged killing by Cunanan made it all the more crucial. Each TV reporter knew that their stations expected *live* reports at 5:00, 6:00 and 10:00 p.m. News Directors would not chance pre-taped stories, given the possibility that at any moment, even *during* a live report, the news could change; Cunanan might even be found or kill again.

At the *Star-Tribune,* Chris Graves never found a second source to prove Cunanan's link to the murder. The newspaper required her to share the name of her confidential source with her boss, and even though her source was Lee Urness, neither the editor nor the attorneys would let such a story run without a second confirming source. Her 6:00 p.m. deadline and end of day sat minutes away, and yet she had nothing to write. Finally, she wrote an abbreviated story using measured words to indicate that someone had killed Gianni Versace and perhaps Cunanan was involved.

She hit the send key on her computer and stood up to leave. She wanted to head home, but the fact that she could not verify her story really ate at her. Before leaving, she picked up the phone and called Lee again.

"Urness here," he said, knowing she was the caller. "Okay, you have some information for me?" he asked. He had no time to chat.

"No. But please, you gotta help me. Is it Cunanan or not? My editor wants me on a plane right now," she pleaded.

"Pack your bags and get your butt on that plane," Lee answered. He heard near panic in her voice. "I have to go. You owe me two," he said tersely, and hung up.

"Oh my God!" Graves exclaimed. She called the composition department. "Take it back. I know it's Cunanan who did the Versace killing."

"How do you know?"

"My source just told me to get to Miami. I can't explain any more than that," she said. "But it *is* Cunanan!"

She ran to Pam Fine and told her.

"How soon can you get on a plane? I need you down there now," Fine said.

"A plane? Well, let me see what…" she said, as she picked up the phone to call the travel office.

"The last flight out is at 6:30," she reported to Fine, nodding at the clock which said 6:10.

"Can you get to the airport in 20 minutes?"

"What? No, that's impossible," she insisted. In her mind's eye she saw Emma waiting for her at home.

"Can you go tomorrow?"Fine asked.

"Yes, first thing."

"Make your plans, then," Fine said.

Graves spent the rest of the evening trying to verify aspects of her story, and cobbling together a piece to make the 10:00 p.m. deadline, with Pam Fine often hanging over her back as she wrote. Early Wednesday morning she boarded a flight to Miami. She sighed as she settled into her seat. Thanks to Andrew Cunanan, she had just started to wean Emma.

On the plane, Graves' reporter-mind went to work. She wanted to hit the ground running. Then it struck her. She knew absolutely no one in Miami, not a cop, a reporter or even a good restaurant. Yet, the newspaper expected her to break many meaty original stories. A major scoop would be better. But without any sources, she worried whether she would be able to get even one good story. Panic replaced planning.

Media stalked Maryann

During mid-May, Maryann Cunanan had returned to California, settling in a tiny house in National City, just south of San Diego. The San Diego FTF had been in regular contact with her since she moved back. By July 15, John Hause and Ann Murphy had learned that Maryann could easily become unstable and emotional. They worked hard to keep reassuring her, keeping her calm and cooperative. They felt confident that should Cunanan try to call his mother, she would not hesitate to notify them.

The Versace murder suddenly threw Maryann into the center of a media storm. She called Hause, screaming at him to protect her from the reporters who had set up camp around her house. It sat on a corner bounded by two streets, and the media covered both of them, making it impossible for her to leave or even stick her head out a door or window.

Unable to catch her outside, the reporters finally entered her back yard, calling to her through her screened windows: "Maryann, come on. Please talk to us. We are your friends," they said, but their pleas only fueled her paranoia.

"You've got to help me!" she screamed at Hause when she got him on the phone.

"Just relax Mrs. Cunanan. We will take care of you. Just give me a few minutes and I'll call you right back," Hause assured her.

The FBI concocted a plan to protect her, and she readily agreed. Two Chevy Suburbans would pull up to her house near midnight. She would have her bags packed, ready to go and as soon as they arrived, agents would whisk her into a van and take her to safety.

Hause assumed the media would follow, so he and Ann Murphy had devised a route to shake them. First, they would drive through a military base and out the other side. He knew that the media would not be allowed on the base.

Once through the first military base, they would drive into San Diego, though the Marine Corp Recruit Depot and out the other side. By then, they would have shaken the media. Then they would drive to Miramar, the Navel facility. Hause and Murphy liked the plan and looked forward to it. It certainly offered more excitement than the endless interviews he had been conducting during the past 10 weeks.

When they arrived at Maryann's house, Hause saw that the media had disappeared, apparently off work. "Must be too late for them," he laughed cynically as he helped Maryann into the van.

Maryann rode next to Ann Murphy. Murphy had spent many hours talking with Maryann, both in person and on the phone. She realized that Maryann had a difficult life, that her emotions flowed effortlessly and could be unpredictable. Murphy saw this as a result of many years of emotional abuse at the hand of her husband, Modesto, who had left her and the family years earlier.

"Maryann, how are you?" Murphy asked.

"Oh, I'm good," she answered, and then looked at Murphy, adding, "Are you a police officer?"

"Yes, I am. FBI," Murphy answered patiently. Maryann would have known this for weeks.

"Do they let girls carry guns?" Maryann asked.

"Yes, yes Maryann, they do," Murphy answered, once again, very patiently.

They drove without incident and without a tail directly to Miramar, where the military put Maryann up in base housing. Once there, Hause and Murphy stayed with her for several hours until she relaxed and felt safe. The least they could do for Maryann was protect her from the newsies, and the most they could hope would be that Andrew would try calling her. The latter they doubted, worrying instead that he would just go on about his random killings.

Chapter 41 ~ Crazy leads flood Miami Beach

Lee had handled hundreds of leads before Versace's murder. Some bordered on the insane, like the New Orleans' man who insisted he had dated Cunanan on June 14. With this new, high profile murder, the Miami Beach PD found itself flooded with leads on top of those the FBI handled.

AMW's phone began ringing immediately as well. Perhaps atypical of those calls came from an anonymous Broward County, Florida man at 7:25 p.m. on July 15. He claimed that Cunanan had showed up at his door on June 25, and stayed with him for a week, leaving on July 1. During the stay, the man claimed that Cunanan refused to leave the house, but did participate in a birthday celebration there on June 27.

The caller claimed that he dropped Cunanan off at University and Cypress on July 1. Especially helpful, the man said that Cunanan had stolen a black sports utility truck; he told the caller that he had previously ditched the red pickup. The caller and Cunanan had been friends for about four years, and they often engaged in sex.

The caller felt they could catch Cunanan quickly as he had just seen Cunanan at the Copa, a club on Federal Highway. No report exists about how police followed up on this call, but for sure, he never knew Andrew Cunanan.

From the fuselage into the fire

Stepping off the plane in Miami, Chris Graves entered a world of reporters foreign to her. She saw hundreds of them scurrying around the airport, working the phones, grabbing their luggage and shoving others aside, all of them trying to get to South Beach first.

Graves stared at the TV reporters, many who looked like they had just stepped out of a Versace *commercial* not into a Versace story. They looked and dressed exquisitely. She looked at her own frumpy appearance, plain pale face and baggy clothes.

She shrugged, sighed and walked out to hail a taxi. The thick, hot humid air slapped her in the face. She hated the heat almost as much as not having a clue where to start. Only slightly higher on her list of things to dislike was the ratty Days Inn Motel into which she checked a few minutes later.

"This has started out well," she said as she dumped her luggage on the bed. She opened up her laptop computer and plugged into the telephone line. Dialing her internet connection, she attempted to send an email; the phone line went dead. She repeated the process and got through, but that phone line continued to plague her in the frustrating days ahead.

Before unpacking a suitcase, her pager sounded. It was Pam Fine, the first of dozens of such pages each time a story broke on CNN or network news. She heard, "Did you see this?" or "CNN says that…," or "Now they're saying…," each time she answered the page. The pressure felt enormous, and competition with reporters from every corner of the globe intensified it.

She called a taxi.

"The Versace Mansion, please," she told the cab driver. She felt that was as good as any place to begin.

"You and everyone else," he said in his Cuban accent.

The taxi's air conditioner fought a failing battle against the oppressive hot air. She had begun to ache from the need to nurse.

"Walk one block east," the taxi driver told her. "You won't have any trouble finding the mansion."

She saw a mass of people crowded together just up ahead and in a few minutes, stood behind them looking at the front of the Versace Mansion. She studied the "palatial estate" and then turned to look across the street where, for the first time, she saw Lummas Park.

To see the park she had to stare around what seemed like an endless line of TV and news crews perched on the berm. Satellite trucks parked along the length of the street.

The size and number of the TV crews astounded her. Many of the on-air personalities looked more like Hollywood celebrities than reporters, and were treated as such by their make-up assistants inside dressing trailers. Each crew had a bevy of technicians and camera operators. Grave's entire crew included her plus Jeff Wheeler and Cheryl Myers, her camera operators. *How can I compete with them?* she worried.

Bernie Grace and his camera operators stood amidst the line of TV crews next to the satellite truck KARE TV had rented. They shared the cost of the expensive live portable broadcast satellite truck with several other smaller stations. KARE TV had risked a lot of money on these reports. Grace and his two camera-operators made that truck their home base.

Graces' ruddy, plain white Midwestern appearance stuck out from the beautifully tanned people who quickly became his soul mates. He had never before seen such a carnival, both of reporters and gawkers. Of course, the Miami Beach gawkers had always been there, but it struck him that they never changed their behavior despite the serious nature of what had happened. They just kept "cruising" Ocean Drive once the police had re-opened the street.

On either side of Grace were TV crews from foreign nations. Reporting in their native tongues added to the clamor that filled the air. He realized that his Miami reports would be unlike any other. He had done hundreds of live TV reports and each presented its own special challenges, not the least of which was the sheer noise that usually worked to distract him. Here, the noise magnified. Just a few feet away on either side of him, reporters did their own live feeds speaking in a foreign language. The noise at the Tower of Babel could not have been more confounding.

During those early live broadcasts, Grace stood across the street from the Versace mansion so viewers could see it behind him. Viewers could also see the cars endlessly cruising past as he talked.

Fifteen seconds remained during his countdown to one of his live reports as a convertible drove slowly past behind him; the camera captured it. Sitting on the trunk of that convertible with her feet dangling into the back seat was one of a countless number of the gorgeous women who populated South Beach; this one had a surprise for him. As he saw his count going to 5-4-3-2-1, the woman pulled her T-shirt up and off, revealing her naked breasts.

With foreign reporters speaking gibberish on each side him, and the likelihood that a bare-breasted woman added unwanted "excitement" to his report, he began. Since no Minnesotans wrote letters to the station, he had to assume the car and girl passed out of camera range before his mind had entered hyper-concentration mode and his report began.

KSTP TV's Tom Hauser, along with photographers Dave Wertheimer, Char Arends and Dan Dwyer, captured close-up footage of Versace's mansion, noticing the blood stains on the steps and finding it unusual that the cops let them get so close to the place. He had arrived early enough to do a live report for the 5:00 p.m. news. Mike Maybay, Hauser's producer, worked out the kinks in the system before the live shot began.

Richard Chin, the *Pioneer Press* reporter, got to Miami late Wednesday afternoon. As quickly as he could he drove to South Beach, parked his car and walked toward the Versace mansion. Even though dusk had begun settling in, the air felt very hot and sticky. He turned on his reporter's mind, beginning to mentally collect and file what he saw.

Up ahead he saw crowds of people milling about on the street as though they had all gathered at a state fair or rock concert. He sensed both fear and excitement had captured the crowd.

"Hey Andrew," someone shouted, snapping him back to reality. "Hey! Andrew," he heard again.

He turned and saw a couple of guys hanging out at a pizza store. And he saw them studying him carefully, wonderment on their faces.

Chuckling to himself, Chin continued his walk toward Versace's. He had been in South Beach all of 10 minutes and Rosario's prediction had already come true. *I wonder how many more times that will happen.*

On day two, the cops herded all the media across the street from the mansion. The cops held regular news conferences, and this served to filter the news stories, making it difficult to report anything different from the "company line." Reporters dug for the few stories they could develop on their own.

That night, Lee took a call from America's Most Wanted. A woman felt sure that she had seen Cunanan standing in the background at a press conference. He wore a red shirt. Lee had never met Richard Chin, and Chin never knew about this caller and years later, could not recall whether he wore a red shirt. He did learn, however, that anyone who looked at all like Cunanan attracted attention. At least one other reporter suffered the same misidentification, a fellow Knight-Ridder reporter from the *Herald*. Jose Garcia* likewise dealt with the not-so-friendly gawkers who stared at him as they did Chin. Back in St. Paul days later, reporters teased Chin, saying, "We heard you got accused of looking like Jose Garcia." Maybe Chin or Garcia wore a red shirt at the press conference.

While the cops kept the media away from the mansion, they could not control the continuous march of partiers who found their way to the mansion steps and had "tourist" photos taken. The partiers wanted their own sordid remembrance of that murder scene, maybe one day to share with their grandchildren. The paradox baffled Hauser as much as did the disappearance of Wanted Posters baffled Lee Urness.

Hauser looked around at the competing TV crews and realized that many of them were not news or crime reporters. The mix included fashion and design reporters along with paparazzi; all were caught up in the frenzy created by the murder of an international icon. Princess "Di's" death could not have had more reporters assigned to it.

Esme Murphy and her WCCO TV crew fought for their piece of reporter real estate. The short, svelte woman in her neat TV blue outfits stared at Versace's mansion. Its size and majesty impressed her, even as she saw the bloodied front steps. She looked up higher to the second story, and saw a beautiful fresh arrangement of Calla Lilies in the window. The contrast between those beautiful flowers and the ugliness of the death scene just below made her shudder.

As the intensity of the first wave of reports relented, and Cunanan had apparently once again disappeared, reporters began blanketing South Beach, looking for their own unique angle. Most often, they tripped over each other as they did the same stories. Still, the suspense created by Cunanan's disappearance, and the hope that he might show himself again left them both excited and tense. He might even kill again.

The reporters longed for the ultimate scoop – finding Andrew Cunanan. The reporter who happened across him, camera in hand (or nearby) would own a Pulitzer Prize, even if it might be presented posthumously. To do so meant visiting South Beach gay clubs and bars after dark and mixing in with all the "beautiful people" who hung out there. Esme Murphy and her crew spent their late evenings wandering through the dimly lit clubs populated with undulating hordes of partiers rocking to endless loud music. The activities of those at the gay clubs were not lost on Murphy who said, "They were very promiscuous." But any discomfort would quickly be jettisoned if one of those dancers was Andrew Cunanan. Had she been able to talk to Lee Urness, he would have told Esme, "Forget it. He'll never show his face in a crowd, no matter how horny he gets. Especially now."

Richard Chin faced a different dilemma than other Twin Cities' reporters because of the heavy coverage provided by the *Herald*. He spent much of his time "chasing his tail," and trying to ignore the continuing stares of gawkers who felt certain he was Cunanan. During one of his reporter forays, he visited a South Beach gay and lesbian resource center. As he walked in the door, the man who greeted Chin studied him carefully.

"Hi. My name is Richard Chin, a reporter with the St. Paul Pioneer Press," Chin said, handing the man his card.

After a moment in which the man looked at the card, at Chin, and back at the card a few times, he said, "If you hadn't given me your card, I would be calling the police right now."

Chin tried to laugh it off, but what he faced the next day felt, at the time, anything but funny.

The media pack's route took them on countless trips north and south as they searched for clues about Cunanan, and their main route was Collins Avenue. Many of them had found lodging far north of South Beach, forcing them to drive in the congestion of Collins Avenue. Their route took them past the docks that harbored expensive yachts, houseboats, sailboats and speedboats. Andrew Martin, the lead reporter for the *Chicago Tribune* made that route one day on his way to the area surrounding the Normandy Plaza Hotel. He saw a man sitting on a bench near the boat docks and thought he looked a lot like Cunanan, but he paid it no mind; many men looked like Cunanan. None of the reporters or police knew that Andrew Cunanan watched them as they fruitlessly searched for him, but never looking in the right place.

While hundreds of reporters combed through South Beach, Lee Urness sat in the midst of a storm of activity. The blur of May 7 had become a blizzard. Several times Lee had to retreat to the safe-haven of his van to attempt to handle all the calls, but once there, his pager never stopped nagging him. From FTF offices nationwide, to FBI headquarters, to local cops everywhere, to Minnesota jurisdictions, to Coleen Rowley and countless media inquiries, the calls continued like the rush of water over Minnehaha Falls.

Lee wanted to get on the street and catch Cunanan, but this he had to leave to others.

He even felt jealous of the reporters. While they flourished in the street action, Lee was relegated to working the telephones. While they stuck microphones into the faces of cops and "witnesses," and busily scribbled on their reporter pads, Lee took reports from others on the ground, writing in an intense scrawl on his legal pads. Lee felt ready to bubble over in frustration.

Chapter 42 ~ Media turns hot

Once Cunanan shot Versace, FBI Headquarters faced intense media pressure. To some in the media, the FBI had appeared to be less than energized by this "gay" killer. Lee knew the truth. Even Interpol had picked up their level of involvement, faxing the Minnesota FTF a copy of their release with the latest information they had on file. Cops everywhere had joined the chase for Cunanan, and his sexual identity played no role, save giving officers some clues where to look and with whom to talk.

The FBI, Fugitive Task Forces and local cops had expended tens of thousands of hours following more than 2,000 leads, all to dead ends. Within minutes of the news of Versace's killing, dozens of leads poured in every hour, amounting to more than 2,000 within days – hundreds alone in Miami and Miami Beach. Each lead had to be evaluated and followed, no matter how obscure or unlikely.

Some gay leaders, however, appeared to be looking for a fight, not an accommodation. Lee read and heard these statements and thought back on how closely he and FBI agents everywhere had worked with the gay community. For some agents, it had felt uncomfortable, but they did it anyway.

Mark Segal, Publisher of *Philadelphia Gay News*, blasted the FBI in an editorial that appeared on August 15. He wrote, "I know who is responsible for the murder of Gianni Versace. It is none other than the FBI. That's right, folks, the FBI – or more accurately, the homophobia at the FBI.

"The point is that we, the gay community, should have been the first phone call the agency made for two basic reasons: We were most at risk and, two, it would be the place he might come for safe harbor.

"Didn't the FBI consider the people of the gay community important enough to be warned by their trusted press that their [sic] was a potential killer in their midst?"

Lee had secured the federal warrant on May 7. He sent Steve Gilkerson to talk to Constance Potter at the Minneapolis Gay Lesbian Community Action Council on May 8, and talked personally with Potter on May 9. Potter offered her group's help, and Lee readily accepted. He gave her one poster that day. By mid-June, he had provided Potter with 500 posters, which she assured would be sent nationwide through the gay and lesbian network. Lee made sure the posters were "new looks," updated photos. Perhaps, Lee thought, Segal was not linked to this national network.

Lee sent the Serial 9 on May 9.

Special Agent Emilio Blasse showed Cunanan's picture all around New York City's gay bars and clubs on May 9. And Blasse provided personal protection to William Norman, Cunanan's former Sugar Daddy, during that same weekend. By then, Special Agents John Hause and Ann Murphy had questioned dozens of gay men in San Diego, and the word about Cunanan had been heard everywhere in that city's gay community. Other California Special Agents, Jeff Knotts and Scott Anderson, had completed a first round of interviews with numerous gay men by May 9.

Lee sent 3,000 wanted posters to Special Agent Keith Evans in Miami. Evans spread a portion of those posters to every bar and club in Miami Beach and surrounding communities. But the managers and employees saw them, not the patrons. The hospitality industry showed very little enthusiasm for publicizing the possibility that a brutal murderer could be in their midst.

In June, New Orleans FBI Special Agents spent a Saturday night with Chuck Loomis, hitting that city's gay bars and clubs and passing out Cunanan's photo.

Every major city had been contacted and Special Agents and local cops had circulated posters or pictures at hundreds of known gay hangouts. By early July, Lee and the Minneapolis office had mailed a wanted poster to every establishment listed in the DAMRON directory, warning them of Cunanan.

Yet Segal protested that the FBI failed in its attempt to work inside the gay community, claiming this was because the FBI had no gay or lesbian agents; the facts proved otherwise.

Gays and lesbians who partied at South Beach had ample access to Cunanan's picture, the four America's Most Wanted segments that had already run, and countless network and local TV and newspaper stories about Cunanan. Segal might well have questioned the *Miami Herald* which, during June and up to July 15, had not once published a story about Andrew Cunanan.

Lee felt very disappointed at these types of charges. He saw the Segal-types as nothing but activists who, "just plain don't like cops."

Lee felt that Segal's ill-advised comments hurt the relationship and co-operation built by the FBI with gay groups. But even more so, Lee felt that had Segal and his gay friends, especially in South Beach, worked harder and cooperated with the FBI, they could have helped stop Cunanan.

ABC News aired a Cunanan special on July 16, the day after Versace's murder. Chris Wallace hosted the show. First, it dug into several different aspects of the case, and included interviews with local cops and FBI agents, as well as Miami and San Diego citizens. Then it turned to the real red meat of the program. Wallace introduced the next segment:

"Joining us now from our Minneapolis affiliate, KSTP, former deputy assistant director of the FBI's criminal division, Nicholas O'Hara. Sarah Pettit is editor-in-chief of *Out* magazine, which has the largest worldwide circulation of any gay and lesbian magazine. And she joins us from New York."

Governor Arne Carlson had appointed O'Hara as the head the Minnesota Bureau of Criminal Apprehension. O'Hara, along with Steve Gilkerson, had started the Minnesota Fugitive Task Force in 1991. He served as Special Agent in Charge in both Omaha and Minneapolis, and while heading the Violent Crimes Division at FBI Headquarters, ran the Top Ten program. A "company man" who was articulate, witty and full of energy, O'Hara made the perfect foil for the lesbian, Sarah Pettit.

As the interview progressed, Wallace finally broached the gay-lesbian versus FBI debate. "How do you try to break through this in a case like this and gain the trust of that community to help you?"

"I've been doing this for 33 years, Chris," O'Hara began, "and there are so many good cops out there that I don't have to talk about that. They are motivated to solve cases regardless of who is involved, whether it is a rich kid, poor kid, gay, lesbian, whatever. We do have some who are maybe turned off by that kind of a lifestyle. But the vast majority are going to go out there and do everything they can to find this guy, bring him to ground, bring him in, arrest him and protect the group that may be at most risk." His answer did not satisfy Sarah Pettit. She smelled discrimination.

"I guess one of the questions I would have is how much we're allowing Mr. Cunanan to call the shots here," Pettit said, "and to what degree we've all had to wait, frankly, for the tragic loss of someone like Gianni Versace to really pay attention to someone who clearly has been in the FBI's line of vision for a lot longer than the last 48 hours."

Clint Van Zandt, a Miami Special Agent, reminded viewers that Cunanan was on the FBI's Top Ten list, and as such, the FBI had committed maximum resources to this case. "So that means that every FBI office in the country has been looking for him prior to this. They just didn't have a strong indication of where he was."

"Except for that red truck in a parking garage in downtown Miami," Pettit needled.

"Which came up after the homicide," Van Zandt reminded her.

"Nick O'Hara, though, let me ask you about that," Wallace said. "Because Mr. Cunanan was on the 10 most wanted list. A lot of people have asked the question that Ms. Pettit is asking – and it's obviously 20/20 hindsight. But does it surprise you that he was able to drive this red pickup that law enforcement authorities knew about, were looking for and was able to elude all of them?"

"Not really, Chris," O'Hara answered immediately, "because there are so many vehicles out there and so few cops to monitor that kind of activity and so many red pickup trucks. I really think, in my own mind, that he was interrupted as he went back to the truck by the individual that pursued him from the Versace shooting.

"And I don't know that I would suggest that he planned on leaving the clothing and the personal ID there. I think that that put him in a bad state. Any time a person loses personal ID like that and he's on the run, it's going to make his life more difficult.

"That doesn't mean he didn't have a vehicle close by. But I'd also like to make a comment, Chris, with regard to Sarah Pettit's remarks, the broad-brush approach to the FBI not being sensitive to gay issues and not hitting this case very hard. And that's absolute nonsense, Ms. Pettit, and you know it."

"Well, I think..." she began.

"Let me finish," O'Hara interrupted her. "Let me just finish now. I've got an agent that's been working this case ever since the murder up there in Chisago County. And he's putting in 12, 14, 16 hours a day as are police officers all over this country. So I think that you need to be a little more realistic as you categorize cops not buying into your gay/lesbian..."

"I have no interest in categorizing anyone," she snapped back at him. "I think we all have an interest in catching..."

"Let me finish. I'm not done," O'Hara said, boring in.

"Mr. O'Hara, let's let Ms. Pettit talk," Wallace interrupted.

"I don't think we – any of us have an interest in seeing this go on one second longer, sir. And I respect the work you do. But Mr. Versace isn't putting in one more 12-hour day, frankly, and neither are the four other people that were killed."

"And I think that we need to recognize that all lives are equivalent, and sometimes gay and lesbian lives are the last ones to get attention when it comes to murder. And there are a lot of people who feel very strongly about that and are very scared and who may, in fact, be at risk here."

"Well, Chris, the thing we have to consider, too, there's 22,000 homicides a year," Van Zandt said, breaking in. "And this individual is very important to catch. But solving 22,000 homicides is one of the top things that any law enforcement agency does on a yearly basis.

"And I think everybody's out there trying as hard as they can, and they're just seeking the cooperation of the community to help them do their job. We need hundreds more, thousands more sets of eyes and ears, and the community out there can provide those."

"Mr. O'Hara, we have less than a minute left," Wallace said. "Based on your long experience in these kinds of high-profile cases, how do you think it will end?"

"I don't know that he's got it planned. But I have great respect for Clint Van Zandt's insight. I think that he [Cunanan] probably has an agenda that he might not be finished yet with, and I want to work with the communities – all communities. Because it isn't just the gay and lesbian community that he's victimized. He has victimized a gentleman up in New Jersey and there was a warrant charged on that today. And there's no suggestion of Mr. Miglin either. There is no suggestion that he is anything other than a straight individual." U.S. Magistrate Judge Robert Kugler had signed the New Jersey warrant charging Cunanan with the first-degree murder of William Reese earlier that day.

Sarah Pettit had only one more response and that was to thank Chris Wallace for including her in the interview.

Lee Urness and thousands of cops echoed O'Hara's words that night. They knew that picking a fight with the cops was a lousy way of winning their cooperation the next time around, yet despite Pettit's and Segal's anti-cop remarks, the cops pushed ahead. A blizzard of leads had created thousands more hours of work for the beleaguered agents.

One reporter snooped back home

While reporters flooded South Beach, the *Los Angeles Times* sought a different angle, sending a reporter to Minneapolis for an exclusive interview with the Task Force Case Agent, Lee Urness.

"Lee," Coleen Rowley explained, "you should talk to this reporter from Los Angeles."

"Hell no. I have no time for that," he said. "Tell her to go home."

Late that evening his home phone rang. Lee heard the voice of that L.A. reporter begging for an interview. He refused.

"How the hell did that reporter get my home phone number?" Lee shouted at Rowley. "It's non-published!"

"Oh they have their ways, just like we do," Rowley answered.

"Well it'll be a cold day in Hell before I talk to her, and you can tell her that."

Rowley told her, but the reporter hung around for three days, nearly camping out at FBI headquarters, before she went home defeated.

HQ pressure cooker

Versace's visibility and standing brought unwanted pressure to the FBI and Miami police. Not only was he an international businessman with the wealth and power such a position offered, his clothing designs draped the bodies of wealthy people across the world. High society and the paparazzi knew Versace. Few had known Jeff Trail, David Madson or Bill Reese. Chicagoans had known Lee Miglin and though they may have frequented his buildings, they did not wear his boots, belts and bras on their bodies.

The cops had worked day and night trying to catch and stop Cunanan. Now, the Minnesota FBI office issued orders that every Special Agent and their clerks were to cancel all vacation and time off plans. The agents knew that such an order came with the job, but it never felt good to shut down plans, and it proved expensive to some.

"Well, there goes $500," one of the agents said. "A nonrefundable plane ticket wasted."

"Gee, that's too bad," Lee teased. "You know, I've had to cancel five of them with my family this summer."

"Well, you're the case agent."

Miami cops under intense pressure

In South Jersey, William Reese's murder had created a flurry of activity that quickly died down into an intense, but routine homicide investigation. In

South Beach, nothing was routine about the investigation of Gianni Versace's murder.

The killer had been identified quickly by the witness and discovery of Reese's truck. The two slugs that cops recovered, the truck's contents, and Cunanan's shed clothes had proved Cunanan's guilt. That part was easy. Finding Cunanan was a different, yet the same, story. The cops felt sure he had not fled from Miami Beach and they began a massive door-to-door search.

Others speculated that Cunanan fled, or would try to flee, from Miami.

"He's not going anywhere," Lee Urness said. "He's out of money. He's got no identification papers. He's got no vehicle. He's not a thief or burglar. Nope. He's holed up somewhere in Miami Beach and we have to find him," he told his fellow agents.

Miami Beach police and FBI agents fanned throughout the city doing their search while Lee and his crew in Minneapolis tried to handle the drumbeat of leads flooding into the office.

Chapter 43 ~ Hitting gold

Vivian Olivia called the Miami Beach Police Department before 9:00 a.m. on July 16. She told them that Andrew Cunanan had hocked a coin at her shop on July 7. Keith Evans, calling from the Miami Beach Police Department's Command Post, immediately reported it to Lee Urness.

"We found that Cunanan pawned a gold coin right here in Miami Beach. The pawn slip has his address and we're on the way," Evans said. "It shows a hotel, the Normandy Plaza, just a few miles north of here."

"Awesome! Let me know as soon as you have anything," Lee answered. He felt they had indeed caught a break, but a break that only filled in a few blanks. That Cunanan had any gold coins had never before been reported to Lee. Had he known, he would most certainly have notified every pawnshop in America.

"First we're going to send out some false cars to draw the newsies away, but we should be there soon," Evans explained. Media types were everywhere in town, stalking the cops as they flew off to leads. The cops did not want a stream of media trucks following them up to the Normandy Plaza Hotel, which sat directly up Collins Avenue five miles north of the police department.

Lee sat back at his desk and smiled. He hated that Cunanan had killed again, but this time he felt they were really close. "Maybe this is the day, folks," Lee said to the task force in the command center. He threw a dart at Cunanan's picture.

Bernie Grace caught wind of the FBI's discovery and somehow managed to follow the *right* FBI car to the Normandy Plaza Hotel. He found the staff there to be very courteous and open to interview, and more importantly, he saw no other reporters. He began putting together a story.

The FBI showed Cunanan's picture to the clerk. She recognized it right away and showed them the name under which he had checked in: Kurt Demars. Demars had been one of Cunanan's close west coast friends. They went to his room, and no one occupied it, but it was picked clean. They knocked on every door in the hotel and talked to those who answered. Some remembered seeing Cunanan, once they saw the pictures, but none had any contact with him and neither did they know where he had gone. He had walked out on July 12 without paying his rent.

Once the FBI finished searching Cunanan's room, Evans called Lee with the news. He had no way of knowing that they had searched the wrong room. The clerk never told them that Cunanan had moved to the third floor.

"Lee, Cunanan lived here from May 12 on, but left on July 12 without paying his rent. We've been in his room and it's empty. There's no clue where he is. He's got to be hiding somewhere in the area, though," Evans reported. Evans had distributed thousands of Wanted Posters. One even now hung at the News Café.

Lee wrote on his notepad, "1800, 7/16, pawnshop lead done." He reminded himself not to get too excited about any lead save for the one that was certain – "we have Cunanan." Still, the FBI *did* have the red pickup truck. Police covered all possible normal exits, but local cops had to admit that was an impossibility to cover all of them. The ocean nearby offered a quick escape if Cunanan could find a boat to steal or hire, though the police had immediately checked all boat rentals and reports of stolen boats, coming up empty. They had checked every taxi pickup and drop off, with the same dismal results.

Rough sailing

Earlier that afternoon, Mr. Volpe and his friend Mr. MosQuera walked down Collins Avenue on their way to Volpe's Bristol sailboat. He kept it moored in Slip 21 at 5445 Collins Avenue. The old boat had not been seaworthy for some time, but Volpe still hung on to it, hopeful that it might prove useful for something.

As the two men came close to Volpe's boat, they spotted a man sitting on a nearby bench. Volpe noticed that the man was reading a book with the same title as one of his own.

Volpe climbed onto his boat and discovered that the top hatch had been opened. It looked like someone had broken into his boat. As best he could he examined the boat's interior from above, and satisfied that no one was on the boat, he climbed down inside. There he saw that the place had been ransacked. Clothing lay strewn about, and two newspapers from July 16 lay in a mess on the floor – the *Miami Herald* and an Italian paper. He saw that at least one book was missing, the one that the man on the bench had been reading.

He and MosQuera climbed back out of the boat, looking for the man they had just seen reading the book. No one was there.

Andrew Cunanan had moved south to the huge, two story houseboat he been eyeing for the last four days. He quickly broke in, just in time to see Volpe and MosQuera come out on the dock. He felt sure they would immediately call the police. In his haste to leave the sailboat, he had carried nothing with him except the clothes on his back and Jeff Trail's Taurus pistol, now Cunanan's last remaining earthly possession.

Cunanan found a pair of binoculars lying on a table and climbed up the stairs to the second floor. From there he could see in every direction, across the canal to the luxury homes, to the north and south on Collins Avenue, to the two luxury hotels across the street. He knew the police would likely be there shortly, though it took Volpe quite a bit of time to leave his boat.

At 4:00 p.m., Volpe and his friend walked into the Miami Beach Police Department. Once they had told security the nature of their visit, they were ushered into a meeting with Sgt. George Navarro. Hearing their story, Navarro dispatched officers to the 5400 block of Collins to conduct a door-to-door search.

Cunanan saw the cops coming. He ran downstairs and made sure the dead bolt was locked on the front door and then moved into the middle of the houseboat, his Taurus at the ready, but hoping the cops would just go away.

The police worked their way along the four blocks of boat slips, knocking on each door and checking to see if they were secured, or if there was any sign of forced entry. They peered into windows and listened. They saw nothing. Although the lead had sounded good – two men identified Cunanan in an area that made sense to the cops – nothing good came of it.

As late as five minutes past midnight two nights later, police re-checked the area. Someone had reported seeing Cunanan in the area of 54th and Collins. Once again, the cops found no one, but Cunanan could see them.

Unable to venture out, Cunanan began searching the cabinets, refrigerator and closets, looking for food. He found nuts, crackers and bottled water to serve his needs until he could fashion some way off that houseboat.

Not that it affected Lee's job or Cunanan's chances for freedom, but on July 17, the Chicago Police Department finally secured an arrest warrant naming Andrew Cunanan as Lee Miglin's murderer. With the discovery of the red pickup truck in Miami Beach, Paul Murray also secured his arrest warrant charging Cunanan with William Reese's murder.

To the ends of the earth, if necessary

"Lee, I think you're going to want to get on this one right away," one of the Command Post assistants said as she handed him a call slip from FBI headquarters.

Lee read the note. It said something about a call the FBI tip-line had received from a caller in Sao Paulo, Brazil. A Sylvia Martinez* had told the FBI that she attended a party at Gianni Versace's Miami Beach mansion on July 13 and while there, freely videotaped the guests. That video, Martinez claimed, showed Cunanan and Versace together. For the right price, Martinez offered the video to the FBI.

Soon, the FBI sent Special Agent Richard Cavalieros to Brazil to obtain the video. Such footage, they hoped, might reveal others at the same party who could steer them to Cunanan.

Cavalieros paid Martinez for this potentially explosive, useful piece of evidence. The tape, indeed, did show a Versace party, but unfortunately, Cunanan never appeared in the video.

Strange claims such as the Brazilian video became the norm after Versace's murder. That same day, an anonymous caller notified the FBI that he had information about Lee Miglin. The caller claimed that it was common knowledge at SAKS Fifth Avenue in Chicago that Miglin was a member of the gay community. Lee knew that if this tip was true, it could spring open a plethora of new leads from others previously afraid to come forward.

Lee notified Terry Thedford to follow up on the lead, but it led nowhere. No one at SAKS took credit for such information. In fact, the end result was to offer stronger proof that Miglin never had been part of the gay community.

Lee believed that if Miglin really had been gay that somewhere, sometime at least one credible lead would be established. Really, he expected several, but no credible lead ever surfaced. The absence of the leads, especially following Versace's murder, led Lee to the conclusion that if some connection had existed between Cunanan and Miglin, it had nothing to do with the older man's sexual identity.

Lee followed up on a lead he had set with the Lubbock, Texas Resident Agent. Bonnie Kates*, an airline traveler, reported that she had flown on the same plane with Andrew Cunanan on July 15. Kates said she had flown from Lubbock to Dallas, and then on to Chicago on that day. Special Agent Steve Powell took her statement.

Kates said that her flight to Chicago left at 5:00 p.m. and that Cunanan sat in a seat across the aisle. When she saw the wanted poster, she felt certain that it had been him. She remembered that when the plane landed in Chicago, Cunanan pushed his way through the cramped airplane aisle, uncaring about how he irritated other passengers.

Agent Powell first confirmed that Kates really had been on the flight and that she did, indeed, work for Nabisco, Inc. as she claimed. He further identified the flight number and requested American Airlines to identify the passengers. This allowed him to identify the individual who Kates had seen on the plane. But at that moment, Cunanan hid on a sailboat moored at 5445 Collins in Miami Beach.

Kevin Rickett followed up on an electronic communication (EC) sent from the Milwaukee, Wisconsin FBI office. It reported on a truck theft that had occurred on July 3 at Iten Chevrolet in Hudson, Wisconsin. Hudson sits on the banks of the St. Croix River just 18 miles east of St. Paul, Minnesota.

Leland Horton*, a felon on supervised release, drove a 1985 Grey Chevy Nova onto the Iten lot that day. Horton had told the car's St. Paul, Minnesota owner that he wanted to take it for a test drive, but had never returned. Now he wanted to trade the Nova for a new truck.

He asked the Iten salesman for the keys to test-drive a brand new red Chevy pickup and having left the lot, once again, never returned. On July 9, Miami, Florida police had recovered Iten's truck at a parking garage. Given that Cunanan's murders began in Minneapolis, the Hudson cop who investigated the first theft felt this might be related to Cunanan's unlawful flight. Horton, though a car and truck thief, and in serious trouble with federal authorities, looked nothing like Cunanan.

Media went anywhere for a story

Richard Chin joined hundreds of reporters who crowded the steps, narthex and sanctuary of Miami's St. Patrick Church on Friday morning. Chin hoped to interview prominent mourners who had come to pay their last respects to Gianni Versace.

Mixed into the crowd of mourners and reporters were dozens of plain clothes FBI agents and Miami Beach Police Officers. They hoped that Cunanan would try to show up to see the effects of his grim handiwork. One of those cops spotted Chin.

"Excuse me sir," Chin heard from the cop who approached him. Chin had a camera strap over his shoulder. His laptop computer lay against his side inside a shoulder bag that hung on the other shoulder.

"Yes sir," Chin answered.

"Could I see some ID, please," the cop asked, and within 30 seconds, three officers surrounded Chin. He handed over his ID and studied the faces of the other police officers. Within a minute, they had been joined by a handful of others.

As the first cop looked at his ID, others began patting down his legs. One asked to see his laptop computer, which he carried to a small alter nearby, opening it to view the files inside. Another cop pulled a Cunanan wanted poster out of his pocket and stared at Chin.

"Would you please give me your social security number, and also, will you tell me where you were born," another cop asked. Chin learned later that the number related to the place of birth in such a way that a cop could quickly recognize if he had been lying to them.

"We don't think you're him," the first cop said after a few minutes of this, "but why don't you stay around."

"Yes sir. I'm not going anywhere," Chin said, "except inside."

As he sat quietly in the service taking notes, he saw a woman sitting nearby who began staring at him – more like glaring angrily. Following the service, Chin joined with dozens of other reporters as they attempted to interview a Miami Beach cop. As he looked up he saw a TV camera focused on him.

Chin felt compelled to file a story on the look-alike issue. He knew from his own experience what it meant, but had no idea how many hundreds of such sightings Lee Urness had followed to the same dead end as those Miami cops in that church.

On the same day mourners gathered at St. Patrick Church, the FBI Director Louis Freeh signed off on a memo carrying "immediate" urgency to all FBI offices. It provided a synopsis of Cunanan's five murders and, in essence, labeled him Public Enemy Number 1. FBI agents everywhere were put on alert – get Andrew Cunanan!

Cunanan came from Canada?

Shelly Mollar* of Toronto called the Ottawa FBI Legal Attaché on July 17. She believed she had astounding news. The Mollar family, as a statement of their Mormon faith, made it a practice to take into their home certain people who seemed without direction, or needed a helping hand. During late June, the Toronto Mormon Mission sent them such a person. Mollar expected the young man, Martin Anders*, to stay a few days, but those days dragged into more than two weeks.

"He seldom left our house, and seemed clandestine, almost never leaving the house," the earnest woman said. "Anders told us he had been staying with a local gay man. He said he was waiting for money."

Anders claimed he had been shot and stabbed in San Diego. Still, Mollar saw Anders as a "model type," a handsome man whom she believed was bisexual or homosexual.

"He was educated and fluent in at least a couple of languages, smooth and delightful, as well as a computer nerd," she added.

He spent a good deal of time using the Mollar's computer and she noticed at least once he dwelt on a page about the "serial killer from San Diego." Anders wanted to know, "if they had caught the serial killer" yet. He looks like he couldn't hurt a fly," Anders had said.

"Do you really think so?" Mollar asked.

"I'm the killer. That's me," he said as he pointed at the picture.

Mollar stared at Cunanan's picture and the resemblance between the two men set her nerves on edge. She needed to find a way to get Anders, or whoever he was, out of the house.

When she learned that Anders had been making long distance phone calls using stolen phone cards, she asked him to leave. He left without incident.

Norton Chiles* also contacted the FBI Toronto LEGAT. The gay man had hosted Anders for three weeks prior to his moving to the Mollar's house. "He stole phone cards from my friends," Chiles reported.

"We have a local resident who claims that Anders might really be Andrew Cunanan, a man wanted on a murder warrant in the states," the LEGAT said. "What do you think?"

"Oh no. Martin? No, certainly not," he insisted.

Both Chiles and Mollar provided the LEGAT with dozens of phone numbers and several addresses Anders had contacted. Despite the near certainty that he was not Cunanan, the FBI still made each contact until fully satisfied that this was not their man.

Chapter 44 ~ Chris Graves searches for something

Chris Graves had hit the ground running on July 16, but she had run in circles. She needed a plan, a plan different from the other reporters who littered the sidewalks of South Beach. *Real* reporters, she told herself, disliked the periodic FBI and Miami Beach Police Department press briefings, spoon-feeding news to reporters.

She saw close-up how desperate national TV news acted as they needed to fill their quota of live shots, and she was not impressed. She saw TV reporters reporting everything, whether newsworthy or factual or relevant – or not. She could not accept that, even *if* her editors would have allowed it. Stories produced in this manner led to misstatement of fact. She heard a TV report that Versace had HIV, and that Cunanan had AIDS. These unverifiable kinds of claims were based on the statements of countless self-aggrandizers who flocked to the story like bees to honey. (During one such media interview, Minneapolis Police Officer Gary Barsness mentioned in passing the possibility that Cunanan might have AIDS. The story spread and took on its own life, suddenly becoming media "gospel." Graves never believed the report because it could not be verified.)

Two days after Versace's killing, Graves overheard a police report that Silvio Alfonso, a prominent doctor and believed to be gay, had been murdered in Miami Springs. She and one of her camera operators immediately hailed a cab, both hopeful and fearful that Cunanan had struck again. She paged Lee on the way. He called her back. "Is this Cunanan?"

"Naw, it's not him," Lee answered.

"Okay, good. But we're headed out there now anyway," she said. Every murder case resulted in the question, "Did Cunanan do this?"

"What's going on down there with the newsies?" Lee asked. His question was more than mere curiosity. He knew that reporters often found information before the cops did.

"It's crazy. The reporters don't know what's going on. It's absolutely wild" she answered.

"Well, if the newsies get a hot lead, that's what I need to know. I'll help you out with some of this stuff, but I have to know what's going on. Some people call the newsies who won't call the cops. You be my eyes and ears," he urged her. He needed everything he could get. And he told no one he was talking to her.

Lee went back to his growing stack of calls.

Graves' pager rang. Her editor wanted a call back right away.

"This is Chris," she said as Fine picked up the phone.

"We saw a story about another murder, some doctor. Do you know about it?"Fine asked.

"We are in the cab on the way already," she sighed. "It's not Cunanan, though. Look, if you would leave me alone I could get some work done." Still, Graves had to go and get the facts to write the story because with Cunanan, even a non-story had legs.

Bernie Grace arrived at Dr. Alfonso's house at the same time as Graves and hundreds of other reporters. He saw a police line already established outside of a fence, a police line that included several Miami Beach police officers sent to assist. Packed against the fence stood the Miami Beach media horde.

Grace and his camera operator got as close as possible. There he saw a Miami Springs police officer working his way down the line of reporters, first standing near a small group, giving his statement and then moving to the next small group. Patiently and with great detail, he gave the report to each group, repeating his performance until he reached the end of the line. In each case, the police officer repeated the same line, "No, we are sure it was not Andrew Cunanan."

Tired and frustrated, Grace and the other TV reporters filed back to Ocean Drive and the waiting satellite trucks to file their non-story. "Today a distinguished doctor who was allegedly gay was murdered here in Miami. Police officers have determined the murderer was not Andrew Cunanan…"

Meanwhile, on July 18, a protected source called Boston FBI to report that he had seen Andrew Cunanan together with Gianni Versace at Club 82 in New York City during early May. He remembered a third man at their table as well. Cunanan wore glasses that night, according to the source, and he could not remember if they left together. New York City FBI agents responded to the lead, tracking down the owner of Club 82, and the man tried to avoid talking to them. FBI agents pressed him, though it was a wasted effort. Lee knew that Versace was in Europe during the time of this sighting.

Lee still worried about Cunanan killing again, no matter how far removed from Miami Beach a potential target might have been. He had noticed that Cunanan had retained in his San Diego apartment an article about another architect, Richard Meier of Los Angeles. Lee called Agent Jeff Knotts to make sure that Meier could be warned and take precautions.

The Minnesota FTF then issued another Electronic Communication directed at the FBI Director and all field offices worldwide. Lee had done this first on May 11, but felt everyone needed a reminder. He wanted all FBI offices to make contact with any gay and lesbian establishments in their areas and especially, with any gay and lesbian organizations.

Lee had learned two important lessons from the beginning of the investigation. First, gay and lesbian leaders were more than willing to help disseminate Cunanan's picture and information about him. Secondly, many in the gay community who had knowledge of or had spotted Cunanan feared calling the police; instead, they called a local gay organization. Lee requested that FBI agents in all offices get out and have face-to-face meetings with these gay groups and community leaders, as the FTF's in 10 cities had done from the beginning.

As that EC spread across the world, Boston FBI received a lead from a woman who claimed that Cunanan had been a patient at Hazeldon's Minnesota drug and treatment center during 1996. The woman said she went through the program with him.

Following such a lead required careful negotiations. The FBI's Behavioral Science Unit (BSU) made discreet inquiries to Hazeldon's director, providing him with all of Cunanan's aliases, but their search of records turned up negative. Cunanan had never been there, just as he had never been at the Betty Ford Clinic, as he had told others.

While the FBI and Miami Beach Police followed up hundreds of leads, the media continued to probe for stories, hoping to trip across a scoop.

Itching for real news

The FBI had done a great job of keeping information about the pawnshop from the media, until Chris Graves decided to walk the streets on July 19. She had decided to end her frustration by doing what she had always done. "You are a reporter," she told herself. "Get hold of yourself. He's just a killer. Do what you always do back home. Develop sources, make your calls."

Then she hit the streets near the Normandy Plaza Hotel, trying to figure out where Cunanan might have gone. She stopped at all the shops and restaurants along the way. In every place, the routine was the same.

"Hello, I am Chris Graves, a reporter with the *Star-Tribune* from Minneapolis, covering the Andrew Cunanan case. I wonder if you know anything about this, or perhaps have seen Cunanan?"

She and Jeff Wheeler, her photographer, dragged themselves through the stifling heat, moving from one store to the next. No one had seen Cunanan or Versace. Most did not want to be bothered, telling her that other reporters had made the same inquiries, as well as police and FBI. She walked down the north side of 71st Street.

"Let's go in here," she said to Wheeler as she studied the stickers on the door of Cash on the Beach. One said "Please Ring Bell." She rang the bell and the door buzzed signaling her to enter. She saw a counter straight ahead and behind the bulletproof glass stood a woman. She waited on the customer who stood on Graves' side of the glass.

"May I help you," the woman asked in the Hispanic accent that had become common to Graves since coming to South Beach.

"No, I can wait. You are busy," Graves said courteously.

Finally, the woman finished her business and Graves stepped up to the window. Her photographer hung back.

"Hi, I am Chris Graves, a reporter from the Minneapolis *Star-Tribune*. About this Cunanan thing. Is there anything you know?" Graves asked, not expecting anything, almost ready to turn and head out to the next shop.

"You so nice," the woman answered. "You so nice. Wait just a minute."

Graves watched the woman go into the back room and emerge with something in her hand. As she returned, she pushed a yellow slip through the opening in the window.

"He passed this coin," she said, nonchalantly.

Graves stared at the receipt that showed Cunanan's signature, his thumbprint, an address for the Normandy Plaza Hotel and a description of a gold coin for which he had received $190. It was dated July 7.

"Have you told the police?" Graves said, astounded at this news. She knew she had read everything made public about the case and could hardly believe that this had gotten past her.

"Oh yes, of course. We must report it within 24 hours," she smiled.

"What did they do?"

"Nothing. They did nothing," the woman, whom Graves came to know as Vivian Olivia, told her. Olivia said nothing about talking with the Miami Beach police or FBI the past Wednesday.

"What about reporters? Surely reporters came here and talked to you," Graves said.

"Yes, but I told them nothing," Olivia smiled.

"Why? Why did you tell me?"Graves asked. Her gut told her she had stumbled across a major scoop.

"Well because you so nice," Vivian answered, smiling back at her.

Graves effusively thanked Vivian and asked permission to take her picture and pictures of the pawn slip and her shop.

She and Wheeler walked around the corner to the Normandy Plaza Hotel. There she found it surprisingly easy to get the management to show her room 322, the last room in which Cunanan had stayed. The dirty, dingy place surprised her, as she had felt sure Cunanan would only stay in fancy digs.

She rushed back to her motel room, calling in along the way. "You are not going to believe what I have," she told her editor. "And it's all ours."

"You have pictures?"

"Jeff is heading out to send them right now. Give me an hour and you will have the story," she said.

Her adrenalin pumped as she banged out the story on her laptop. Other than frustration with the phone line as she sent the story back to Minneapolis, this day had given her a thrill reporters dream of – an exclusive scoop in a huge story! The heat and humidity had been worth it all for this one moment.

One unintended, but appreciated result of her scoop was that her editor quit paging her so often.

Seeing Andy's real room

That evening, KSTP TV reporter Tom Hauser prepared for yet another live report of really not much news. Just before going on the air, sources at the ABC Network tipped him off that Chuck Goudie of their ABC Chicago affiliate had discovered the real room Cunanan used at the Normandy Plaza Hotel, and already had a crew there. (Graves had come and gone by then.) Strewn about Room 322 were magazines and books Cunanan had used for entertainment. The FBI had not yet seen the room. They had searched one of the rooms Cunanan used when he first checked in, but not his last room. As soon as he could, Goudie sent the footage to ABC. The FBI would later dispatch an agent to fingerprint Goudie, worried that he had disturbed some of the materials during his camera shoot.

Hauser sent one of his cameramen directly to the Normandy Plaza Hotel while the other stayed to do his live shot. Hauser's tip allowed him to broadcast a clip from ABC's footage to the curious eyes back home. Following this, the FBI went back to the right room and taped it off, ready to do their own search.

"How in the hell could this happen?" Lee asked Rickett when he heard about this second trip to the Normandy Plaza Hotel. "I mean, here they are, the FBI, walks into that place a few days ago. Versace's dead. They know Cunanan had lived there, and yet not a single person at the Normandy Plaza Hotel thought to mention he had moved to a different room? Go figure," Lee said in a huff. Lee believed that someone at the front desk should have at least mentioned that Cunanan had changed rooms and that, in fact, he had not yet paid the rent on 322. Or when the cops canvassed the building, someone should have said something. But no one had said a thing.

Miami Beach Police Sergeant Gary Schiaffo simply said, "Those people at the Normandy are not the sharpest."

In room 322, the FBI found several publications, books and magazines. None helped them find Cunanan, but they did reflect on his wide variety of interests. Books included:

Jean Nouvel
Phaidon Guide to Furniture
Miller's Antiques Checklist – Art Deco
Claudius the God by Robert Graves
How the Irish Saved Civilization, by Thomas
I, Claudius by Robert Graves
A History of Civilizations by Fernand Braudel
The Romantic Rebellion by Kenneth Clark
Slim by Slim Keith with Annette Tapeau
In All His Glory by Shelly Bedell Smith
The Man Who Was Vogue by Cardine Seebohn
The Glitter and the Gold by Consuelo Vanderbilt Balsan
The History of Photography by Beaumont Newhall
History of Art by H.W. Janson
The Britannica Encyclopedia of American Art
Stills by Snowdon
Just Looking by John Updike
Francis Bacon by L. Growing and Sam Hunter
Mainstreams of Modern Art by Canady
Modern Art
French

The Arts and Crafts Movement by Elizabeth Cumming

Not just satisfied with these books and publications, Cunanan kept numerous magazines. Some of these he bought at Pleasure Emporium in South Beach where the manager and a store clerk remembered seeing him – weeks earlier. Cunanan's collection showed that he searched for current events stories, and stories about himself.

He had kept the *Time Magazine* dated May 19, 1997 that contained an article about him titled "DEATH AT EVERY STOP, ONE MAN, STILL AT LARGE, MAY BE THE CONNECTION BETWEEN BRUTAL KILLINGS IN THREE DIFFERENT STATES."

As well, he kept the *Newsweek* dated May 19, 1997 with an article about him titled "A Lethal Road Trip."

Nothing in either of these articles left him standing as anything much more than a crazed, gay killer. Certainly, anyone remembering him in light of these writings would easily forget him.

Besides these two magazines, Cunanan had the tenth anniversary edition of *Detour*, *Surfer* and *National Enquirer*. Sexual stimulation came from five other magazines he had left behind: *Urge, Hunk, Jock, Honcho, Ram, Hard, Euroboy*, three editions of *XXX Showcase*, and five editions of *Manshots*. The books, magazines and newspapers gave an insight into both his eclectic mind and preoccupation with sex.

Cunanan left little else behind. Investigators found an Oster hair clipper and a Walgreen's receipt for a girdle he had bought on June 15, for which he paid $22.18. The girdle left investigators wondering if Cunanan had dressed as a woman when he left the place, but never did they find anything that indicated this had been true – no wig, make-up, false breasts, dresses, shoes.

But Cunanan had taken his clothes and any other item of his remaining possessions when he walked away from the place on July 12.

Chapter 45 ~ Ginny up the resources

Principals in the Cunanan case eventually came to view their work on the case in two periods: BGV and AGV – that is, Before Gianni Versace and After Gianni Versace. Although Lee had felt the hectic pace and immense pressure since May 7, hundreds more began to feel it on July 15 – AGV. The dribble of leads Lee and the Minneapolis team had received in the weeks BGV exploded into an unmanageable flow AGV. Headquarters FBI heard the explosion and moved quickly to do something about it. Kevin Rickett got the call.

Rickett's parents had come to the Twin Cities to visit him and his family. He decided to steal a few hours away from Cunanan to breakfast with them on Saturday morning. The noisy, busy Perkins restaurant raised his spirits, as did just taking a break from the case.

Just after ordering breakfast his cell phone rang. He saw that it was the FBI office and picked up. "Rickett here, what's up?"

"We have the Deputy Director on the line. He wants to talk to you," he heard. *The Deputy Director? Bill Esposito calling me? What gives?* "He said he couldn't get ahold of the ASAC, so he wants you. He asked for the FBI Case Agent."

"Ah, okay. Put him through," Rickett said. He heard a click. "Mr. Esposito, this is Special Agent Kevin Rickett."

"Oh yes. Listen, on this Cunanan case. By the end of the day I want you to set up 24-hour-a-day command posts in Minneapolis, San Francisco, San Diego, New York City, Chicago – and maybe more later," Esposito said. Miami had set up a Command Post on Thursday.

"Yes sir, I'll get it done," Rickett answered. *Today? Well, forget family time.*

All the principals, including Esposito, had begun doing two-a-day conference calls on July 17, so the Deputy Director kept a daily tab on progress in the case.

"And anything else you need, let me know," Esposito said.

"I will sir."

"I've got to run," Esposito said, and their conversation ended. Esposito also activated the FBI's Special Investigation Operations Center (SIOC) in Washington, D.C. to assist Minneapolis, and he turned on its toll-free tip line. They routed all their calls to Minneapolis.

"Um, I'm sorry, but I have to go," Rickett said to his parents.

"Will we see you later?"

"I'm not sure. Not today. I'll try to see you later, but it's a pretty big job," he said. As soon he said goodbye to his parents, he called Lee to explain what Esposito wanted from him. Lee was glad to hear it. It meant that the Cunanan case would receive the FBI's highest priority.

Rickett never again saw his parents during their visit, and he seldom saw his wife and children. For the duration of the case, he stayed at the Minneapolis Command Post (CP), going home briefly every other day to change clothes, shower and see his family.

Rickett had never before been solely responsible for a Command Post, save ordering them set up in other cities. Given his authority by the Deputy Director and a Top Ten case, he knew the agents in other cities would get on it right away. Many of them had already felt the same AGV pressure.

In Minneapolis, the FBI offices sit on the Eleventh Floor of a downtown office tower. A stuffy, 14' x 20' training room just down the hall from Coleen Rowley had been pre-configured, ready to transition into a command post. Several computers were set up on folding tables along one wall, with fax machines and copiers on a similar table across the room. Workstations were equipped on folding tables in the middle of the room. Several phones were connected, and a TV monitor set up. The FBI assigned additional Special Agents and their clerks to the command post. Within hours, Minneapolis' CP was operating while, at the same time, similar operations came on line at the other major city FBI offices. The Special Agents immediately began working leads that poured in after Versace's murder.

Minneapolis had six photos of Cunanan, and all looked so different from each other. *We're going to get a million phone calls on this because he looks like an average guy*, Rickett thought. He, like Lee, had begun to see Cunanan everywhere he went; it seemed like hundreds of times a day. Cunanan had no outstanding physical characteristics or anomalies. He looked like a million other guys.

"Get ready for a ton of sightings," Rickett told the others, "especially Hispanic or Asian; maybe even Middle Eastern. And some will be bizarre."

The FBI publicized its hotline phone number that rang in its D.C. headquarters. Agents there immediately forwarded all sighting calls to Minneapolis, either by fax or phone. Hot leads, described as those in which someone claimed Cunanan stood within their view or had just left, were called to Minneapolis. Clerks typed the leads as agents called them out to the FBI agent closest to the action. Usually before the paperwork could be faxed out, the agents were on their way.

Other, less urgent leads were faxed to the Minneapolis CP. These agents parceled out by their apparent urgency or priority to the agent closest to the lead. More than 2,000 leads poured in within days.

Lee read all the leads as they came in, searching for names or other clues that tied to his knowledge base. Arriving before 7:00 a.m. each morning, Lee sorted through 50-100 new leads that had come in during the night, and continued the routine all day long. When he saw something he thought was particularly hot, he walked to an office down the hall to call it out. With luck, he crawled into bed by 3:00 a.m. each morning, and then made it back to the Command Post by 7:00 a.m.

While Rickett ran the CP, Lee continued to contact the team of agents with whom he had worked since May. Especially on the west coast, Lee asked them all to re-interview key contacts, some for the third or fourth time. "If C is ever going to call any one, this is the time," Lee told them. But Cunanan never called anyone, even though the FBI began receiving calls from some who claimed otherwise.

Lee spent most of his time in the command post while the rest of the FTF worked out of the office down the street. He allowed himself one luxury, a quick meal at Cuzzy's where Mike the cook, one of the owners or a waitress greeted him with, "You ever gonna catch this guy?"For a Cuzzy's burger, Lee could suffer the worst of their reproaches.

Back on TV and sightings explode

The murder of Gianni Versace fueled America's Most Wanted desire to find Cunanan. Doing so would not only stop his murderous spree, but would win them rating points beyond speculation. They aired their fifth segment on Cunanan on July 19, four days after Versace's murder.

Lee knew there would be an explosion of sightings from this showing, as between the FBI and Miami Beach Police Department, more than 1,000 leads had already been received just since Versace's murder. At least this time around, Lee would have the help of the FBI's SIOC and 10 Command Posts.

AMW callers that night saw Cunanan in:

- A supermarket in Fort Lauderdale, Florida.
- A Daytona Beach bar.

- The Hilton Casino in Atlantic City, New Jersey.
- The American Video store in Madisonville, Kentucky.
- A white Ford Ranger on Portola Boulevard in Livermore, California.
- A bus headed for Princeton, New Jersey.
- The Shifting Sands Resort at Treasure Island, Florida on July 9 and 12.
- Westminster Village in Houston, Texas, walking to apartment 993.
- Galveston, Texas, and he had been there for two to three days.
- A McDonalds in Waycross, Georgia.
- Macy's, New York City, and then going down a stairway to the subway.
- The Philadelphia Airport at 2:00 a.m. near the luggage rack.
- The Woodmont in Coral Springs, Florida two or three weeks earlier.
- New Brunswick, carrying a "USA Today" and acting "funny."
- The crowd at a gay pride festival in Madison, Wisconsin.
- A campground in Shafter, California.
- A motor home, driving through Texas on his way to Mexico, traveling with a wealthy man.
- A gay club in Memphis.
- Denny's at Alamonte Springs, Florida.
- The Brick Plaza Shopping Center at Bricktown, New Jersey.
- A gold Mercedes, driving on I-40, but gave no location.
- The Mesabi Mall, in Hibbing, Minnesota.
- A brand new teal green Cadillac, driving north on I-495 in Maryland.
- Sun Prairie, Wisconsin, driving a blue Fiero.
- Filene's at a mall in South Portland, Maine (but had seen him on May 23 or 27).
- In Salem County, New Jersey, visiting a gay doctor, who the caller named.
- Las Vegas, with a homosexual friend of the caller.
- A Publix store in Atlanta, Georgia.
- A healing service at a church in Orlando.
- The Harlem Bar in Gloucester, New Jersey.
- A Chicago bar.

- The Red Neck Bar in Columbus, Ohio.
- Daytona Beach, driving west on I-92.
- The Ruby Tuesdays' restaurant in Raleigh, North Carolina.
- Kitchener, Ontario, where this couple picked him up and gave him a ride to their town. They talked about religion.
- Asheboro, North Carolina.
- The Great Expectations shop at the Edison Mall in Fort Myers, Florida. The caller claimed she had cut his hair the prior day.
- Panama City, Florida, walking along a walkway.
- The Merritt Square Mall at Cocoa Beach, Florida.
- At Delchamps Liquor Store in Ocean Springs, Mississippi.
- A swimming pool at the Budgetel Inn in Greens Point, Texas.
- The Dunkin' Donuts at Delray Beach, Florida.
- A Toyota driving north on Route 287 in New Jersey.
- The Market Basket at Seabrook, New Hampshire.
- The baseball stadium, watching the Florida Marlins game.
- A gay bar in Reno, a month earlier.
- The Las Vega airport.
- The Delchamps Liquor Store at Pensacola, Florida.
- An abandoned building in Detroit.
- A gay club on Rampart Street in New Orleans.
- The Rockaway Bar in Queens, New York.
- Secaucus, New Jersey, at the Hoolihans in Mill Creek on Route 3.
- Fort Lauderdale on a big yacht, just 30 minutes before calling AMW.
- The Exxon Station in Lambertville, New Jersey.
- A house staying with a fellow in San Marino, Florida.
- A Jeep Cherokee, driving on I-40 near Nashville.
- A Shell gas station in St. Petersburg, Florida, just 90 minutes earlier.
- The Sahara Pavilion at Las Vegas, receiving a total body waxing, including his private parts.
- A phone booth in Las Vegas, using a pay phone just 20 minutes earlier.
- The Caraway Hospital in Birmingham, Alabama, picking up another homosexual.

- The Grand Strand Hospital in Myrtle Beach, South Carolina, where he was being treated for extreme drunkenness.
- A payphone in Chula Vista, Florida.
- San Mateo, California at the Bay Meadows Race Track. The caller said Cunanan was there at that moment.
- A blue Taurus near Tampa, Florida.
- A shopping mall in Boca Raton, just 30 minutes earlier.
- A red Taurus, driving near Orlando with another man.
- A friend's house in Hollywood, Florida, and the caller named the friend.
- A dark Blazer driving on Mt. Diablo Boulevard Walnut Creek, California.
- The Little Champ Convenience Store in Jacksonville, just two minutes earlier!
- Dallas, reading a "People" magazine.
- The Tampa Bay mall.
- A car on Highway 89-A in Cottonwoods, Arizona.
- A bar in Redlands, California.
- The Los Angeles airport buying a ticket for Guam.
- Redlands, California where he followed the caller home and asked to use his telephone.
- Palm Springs, California where he partied with Cunanan at the Levi Leather Bar.
- Miami Beach at 14th and Ocean Drive, three blocks from Versace's. The caller thought he had seen him sometime around 5:00 p.m. that same day.
- The Family Dollar Discount Store in Fort Lauderdale.
- The Peruvian Restaurant in Miami Beach, eating with another guy.
- Memphis, Tennessee at a travel agency trying to buy a one-way ticket to Amsterdam, leaving from Tampa Bay.
- Montgomery, Alabama, driving a Cadillac with Florida plates.
- Alfareda, Georgia on the 16th, talking with one of the caller's friends.
- St. Augustine, Florida, at the L'il Champ Food Store where he bought a root beer from the caller.
- A Safeway Store in Annandale, Virginia. He came through the caller's lane.

- Camden Yards, the home of the Baltimore Orioles baseball team. The caller said that Cunanan bought his ticket off the internet and eventually wanted to get back to Florida, where he was "Going to see my man."
- The Treasure Bay Casino in Biloxi, Mississippi.
- The parking lot outside of CCC Counseling in Naples, Florida, where he stood arguing with a woman.
- A commuter train traveling from Miami to Palm Beach. Cunanan watched the news on a portable TV.
- A car in Alta Mote Springs, Florida.
- A car in Bellevue, Florida.
- The Gatehouse Green Apartments located on Broward Boulevard in Plantation, Florida.
- The courthouse at South Haven, Mississippi.
- A Publix Supermarket off 15th Avenue NE in Miami. The caller said he saw him just 35 minutes earlier and that Cunanan had been trying to make a photocopy of a passport.
- An art gallery in Lakeworth, Florida.
- A red SUV driving north on Route 29 near Warrington, Virginia.
- A Salvation Army facility in Hopetown, Florida.
- Fort Myers, Florida, where he was walking on Estera Boulevard.
- Hollywood, Florida, walking on Johnson Street and drinking a beer that was sticking out of a brown bag.
- The Sonesta Beach Hotel in Key Biscayne, Florida, but had seen him a week earlier.
- A bar in Wichita, Kansas.
- A car driving in Tampa Bay.
- Fort Lauderdale, going east on Park Drive.
- A Wal-Mart Store in Panama City, Florida.
- The Kenoer Restaurant in Tustin, California.
- The Winn-Dixie Grocery Store in Greenacres, Florida.
- A car on I-44 in Virginia Beach, Virginia.
- The Bottom Line bar, a gay club in Fort Myers, Florida.
- The Tara Vita Community near Phoenix, Arizona. A woman there felt sure she saw him the day before, and felt so upset about it that she cried the whole time she gave the report. She said that Cunanan had lived in the area previously, and she felt too frightened to call the police.

- A car driving east on US 50 near Ocean City, Maryland.
- The stylists' chair at the Cut-N-Run in Sacramento, California. The caller believed she had cut his hair there on Thursday.
- The Holiday Inn near Indian Creek in Miami Beach. The caller saw him that same day staying in a room on the 10th floor, and saw him in the lobby asking for change.
- Gainesville, Florida, only these sightings had occurred a month earlier.
- The Normandy Plaza Hotel in Miami Beach. The caller remembered seeing him two weeks earlier. By this time, of course, FBI and Miami Beach police had been all through the Normandy. The caller added that Cunanan had asked him how to get to Haulaver Beach, in Hollandale, Florida.
- The Publix supermarket on Hammocks Boulevard in Miami. Cunanan spoke Spanish and bought milk, cheese and ham.
- Miami Beach, walking south on Collins Avenue south of 2nd Street around Noon that day.
- Toledo, Ohio where a man picked Cunanan up. Cunanan had been hitchhiking from Wildwood, Illinois and was heading toward Iowa. The caller "bet his truck" that this had been Cunanan.
- A Miami Beach apartment on West 47th Street. Cunanan was staying with the caller and her friend.
- An office building in White Plains, New York.
- A McDonalds at 71st and Collins, across the street from the Normandy Plaza Hotel in Miami Beach. The caller saw him there a week earlier, with a white woman. He carried a backpack, rode a bike and had probably checked into a cheap hotel on Espanola Way near the Miami Beach Police Station.
- Tallahassee, Florida, dressed as a woman and claiming he would kill again. The cross-dressing Cunanan was working there as a prostitute and planned to leave the country.

There were a series of July 19 reports of Cunanan driving a black Pathfinder.

- Driving north near St. Louis, Missouri.
- Near Jacksonville, Florida.

- Driving north on I-95 near Stafford, Virginia.
- Washington, D.C., on the East-West Highway near 16th Street.
- A tow truck driver noted that he had pulled a black Pathfinder with Florida plates the day before.
- In South Carolina on July 15, sometime after 5:30 p.m.

And there were a series of callers who had information they thought would be useful.

- A Dallas caller said that Cunanan had a lover named Bob in the same town, and provided the phone number. He felt that Cunanan and Bob were meeting each other that same evening.
- The caller urged the FBI to check out Mama Leon's Deli in Southside, Florida. The caller felt sure Cunanan was dressing as a woman with silver hair, and he desperately wanted to get to Akron, Ohio.
- A psychic saw a mind picture of Cunanan driving a Cadillac near Tallahassee, Florida. He had a knife and was very dangerous, desperate. He was working as a gay prostitute and had no money. He had stolen money and a Rolex that he planned to sell. He was a very smart man who missed his mother.
- Another psychic, this one from California, saw Cunanan coming to the gay march in northern California where he would rig explosives. Cunanan would dress as a police officer or fire fighter. In his vision, he saw a hotel in Chinatown. Cunanan would do this because he is HIV positive and in a rage against gays; he wanted to become famous. Or, he might commit suicide.
- The caller's brother served time in a San Bruno, California jail and knew Cunanan, even knew where he was at the moment.
- An elderly Las Vegas woman wanted the FBI to know that Cunanan might dress as an old lady.
- A Scottsdale, Arizona caller felt certain Cunanan had been in her town on June 11, staying with a wealthy gay man. Cunanan said he came from Miami, spoke five languages and was in the U.S. illegally. She was really worried because a gay friend of hers was missing.

- This caller claimed he had just spoken on the phone to Cunanan for 92 minutes. The AMW clerk reported that the caller was very nervous, and so she doubted his veracity.
- The caller wanted AMW to know there was a Boston serial killer with the last name of DeSilva, and that he and Cunanan might be related.
- This west coast caller said he knew Cunanan from the warehouse district and last saw him at A Different Light and the Midnight Sun.
- A fellow Thrifty Drug employee called to say that he had worked with Cunanan in the early 1990s.
- The Norfolk, Virginia caller insisted he had lived with Cunanan for five months during 1989 and named an Oakland, California man and woman with whom they both lived.
- This San Diego caller mentioned that Cunanan knew a man named Fred Escone*. Lee found that Escone's name did not appear on his list.
- From Denver, a caller who had lived in Miami suggested that Cunanan would go to Orlando and hide out at the Parliament House, a gay resort, where he could achieve anonymity.
- A Cleveland, Tennessee caller worried that the murder of Marty Davis, a gay man killed after Versace, might somehow be connected to Cunanan.
- A caller suggested that Cunanan might be using the website at www.fur.com because it catered to "his sexual preference."
- Another caller advised that for sure, Cunanan would go to Key West, Florida because there was a huge gay population there, and they never watched the news. He suggested further that there was a lot of money to be had in Key West, and that Cunanan would never again go north.
- An anonymous caller from Columbia, South Carolina said that Cunanan had called him an hour earlier, and that he was heading into Columbia. He told the man that he was eventually heading to Myrtle Beach.
- A Memphis, Tennessee caller complained that a man named Charles had been stalking her for two years. She knew Charles to be a bi-sexual gigolo who traveled extensively. She felt sure that if the cops contacted Charles, he could help them find Cunanan.

- The Chief of Police in Pascagoula, Mississippi, called to request a photo. He believed he had Cunanan sitting in his jail.
- A male model suggested that Versace's real killer was a former lover, and that police check out the Ford Modeling Agency in Miami Beach for more information.

And for the first time, AMW sent copies of emails to Lee.

- A San Francisco woman suggested Cunanan might go to New Orleans.
- A Miami writer said he saw him on 15th and 70th the night before and Cunanan swore at him
- A Daytona Beach writer suggested Cunanan might dress as a woman.
- A Mississippi writer saw him driving a black SUV.
- A Phoenix writer said she had a "feeling" that Cunanan was making a circle of the United States that would end up in Phoenix and she knew someone who would be the last victim.
- A Canadian writer suggested that if Cunanan was really gay, he would probably cross-dress, so the cops should use K-9's to catch him.
- Another Canadian felt sure he saw Cunanan in Edmonton a week earlier, that he would be trying to cross to the U.S. through the woods and would be cross-dressing.
- One writer suggested a long string of internet website maneuvers that would result in downloading a picture of Cunanan. The writer felt sure that if it was not Cunanan, it certainly was a "twin to him."
- From Jacksonville, a writer expressed deep sorrow for not writing earlier. She felt she saw Cunanan early in June at an area shopping center. Cunanan was riding along in a black car with three others. The new Eckerd Drug Store had just opened that day, and she actually talked with Cunanan for a while: "He was ever so charming."
- A writer wanted to know if there was home video of Cunanan.
- From Coral Springs, Florida a woman who said she had worked with law enforcement on previous cases had an intuition that

Cunanan had been in Florida, and she had always been right about such things. She believed he was headed to New Orleans.

- This caller saw a comment in a chat room that Cunanan was a cross-dresser.
- Another caller had seen numerous Andrew Cunanan's on AOL. "Maybe he is carrying a laptop?"
- A San Francisco caller who identified himself by name claimed he saw Cunanan that day at Milpitas in the Great Mall. The caller felt scared.
- Steve wrote a long dissertation on his impressions. He had "felt" for some time that Cunanan had killed a person, wrapped him in strips of cloth, and left him in the woods in northern Florida. He had not closely followed the news about Cunanan, but did notice the Reese and Versace murders. Only July 18, he felt sure that Cunanan planned a long route by auto back to California, and named the cities through which he would pass. He felt that Cunanan would kill celebrities in each city, and finally, back home, would go after members of the gay community whom he believed had wronged him. He emphasized that these were only his impressions, and he felt foolish for sharing them.

Chapter 46 ~ Time to go home

By Sunday night, Twin Cities' media bosses knew they had exhausted their news teams and the time had come to bring them home, albeit reluctantly. Each reporter had a sense that something could break at any moment, but budgetary concerns and physical exhaustion dictated that they should leave.

Tom Houser, Esme Murphy and Bernie Grace, along with their camera operators, climbed on the plane. If anything broke, they could rely on network TV news to cover it. Each left feeling relieved but disappointed, not having the chance to see the arrest or demise of the vicious killer. They wondered where and when it would end, if Cunanan had somehow fled Miami, and if he would strike again in another city.

Chris Grave's skin was crimson red from sunburn, her milk had dried up and she missed her baby Emma. She looked forward to getting home. As she flew back to the Twin Cities, the *Star-Tribune* sent Anne O'Connor to relieve her, just in case something broke.

Cunanan, a "model" citizen?

As reporters flew back home, an Atlanta, Georgian named Steven Bryant* called the FBI hotline. He felt certain he had spotted Cunanan in a series of advertisements in a 1991 edition of the "International Male" clothing catalog. Finding the edition, he looked carefully at the pictures to make sure the man in the ad really was Cunanan. Armed with his conviction, Bryant had contacted the FBI to provide them with this *critical* lead.

FBI Special Agent Barry Witrick met with Bryant and viewed the ad. Bryant insisted that Witrick take the magazine with him, wanting only to be sure that the FBI would return it when it had finished its investigation of the matter.

Witrick returned to his office and dictated the official memo, concluding with his well reasoned, but less than profound decision: "Atlanta is conducting no further investigation at Winder, Georgia." Some time later, the FBI returned Mr. Bryant's magazine with a thank you note from the SAC.

More press boredom ahead

Back home, Chris Graves exchanged Miami's humid heat for Minnesota's humid heat and did so without complaint. The newsroom chaos had escalated. *No rest for the wicked!* she laughed as she settled in at her messy workstation.

"Annie, how's it going out there?" she asked when her peer called from Miami.

"Hot, humid, and crazy," Anne said.

"Tell me about it."

"But I got a great hotel, right on the beach," she said. "I imagine I'll spend some time there."

As Anne O'Connor traveled to Miami, she had felt the same frustration as Graves had on her trip. *So what am I supposed to write? Versace is dead and buried. Cunanan is hiding.*

O'Connor, like Graves, hated the heat and humidity, but at least had packed light clothes. She fully expected her days to be occupied walking on the beach, waiting for the next development which, she knew, could be hundreds of miles away in another city. She could not imagine that any new Miami Beach story was left to be told, given the media horde had combed the area since July 16.

She reasoned that the FBI would have quickly shut down Cunanan's avenues of escape as best they could, but from Miami Beach, there were still dozens of ways to flee. For all anyone knew, Cunanan had done just that.

O'Connor hated staged news conferences where all the "reporters" waited like cattle for their daily feed. FBI and police spokesmen periodically paraded to a bank of microphones as half-asleep camera operators scurried to take up their positions. Alongside, shoved in between TV cameras, stood a remnant of the media horde, all trying to pick up anything worth reporting. O'Connor saw that far too many of the members of the reporter pack were satisfied with this press conference pabulum, but to her, it was not reporting. Reporting meant digging out stories from original sources, and here in Miami Beach she felt herself a failure. She meant to keep pushing for a scoop in between sunbathing trips.

Face-to-face conference

Headquarters FBI decided it needed to stave off charges that they were not doing enough to apprehend Cunanan. They knew that Lee Urness and Kevin Rickett, along with hundreds of Special Agents in nearly every state had worked diligently to find the killer, but they also knew he remained at large. The best remedy, HQ felt, was to bring the principal investigators to Quantico for a conclave.

Paul Murray, in New Jersey, declared the idea dead on contact. He sent a member of the New Jersey State Police in his stead, and he let Lee know about his decision.

"Even B.S.U. wants to help now," Murray laughed, referring to the Behavioral Science Unit that had turned Lee down when he asked for help during May.

"Well, I'm not going," Lee told Murray. He told Kevin Rickett the same thing. "I don't have time to go."

"Maybe I should go," Rickett suggested.

"No, you're needed here. We've got a guy to catch," Lee said. "We can send somebody." They sent Special Agent Greg Jones who had been assigned to them during May, the one Lee had sent to monitor AMW airings.

For the next two days, agents and cops from ten jurisdictions plus FBI headquarters did their best to dissect everything they knew about the case. They hoped that their collective reasoning would result in a catch, but it was not to be.

Conferencing again

At 10:00 a.m., July 22, Special Agents from nine major cities joined with FBI Headquarters officials, including Deputy Director Bill Esposito, for their regular conference call.

Miami reported that they had been tracking phone calls made from pay phones near the Normandy Plaza Hotel and were rechecking all other leads. Sylvester Stallone and Madonna were both due in town, and Miami had security worries, fearful that Cunanan may have chosen one of them as another celebrity victim.

San Diego had acquired a VCR tape Cunanan made in Hawaii. It could help further identify his voice and personal characteristics. Maryann Cunanan had requested making a public statement to clear up some of what she saw as media misstatements. Agents had hidden her away at Miramar to protect her from reporters who had been stalking her. She wanted to move somewhere with her daughter, Gina. Someone asked about Cunanan's lifestyle, prompting remarks that he might try to flee to New Orleans, and that while he had, in the past, shaved off his body hair as a fashion statement, it was unlikely he would dress like a woman.

San Francisco reported that Gina, Andrew's sister, did not want to go on TV to make a plea. Far too emotional, she said.

Los Angeles reported that Liz Cote had prepared a statement and it had been faxed to headquarters. Liz had been Cunanan's closest friend since junior high. Agents had interviewed Santana Romero*, another long-time Cunanan friend. Romero claimed that Cunanan had called him before Versace's murder.

"He was nervous and agitated," Romero claimed. Cunanan needed help getting a passport so he could flee to the Philippines. As Lee heard this, he held his tongue, but not his mind. *What bunk! Cunanan never called anyone.* Since Versace's death, dozens of such claims had turned up.

Romero listed several other names that he claimed were Cunanan's friends. Lee listened and wrote them down, checking them against his Rapid Start file.

In some strange twist of logic, Romero claimed that Cunanan was not really gay, but rather, he was a prostitute. Cunanan had asked him which United States airport was the busiest. "O'Hare," and Romero claimed Cunanan planned to fly there. He never did, and Lee considered this to be bunk, too.

San Francisco jumped in again. An informant claimed that Cunanan was obsessed with a woman named Laura Koski, and they planned to get a trap and trace on her phone. The same informant believed that Cunanan could have contact with Gary Elly. Cunanan might even be hiding nearby. Agents had planned a trap and trace on Elly's phone as well.

Chicago reported on their investigation of Lee Miglin's gold coins. Duke Miglin claimed his dad had seven gold coins and three 1- ounce gold bars with serial numbers; the word "Credit Suisse" had been embossed on them. All of these were missing, Duke claimed. Duke said that Miglin's company had given them to employees as a bonus, and they were checking on the serial numbers.

New York agents had asked for help from Baltimore agents. They were doing an internet search of the email address <u>ACUNANAN86@AOL.COM</u>, an address a west coast friend had claimed Cunanan used to write to him in recent days. A Pennsylvania caller claimed that Cunanan planned to kill Elton John at an upcoming concert. They were doing a house search at that moment on East 64th Street, following up on a Cunanan sighting. New York hosted a huge fashion show at that time, so police had increased security.

Philadelphia agents requested that Miami send the evidence seized from Reese's red pick-up truck to FBI headquarters. They needed good fingerprints for purposes of building their case against Cunanan.

Kevin Rickett reported that America's Most Wanted had come to Minneapolis that day to tape a segment for their next show. Rickett urged Miami to send the magazines found at Cunanan's motel room to headquarters.

The agents agreed that Liz Cote's offer to do a press conference was a good idea and the sooner the better. They expected another America's Most Wanted segment the following Saturday. Esposito wanted to know if there was anything else headquarters could do to help.

"Raise the reward money," Rickett said.

"How much?"

"100 thousand dollars," Rickett answered.

"You got it," the Deputy Director responded.

Lee disagreed with this approach and urged them to wait. "Let's see what happens," he said. They agreed to wait, and Cunanan spared them raising the dollar amount.

Check foreign ports

FBI and local police had done a thorough inventory of everything found in Cunanan's Normandy Plaza Hotel room. Yet, on July 22, one of the housekeepers remembered another fact she believed would be helpful.

"I saw that he had a passport, but it was not in the name 'Cunanan,'" she told investigators. "It was that name he used to check in."

"Kurt Demars?" the agent asked.

"Yes, that is it. And I think it was a French passport. Could that be right?" she asked.

"It could be. Thank you for your help," the agent said.

Lee had contacted the French Embassy as early as May 5, and doubted that Cunanan would ever attempt to leave the country. Still, the lead demanded immediate action.

A photo array and all pertinent information about Cunanan were sent overnight to the Paris LEGAT. To ensure that Cunanan never slipped into the country under an alias, the LEGAT planned to run a check for passports issued to Andrew Phillip Cunanan, Drew Cunningham, Andrew Phillip De-Silva, and Kurt Matthew Demars.

Cunanan, however, never went to Paris. During his two-month Miami Beach cloister, Cunanan never ventured more than a few miles from the Normandy Plaza Hotel, and went nowhere near an airport.

Chapter 47 ~ Could Cunanan go down shooting?

Lee's edginess, Versace's killing and the hyperactivity of east coast media told Lee that Cunanan's days were numbered. Soon the FBI or a local cop would find him. *Would there be a shootout? It wouldn't be much of one; he's only got four bullets left. Did he find another gun somewhere? Doubtful, unless he tripped across one. He'll never kill again just to get a gun. But he killed Bill Reese for a ride.*

In 27 years of law enforcement, Lee had drawn his weapon numerous times. He had never been in a shootout and had, in fact, only once even fired at a crook. A shootout with Cunanan would be nothing like those in the old days before SWAT teams had been invented. Lee's mind drifted back to stories he had heard about the morning of February 6, 1956 and a small town liquor store.

The telephone next to Douglas County Sheriff Bennie Urness' bed rang at 4:00 a.m.

"Sheriff, somebody's broken into the Garfield liquor store," a town resident reported.

Before he could say "thank you," Bennie started pulling his pants on and reached for a shirt. He dialed his deputy, his son Howard.

"Get up," Bennie said. "I'm waking Luther now. We'll pick you up and let's go." Bennie woke up Luther Urness, Howard's brother, home on a college break, and told him to get ready. Luther was also a deputy sheriff.

Within minutes, Bennie and Luther headed out into the frigid Minnesota winter air and jumped into the 1956 Buick that the sheriff provided the county. They picked up Howard, who lived a few blocks away. Bennie drove 100 miles per hour toward Garfield, just seven miles away.

"I'm turning out the lights," Bennie said when they were two miles out of town. He meant to catch the burglars, not scare them off. Driving 100 miles per hour in the dark was just an occupational necessity.

They rolled to a stop in front of the liquor store and turned off the engine. The three cops started to get out of the car when they saw movement at the store's side door. Within seconds, bullets from a .38 WCF pistol and a .45 flew at them, one of which hit the Buick's front bumper, leaving a gaping hole in the grill. Another flew dangerously close to Bennie's shoulder.

Howard raised his .38 and let rip in the direction of the gunfire, while Bennie ran for the front door. Luther ran to the back.

One of Howard's slugs hit two of the men in their right shoulders, and they ran back into the building. There they faced Bennie, his automatic shotgun raised at eye level.

"Drop your weapons or I'll blast your head off!" Bennie ordered. The men immediately complied.

The third burglar ran toward the back of the building. As he came around the corner, Luther ordered him to drop his weapon, and when he refused, Luther unloaded one round from his .12-guage shotgun, hitting Clarence Salmey just below the knee; he went down.

Bennie, Howard and Luther loaded two of the crooks into the Buick and sent Salmey to the hospital in Alexandria where Andrew Urness, Bennie's brother, guarded him. Bennie booked Clement Ransom, the leader of the gang, and his sidekick John Hoffman, into the country jail. Their shoulder injuries were only surface wounds, but enough to stop them. The only injury suffered by the cops was a huge hole in the Buick's grill and a disrupted night's sleep. They felt fortunate.

Ransom, Salmey and Hoffman had met the Urness family; they lost.

Early the next day, investigators needed to collect evidence at the crime scene. Bennie's criminal complaint had listed burglary and assault with a weapon.

Ransom had quickly come to respect Bennie Urness. "I just was shooting at his headlights to scare him away. But he doesn't scare easily." At 60 plus years of age, not much scared Bennie.

Even though three sheriffs witnessed the robbery in action and stopped it, securing a conviction required careful processing of the crime scene. They needed all the evidence they could muster to put these three career criminals in prison for life.

Bill Morris, a retired FBI agent working for the Minnesota BCA, began his assessment of the crime scene. Howard assisted him. While they were doing this, 10-year old Lee Urness went to the jail where he visited with Clement Ransom. Bars separated the boy from the man as they talked.

"Kid, don't ever get on this side of the bars," Ransom told Lee. Ransom had told Lee that all three men were ex-cons.

"No sir, I won't," Lee answered.

"So that deputy's your daddy?"

"Yes sir, he is," Lee said.

"Well, we thought he fired a machine gun at us the way he fired so fast. That's why we gave up right away," he laughed. Howard had fired six rounds, emptying his gun.

Agent Morris collected evidence at the liquor store. There he found bolt cutters, a sledgehammer and chisels, among other burglary tools. He spotted a pint bottle of whiskey wrapped in cotton in a box. It had only a few ounces of the yellow liquid in the bottom. He thought it strange that burglars would drink on the job; nevertheless, he put the bottle in his back seat next to the burglary tools.

Morris drove back to Alexandria on the worn, bumpy pavement of Highway 52. As he drove, he kept thinking about the bottle of whiskey. *Why a bottle of whiskey? That makes no sense. Unless it's not whiskey!* The realization hit him like a 30 below arctic blast. *That's nitro in there!!!*

Morris slowed to 10 miles per hour. His hands tightened on the steering wheel. In moments, his knuckles turned white. In the rear-view mirror he saw Howard Urness driving behind him.

Howard, frustrated by Morris' slow pace, finally pulled alongside and stared at him, wondering what had gotten into the man. *Is he sick or something?* He saw Morris shaking his head back and forth, his two hands holding tight to the steering wheel, positioned at 11:00 and 1:00. Morris stared ahead, refusing to make even make eye contact with Howard.

Howard dropped back and stayed behind Morris as they drove into town. He felt sure that Morris had lost his mind. He watched Morris' car pull slowly up in front of the jail. The door opened slowly and Morris got out. To Howard, Morris looked like a man suffering intense pain. Morris walked gingerly away from his car after closing the door softly, but not latching it.

"What was that all about? You all right?" Howard asked as the white-faced man came toward him.

"Nitro," Morris said. "There's nitro glycerin in my back seat." He walked passed Howard. "Your daddy got any real whiskey in there?"

Lee loved listening to stories like this one often retold by Bill Morris. Lee had long known that arresting cops always run great risks. Morris showed him even the follow up at a crime scene carried its own hazards.

As Lee replayed that scene, he wondered how Cunanan would go down. Out of money, and convinced that he was still somewhere in Miami Beach, Lee hoped Cunanan would not take anyone else to Hell with him.

High tech touching

Leads continued to pour into the Command Post. Lee searched them carefully, hoping to spot the one that would end the chase.

During the morning of July 23, an anonymous caller, who identified himself only by his email address and appearance – black, gay "queen" – contacted the FBI hotline to tell them about a gay man he knew, Aaron Donaldson*, from Washington State. Donaldson, he said, had been exchanging email with Cunanan for quite some time, the last email arriving at 9:00 p.m. the night before, on July 22. The self-employed computer consultant claimed to know Cunanan as Andy DeSilva. Donaldson said he knew Cunanan from his days in San Diego and Los Angeles, and since moving to Seattle, had become a volunteer with the Lambert House.

"I saw Donaldson send the July 22 email," the caller claimed. "He used the internet at a public library computer."

"Why do you think he wrote to Andrew Cunanan?" the FBI agent asked.

"Because he called him by name, and had said that he thought Cunanan was crazy for using the internet this way," he answered.

"Thanks for your call," the agent said. "And again, your name is…"

"No sir, I can't tell you that," the caller said.

"Okay. Well, we'll get right on it." The agent said good-bye and wrote the lead report.

FBI agents immediately tracked down Donaldson, and set leads in San Diego to verify other aspects of the story. Since the caller claimed that Donaldson knew Cunanan's' current address, the lead had immediate concern.

Lee reviewed the lead report and shook his head in disbelief.

"Cunanan doesn't know anything about computers," Lee said. None of the magazines Cunanan left behind, or his notes, credit cards, bills or interviews with those who knew him indicated that Cunanan used computers. During 1997, email had still remained a mystery to many people, and finding access to a computer to spend this amount of time with a guy he did not know made no sense. If Donaldson had received an email marked 9:00 p.m. PDT, July 22 from Cunanan, it would have meant that Cunanan sent it at midnight, if he still hung around Miami.

"Nope, this is not our guy," Lee said. "It might be someone claiming to be Cunanan, or maybe our caller has something against this Donaldson guy. But I'm telling you, C does not use computers."

Chapter 48 ~ July 23, 1997

Minneapolis, MN

Lee walked into the Command Post that morning where he was met by Coleen Rowley.

"I've got a surprise for you," she said smiling.

"Surprise? What surprise?"

"You're on TV today. America's Most Wanted is here, waiting for you," she explained.

"No way. Aw come on, you can't be serious," Lee protested. "Tell me you're kidding."

"No, not kidding. FBI approved it, and you're the star," she laughed as she led him to a room where a TV crew waited.

All Lee wanted to do was catch Cunanan, but in this he had no choice. He doubted that this interview would make a difference. They needed a break in the case, not a camera crew in the place.

"Special Agent Urness," a young TV reporter greeted him as he walked into the conference room.

"No, I'm not FBI. I'm with the Minnesota BCA, and the Fugitive Task Force," he corrected her.

"Okay, well I'm Barb Schmidt with America's Most Wanted. We want to do a story about the inner workings of the Fugitive Task Force and the Command Post in this Cunanan case. Coleen Rowley tells me I need to talk to you." Donna Brant had never warned Lee about this interview. He made a mental note to give her hell.

Schmidt explained the process, and it began with powdering Lee's face. "Your forehead is shiny, too," she said as she finished the bridge of his nose.

"Now, look at me when you talk, not at the camera. Just ignore them," she ordered.

"Yes ma'am, no problem," he said, trying to loosen her up. *What's with her? Shorts too tight or something?*

The questions began. The room got warm and Lee fidgeted.

"Cut!" Schmidt said to the camera operators more than once during the interview. "I need to powder you again," she said to Lee. She picked up the powder puff and began dabbing his forehead.

"You do windows, too?" he teased. She never broke a smile.

453

The camera crew moved to the Command Post where they filmed the team going about their work.

Finally, the TV crew packed up and left.

"Remind me again why I hate the newsies," Lee said to Rickett as he wiped the powder off his nose. He hated wasting time, and to him, this interview would do nothing to help catch Cunanan, and that was the only thing about which he cared. "The next time I talk to the media I want it to be in front of C's cage or casket," he snarled.

The next time he talked to the media, Lee came as close as he ever would to Cunanan's casket. And it pleased him.

July 23, 1997, all across the country
The last conference call

On July 23, as had become daily procedure since the Versace murder, agents in nine cities and officers from FBI headquarters sat down for a conference call. None of them knew that it would be their last on the Cunanan case. At the same time, officers from several cities were still in Quantico, sitting across the table, working to piece together all known facts.

Minneapolis reported that 1,143 calls had already been entered in Rapid Start. These calls, of course, did not include those not yet reported from other jurisdictions, and especially from Miami Beach, which was snowed under by hundreds of their own. Lee reported that America's Most Wanted planned to do a major feature during their July 26 airing.

Seattle had a lead on the man who claimed to be emailing Cunanan, including one the prior night. Another caller had information that Cunanan claimed a friendship with Debbie Harry, a singer in the girl band "Blondie."

Headquarters reported that Liz Cote would tape an appeal to Cunanan to give himself up. They planned to distribute it to the media later that day. They also suggested that FBI Director Louis Freeh, during his regular Thursday press conference, could disseminate any needful information.

Miami reported that the gold coin recovered at Cash on the Beach had been positively linked to Miglin.

San Diego reported that Maryann Cunanan planned to leave the area on July 25, but they would keep in contact with her. They suggested that a single office with a computer squad be assigned to follow up leads sent through the FBI internet site. The next weekend would be the big San Diego gay pride celebration, they said, but there was no indication Cunanan would attend.

New York had contacted all of Cunanan's relatives in that area. They were tracking an email received by a New York TV station in which someone claiming to be Cunanan said he would be in the New York City area; that is where his next victim resided. They had already traced the email address and were contacting the owner. They discussed how they should handle false email leads.

Los Angeles planned to have the Liz Cote interview taped that same afternoon. Tom Schell, a retired ABC TV reporter, agreed to do the interview. They had set a trap and trace on Cote's phone line, in case Cunanan called her.

Chicago planned to enter the serial numbers of all the gold coins and bars reported as stolen from Miglin's house into the NCIC database. They hoped that all pawnshops would do a search of their records for the missing gold (none ever reported back).

San Francisco planned to talk with Gary Elly about how Cunanan would view Liz Cote's plea, whether he would see it as a police ploy. Numerous friends of Cunanan had reported that they received phone calls from individuals who represented themselves as FBI agents or cops and wanted statements from them, but these "agents" left no call back numbers. It appeared that they were reporters looking for a scoop.

FBI Director Freeh had urged Bill Esposito to hold a press conference to announce that the reward for Cunanan had been increased to $100,000. Lee argued against such an announcement; Esposito never did announce it.

Neither Boston nor Philadelphia had anything new to offer.

"Well," Lee said, once the conference call ended, "let's look into the crystal ball and see if Andy is there." Lee saw a stack of leads, a well-oiled investigative effort and endless hours of work; but he never saw a houseboat in Miami Beach.

July 23, 1997, South Miami Beach, FL

Andrew Cunanan knew the end of his life would come soon. The man he had once known, the happy life-of-the-party Andrew, had been dead for nearly three months. The FBI Fugitive Task Force had cut off all means of escape. And with the murder of Gianni Versace, the gay community had turned against him, demanding swift justice. He knew that when the cops found him he could not let himself be arrested. He could never survive in a prison. If the cops came, a shootout would ensue. With four bullets in his gun, he could only lose, and the enraged cops would fill his beautiful body with lead; they would destroy his good looks. He could not let that happen to him. He needed to execute his own judgment on the killer Cunanan.

Wearing only his white boxer shorts, he walked into the spacious second floor master bedroom of the houseboat, his bare feat padding across the short-napped tan carpet. He looked at the queen-sized bed, saw the thick light blue comforter lying in disarray, clinging to the brown sheets as if trying to keep from falling off the bed.

The model-sized tail end of a pink Cadillac that served as a radio hung on the wall next to the bed, just above a nightstand. Two prints of paintings by the deceased gay artist William Gatewood hung on the wall above the bed. Gatewood had died of complications related to AIDS. Some people speculated that Cunanan had AIDS, and that is why he started killing, in some sort of attack on the gay lifestyle that had supposedly condemned him to death. But he did not have AIDS.

He held the Taurus in his hand.

He had left the binoculars downstairs.

Just before 3:30 p.m., Cunanan heard footsteps on the deck. He looked out the window and saw a red Ford pickup truck parked across the nearby boulevard, but could not see the driver. He heard footsteps in the hallway leading to the front door downstairs. He knew he had locked the deadbolt, and at least twice, police had knocked the door. Perhaps this one would go away, too, though it mattered little. The stash of stale crackers and nuts had run out. He had no more food or potable water.

Fernando Carreira, and his wife Luz Rodriguez, stood at the door. Carreira worked as the boat's caretaker. The old 50' x 32' two-story boat was no longer seaworthy, and had a tendency to leak. Carreira's duties included checking on the boat twice a week to make sure the pumps were working.

Carreira noticed a light on inside the boat and saw that the curtains on the west side sliding glass had been closed. He felt sure that they were open the last time he had been at the boat.

Carreira stuck his key in the bottom door lock and discovered it was unlocked, but the door would not open. He saw that the dead bolt had been set, something he never did because it was difficult to unlock. In his frustration as he jiggled his key in the deadbolt lock, he yelled at Luz and pounded on the door.

Cunanan stood at the top of the stairs, unsure of what to expect once the door opened if, in fact, it did at all. He heard the bolt slide and saw the doorknob turn. Fear enveloped him as he held the Taurus close, wondering what might happen next.

Carreira pushed the door open and glanced in. He saw that the loveseat and TV were set at an odd angle, as though made into a barricade. A pair of brown sandals lay next to the chair. He knew something was wrong, and felt sure someone had been on the boat, though he had no idea if they were still there. He reached into his belt and withdrew his .38 revolver, holding it out in front of him. "Hello!" he yelled.

Cunanan stood staring down at this unknown man carrying a gun, who slowly worked his way into the boat. Was he a cop? Was he the boat's owner?

Cunanan needed money. He needed a ride. He needed another gun. Fernando Carreira had all three. But Cunanan never moved toward Carreira and the man never saw him staring down from the open stairwell.

Cunanan walked to the bed and sat down on the right side. For a moment, he stared at the Taurus.

He reached out his left hand and grabbed the top of a bed pillow, propping it up against the great sweeping ivory-colored headboard. He laid his head back against the pillow and rested his shoulders in its middle. It felt good, warm and comfortable. At another time, he would be welcoming a young blond boy into his arms.

The air conditioner in the wall to his left sent cool air across his body. He shivered, but not from the breeze.

He laid his left arm alongside his body and with his right hand; he raised the Taurus toward his face. He stared at the barrel once more. Only one decision remained, and that was the best entry point.

He opened his mouth and pointed the barrel of the gun inside, took one deep breath and squeezed the trigger.

The Taurus exploded violently, sending a slug screaming into his cranium, and there it lodged. The pressure blew out his eardrums, sending blood and tissue flying, attaching itself to the headboard and bed linens. His arm fell down to the right, and his right hand rested on top of the fly of his boxer shorts with the gun underneath. His hand still clutched the Taurus's grip. His body went limp. Blood flowed from his mouth, nose and ears, running down his hairy chest and soaking his boxer shorts.

Andrew Cunanan had sewn the last stitch of his deadly design.

What the...

Startled by the noise of gunfire and fearful that it was directed at them, Carreira and his wife ran from the houseboat and hid behind the pickup truck. He reached for his cell phone and called his son; the cell phone screen blinked back 3:30 p.m. at him. Carreira and his wife sat waiting while the son called police. He had no clue who was on the houseboat, but someone inside had just shot a gun, and he wanted no part of it.

Within minutes, Officer Andrew Kuncas arrived. Carreira told him about the gunshot, but no one had come off the boat since then. Kuncas told him to move up onto Collins and wait.

Miami Beach Sgt. Gary Schiaffo stood at a drycleaners in Miami Beach when he heard about shots fired at a potential burglary on or near a houseboat on 52nd and Collins. He remembered something about a Cunanan sighting near there, and grabbing his clean clothes, headed to the scene. When he arrived, Kuncas and other officers were diverting traffic on Collins. Schiaffo ordered the street shut down between 52nd and 56th, creating huge headaches for Miami Beach commuters who had only one other north/south option, and that lay on a narrow residential street on the west side of the canal.

Schiaffo found Carreira and heard his story, then called Sgt. George Navarro. Navarro assigned him as lead investigator.

Schiaffo assigned Officer Mike Jaccarino to guard the door. Schiaffo labeled Jaccarino as "a bull dog, and I told him no one, absolutely no one gets on the boat without my permission."

A bevy of Miami Beach Police Officers, the FDLE and FBI agents soon followed. Everyone braced for action, but the decision of when and how to go in had to wait for a plan.

Schiaffo realized that anyone still on the houseboat would have an easy swim across the canal, diving off the back of the boat. He called for squads to watch the west side of the canal. Then he ordered that two perimeters be set up in front of the houseboat, first at the closest curb on the west side of Collins, and then on the east curb across the eight-lane street.

Within minutes, FBI agents, Miami Beach police, FDLE agents and the Miami Beach SWAT team had assembled at the site. They were ready to board the boat.

Frustration turns to a long vigil

Police officers started shutting down Collins at about the same time that a frustrated Anne O'Connor had prepared to leave her hotel. She wore a pair of sandals and a light-colored sleeveless sundress to fend off the oppressive heat and humidity. She wanted to hit the streets to do some real reporting, and had decided to drive to the Normandy Plaza Hotel. She hoped to get lucky and find something missed by all the others.

As she began to drive away, she noticed the police closing down Collins Avenue, and her news nose told her something had happened. She parked her car and followed the police down closer to the boat docks. She managed to get inside the first perimeter where she began her vigil.

"Chris," she said as she dialed the *Star-Tribune* newsroom on her cell phone, "something big is happening here, but the police aren't saying anything. See if anything's going on."

"Where are you?" Graves asked, already dialing up her internet news sources.

"I'm near some boat docks inside the police lines," she bragged.

"Fantastic! Stay there. I'll get back to you as soon as I can," she said.

Graves found nothing about the incident on the internet. She scanned the TV networks and saw nothing. She called Lee and got no response. No one at the paper could find anything going on. She called O'Connor back.

"Annie, I can't find anything at all. What do you see?"

"Just a lot of cops and FBI standing around near a houseboat. And they are saying nothing," she said. She had remained quiet, trying to eavesdrop. She felt, though, that this was big. Even if it was a false sighting, as long as it was Cunanan-related, she finally had a story to write from her bird's-eye view. She planted herself on the spot, letting nothing drag her away until she knew for sure what the cops were doing.

Soon after, the other remnants of the Versace media horde got wind that something had happened up on Collins and raced north. They set up in a parking lot next to the Imperial House on the east side of Collins Avenue, but were confined to report from the sidewalks across the street.

We might have something

Coleen Rowley ran down the hall to the Command Post with the news. "Miami thinks they could have him on a houseboat," she said breathlessly. "They got a call near Versace's mansion."

Lee paged Keith Evans and it took very little time to get a response.

"Lee, you'll want to take this call now," Rickett said as he answered the phone.

"Urness here," Lee said.

An agent in the Miami Command Post had called. "Keith Evans asked me to call. We don't know if there's anyone in there. All we have is the report of the caretaker who says he heard a shot. The squads are on their way."

"Where's this houseboat?" Lee asked.

"On Collins Avenue, a few miles north of Versace's."

"Sounds promising," Lee said.

"You'll never believe this, but just this week, two cops had checked out a Cunanan sighting near the houseboat during a canvass of the area," the agent said.

"Okay," Lee said, measuring his answer. If he had kept a clicker to count all the Cunanan sightings during the past 11 weeks, this one would be at least somewhere near 3,500. So as much as he hoped it was *the* sighting, he refused to get too excited. "It does sound possible. Keep me posted."

"Wouldn't it be nice if this ended it?" Lee said to Rickett as he hung up the phone.

Tension in the Command Post had run high each day since the Versace murder, as the frustrated agents continued to chase down hundreds of new sightings. This news from Miami brought some temporary relief and hope to the exhausted crew.

Everyone in the Command Post understood that it could be hours before any of them knew whether this was the final act, or if the guy on the boat was just another nobody. "Hell, maybe all the caretaker heard was a cork pop in a champagne bottle," Lee chuckled.

Lee returned to his stack of paperwork, reviewing other leads, writing notes, checking records, but kept an ear tuned to the Command Post chatter. Lee had trained himself not to get excited at any lead, until the final one when a medical examiner had officially identified Cunanan. He remembered that a short time earlier, everyone had been convinced that agents cornered Cunanan in Yosemite, and it turned out to be a false sighting. Still, the location gave this one a measure of credibility – south Florida, close to Versace's mansion.

Liz pleads for Andrew to do the right thing

Veteran ABC News Network Reporter Tom Schell had law enforcement friends in high places and many cities. Even though he had retired from ABC in 1992, he regularly got calls from reporters almost every time the word "FBI" adjoined a current case.

Schell recalled with pleasure a parting compliment he received from one of his FBI agent friends. The man approached him and said, "We don't respect you."

"Oh?" the somewhat surprised reporter answered.

"We trust you. Do you know the difference?" the agent asked.

"Yes," Schell answered. It had taken him 30 years to develop that level of trust and he worked hard to protect it.

When the Los Angeles FBI office called during one of those difficult post-Versace days, he said "yes" without hesitation. They had won an agreement from Elizabeth "Liz" Cote, Cunanan's best friend – perhaps only real friend. Liz had agreed to tape an appeal to Cunanan to give himself up, and the FBI wanted the taped segment to be of professional quality. They asked Schell to do the interview. Once taped, the FBI planned to send the video to every possible media outlet for distribution, hoping that Cunanan would see it.

At the time Tom Schell interviewed Liz, Cunanan hid on a houseboat in Miami Beach. The dead Cunanan never saw the interview, though it did air on the evening of July 23. Because police authorities in Miami Beach had told the media that there was no body on the houseboat, Liz' plea still seemed valid and it played on national news. Even in this bizarre order of events, Cunanan seemed to be minutes ahead of the police.

"The Andrew Cunanan I know is not a violent person," Cote said, looking directly into the camera. "The Andrew Cunanan, who is the godfather of my children is not a thief. The Andrew Cunanan I know is close to God and knows that whatever has happened, He will always forgive. Andrew, wherever you are, please stop what you are doing."

Liz knew the old Cunanan well. She knew nothing about the new, violent amoral man.

Liz's plea literally fell on deaf ears, caused by the explosive blast of a .40 caliber bullet. Her plea was too late to save Cunanan's wretched life from its final self-destruction. Certainly, Lee felt, Hell had reserved a place for his kind.

So why are we waiting?

The Miami Beach SWAT team had assembled. Sgt. Schiaffo felt it was time to fire the tear gas and get ready to board the houseboat. But "higher ups" somewhere had insisted that they wait for the Miami-Dade Special Response Team (SRT). That meant standing around. Standing around made the cops, media and FBI agents everywhere nervous.

Time crept along slowly. Anne O'Connor's cell phone battery finally went dead and her body begged for food and relief. She thought about walking back to the car, but it was blocks away, and she did not want to lose her spot. Still there was no news. She had begun to think of her location as "my territory," and meant to stay there as long as it took. Then she saw a policeman approaching.

"Ma'am, who are you?" he asked.

"I'm a reporter," she answered.

"Oh, well you can't be here. You'll have to move back behind the line," he said, motioning for her to start walking across the street.

It did no good to protest.

Now back behind the police line, she joined the media pack that all waited for the pre-packaged news bites that the cops were occasionally offering. And they offered very little. So they waited...and waited...and waited.

Chapter 49 ~ Lee's wait continued

Sometime around 5:00 p.m. CDT, Lee got a call.

"They're going to gas the houseboat," his contact told him.

"Keep me posted," Lee said.

By 5:30 p.m., Lee got tired of waiting. As promising as the lead sounded to him, he decided to squeeze in some family time. Kari and her softball team were scheduled to scrimmage the Burnsville Blaze; both teams prepared for a regional tournament in Sioux Falls two days later.

"Hey Kevin, I've got a softball practice down in Burnsville," Lee said. For a solid week, he had worked 16-hour days and averaged less than four hours of sleep each night. "I'm going to get out of here for a while. I can catch a few innings of Kari's game. If anything breaks, call me right away."

Earlier that week, Lee told Kari that he could not go to the regional tournament in Sioux Falls. The weekend tournament preceded the nationals and ranked as the single most important games of her young life. She and Lee felt very disappointed.

Lee left the Command Post feeling very frustrated, and drove to the ballpark. He fought the urge to hope that finally this mess could end.

"So, is it CunaHAN?" Jesse asked, beaming at him as he got to the ballfield.

"We don't know," he said, trying to hide his frustration. "We really don't know." He saw the looks on the other parents' faces, all turned toward him like a choir following its director. Lee shrugged his shoulders and said, "I don't know. I sure hope so. But it doesn't make sense."

Lee had carried his personal cell phone with him, a purchase he had made during June just because of the Cunanan case. As the scrimmage began, Lee handed the cell phone to Kathy and headed out to first base. He had a hard time concentrating on the game, but felt glad to be out in the open air. *Who knows when I get to the next one of these?* he reminded himself. During the next hour, Lee's uneasiness kept him from enjoying the beautiful summer evening with "Little Bear" and the Lakers. His mind kept wandering to a Miami houseboat.

Gas marks entry

The Miami-Dade SRT finally assembled near the houseboat. Before going in, FBI Special Agent Manny Cereus arranged to have a hard-wired phone thrown into the houseboat. At 7:30 p.m. EDT, he attempted to make contact with the person inside, hoping to negotiate surrender. But a corpse could not talk on the phone.

Just before 8:00 p.m. EDT, reporters saw SRT members positioning themselves. It looked as though an assault was about to begin. At 8:01 p.m., the SRT fired five rounds of tear gas into the houseboat. They waited. Nothing happened. At 8:13 p.m., they fired three more rounds of gas into the houseboat. They waited, and again, nothing happened. The lack of response meant that if indeed, someone really was on that houseboat and had fired a weapon, either that person had escaped or was dead.

The SRT finally searched the boat around 8:25 p.m. EDT. They declared the area all clear. Nothing living was on that houseboat, but the sheer volume of gas fired into the boat made further investigation impossible. Miami Beach Fire Department personnel set up fans to aerate the boat.

At the Minneapolis Command Post, Kevin Rickett kept an eye on the TV monitor tuned to CNN, just in case the newsies had information they could use. All the agents saw was the same thing as did Anne O'Connor and her peers in Miami Beach.

"The houseboat is empty," an FBI spokesman said. The reporter pack felt stunned, and was left wondering about all the fuss and activity of the afternoon and evening. They continued to wait because even a story that it was *not* Cunanan was a story. Upon hearing the news, heads dropped in FBI Command Posts across the country. Rickett called Lee with the bad news.

"The locals just said no one was on the houseboat," Rickett told Lee.

"Damn! So what's all the fuss then? What's going on down there?" Lee asked.

"Well, we don't know. I think there's more going on. I'll call you if anything changes," Rickett said.

Lee handed the phone back to Kathy and shook his head, walking slowly back to the dugout.

Kevin watched the CNN coverage as the police continued their activity in and around the houseboat.

At about 8:55 p.m., Officer Jaccarino asked Fernando Carreira to sign a search warrant waiver to let investigators enter the boat. Minutes later, the

SRT reported to police near the boat that they had, indeed, found a body on the boat. No one told the media. Someone did call Kevin Rickett in Minneapolis and let him know the answer would be forthcoming soon. Once again, he called Lee's cell phone.

As Lee stood in the first base coach's box, he saw Kathy waving at him, telling him to hurry.

"What's up?" he asked as he came close.

"It's Kevin" she said, handing him the cell phone.

"Hey, what's up?" Lee asked.

"There is a body on the boat. I think we've got him. I can't say much over the phone," Rickett said, "but you better get back here." Lee's cell phone was not encrypted. They had to guard their conversations.

"Good news," Lee whispered to Kathy, "I think it's over, but don't tell anyone here." He saw the broad smile break out on her face.

Lee ran to the van and drove straight to headquarters, making the 15-minute trip in 10 minutes.

"Lee, there *is* a body in there," Rickett told him as he walked in. "I have no idea why they said there wasn't one. They're going in for a closer look. We're waiting for the call."

The agents' Command Post phones continued to ring, and they continued to answer and write their notes about new sightings. But each agent kept one eye on the TV monitor and an ear listening to "the" call they hoped would come soon. Patience eluded them. Instead, tension mounted.

In Florida, many in the media pack had grown restless and were talking about leaving the scene. Anne O'Connor had grown tired and irritated.

In California, Tom Schell had been watching the developments with interest. His phone rang and he smiled at the news he heard. He called ABC news in New York and learned they were about to pull out their reporters. "No, you don't want to do that. Trust me, it's him. Stay there."

Got him!

AT 9:38 p.m. EDT Sgt. Navarro and FBI Agent Evans decided to enter the houseboat for the express purpose of identifying the body. As they walked onto the boat, the remnants of tear gas tore at their eyes, nose and throat. They fought against the pungent gas as they made it to the second floor where they got a good look at the dead body. Evans saw for certain it was Andrew Cunanan. The two men made a hasty retreat from the boat, but still said nothing to the media waiting nearby. Miami Beach Police Chief Richard Berreto, who had come to the scene earlier, learned the good news along with the other cops at the scene.

Keith Evans walked off to the side to call Minneapolis.

Lee paced the Command Post, staring at the clock through exhausted eyes. He remained hopeful. He fought against the emotional release for which he longed; not wanting to be let down if the news was bad. He expected bad news. The hands on the clock crawled along, teasing him with their slow motion dance.

"Lee, line three is Evans," Rickett told him.

Lee took the phone in his hand.

"Urness here," Lee said, trying to hide his emotions. No one could see the butterflies in a state of heightened scramble that flittered through his gut. Lee looked around the room at the anxious faces of six Special Agents, including Kevin Rickett, four clerks and the ASAC, Mike Waldner. All hoped to hear the same thing.

The room went dead quiet as the agents studied Lee's face in that instant between announcing himself to the caller and the words they hoped to hear. They knew that America's largest and most intense manhunt might be coming to a close – or it might not. The busy, cluttered Command Post reflected the chaotic days since Versace's murder. An overwhelming volume of information collected by cops from all across America, recorded on an endless stream of paper and reports sat in stacks and files at worktables all around the room.

Lee braced himself to hear that, once again, the lucky bad guy had slipped through their hands, that the bad guy was someone else, or no one else.

But Evans relayed good news. As he did, adrenaline pulsated through Lee's body, his eyes welled up and he took a deep breath.

"He pled guilty," he told the agents. "It's him." Then he walked to a nearby easel and wrote in two-foot tall letters on the blank pad hanging there, "D.R.T." – Dead Right There.

Get out of those pajamas

Coleen Rowley had just gotten home. She had pulled on a pair of pajamas and meant to spend a few minutes relaxing before going to bed. She looked in on her sleeping children and talked for a few minutes with her husband. The phone rang.

"Hello," she said.

"Coleen, this is Rickett. They got him. It's him on the houseboat."

"All right! Okay, I'm coming back," she said.

Rowley got back as quickly as she could. Her pager sounded as she pulled into the basement parking garage at the FBI. She saw a message from Chris Graves.

Out of her car, Rowley picked up an FBI phone in the basement parking lot. She dialed Graves.

"This is Coleen Rowley. I see you paged me," she said as Graves picked up.

"Coleen! Great, thanks for calling. ABC is saying they think it's Cunanan on the houseboat. What can you say?"

"All I can say is that it is not official. We're waiting for confirmation now. I'm going into the office and will let you know once we know for sure," Rowley said before hanging up. She and the rest of the team would spend the next six-and-a-half hours waiting for that official confirmation.

In Maryland, America's Most Wanted producer Donna Brant had just gotten home when her mother called. "Turn on ABC right now. There's news about a body on a houseboat in Florida." The story speculated that it might be Andrew Cunanan, although no confirmation of that fact had been given to the media.

Within seconds of that call came another, this one from her boss at AMW. Their last Cunanan episode had just aired on July 19.

"Donna, this is…"

"I'm already on it," she said and hung up. Though she had yet to make a call, her mind had already conceived a plan. She called Lee Urness' pager and he called her back.

"Lee, what is going on down in Miami Beach? Is it Cunanan?" she asked.

"Well, yeah, it is him but it hasn't been released officially yet. Better get your crew cranking," he said.

Brant called Lance Heflin, her producer, and laid out her plan. She let him carry the burden. Heflin tracked down the AMW tape crew that even then was hanging out in South Beach, filming their next episode. John Walsh was with them.

In Minneapolis, Lee and Kevin Rickett fumed, angry that Miami FBI officials, or whomever it was, refused to release the information to the media.

Miami wanted to be perfectly certain, even though Keith Evans knew beyond doubt that Cunanan lay dead on that boat. That meant doing a full crime scene investigation; that meant waiting until the gas had been expelled enough to allow Sgt. Schiaffo's crew onto the boat. Schiaffo first tried entering the boat at midnight, only to find that the powdered residue from the gas rendered it inaccessible. He had to wait until nearly 1:40 a.m. before beginning to process the scene.

In the meantime, police had discovered that a man named Torsten Reineck owned the boat. Reineck also owned a gay club in Las Vegas, and was wanted on a German warrant for fraud. He had made a lame attempt to sell the houseboat only days before Cunanan moved in, and this intrigue created its own story sidebar. But no one ever drew a straight line between Cunanan and Reineck, even if the events seemed far from coincidental.

Late in the evening, Keith Evans called Lee again. He needed to know the serial number of the Taurus.

"Is there some question?" Lee asked as he read off the numbers.

"No. No one had it out here, that's all," the exhausted man answered. Upon hearing the numbers Lee related, Evans added, "That's a match."

Miami cops and the FBI continued to refuse to say anything. Anne O'Connor and the other reporters kept on waiting. From their perch in front of the Imperial House, they ordered pizza, subways, sodas and beer. The reporters were not looking for sympathy; they just wanted to know what was going on, and they were growing tired of waiting.

AMW waited for nothing

"Get over to this houseboat in South Beach," Lance Heflin said when he found John Walsh. "It is Cunanan and he's dead."

Walsh immediately called his Miami Beach Police Department friend, Chief of Police Richard Berreto, who had been at the sight for more than two hours. Walsh's crew loaded into a limo and sped to the houseboat. They were about to scoop everyone and in the process, make many other reporters jealous, and not a few, downright angry.

Anne O'Connor had never felt so physically rotten, at least covering a story. She had been at the crime scene since late afternoon. She never left.

Earlier that day she had suffered the embarrassment of being advised on her wardrobe by a Miami cop.

"Ma'am, I really think you need to get a hat, some sun tan lotion and water or you're gonna fall over," he said, and he meant it. O'Connor's skin had turned beet red and she had become dehydrated. Still she feared leaving her spot. And even now, nearing 10:30 p.m., she still knew very little. Neither had anyone else in the media pack, save those from ABC whose angel had delivered the news to New York, and even that was speculative until an FBI or Miami Beach officer made it official.

Then near 10:30 p.m., O'Connor heard a rustle in the reporter pack as a few limousines pulled up and stopped. She strained to see who got out. Paul Phillips, Miami FBI Special Agent in Charge got out of one. He wore a tuxedo; Cunanan's suicide had pulled Phillips away from a reception. Greg Jones, the Miami ASAC, also wore a tuxedo as he arrived at the scene. Other officials soon followed. O'Connor hoped they had just been waiting for these agents to arrive and that finally, someone would explain everything.

Then another limo pulled up and O'Connor saw a man get out. He had coiffed blond hair and a sculptured body. The face looked very familiar. The man walked quickly toward the police line and much to her shock, one of the officers lifted the tape and let him underneath. She realized then it was John Walsh.

A few minutes later, John Walsh stood nearby as the police announced to the world that the chase for Andrew Cunanan had finally come to end. Yes, they had found him dead on the houseboat, although investigators had not yet completed their work.

Anne O'Connor felt as though someone had punctured a balloon, releasing energy pent up for nearly three months. Relieved that Cunanan would never again murder, the way the media got the story ate at her. She had stood guard in the humid Miami heat, hearing nothing, speculating, wondering since late that afternoon. Just like that, John Walsh beat them all to the punch. Irritation mixed with jealousy. It should have been her scoop.

Still, the Cunanan news could not be reported until investigators completed their work and issued an official statement.

The Minneapolis newsies demanded an update, and as the Originating Office, local and national news turned to Coleen Rowley for the official statement. She went across the street from the FBI office and stood under a bright streetlight just before 10:00 p.m. CDT. She told the media that though a body had been found on the houseboat, there was no official confirmation that Cunanan was dead; she could give them nothing more. Lee snuck out to stand in the back of the media pack, wanting to hear what she said. It burned him that Miami had made her job so hard by withholding the news, that they *knew* it was Cunanan.

It was past 5:15 a.m. EDT when the Medical Examiner finally went on the boat with Schiaffo. By 5:30 a.m. EDT, they could report back to Minneapolis. Yes, officially Andrew Cunanan was dead. Anne O'Connor, who was the first reporter on the scene at Cunanan's first murder, and now the first reporter at the scene of his suicide, could finally file a story and go to bed.

Lee, Kevin Rickett, Coleen Rowley and the other agents at the Command Post had waited around for the official confirmation. Fingerprints, ballistics, a red pick-up truck and a photo-lineup all proved the dead guy was Andrew Cunanan. The chase had ended.

Lee drove home a happier man. He tuned his car radio back to KQQL 107.9, and once again enjoyed the Golden Oldies, although he left his police monitors turned off.

He had hoped to see Cunanan, learn his motives, and discover how he had eluded police for so long. He wanted to evaluate his own work, although he felt he had done everything possible to apprehend the killer. These thoughts were not second-guessing; they were thoughts of success, and the desire to learn from the experience.

He walked into his house a few minutes later and went to the liquor cabinet. *So what if it's almost 7:00 a.m.!* He poured himself a double shot of Jack Daniels; he skipped adding the 7-Up. Sitting at the kitchen table, his mind continued to play and replay events of the past 79 days.

The phone rang.

"They want the dental records," Rickett said.

"They've got them at Chicago PD," Lee said. He returned to sipping his drink.

The morning sun rose and brought light to the birds already busy at their work. Lee heard their noisy clatter as they celebrated a new day. He chuckled to himself. For the first time in 79 days he really saw the sunrise, and it felt good.

Up since 7:00 a.m. the previous day, Lee slept peacefully until late morning. He hoped a few hours of work would tie up loose ends.

Chapter 50 ~ A little face time

Now that Cunanan was dead, Lee felt better about letting America's Most Wanted film him. He greatly appreciated the work that Donna Brant and her crew had done, despite the tens of thousands of hours agents spent chasing down dead end leads. He knew that almost any one of them could have led them to Cunanan. He much preferred dead end leads to no leads.

He met the film crew at FBI headquarters, and they taped him for well over an hour. They took footage of the Command Post as well. Lee made sure to credit the entire team of agents across the country. He had no need or desire for personal acclaim.

Lee still needed to check in with his BCA chief, Nick O'Hara. As Lee entered his office that day, O'Hara stood and walked around his desk toward Lee. He reached his hand out to the exhausted agent, and smiled broadly as they shook hands.

O'Hara had a small present for Lee, a booklet of all of the FBI's Top Ten Most Wanted cases from the program's inception. The booklet began with a story about the Top Ten and then a list of each of the crooks that made the grade. O'Hara pointed to the last entry.

"Andrew Cunanan. See, that's your name there next to his," O'Hara said smiling. "You are the first non-FBI agent to make this list. You did an excellent job, Lee. Excellent. I am proud of you."

Having a ball...finally!

Friday morning, July 25, Lee rolled out of bed. The Cunanan chase details replaying continuously in his memory, Lee focused on the events of July 23. It brought a smile to his face and he could feel his body had relaxed Minutes later, he sat watching the cardinals come and go from his birdfeeder. They looked happy and free, ready to enjoy their day. He felt the same way.

Soon, Lee, Kathy and Kari drove down I-35 on their way to South Dakota. Andrew Cunanan no longer owned his life.

As the regional softball tournament began later that day, he watched his girls warming up.

"You caught CunaHAN," Jessie said, a wide grin on her face.

"Yes. Yes we did."

If his pager sounded that weekend, no one heard it. It sat at home.

Epilogue

No AIDS; Scrambled motives

Why did Andrew Cunanan murder Gianni Versace? No definitive answer exists; speculation abounds.

For certain, the autopsy performed on Cunanan's body proved he did <u>not</u> have AIDS nor was he HIV positive. Speculation that he blamed gays in general or Versace in particular for AIDS held no merit.

Lee Urness came to know Cunanan in a way unlike any other person. His 79-day chase of the murderer included constant analysis of Cunanan's personality and habits both before and during the chase. For months following the suicide, Lee continued to sort through what he had learned about the man. From this, he arrived at his own conclusions.

Andrew Cunanan left San Diego behind on April 25, 1997. At the same time, he left behind the old Cunanan. He had been forced to confront an entirely different life, and had not prepared at all for the change. And he had begun to use steroids to build his physique as a means to attract younger men and especially, David Madson.

Jeff Trail provided a barrier to Cunanan's new life, but he never meant to murder him. His childish anger overcame him, fed by steroids, and it exploded in a brutal murder.

Now a murderer, survival became Cunanan's utmost concern, and achieving some form of immortality. David Madson would and could not participate in Cunanan's new life and had been the only witness to his brutal murder of Trail. Madson had to die.

Cunanan needed money and companionship. He needed a place to lay low, to get lost in a crowd, but he had nowhere to go. Lee Miglin offered him money and a car. Cunanan's explosive fit of rage in Miglin's garage resulted in the most brutal of Cunanan's murders.

William Reese's tragic murder was sparked by the media's release of how the police were tracking Cunanan. He died simply because he had a red pickup truck and crossed Cunanan's path at the wrong time.

Cunanan's motive to murder Versace, then, became an extension of the circumstances that followed the murder of Trail, Madson, Miglin and Reese. Versace offered Cunanan a sordid form of immortality.

Once he dispatched Versace, the grand design of his last days had been completed. Though suicide took his life, Versace's murder had bestowed on him immortal, evil notoriety.

Cleaning up afterwards

A hot dispute ensued over ownership of the .40 caliber Taurus pistol. The Trail family wanted it back, but the FBI wanted it destroyed. Agent Paul Murray, with Lee's help, won a federal court order allowing Keith Evans to return the gun to New Jersey. Finally, in 2000, New Jersey police officials destroyed the gun, while at least one member of the Trail family watched.

Though Cunanan had killed himself, thereby solving five murders, each jurisdiction still had to close out their investigations. This meant gathering together evidence and dispersing it to the proper jurisdiction, retaining what was necessary and destroying the balance. Finally, it meant writing the closing forms. In five cities, police files were set into boxes to collect dust alongside other solved and completed cases. The local and state police, FBI and FTF agents and media, worn out from the long chase, picked up new cases, new stories, but none quite like Andrew Cunanan.

Had been almost everywhere

Lee kept a small legal-sized map of the United States in one of his files. As sightings of Cunanan poured in, he checked off each state where he had been seen. When the chase ended, Cunanan had been spotted in every state except North Dakota and Alaska. He had also been seen in Puerto Rico, Tokyo, Paris and London. And many times, he was seen at the same time on the same date in several different locations.

The greatest majority of these sightings had been driven by media exposure offered by America's Most Wanted. Even though each report burned police and FBI time, perhaps even diverting them from useful investigation, Lee and most cops greatly appreciated getting them. Every time they chased down a lead, no matter how strange, they had gained another chance to cut Cunanan off from escape.

Career finally ended

In 1999, Lee suffered an injury to his leg during a car accident. As a result, his knee tends to stiffen and cause pain during long periods of sitting. In

his work chasing fugitives, he often had to sit for hours at a time doing surveillance. With his banged-up knee, that became impossible. Lee retired from
police work during 1999.

The upside of his retirement is that he has ample time to make every one
of Kari's softball games, visit his lake cabin and get on Kathy's nerves as he
hangs around the house.